Comprehension FIRST

INQUIRY INTO BIG IDEAS

USING IMPORTANT QUESTIONS

Claudia Cornett

Holcomb Hathaway, Publishers

Scottsdale, Arizona

Library of Congress Cataloging-in-Publication Data

Cornett, Claudia E.
    Comprehension first : inquiry into big ideas using important questions /
Claudia Cornett.
        p. cm.
    ISBN 978-1-890871-98-7
    1. Reading comprehension.   2. Content area reading.   I. Title.
        LB1573.7.C67 2010
        372.47—dc22

                                                    2009031509

Please note: The author and publisher have made every effort to provide current website addresses in this book. However, because web addresses change constantly, it is inevitable that some of the URLs listed here will change following publication of this book.

Holcomb Hathaway, Publishers, Inc.
8700 E. Via de Ventura Blvd., Suite 265
Scottsdale, Arizona 85258
480-991-7881
www.hh-pub.com

10 9 8 7 6 5 4 3 2

ISBN 978-1-890871-98-7

Printed in the United States of America.

Contents

❷ Comprehension Problem Solving   25
INQUIRY INTO BIG IDEAS USING IMPORTANT QUESTIONS

Teachers, Context, and the Comprehension Task   51

Assessing to Differentiate Instruction   79

5 Explicit Teaching of Comprehension Strategies and Text Characteristics   117

6 Using Motivation Strategies to Engage Comprehension   153

7 Using Questioning to Promote Discussion and Conversation   181

8   Teaching Vocabulary and Fluency for Comprehension   221

Teaching Diverse Response Options to Show Comprehension   269

10 Organizing Main Events with Embedded Comprehension Practices   303

Appendices   349

See p. 349 for a complete list of appendix tools and page numbers

LIST OF READY RESOURCES

Foreword

BY BRIAN CAMBOURNE

fter more than 50 years of teaching reading, I'm hearing more comments such as "Dick/Jane can read fluently at a high level but don't have a clue about what they read."

This rings alarm bells. It suggests reading is merely decoding-to-sound and implies comprehension is secondary to decoding. Such views can alienate students from deep engagement in life-long reading.

Let me explain. An alphabetic writing system gives the illusion that reading is translating visual symbols into their phonetic equivalents. You decode the graphic symbols into the sounds they represent, blend them, and then hear words inside your head to which you attach meanings. This is "comprehension." Given this illusion it's common sense that you must first learn to decode. This means mastering phonics before you can comprehend.

Unfortunately, illusions can acquire the status of irrefutable truths. Our perceptual system creates the illusion that the Earth is flat. For thousands of years a "flat Earth" assumption was basic to navigation theory. If you sailed too far you would fall off the edge of the Earth.

Just as this affected how sailors navigated, the illusion that readers cannot comprehend an alphabetic text until they have first decoded it to sound has had a strong impact on reading education. It too has acquired the status of an absolute truth around which a set of self-affirming theoretical principles has also developed.

Yet a definitive experiment that proves the illusion has never been done. Nowhere can I find an experiment that conclusively proves that comprehending alphabetic print demands readers must first convert visual symbols to sound. Nowhere.

On the other hand, evidence that challenges the illusion is continually emerging. The deaf are one example. They have no access to sound. In theory they can't decode to sound. But they learn to read. How?

Then there are homonyms such as *rite* and *right*. Decoding these produces identical sounds, yet we can still work out what they mean. How? Are there lexical and grammatical cues embedded in the visual shape that take precedence over sound?

Homographs (words spelled the same but pronounced differently) are another example. In the sentence "He wound the bandage around the wound" it is impossible to say either homograph correctly until after the meaning has been accessed. Perhaps decoding to sound works for all words except homonyms and homographs? That doesn't make sense.

The ecological research I've completed in schools has convinced me that a "reading-is-decoding" definition of reading unintentionally creates teaching practices that alienate many less advantaged children from deep engagement in life-long reading. Teacher Kelly Gallagher has identified this phenomenon as "Read-i-cide," defined thus: "The systematic killing of love of reading, often exacerbated by the inane, mind-numbing practices found in schools."

Some approaches to decoding demand hours of intensive drill and practice on small "bits" of language that are devoid of meaning, before meaningful texts can be read. Meaning-making is put on hold until decoding skills are developed. This makes it hard for learners to do what evolution designed them to do—go straight to meaning from visual symbol using linguistic clues other than sound, clues such as spelling, syntax, and background knowledge.

A decoding-first theory assumes comprehension can be fixed up after decoding is mastered. Evolution theory suggests meaning is paramount from the start—not something that can be added later. The examples above indicate it is possible to access meaning without first accessing sound.

Does this mean I advocate a "zero-phonics" approach for literacy education? No. I ask that we teach phonics mindfully not mindlessly. Mindful literacy instruction teaches children to decode symbols, but puts meaning on the front burner. The title of this book calls this approach "Comprehension First."

In *Comprehension First*, Claudia Cornett has synthesized research and professional wisdom to explain why children should be respected as meaning generators. Her definition of literacy challenges educators to focus on the big picture, the human need to create meaning *from* and *in* diverse communication forms. Cornett describes abundant instructional strategies to show teachers how to emphasize meaning-making while teaching students to purposefully decode symbols in 21st-century print, digital, and multimedia texts. It makes sense to teach even our youngest students to ask important questions that lead to "big ideas" derived from texts—the process Cornett calls "Comprehension Problem Solving."

I have been communicating this message in various abbreviated "sound-byte" formats and forums for many years. I am overjoyed that there's now a book dedicated to treating the concept of "comprehension" in depth, at length, and in a scholarly fashion.

Brian Cambourne is an Associate Professor and a Principal Fellow on the faculty of education at the University of Wollongong, Australia.

Preface

Identification of best comprehension practices is "one of the nation's highest priorities."

RAND, 2002, p. xvi

When my husband and I were remodeling our house, we were lucky to find an expert carpenter. Dale honed his craft during decades of experience, and he will not be hurried. He was quick to point out the futility of moving one wire or cutting a single board before "grasping the concept." In the world of expert carpentry, understanding is paramount.

In the past two decades the reading performance of adolescents and young adults has declined sharply, as has voluntary reading. At the same time, students now spend hours online *reading*, *writing*, and *creating* new texts, ranging from collaborative works produced through FanFiction.net to "anime" movie videos. We as teachers of literacy and new literacies can no longer rely on a comprehension blueprint that is outdated. Some favored instructional tools and materials of the last century are simply inappropriate for a quality third-millennium education. Our students may face a future of closed doors if they lack essential comprehension strategies. It has never been more important for educators to "grasp the concept" of the kind of comprehension required for Literacy 2.0 and its place in the literacy hierarchy.

As recently as ten years ago, teachers admitted that they did not know how to teach comprehension. Many teachers continue to believe most students can achieve comprehension success just by doing a lot of reading (Block & Pressley, 2007), and confusion persists about key definitions and concepts such as comprehension *strategies* versus *skills*. Too often, reading is motivated by using external tools such as praise, stickers, coupons, and grades, which hold temporary engagement potential, at best. Vocabulary instruction is sometimes weighted in the direction of pronouncing and spelling words rather than concept development. Discussion questions frequently continue to come from teacher's manuals and call for low-level thinking—a pattern that seems most common in schools that serve at-risk children.

As Brain Cambourne explained in the Foreword, change in comprehension instruction is overdue. Fortunately, we have abundant research to guide our efforts.

A COMPREHENSION REVOLUTION

Comprehension is a complex concept. Effective comprehension instruction is also complex, because it must take into account the many factors that determine comprehension success. However, as Knight (2009) reminds us, "Few people do more thinking on the job than a teacher standing in front of 27 students" (p. 511). Teachers are willing and able to take on complicated tasks . . . if. The "if" has to do with a critical condition for changing pedagogy: we must believe the cause is great. One of the great causes in literacy today is the need to revise our concept of comprehension to give meaning-making top priority. In this book, I describe comprehension as a multifaceted problem-solving process. There is no doubt that *all teachers* have the capacity to grasp this concept and use the process to design quality comprehension instruction. Such understanding will allow educators to bring to bear knowledge of best instructional practices to solve comprehension problems that beleaguer too many of our children.

Change is in the works. Comprehension instruction appears to be increasingly informed by contemporary research. I recently visited a school where students had created a podcast to show their comprehension of "big ideas" from a Civil War unit. Posted on the walls were strategies ("skip and come back" and "chunk") for "solving" words. I also saw evidence of comprehension strategies: in a first-grade class, the students had made art to illustrate diverse mental images they had constructed from a book read to them. A three-foot-high W filled a bulletin board, with the 5 W questions (who, what, when, where, why) written on its points. (We need an extra point for the important question "How?"!)

Today's teachers work hard and know a lot. But one of the difficult challenges we face is prioritizing instructional time. Inquiry-based comprehension is currently not job one. If the war on illiteracy is to be waged more intelligently, we need a "surge" in comprehension instruction that responds to a new view of literacy—one that acknowledges the need to make sense of a myriad of diverse texts.

To teach effectively, we as teachers need information about "high-leverage teaching practices that are proven and powerful" (Knight, 2009, p. 512). However, teachers still are not receiving adequate pre-service preparation or ongoing professional development focused on comprehension (RAND, 2002). This book is a resource to help fill the gap for both pre-service and in-service teachers.

INQUIRY INTO BIG IDEAS USING IMPORTANT QUESTIONS

The Comprehension Problem Solving (CPS) process described in *Comprehension First* comprises the thinking strategies (e.g., predicting and imaging) that capable comprehenders use to "extract and construct" big ideas from traditional print texts and contemporary digital/multimedia ones. Using this process in the service of the comprehension product is crucial to excellent instruction. Central to the process is asking important questions that lead to *worthy* big ideas—ideas that grow from reading and understanding more than a sentence or paragraph. Asking important questions activates personal inquiry into the meaning of texts, which increases motivation to learn.

Important questions. *Comprehension First* focuses on the following umbrella questions:

1. What is known about the nature of comprehension?
2. Why should comprehension be given priority in planning and teaching?
3. What is elemental to quality comprehension instruction?

Big ideas. This book is a digest of ideas that connect to the three crucial umbrella questions. Some of the biggest ideas are:

- Unless comprehension is the top priority, the most needy students are unlikely to make progress.
- Comprehension is both a problem-solving process and a product.
- Elevated comprehension is a result of inquiry, which is an intensely personal form of problem solving.
- The Comprehension Problem Solving process orchestrates research-based strategies to make sense of diverse print and non-print texts.
- Comprehension Problem Solving needs to produce big ideas that are both found in and created from word-based, digital, and multimedia texts.
- Excellent comprehension instruction results from embedding best teaching practices in main literacy events and in all content instruction. Although the idea of best practices is not without controversy (Reinking, 2007), I choose to use the label as it is generally understood. Best practices are the best ways we know to teach comprehension, *given our current knowledge base*. They are not written in stone and may change over time as the research base about "what works" to increase comprehension grows.
- Assessment is needed to differentiate comprehension instruction (1) for learners' strengths and needs, (2) for various texts, and (3) for comprehension tasks.
- Knowledgeable teachers need to take center stage in any reform of comprehension instruction.

Big Ideas are featured at the end of each chapter in this book and link back to the Important Questions that open each chapter. However, the *most* important questions are ones readers generate for themselves and use before, during, and after reading. I urge readers to generate personal questions while they read in order to participate fully in the inquiry-based, problem solving process used by effective readers, writers, scientists, and artists. Comprehension Problem Solving is just such a process.

TEXT ORGANIZATION

Chapter 1 introduces the challenges that surround comprehension achievement and instruction. It provides definitions important for understanding inquiry-based comprehension and describes the factors that are most influential in comprehension success.

Chapters 2 through 10 describe the essential knowledge base and the pedagogy that teachers need in order to implement nine comprehension best practices in a flexible manner. These chapters build on one another, with Chapter 10 showing how the "comprehension first" proposal can be integrated into main literacy events. Each of the chapters continually returns to the premise that an inquiry-based problem solving process, in which students find and construct big ideas, is at the heart of comprehension success.

TEXT FEATURES

The following features of this book are intended to help readers grasp the overall concept of comprehension:

- *Chapter Preview:* A brief introduction previews the chapter's big ideas to help readers activate prior knowledge and get a big-picture view of the chapter and how it relates to comprehension as an inquiry-based problem-solving process.

- *Important Questions:* These opening questions act as scaffolds on which to construct big ideas. I also designed them to elicit additional questions from readers.

- *Classroom Snapshots:* Vignettes of teachers grappling with how to teach comprehension provide big-picture examples of key concepts in action and the chance for readers to critique teaching practices.

- *Ready Resources:* These features highlight and illustrate "need to know" information.

- *Chapter Big Ideas:* This list summarizes the chapter's big ideas to jump-start generation of a personal list.

- *Response Options:* These activity options provide opportunities for readers to engage in instructional problem solving.

- *Differentiation tools and discussions:* These elements include principles and basic ways teachers can adjust instruction for diverse students, including English learners.

- *Assessment strategies:* Ideas and examples for using formative tools with an emphasis on helping students monitor their own comprehension growth.

- *Technology:* Resources and ideas for the appropriate use of electronic texts are integrated throughout the book, with focus on use of the Internet. Boxes highlight online resources and include useful URLs.

- *New literacies:* An expanded view of the concepts of *literacy* and *text* is used throughout this book. Arts-based and digital texts are treated as significant contributors in comprehension instruction.

- *Appendices:* To assist teachers with implementing comprehension practices, the book includes an extensive compilation of additional resources, including worksheets, rubrics, and checklists, perforated for ease of use.

- *Instructor materials.* An instructor's manual and PowerPoint presentation are available to those adopting this book for classroom use.

Visit YouTube (search for "Comprehension First") to hear my introduction to this book and to learn more about its purpose, the important questions I hope to answer, and the big ideas about a meaning-making process that results in comprehension.

Please note: The names of teachers in this book are pseudonyms. Many of the lessons featured in the snapshots represent composites.

THE LITERACY BRIDGE

The comprehension model described in this book responds to calls from literacy experts and professional associations and organizations, such as the Partnership for 21st Century Skills, for inquiry-based instruction that prepares students to think critically. Inquiry-based comprehension instruction acknowledges that we have entered the age of multiple literacies, with non-print, electronic, and multimedia texts growing in popularity. Youth and adults alike must become nimble thinkers who can navigate hypertext, judge the credentials of websites, and intelligently use Literacy 2.0 communication tools, while also developing traditional print comprehension. Our students have one foot planted in a print-dominated world and the other in a future rich in technology-dominated communication. In Shel Silverstein's words, knowledgeable teachers are the bridge that can take students "halfway there."*

*S. Silverstein. (1981). The Bridge. *A Light in the Attic.* New York: Harper and Row.

Acknowledgments

No book is ever created by a writer alone and this one is no exception. Without the many teacher colleagues I have worked with over the years I would not have so many stories to tell. I thank all those teachers and principals in schools throughout the United States who have made my professional life and this book so much richer.

I also wish to thank those folks who took the time to offer so many useful comments and give their unique perspectives on early drafts of this book. In particular, these reviewers were most helpful: Julie Ankrum, University of Pittsburgh at Johnstown; Christine Best, Regis University; Jeanne Clidas, Roberts Wesleyan University; Jeanne Cobb, Coastal Carolina University; Joyce Cockson, freelance consultant, Omaha; Beverly DeVries, Southern Nazarene University; Connie Dierking, University of Central Florida; Mariam Jean Dreher, University of Maryland; Leigh Hall, The University of North Carolina at Chapel Hill; Peter Hilton, St. Xavier University; Wendy C. Kasten, Kent State University; Leah Kinniburgh, University of South Alabama; Angela Rutherford, The University of Mississippi; Tabatha Scharlach, University of Central Florida; Pamela Solvie, University of Minnesota; Lois Stover, University of Maryland Baltimore County; Judith Trotter, College of Charleston; Gary Wilhite, Southern Illinois University; and Thea Williams-Black, The University of Mississippi.

I have worked with many publishers over the years and none has ever taken as much care as Holcomb Hathaway. Colette Kelly and Gay Pauley live the company motto of "exceeding expectations one book at a time." I thank them both for their faith in this project, and their expertise in producing a text we can be proud to share with educators. And to Colette I have to say, after these many years of friendship, we finally did it!

Finally, I must thank my very best friend in all the world for all that he does and is. First and last, time present and time past, there is Charles. His wonderful advice and research skills have been invaluable, along with the many meals he has cooked. And, once again he made me laugh every day.

About the Author

Claudia Cornett is Professor Emerita of Education at Wittenberg University. During her tenure at Wittenberg she directed the Reading Center and taught graduate and undergraduate courses in literature, literacy methodology, and arts integration. In 1989 she received Wittenberg's highest teaching honor, the Distinguished Teaching Award.

Before moving to the college level Claudia taught grades 1 through 8 and was a reading specialist. She earned her Ph.D. in Curriculum and Instruction from Miami University.

Claudia is the author of numerous books and articles about literacy, arts integration, bibliotherapy, literature discussion strategies, comprehension instruction, a problem-solving approach to phonics, and the strategic use of humor. Her most recent books include a fourth edition of *Creating Meaning through Literature and the Arts* (Allyn & Bacon/Pearson, 2011), and *Learning through Laughter II* (Phi Delta Kappa, 2003). In 2006, the International Reading Association published her article "Center stage: Arts-based read alouds."

Claudia also developed and is featured in *Sounds Abound*, an instructional television series on early literacy, broadcast on PBS stations during school programming. During 2004 and 2005 she hosted a weekly segment on local educational TV called "Art Chat," featuring interviews with artists in their studios.

Claudia regularly conducts keynote talks and professional development for educators on comprehension problem solving and arts integration throughout the United States, Europe, and Canada. Her current research focuses on literacy issues using an arts-based teaching model.

Claudia lives with her husband, a school superintendent, in historic Lebanon, Ohio. They both enjoy traveling, theatre, ballroom dancing, boating, antiques, and lots of reading. She can be reached at ccornett@wittenberg.edu.

Comprehension Definitions, Issues, and Directions

preview

This chapter introduces the concept of "comprehension first" and explores why inquiry-based comprehension instruction needs to be a high priority in the classroom. I begin to build, and help you build, a new view of comprehension that is more consistent with 21st-century demands. The chapter includes

- definitions of *comprehension, big ideas, inquiry,* and other key concepts that relate to literacy.
- an introduction to the information teachers need to evaluate comprehension instructional options.
- a profile of common comprehension problems and common literacy needs of all learners.
- an overview of the five factors that influence comprehension success.

important questions

Use these questions to guide your thinking during reading.

1. What does "comprehension first" mean? Why is this concept vital?

2. How does a teacher's definition of comprehension affect how he or she teaches?

3. How would the adoption of a definition of literacy that considers real-world demands (including workplace expectations and technology) change comprehension instruction?

4. What is the status of student reading/comprehension achievement in the United States? What does the current status suggest about instruction?

5. What are common characteristics of students with comprehension difficulties?

6. What conditions are recommended to meet children's basic literacy needs?

7. What five factors influence comprehension, and how are they important to boosting achievement?

8. What role can Comprehension Problem Solving (CPS) play in putting comprehension first?

Introduction

The goal is lifetime, not school time readers.

JIM TRELEASE

A book's title should say a lot. In fact, an effective way to start a discussion about a book is to ask, "What does the title mean?" A good title captures the book's big idea on several levels. For example, the title of *Charlotte's Web* doesn't simply refer to the literal web the spider spins. At a deeper level, the web has to do with qualities that, when woven together, create true friendship—qualities such as listening, compassion, and self-sacrifice. Charlotte's web is also her tool for snaring food—an instrument of survival for Charlotte, but also a deadly trap for other creatures. Readers are forced to consider how life is connected to death in the great web of existence. This is a very big idea.

The title of the book you are holding is also intended to operate on several levels. "Comprehension First" summarizes the biggest idea in teaching reading today (RAND Reading Study Group, 2002, p. xi). No Child Left Behind (NCLB) legislation put reading on the front burner, but the research report that informed this law emphasized that its components are not equal. Four of the NCLB components (phonemic awareness, phonics, fluency, and vocabulary) are *means* to reach the fifth: comprehension (National Reading Panel, 2000). Literacy experts widely acknowledge comprehension to be the goal of reading, with other components serving as sub-skills. Comprehension is what reading is all about. Indeed, comprehension is the "sine qua non of reading" (Beck & McKeown, 1998).

The title *Comprehension First* is also a play on "Reading First," the name of the program through which schools received funds to implement the reading portion of NCLB. Unfortunately, many Reading First schools missed essential details or misread key research conclusions regarding the subordination of phonemic awareness, phonics, vocabulary, and fluency to comprehension (Walker, H., 2009). As a result, many programs taught sub-skills as curricular ends. Six billion dollars later, students in Reading First schools comprehend no better than students in schools that did not receive funds (Institute for Educational Sciences, 2008).

Moving comprehension to the front of the instructional line for all American students is long overdue (Walker, B., 2009). To do that, clear, understandable definitions for key literacy concepts are needed.

classroom snapshot

OPERATING DEFINITIONS

What a person knows and believes influences how she or he acts. It follows that any teacher's definition of comprehension determines the nature of his or her instructional practices. Consider the following short classroom snapshots. Think about how each teacher *implicitly* defines comprehension.

Teacher A is working with a small group. She instructs the students to read a short picture book independently. After they all seem to be finished, Teacher A begins with questions, such as, "Who were the characters?" and "What happened first, second, third, and so on, in the story?" Teacher A informally assesses, using a clipboard to record "correct" and "incorrect" answers.

Teacher B distributes a set of questions to guide the reading of part of a chapter in the social studies book. He asks the students to read silently and use sticky notes to mark parts of the text that help answer the questions. The students then individually write answers to the questions, using the text. At the end of the class, Teacher B collects their answers and grades the papers.

Teacher C tells her students to read a short story and focus on being able to retell what it is about. After they read, she gives the students a story map and asks them to fill in information about the characters, setting, plot events, and themes. Teacher C uses a rubric to grade each student's work, with "very detailed and accurate" being the criteria for an A in comprehension.

Teacher D prepares a multiple-choice worksheet for students to show their comprehension of a science article. The worksheet directs students to identify main ideas and details stated in the article. The students read the article and then work in small groups. Teacher D collects one worksheet from each group, at random, and everyone in the group gets the same comprehension grade.

None of these teachers has explicitly defined what is involved in comprehension, but their teaching strategies and activities do give clues about their knowledge and beliefs. Decide for yourself what their behaviors imply. You will be invited to reexamine these snapshots at the end of this chapter, or you may choose to look ahead now to Snapshots Revisited on page 21.

Why Comprehension First?

As in the fable of the blind men who attempted to comprehend an elephant by each examining only one body part, each of Teachers A–D seems to use pieces of the whole of effective comprehension instruction. None explicitly states what comprehension is, but it is apparent that these teachers all operate on the basis of some unstated definition. Moreover, while Teachers A–D all use *common* comprehension practices, they all also deviate from instructional principles agreed upon by literacy experts. For example, the practices of merely calling attention to comprehension skills (e.g., "Each paragraph has a main idea") and of assigning reading followed by testing information recall came into question over 30 years ago (Durkin, 1978–79). Nonetheless, many teachers continue to rely on questioning for recall, with only about 6 percent asking higher-level questions that require students to connect textual information to their lives and feelings (Taylor et al., 1999).

Concerns about traditional methods of learning come from psychologists, such as scholar Ellen Langer. Langer (1997) argues that students are taught to engage in "mindless behavior" when traditional methods focus on overlearning a task, with the implication that there is only one way to do it, regardless of the conditions. Quality comprehension instruction aims to develop "mindful" learners by teaching them to use strategies flexibly, from the beginning. However, even "accomplished" teachers continue to use a paucity of effective comprehension practices; fewer than 1 percent of teachers provide quality instruction for comprehension skills and strategies (Taylor et al., 1999). Pressley (2001) concludes that "there is no evidence of much comprehension strategies instruction occurring extensively now and certainly no evidence of children being taught such strategies to the point that they use them in a self-regulated fashion, which is the goal of such instruction" (*not paginated*).

When it comes to learning anything, time on task matters, but time devoted to comprehension instruction remains a fraction of the literacy instructional budget. Since comprehension is widely acknowledged to be the essence of reading, we need to reorder our instructional agendas and reallocate time in order to put comprehension first. There is some movement in that direction (Block, Paris, & Whiteley, 2008; Brown, 2008). In one study, time spent on comprehension instruction was found to have increased to 25 percent from the less than 1 percent Durkin observed in 1978 (Block, 2004). But what is important isn't just *how much* time is spent on comprehension, but how the time is spent. This book explores how comprehension instructional time can be spent to achieve the best results.

Educational research, such as that of Dolores Durkin, continues to inform comprehension instruction, but there is a change force operating today that is even more powerful than this research. The worldwide communication revolution is now going full-steam, driven by the engine of technology. This communication revolution makes an education revolution necessary, and, according to Pressley (2000), educators are poised for one in the teaching of reading. Learning is "no longer fixed in time and space" (Richardson, 2009,

p. 29). In a world where students blog, twitter, tweet, and flickr, it behooves educators to consider the kind of comprehension instruction that will prepare students for "mindful" thinking about texts from sources such as MySpace, Facebook, and YouTube. Martin Luther King's concept of the "fierce urgency of now" applies. To begin with, we need to reconsider our definitions of comprehension, literacy, and reading in light of the realities of the 21st century. Instruction must be crafted to align with these key literacy concepts.

Definitions Matter

Definitions provide focus and serve as goals or destinations. Goals give vision; without vision, "the teacher is left to sway and sputter as a candle facing the winds of curricular change" (Gambrell, Malloy, & Mazzoni, 2007, p. 17). To focus instruction, each teacher needs to self-assess what he or she knows about comprehension (the destination) and then determine the instruction students need to get there (the route).

Comprehension can be conceived as an inquiry-based problem-solving process. The Comprehension Problem Solving (CPS) process that is a focus of this book incorporates thinking strategies and questions at the heart of this process. The goal of CPS is to construct meaning from diverse texts by deriving and generating big ideas. When CPS is placed at the center of literacy and content area instruction, comprehension is moved to the forefront of education where it belongs.

The following key definitions were synthesized from sources educators customarily use to design instructional programs in any literacy area. These sources included decades of literacy research, constructivist philosophy (beliefs about how people make meaning), and professional wisdom gained from accumulated teaching experience. Constructivist theory (e.g., see Cambourne, 2002) assumes people can and should create their own understandings—so I offer these definitions as drafts to help you

- self-assess your current understanding.
- create personally meaningful definitions, with these as possible starting points.
- derive instructional ideas congruent with the definitions (i.e., develop if-then statements).

These key concepts can become part of your personal dictionary for curricular decision making. Understanding them is foundational to envisioning comprehension instruction suited to the needs of 21st-century students.

LITERACY

Literacy is the ability to communicate thoughts, ideas, feelings, and emotions effectively through comprehension (understanding) and composition (expression). Central vehicles of communication are (1) the language arts (listening, reading, speaking, and writing) and (2) the fine and performing arts (visual art, drama/theatre, dance, and music). In the 21st century it is widely acknowledged that students require "new literacies." A multidimensional view of literacy now includes technological/computer literacy (i.e., ability to use the Internet; to "blog," or produce a weblog, as well as to read blogs; to play console games; and to send and read instant messages) and math literacy (Biancarosa & Snow, 2004; Braunger & Lewis, 2006; Gambrell, Malloy, & Mazzoni, 2007).

READING

Reading, one aspect of literacy, focuses on constructing or making meaning using information *received* from word-based and non–word-based texts such as works of art. Eisner points out that we can "take" meaning from texts, but the meaning we "make" is more important (2002a). Taking meaning involves finding or extracting literal information. *Making* meaning is a more active process, one that requires thoughtful interaction with texts. "Making meaning" summarizes the central problem to be solved when a reader encounters a text (NCTE, 2004)—with "meaning" including thoughts, ideas, feelings, and emotions (see the definition of "literacy" above). A paraphrase of the definition for reading is "constructing, creating, or composing sense from any text."

COMPREHENSION

Comprehension is both a process and a product. It is cognitive action that takes the form of a *problem-solving process* used to take and make meaning from print and non-print texts. In other words, comprehension involves both "extracting and constructing" generalizations, theme statements, or *big ideas* from any text used for information or enjoyment (NCTE, 2004; RAND Reading Study Group, 2002). Comprehension is also the *end product* of the problem-solving process, that is, the content or ideas learned from reading, viewing, or listening to a text.

Comprehension (understanding) and composition (expression) both involve *created meaning*. Prior to the 21st century, definitions of comprehension focused on "intentional thinking," and "meaning construction" related to the interaction between a word-based text and a reader (Durkin, 1993; Harris & Hodges, 1995). In literacy education, *composition* meant written expression using words.

Today it is acknowledged that readers use common comprehension processes, such as prediction and analysis, to understand both word-based and wordless texts and combinations of the two, such as multimedia work (Cornett, 2011; Gambrell, Malloy, & Mazzoni, 2007; NCTE, 2004). Comprehension is the goal across disciplines, and it is achieved through the purposeful use of a common body of thinking strategies. In addition, we now understand that expression of meaning (composition) can result in word-based (oral or written) and wordless forms, such as visual art, music, and dance compositions.

TEXT

A text can be any word-based or non–word-based source of meaning (ideas and/or feelings). It is no longer useful to conceive of literacy solely in terms of reading and writing word-based texts. We are in the midst of an "explosion of alternative texts that . . . incorporate multimedia and electronic options" (RAND Reading Study Group, 2002, p. xv and 14). While word-based texts still occupy pride of place in schooling, visual texts, such as the ancient Chauvet cave paintings in France, are evidence that humans communicated through arts-based texts thousands of years before written words were used. Indeed, written texts began to appear only about 5,000 years ago (e.g., symbolic language, such as cuneiform).

We seem to have gone "back to the future" with the increasing use of arts-based or non-verbal texts to understand and express meaning. Visual and musical texts rich in movement and drama now dominate communication technologies such as the iPhone. Why? Because arts-based texts expand communication to include ideas and feelings that are often "beyond words" (Eisner, 2002b). The nature of modern communication demands that we teach students "multiple and overlapping forms of literacy, including digital, visual, spoken and printed forms that constitute the act of constructing and expressing meaning today" (Gambrell, Malloy, & Mazzoni, 2007, p. 42).

BIG IDEAS

Big ideas are complete thoughts that grow out of themes in literature and generalizations in content areas. Big ideas are core truths about people and the world. They represent the life lessons and deep understandings readers, listeners, and viewers take from verbal and non-verbal texts. They are more than the main ideas of paragraphs. Big ideas are associated with whole texts (Walmsley, 2006). They are the main points of books, plays, and films. Big ideas take these forms: moral, theme, thesis, contention, argument, conclusion, proposal, proposition, claim, premise, assumption, hypothesis, postulation, or supposition.

Big ideas are the most important meanings that readers, listeners, and viewers take and make from texts. *Concepts* are the seeds of big ideas. For example, the concepts of love, loneliness, and greed become big ideas when they appear in statements such as: *There are different kinds of love. You can be lonely even in a crowd. Greed is a sign of fear of loss.*

In literature, big ideas are conclusions that the author may state explicitly or directly. They may also be hidden or implied. Authors and artists state or imply big ideas by giving clues that readers can use to synthesize understanding. In the literary arts, a theme can become a big idea when the author expands the theme into a full statement. In nonfiction texts, big ideas may be called generalizations. Big ideas represent messages from whole texts (Walmsley, 2006). On a large scale, big ideas form the basis of theories like the "Big Bang" or evolution, which are supported by premise statements or assumptions.

IMPORTANT QUESTIONS

The path to extracting and constructing big ideas is to ask questions before, during, and after reading, listening to, or viewing a text. *Important questions* are open-ended queries people make as they work through the scientific method, the writing process, or the Comprehension Problem Solving process. These questions have a range of possible answers and often begin with *Why, How,* or *What if.*

Important questions lead to big ideas. The ability to ask such questions is an essential skill all teachers need in order to provide effective comprehension instruction. More important, students need to be taught to self-question before, during, and after encountering any text if they are to become independent and continue to develop comprehension abilities.

INQUIRY

The subtitle of this book includes the key word *inquiry.* This word means more than a teacher's questioning to test student recall. Inquiry is a *personal* search for meaning set in motion by interest in a problem. The problem may be straightforward, or it may involve a complex series of questions. When teachers raise provocative questions and encourage students to ask their own, students are more likely to assume an inquiring stance.

Inquiry involves a quest, and quests always engage problem-solving thinking. For example, I become an inquirer when I search the Internet for the best route to Nashville, where I'm going to teach at a summer institute. The problem is personally relevant, and the question is obvious: How can I get to Nashville from Cincinnati on good roads and in good time?

More complex inquiry occurs when I choose to read a memoir such as *Reading Lolita in Tehran* (Nafisi, 2003), about an Iranian literature professor who, after losing her job, invited a group of female students to her home each week to study banned books. While I might begin with the problem of needing some pleasurable reading for relaxation, I also start with questions based on the book's reputation: What would motivate a teacher to do something so blatantly illegal, by Iranian standards? How might I myself respond to living under a tyrannical regime, without basic freedoms, especially for women? Personal questions like these cause me to become more mindful about what I read, even when I am reading for pleasure. My choice to inquire about big ideas increases my reading pleasure, because inquiry increases engagement. As I read Nafisi's memoir, I generate more questions: How can good literature cause students to think more independently? What leads this teacher to take such risks? How much would I risk to remain free to teach material I thought was right, and in a manner I thought was justified?

In summary, inquiry is personal meaning making, directed by questioning, used throughout the before/during/after comprehension process. Inquiry is investigation into a problem. For comprehension purposes, the overarching problem for the reader is how to make sense from texts in ways that are personally meaningful. Inquiry centers on ongoing questioning of your own thinking and of other sources or texts that you consult during problem solving. The result of inquiry is that, when readers take this stance from the beginning, they comprehend more and better (Gambrell, Malloy, & Mazzoni, 2007).

Next, I discuss comprehension achievement as part of the purpose of this chapter, which is to establish the need for changing comprehension instruction.

Comprehension Achievement: Facts and Issues

f this book were a newspaper, these might be the headlines:

Society and Workplace Demand Higher Proficiencies Than Schools

High School Graduates Not Prepared for Post-Secondary Options

Reading Declines Have Serious Civic, Social, Cultural, and Economic Implications

These fictional headlines are drawn from real stories about the state of American literacy achievement (Gambrell, Malloy, & Mazzoni, 2007, and Pennsylvania Department of Education, 2004; Torgesen, 2006; and NEA, 2007, respectively).

Thirty-eight percent of employers rate high school graduates deficient in reading comprehension, and 72 percent rate graduates deficient in writing. These facts are most troubling in light of the strong correlation between reading prowess and higher income and more job opportunities. In addition, individuals who read better (i.e., comprehend better) also vote more, volunteer more, and do more charity work. Readers also attend more cultural arts events, exercise more, and are more involved in sports (NEA, 2007).

This information, as well as that in the following sections, shows why the time is right for a revolution in teaching to put comprehension first.

WHAT DO THE TEST SCORES SHOW?

At present, the National Assessment of Educational Progress (NAEP), our only nationwide standardized test, reports that overall reading scores of high school students remain inadequate and flat, having changed little in decades (U.S. Dept. of Education, 2003–2007). Alarming gaps between poor and affluent, majority and minority students persist. Progress benchmarks for fourth and eighth graders are not resulting in high percentages of high schoolers who successfully comprehend the real-world variety of texts. Merely measuring success grade by grade has not worked. Nor has an instructional model based on the premise that phonemic awareness + phonics + sight words = increased comprehension (IES, 2008). This model is analogous to assembling computer parts only to find that the finished machine can't access the Internet. Putting pieces together doesn't automatically make a coherent whole. This was dramatically demonstrated with the multi-billion-dollar Reading First experiment, which concentrated on reading sub-skills and produced no significant differences in comprehension. As one principal put it, "We missed the boat" (Walker, H., 2009, p. 18).

IS TESTING *MORE* A SOLUTION?

Testing has become a preoccupation of politicians and educators. Is it helping to address the comprehension issues that the "headlines" above suggest?

Recently I visited a Tennessee school where a kindergarten teacher was preparing for a weekly individual check of reading rate and accuracy with a young boy.

"They just can't do it," she whispered to me. "Some of these babies can't button their shirts, and I'm drilling them on sight words. They have to have 40 by year's end. I hate it and so do they."

I listened and watched as the small boy struggled through the task. He pushed his stubby index finger along the page as if mashing harder might help. Repeatedly he looked up at his teacher, who was forbidden to help him. She eventually rubbed his back and told him to go on back to the classroom.

"The whole school goes through this every Friday," she said sadly. "It is such a waste."

I've heard teachers in dozens of states express the same feelings. State and local testing eats away at precious teaching time. Testing is conducted too often and is too threatening. In Ohio, I met a teacher who also ran a hog farm. He put it this way: "My hogs won't get any fatter if I weigh them more often." Such down-home wisdom is refreshing in the face of increased demands for testing—especially since there is no research that shows more testing will boost student achievement.

Despite the Reading First schools' poor showing in comprehension achievement (IES, 2008), scores at the elementary level have improved in some districts. The reasons why, however, are not clear. Before No Child Left Behind legislation went into effect, school districts had already been aligning curricula to focus on student performance standards created by professional associations such as the International Reading Association (IRA) and the National Council of Teachers of English. Any claims that federally mandated reform has caused improvements have to account for the effects of the pre-existing standards movement.

WHAT IF THE TESTS WERE CHANGED?

High school graduates now face a workplace that often requires employees to comprehend and navigate complex texts, including Internet multimedia hypertext. It is no longer enough to be able to read words from left to right and follow literal directions. Workers are expected to solve problems creatively, employing judgment and using diverse texts, including digital sources (Gambrell, Malloy, & Mazzoni, 2007; Partnership for 21st Century Skills, 2008).

Educators across the country know this. For example, on Florida's state test, the proportion of thoughtful questions increases progressively. At the third grade, 30 percent of the questions require higher-order thinking; by the tenth grade, 70 percent of the questions require higher-order thinking. In addition, in response to the need for readers' stamina to increase progressively, the average length of test passages grows from 325 words at the third grade to

1008 words by the tenth grade (Torgesen, 2006). Unfortunately, comprehension achievement hasn't increased. Florida students showed a steady *decrease*, with 71 percent at grade level in grade four and only 32 percent at grade level by grade ten. Asking higher-order questions on tests and giving students more to read has not resulted in improvement.

HOW DO DEFINITIONS AFFECT ASSESSMENT?

How schools *define* reading affects educational goals, assessment methods, and, in turn, results. One district may decide that reading ability can be assessed by asking students to choose the main idea from multiple-choice items, while another expects students to read a passage and generate a statement of an important theme. These two very different tasks imply contrasting definitions—one relies on literal thinking and the other on synthesis of ideas to construct meaning.

At the state level, education leaders can choose to buy or make their own tests, use their own definition of reading, and set levels for appropriate progress and proficiency. For example, one test used in many states, labeled a reading fluency test, assesses accurate and speedy word pronunciation. The assumption is that word pronunciation is a way to measure reading achievement, despite research that shows a low correlation between comprehension and word pronunciation (Duke, 2001; Duke, Pressley, & Hilden, 2005; Pressley, 2006). Essentially, schools can choose simplistic definitions of reading, teach to those goals, and get what they teach—low levels of thinking. Under such circumstances, it is not surprising to find high school students who cannot comprehend even at a basic level.

WHY AREN'T THE READING COMPONENTS EQUAL?

As mentioned previously, the misreading of NCLB, and Reading First in particular, has caused schools in many states to emphasize reading components other than comprehension (Walker, H., 2009). According to the National Reading Panel report used in NCLB legislation, phonics, phonemic awareness, vocabulary, and fluency are building blocks to comprehension. Members of the professional reading community varied in their support for NCLB, but they are in consensus about this point: there is no reading without comprehension. Comprehension is the tabletop; the other components are supporting legs. School districts and states that concentrate instruction and assessment on the four sub-skills, without subordinating them to comprehension, end up winning little battles but losing the war against illiteracy (IES, 2008).

Although research has established a strong correlation between vocabulary development and comprehension success (e.g., see Graves & Watts-Taffe, 2002; National Reading Panel, 2000), correlation between phonics and comprehension achievement is far from strong. Phonics skill does not guarantee comprehension, and the correlation becomes weaker as students mature. The same is true for oral reading fluency (narrowly defined as accurate and speedy word pronunciation) and comprehension (e.g., Nation & Snowling, 1998; Paris et al., 2005). In fact,

The Role of Phonics in Comprehension

The complicated relationship between word recognition (e.g., using phonics to decode) and comprehension was demonstrated in one study of students ranging from 7.5 to 9.5 years old. Thirteen and a half percent had good word recognition but poor comprehension. An examination of *low-performing* readers of the same age showed that 27.8 percent had good word recognition but poor comprehension (Shankweiler et al., 1999). Low-performing readers have a much greater than average tendency to show good word recognition and poor comprehension.

In a confirming study, 3 percent of fourth graders demonstrated good word recognition but poor comprehension, while 19.5 percent of fourth graders with reading difficulties had good word recognition but poor comprehension (Duke, 2007, citing Catts & Hogan).

It is simplistic and unwarranted to assume that all low-performing readers need more phonics or sight word instruction. Phonics is one tool to decode words, and it may or may not lead to comprehension. It is not *the* solution to comprehension problems.

An American Federation of Teachers publication puts it this way: "A child cannot understand what he cannot decode, but what he decodes is meaningless unless he can understand it" (Moats, 1999, p. 18).

---

there are documented cases of hyperlexic students who read words aloud very well but have no understanding (e.g., Nation, 1999; Sparks, 2004).

A concept of reading based on a narrow interpretation of the five-component reading model misrepresents what good readers do and what struggling readers need. Comprehension is much more complex than building up skills related to phonemes, spelling–sound patterns, and word pronunciation accuracy and speed.

To help remedy the shortcomings of this model, the two immediate past presidents of the IRA have proposed additional components (e.g., motivation, integrating writing with reading) to map more accurately the route to comprehension success (Allington, 2005c; Gambrell, Malloy, & Mazzoni, 2007). The comprehension practices suggested in this book reflect these recommendations, as well as those of other literacy experts.

WHAT IS THE STATE OF READING ACHIEVEMENT IN THE UNITED STATES?

A conservative estimate is that some 11 million adult Americans are illiterate. These individuals are not able to comprehend well enough "to function in society, to achieve one's goals, and to develop one's knowledge and potential" (U.S. Dept. of Education, 2005). Ready Resource 1.1 summarizes aspects of the illiteracy problem. Take a look and decide for yourself.

1. How do American students stack up internationally?
2. What seems to be the relationship between poverty and achievement?
3. What happens at the high school level that might stymie comprehension achievement?

Research digest: reading/comprehension achievement.

Failure to learn to read reflects an educational and public health problem affecting economic security and overall well being.

REID LYON, NATIONAL INSTITUTE FOR CHILD HEALTH AND DEVELOPMENT

- 20 percent of Americans read at the second-grade level or below.
- 34 percent of all fourth graders scored below basic.
- Fourth graders have made steady gains since 1992, but in some states the percentage below basic is as high as 61 percent (DC), 48 percent (LA), and 49 percent (MI).
- 60 percent of students have some degree of problem in learning to read. Only about one in three children learns to read with relative ease.

INTERNATIONAL GAP

- American fourth graders rank among the best in the world, but the ranking steadily declines after fourth grade.
- In international comparisons of reading, American eleventh graders place close to the bottom, behind students from developing countries such as the Philippines and Indonesia.
- Reading achievement in the United States has declined for twelfth graders since 1992.

MAJORITY/MINORITY GAP

- Gaps persist for poor children, ethnic/linguistic minorities, and urban children in comparison with richer Caucasian and Asian counterparts.
- African American students have made gains, but a 27-point gap between black and white fourth graders remains.
- While 34 percent of fourth graders are below basic proficiency (unable to read a simple book with fluency), the level is as high as 57 percent among African Americans and Hispanics.

- 40 percent of African American and Hispanic high school students cannot read at the basic level. (According to the 2000 Census, more than 380 languages and dialects are spoken in the United States, with Spanish second to English. Since 1990, the Hispanic population has grown 60 percent.)

RICH/POOR GAP

- 75 percent of dropouts report reading difficulties. Most are from poor families.
- Disadvantaged children may start school with half the vocabulary of a middle-class student.
- Low-income kindergartners speak 5,000 words on average, versus 20,000 for middle-class children.
- Advantaged children have had, on average, 5,000+ books read to them by kindergarten.
- By middle school, low socioeconomic status can be two grades behind.

GENDER GAP

- 20 percent of high school girls and 33 percent of boys can't read at the basic level. (The NAEP underestimates the problem, because dropouts don't take tests.)

LAWFUL/CRIMINAL GAP

- 50 percent of youths with criminal records have reading problems. Some states predict the size of prisons needed in the next decade on the basis of fourth grade failure rates (*USA Today*, p. 2A).
- 58 percent of drug abusers have a history of reading problems.

READY RESOURCE

1.1

Sources: Allington, 2002a; Hart & Risley, 2003; McCardle & Chhabra, 2004; NAAL, 2005; National Center for Education Statistics, 2007; NAEP, 2003–2007; RAND Reading Study Group, 2002; Snow, 2004; *USA Today*, 2001.

4. What patterns of achievement do you notice among differing groups (e.g., majority vs. minorities; differing genders)?

5. Which factors associated with reading failure could educators address, and how might they do this?

Howard Gardner, noted multiple intelligences theorist, points out that it is possible to forecast a student's chance of completing college and eventual income by the child's ZIP code. Indeed, statistics support his conclusion. Children who live in poor communities are more likely to have low achievement. Of course, many students from minority groups are poor (Au, 2002). Other disturbing facts include:

- On average, children who watched one hour of television a day scored 224 on the NAEP, those who watched four to five hours per day scored 213, and those who watched six or more hours scored 196. The last statistic was found in 13 percent of white students, 20 percent of Hispanics, and 40 percent of blacks.

- One quarter of African American and Hispanic students change schools each year, and they change more than three times by third grade; this is true for 13 percent of whites.

- 38 percent of black children, versus 75 percent of whites, live with two parents. (U.S. Dept. of Education, 1992–2000)

Then there is the "mother factor" (Guthrie, 2004). The odds are that a student who is rich, female, Asian, or Caucasian and has an educated mother won't have trouble learning to read. If the student is a poor male from an ethnic or linguistic minority and has an uneducated mother, he is likely to have trouble learning to read. At least that's what the numbers predict.

Teachers can't alter the ethnicities, genders, or family incomes of students. We can't boost the education level of our students' mothers. So what can educators do? To find solutions, we must have a clear grasp of the extent of comprehension achievement problems. We have to know the facts and acknowledge that there are "no quick fixes" (Allington & Walmsley, 2007).

If we keep doing what we've been doing, the bottom line will stay the same. Right now, the truth is that children usually don't close the gap. Most never catch up (Juel, 1988). Here are some additional statistics:

- Two-thirds of students with disabilities have learning disabilities, and the bulk of those students have reading problems.

- There is a 90 percent chance that a poor reader at the end of first grade will still be a poor reader in grade four (Juel, 1988).

- Almost 75 percent of students with reading disabilities in third grade still have problems in ninth grade (Francis et al., 1996).

- Comprehension is the biggest problem for struggling readers from third grade on (Farstrup & Samuels, 2002; RAND Reading Study Group, 2002).

The hope lies in doing things differently. That means a revolution in comprehension instruction.

Solving the Problem:
A Comprehension Revolution

The promise of revolutionizing comprehension instruction lies with teachers who will reject conventional practices and embrace "inventional" thinking needed for success in the third millennium. We need teachers who can "think unconventionally, question the herd, imagine new scenarios, and produce astonishing work" (Partnership for 21st Century Skills, 2008). What's more, we need teachers who can teach their students to think in these ways. How can we accomplish this revolution? In a nutshell, we must re-vision the concept of comprehension in light of 21st-century living conditions.

PUTTING COMPREHENSION FIRST

Putting comprehension first on the literacy agenda means more than adding minutes to comprehension instruction. Creative thinking is necessary to produce a different kind of instruction. Of course, all quality instruction depends on assessment to determine the learner's strengths and needs, followed by alignment of instructional practices with assessment results. Key instructional practices include:

- creating supportive learning contexts.
- clearly defining the comprehension task (both process and product).
- teaching students how to manage diverse texts.
- implementing a full range of the best comprehension teaching practices currently available.

When comprehension is put first, it follows that instructional time will be suitably apportioned. Although comprehension of print text presupposes a degree of accomplishment in sub-skills such as phonemic awareness, the alphabet, and word knowledge, putting children on a diet of these sub-skills until print fluency is attained is not warranted. In other words, thought-provoking comprehension instruction should not be withheld until children are expert word decoders. The Comprehension Problem Solving process outlined in this book includes strategies that have been successfully taught to kindergartners (Block & Pressley, 2007). Indeed, the prospect for all students to become active meaning makers depends on laying a solid foundation of comprehension strategy use in the primary grades alongside fundamental sub-skills. Educators must then continue to provide research-based comprehension instruction through middle and high school to assure all students are put on the road to a lifetime of literacy growth.

DIFFERENTIATING INSTRUCTION

In the past decade, states and local school districts have adopted many literacy policies and programs (e.g., high-stakes testing, teacher credentialing, and a raft of interventions) to address student achievement concerns. But no one strategy, method, or program has been found to be superior for *all* students (IRA, 2002; RAND Reading Study Group, 2002, p. xii). Nor is one likely to ever be found superior for all students. What can states and local school districts do to meet the challenge of teaching comprehension in such a manner that all students become adept at meaning making? Many choose to adopt a commercial basal series or another published program. The more promising approach, however, is one that is synthesized from comprehension research and adapted for particular students at particular schools (Pressley, 2006). This kind of custom-designed or "differentiated" instruction cannot be scripted or rigidly paced out. It is not the easiest way to teach, but it is key to the comprehension revolution.

Using "Five Factors" that influence comprehension success

Differentiated instruction draws from information about the educational context that is much more particular than the broad achievement statistics previously summarized. Picture successful comprehension as a textured fabric woven together with five threads. These "threads" are the specific characteristics of (1) learners, (2) texts, (3) tasks, (4) contexts, and (5) teaching (Lipson & Wixson, 1997; RAND, 2002). Considering comprehension from these five perspectives can give you fresh viewpoints about assessment and planning for inventive comprehension instruction. To get started, look at Ready Resource 1.2, which lists key questions linked to the Five Factors. These Five Factors are discussed further throughout this book.

Zeroing in on comprehension difficulties

Of course, any comprehension revolution must address comprehension difficulties. Interactions among the Five Factors of comprehension create an infinite variety of learner profiles. Finding *the* cause of an individual child's comprehension troubles is unlikely—multiple causes are the norm. It is important, however, to be aware of common patterns (RAND, 2002). Familiarity with the range of symptoms of comprehension difficulties will aid a teacher's understanding and help guide assessment and intervention. Here are examples of comprehension difficulties, using the Five Factors as organizers:

1. *Learner factors.* Ready Resource 1.3 summarizes common patterns.
2. *Context factors.* The place of learning may be physically uncomfortable or psychologically threatening.
3. *Text factors.* Diverse, stimulating, and appropriately leveled materials may not be available, or texts may be too restrictive (e.g., workbooks or computer drills used as mainstays).
4. *Task factors.* The comprehension task may be defined narrowly, with a focus on word-level tasks or memory-level thinking rather than problem solving to construct big ideas.

Five Factors of comprehension.

BIG IDEAS

Text comprehension varies because of the influence of these Five Factors. When educators use these factors to guide assessment and planning, the result is differentiated instruction that addresses diverse needs of students.

1 LEARNER
What are key characteristics of the person doing the reading, viewing, or listening?

2 TEXT
What are key characteristics of the text being read, viewed, or listened to?

COMPREHENSION

3 TASK
How is the act of comprehension defined? What is the expected outcome of product? Why and how is the text being used?

4 TEACHER/TEACHING
What are key characteristics of the teacher and the teaching strategies used?

5 CONTEXT
What are key characteristics concerning where, when, and with whom the text is being used?

READY RESOURCE

1.2

Sources: Fountas & Pinnell, 2006; Lipson & Wixson, 1997; RAND Reading Study Group, 2002.

5. *Teaching factors.* Comprehension instruction may be too limited or at too low a level. Teachers may not present themselves as literacy models, leaving a void that can hamper learners who have no other source of inspiration and insight regarding how to think about texts.

Designing differentiated interventions

Once the teacher has identified a specific problem or problems, the best intervention may not be directly connected to the problem. For example, if the comprehension problem is weak short-term memory, memory work is not a guaranteed solution to the problem (Duke, 2007). Low achievers need instruction that meets their unique needs, not repetition of the same methods that have not worked (RAND, 2002).

Comprehension problems must be addressed student by student, on the basis of assessment evidence that details the most likely contributors to the problem. Thoughtful teachers, well versed in cutting-edge comprehension research, decide which interventions promise the greatest comprehension gains given the instructional time available. The Five Factors previously discussed serve as organizers for assessment and subsequent instructional planning.

Am I suggesting an Individualized Educational Plan (IEP) for every child? No. Research suggests that for most students, teachers should spend the bulk of their time on key instructional events, such as engaged independent read-

READY RESOURCE 1.3

Learner characteristics: common comprehension difficulties.

- **Background:** inadequate experiences; failure to apply relevant prior knowledge to a text
- **Motivation:** unclear goals, lack of interest in the text or activity, or dependency rather than an independent orientation
- **Engagement:** inadequate amounts of reading practice that focuses on lack of active meaning construction
- **Memory:** problems with short-term or working memory
- **Oral language:** problems with listening or speaking (English), which are foundations for reading and writing
- **Comprehension strategies:** lack of or inappropriate use of a repertoire of problem-solving tools to make sense of diverse texts

- **Reading concept:** an incorrect idea of what reading and comprehension entail, so the reader may be passive or have low-level thinking
- **Vocabulary:** inadequate body of concepts and words that the reader recognizes automatically
- **Decoding:** insufficient tools to problem-solve unknown words
- **Fluency:** inability to read with expression, accuracy, and rate, which demonstrate understanding of word-based texts
- **Written language:** difficulties with processing the details and patterns in print that are needed to extract and construct meaning

ing and deep text discussions, that are embedded with the teaching of the comprehension strategies that comprise Comprehension Problem Solving. In the following chapters these main instructional literacy events are described. However, teachers often need more than a year to acquire and then effectively implement a full repertoire of research-backed comprehension instructional practices. Their success depends on the motivation to take on this study. This book is intended to be a tool for such work.

Learner Needs: Conditions for Success

This chapter has introduced the problems and possibilities surrounding comprehension. The path to success described in this book is not straight, and it can seem thorny, especially when teachers are challenged to consider the complexities of comprehension rather than implement a simple instructional recipe. How can teachers apply and adapt so much information for use with real children? It will take the rest of the book to answer that question, but bringing it down to thinking about a specific child will help.

Consider the case of Anna. She is in the third grade and can pronounce the first three hundred high-frequency words perfectly. But when Anna reads aloud, the words sound like a list. She does not put them together expressively, with phrasing and varied rate. Anna pronounces the words accurately and quickly, but when asked about what she is thinking, she is clueless. She says reading is "pronouncing words right" and "answering the teacher's questions." She is unable to name a single person in her life that she thinks is a good reader, except Torey, who "gets all A's." Anna says she hates reading, because it is boring. She says texting her friends is fun. When asked what she does when she doesn't understand what she reads, she again seems puzzled, but after a while she says, "ask the teacher."

These are just a few bits of information gained from an assessment that included an extensive interview with Anna. But it is enough for us to practice some instructional problem solving, using the Five Factors as anchors. Begin by comparing the information on Anna with the common difficulties listed in Ready Resource 1.3. What do you notice? What else would you want to know about Anna? How might you get more information?

Next, consider how students' literacy and comprehension development depend on their experiencing conditions that meet their needs. While children vary greatly, they also possess *common* needs (e.g., NCTE, 2004). The following key conditions reflect common learner needs. From these categories, try pulling ideas that might help meet Anna's needs.

CONTEXT

- *Learning spaces:* classrooms that are physically and psychologically supportive of inquiry into the meanings of diverse texts. A variety of appropriate materials is available, and the teacher's personality and disposition create a culture of respect and optimism.

TEXT

- *Engagement:* large blocks of time allotted for engaged reading, listening, and viewing; interaction with a variety of content-rich texts that take the diverse forms typical of the 21st century

TASK

- *Comprehension concept instruction:* explicit teaching (e.g., demonstrating) about the definition of comprehension, with focus on active meaning making by students. For example, students come to understand that reading is making meaning or sense from text, which is more than literal-level thinking about text.

- *Instruction in fundamental sub-skills:* teaching that includes (1) decoding, (2) word study, and (3) fluency. Students gain a solid repertoire of tools for independently problem-solving unknown words; receive vocabulary instruction that creates interest in words and focuses on concept development, wide reading, and discussion; and develop clarity about how to (a) apply "musical" elements to *express* understanding, (b) use flexible rates, and (c) increase the body of words they can accurately pronounce.

TEACHERS AND TEACHING

- *Literacy models:* opportunities to interact with people who show they enjoy reading and demonstrate how to comprehend well. For many students, the teacher must take the first position in providing a clear vision of how successful comprehenders think about texts.

- *Motivation:* teacher use of engagement strategies directed at activating students' intrinsic motivation. This happens when students: (a) are learning important content, (b) can pursue their own interests, (c) have choices, (d) have opportunities to do group work, and (e) have chances to perform or exhibit for an audience (Guthrie, 2002; NCTE, 2004).

- *Strategy instruction:* explicit teaching and scaffolded practice to help students learn a set of thinking tools for making sense of texts (Pressley, 2002).

- *Discussions:* high-level talk about important content (e.g., science and social studies) that invites students to inquire into big ideas and encourages students to generate important questions (Pearson, Harvey, & Goudis, 2005).

- *Assessment:* a variety of ways for students to show their strengths and needs so that teachers have solid information for planning differentiated instruction. Students also need tools that help them understand and participate in gauging their own progress.

- *Instructional routines:* main events that regularly occur during a literacy block of time, as well as instructional habits (e.g., asking open or "fat" questions that provoke diverse responses) embedded in content instruction.

- *Response options:* instruction that enables students to create verbal and nonverbal texts that show understanding and that others can read, listen to, or view.

snapshot revisited

I invite you to review the snapshots of Teachers A, B, C, and D in light of this chapter. My thoughts about the teachers' comprehension definitions and instructional practices are outlined below; compare with your own thoughts.

Teacher A

The use of literature and observation-based assessment is important. However, there is no evidence of purpose setting—and purpose is integral to inquiry-based problem solving that produces comprehension. There are many reasons to read: to get specific details from a recipe, to uplift your spirits with a poem, or to gain a new perspective from a newspaper cartoon. Such purposes set specific comprehension processes in motion and direct the nature of the problem-solving process that readers use to make sense of texts. A teacher may assign some purposes, but students need to learn to select their own purposes.

All the questions Teacher A asks require literal responses. This teacher seems to have a surface or low-level definition of comprehension: literal memory of literary elements—no meaning construction by students.

Teacher B

A purpose is set, and the sticky notes could be helpful. Reading instruction in the content area of social studies is embedded. However, there is no discussion, which is a high-priority comprehension strategy. I wonder about the types of questions this teacher uses; they seem to emphasize right-or-wrong answers. Teacher B seems to think comprehension means extracting information to answer his questions using specific text references—no student construction of meaning.

Teacher C

The teacher provides a focus and uses a story map as a scaffold. She uses a rubric for grading, which would make the criteria for grading clearer. The teacher gives students a purpose—read to retell—but if this purpose is used exclusively, students will think comprehending means recalling facts. Even when retelling involves paraphrasing, it focuses on memory of facts and not on constructing big ideas. This teacher seems to think comprehension means recalling and retelling facts.

Teacher D

The worksheet focuses on explicit main ideas, but main ideas reside in paragraphs. Main ideas may not at all represent big ideas in whole texts. What's more, limiting students' focus to ex-plicitly stated ideas denies the existence of *implicit* ideas, which even young children can and should be taught to derive (Walmsley, 2006). Use of collaborative groups provides attention to the social nature of literacy, but testing comprehension after reading is not teaching compre-hension. Comprehension accumulates as readers engage in the meaning-making process before, during, and after reading. To get at the heart of comprehension—making sense by focusing on big ideas—the multiple-choice questions would need to be more than choices among literal facts. To create meaning or sense, the reader has to pull together important information in a text, connect it to his or her prior knowledge, and construct supportable conclusions about the big ideas. Understanding involves a mental leap that relies on a set of strategies for problem solving for meaning. Teacher D seems to think comprehension means picking out the stated main ideas and supportive details.

In general, it is of great concern that Teachers A through D do no modeling of important *comprehending* strategies (teaching process) that would lead to *comprehension* of found and constructed big ideas (product). They all fall into a "mentioning and testing" pattern of comprehension instruction that has not proved effective.

Conclusion

Six hours of instruction a day for 180 days cannot overcome the effects of a deprived and impoverished home environment for 18 hours a day for 365 days a year.

W. MATHIS, 2005, p. 590

This book attempts to make a case against this quote. Chapter 1 began the case by previewing a different kind of comprehension instruction than what is currently the norm. The chapter acknowledged issues faced by American teachers that relate to comprehension and presented key literacy definitions in order to lay a foundation for considering a more contemporary approach. It presented a brief profile of our national comprehension problems, which included an overview of the dimensions of our unacceptable achievement levels. I discussed sluggishness in implementing an impressive body of research on comprehension instruction was discussed and outlined major findings about basic needs for literacy success.

Unfortunately, few teachers currently receive adequate pre-service preparation or ongoing professional development focused on reading comprehension (RAND, 2002). Comprehension achievement is a condition that can be changed, but change depends on teachers. In a world that is seeing rapid changes in communication, teachers must move beyond last-century literacy definitions and practices. A first step is putting comprehension first.

CHAPTER 1 big ideas

Big ideas are the key product of comprehension, and the most important big ideas are the ones you generate yourself. The following examples from this chapter may help you jump-start your own synthesis.

1. A teacher's definition of literacy, reading, and comprehension changes how she or he actually teaches.

2. Comprehension includes extracting information but focuses on constructing meaning.

3. A 21st-century definition of literacy, based on the abilities needed to succeed outside of school, should determine the nature of comprehension instruction.

4. The concept of *text* has evolved to include non-verbal materials, non-print works, and digital texts.

5. Low reading/comprehension achievement reflects an educational and public health problem affecting our nation's economic security and overall well-being.

6. Comprehension difficulties manifest in a range of characteristics related to these Five Factors: the nature of the learners, the learning context, the task of comprehension, text characteristics, and teaching qualities.

7. All students, regardless of their idiosyncrasies, have common needs that must be met for literacy development to proceed successfully.

8. Comprehension research has reached a critical mass—enough to support an instructional revolution.

9. Teaching students how to do inquiry-based problem solving with diverse texts is a promising approach to comprehension.

a look ahead

Reading is not an innate skill. On the alphabet level, there are 26 letters, 44 sounds, and more than 70 ways to spell these sounds, many of which cannot be understood through logic. Comprehension, however, is different. Comprehension involves executing coordinated thinking to solve problems. Problem solving is how humans have survived for millennia, and it is why we thrive. In Chapter 1 I previewed an inquiry-based approach that focuses on teaching students to use problem-solving strategies to construct meaning from diverse texts. The Comprehension Problem Solving process guides readers in deriving big ideas by way of self-questioning. Chapter 2 describes this approach, which assumes that problem solving *is* an innate skill.

CHAPTER 1 response options

Comprehension is facilitated when readers engage in problem solving to make meaning of texts. Following are suggested responses to this chapter that individuals or, preferably, small groups may use in the comprehension process.

1. List three to five of the biggest ideas that now make sense to you about (a) what comprehension includes and (b) how it should be taught. Explain your reasons for your choices.

2. Return to the opening questions to check your understanding. List points that you think you need to learn more about.

3. Create "if–then" statements about instruction, using the definitions of literacy, reading, comprehension, text, inquiry, and so on. For example, "IF literacy is the ability for effective communication of thoughts and feelings through comprehension and composition of diverse texts, THEN teachers should . . ."

4. Based on the concept of comprehension introduced in this chapter, suggest one way to change the instructional practices of each of Teachers A–D to increase students' comprehension.

5. Create a song, poem, or piece of visual art that expresses a definition of comprehension that focuses on making meaning from diverse texts.

6. Choose one of the common comprehension difficulties students encounter (see Ready Resource 1.3). Describe how you might address that difficulty, using the list of conditions most learners need for success. Alternatively, share your ideas for helping Anna, who was described in the section called "Learner Needs: Conditions for Success."

7. Use the Five Factors to analyze your own comprehension of this chapter. Use the key questions listed in Ready Resource 1.2.

8. Pretend that you have made it to round two in an interview process for a teaching position in a school that has a track record of low comprehension achievement. The principal invites you to explain to a teacher team the cutting edge views you have to revolutionize instruction. Outline key talking points about "comprehension first" that you will present.

Comprehension Problem Solving

INQUIRY INTO BIG IDEAS USING IMPORTANT QUESTIONS

preview

This chapter gives the rationale for the Comprehension Problem Solving process and describes the process in full. The process includes strategies, organized in a BEFORE/DURING/AFTER framework, to help readers make sense of diverse texts common in the 21st century. The chapter discusses unique features of CPS, including the central role of questions as a way to engage an inquiry stance and the focus on the product of the comprehension process: big ideas. Examples and sources of big ideas are provided.

important questions

1. How is CPS different from other strategy groupings?
2. What is meant by comprehension process versus comprehension product?
3. What role do questions play in CPS?
4. How do questions engage inquiry?
5. How are comprehension skills different from strategies, and why is it important for teachers to know the difference?
6. How are inquiry and problem solving integral to comprehension?
7. Why is it important for big ideas be the focus of comprehension?
8. What does the concept of "comprehension first" suggest for planning and teaching in the literacy curriculum and in other curricular areas?

Introduction

his chapter continues the investigation into the umbrella questions introduced in Chapter 1:

1. How and why should comprehension be given instructional priority—that is, be put first?
2. What is elemental to quality comprehension instruction?
3. How can comprehension instruction become inquiry-based, embedded in all instruction, and responsive to diverse students and texts?

Chapter 1 described the comprehension achievement problem and explained the impetus for a revolution in comprehension instruction. It previewed general instructional interventions and discussed ineffective strategies. For example, the strategies of merely mentioning thinking skills and of simply assigning reading followed by testing recall have not proven effective (Durkin, 1978–1979). Although an avalanche of research has suggested the kinds of changes that are needed in comprehension instruction, very few recommended practices have been implemented in daily instructional repertoires. Even very effective elementary teachers may not use comprehension practices considered most promising, despite repeated calls for different instruction (e.g., see NRP, 2000, Chapter 4). In particular, there is little comprehension *strategy* instruction and even less strategy instruction of the quality that results in students' independent unprompted problem solving of texts (Pressley, 2006).

Students' increased comprehension achievement is the goal. Putting comprehension first in the literacy program and in content area instruction would clearly be a step in the right direction. Making comprehension the priority requires developing teachers' knowledge and pedagogical expertise. One place to begin is with teachers doing a self-assessment of their knowledge about mental actions that successful comprehenders use. This chapter focuses on this knowledge base and, in particular, the roles that Comprehension Problem Solving, inquiry, and a big idea focus play in understanding verbal and non-verbal, print and non-print texts. Subsequent chapters address the question of *how* to teach students to use CPS independently and flexibly, using nine research-based best practices. Instruction of this kind would speak to the learner needs discussed in Chapter 1 and address comprehension difficulties that students commonly experience (refer back to Ready Resource 1.3 on p. 18).

Comprehension Problem Solving

Comprehension Problem Solving is a part of an inquiry-based approach to comprehension (see Ready Resource 2.1 below, and see Appendix B.4 for a copy-friendly version of this resource). It acknowledges that the ultimate goal of comprehension instruction is for learners to know *how, when, where,* and *why* to use problem-solving strategies *to understand,* whether they are reading for pleasure or for information. Another way of saying this is that comprehending content is the central problem all readers face when approaching any text, be it fiction, nonfiction, word-based, or wordless, and *problem-solving* strategies are necessary to achieve this comprehension goal.

Comprehension Problem Solving process.

BEFORE *Reading, viewing, or listening to a text*

Purpose-set. Create motivation, by focusing on the goal of comprehension.
- What's the problem? Why am I using this text?

Predict and connect. Overview the text to activate prior knowledge. Link the text to your own experiences, to other texts, and to what you know about the world.
- What is the text like, and how is the text organized?
- What do I already know about this problem or topic?
- What information or experiences do I predict this text will provide?

DURING *Gathering data by taking and making meaning from the text*

Determine important concepts. Use text clues as evidence.
- What does the author want me to think? Why?
- What do I think are key concepts or topics that might lead to big ideas?
- What facts or details (evidence) make me think these concepts or topics are key?

Infer conclusions. Use previous evidence to decide.
- What do I predict so far?

READY RESOURCE 2.1

(continued)

Comprehension Problem Solving process, continued.

READY RESOURCE

2.1

Image. Use your imagination to think about the text.

- What visual images can I make in my head?
- What feelings, smells, tastes, and sounds do I connect to the text?

Question and wonder. Speculate by questioning.

- Ask the Five W + H questions (who, what, when, where, why, and how).
- What predictions about important ideas are confirmed? Which ones should be rejected?
- What new predictions can I make about what is most important in the text?
- What new connections can I make (text–self, text–text, text–world)?

Monitor. Check whether you are making sense.

- Am I understanding? If not . . .
- Which Comprehension or Word Fix-Ups should I use? (See Ready Resources 5.5 and 8.11).

Analyze/critique. Zoom in–zoom out. Use text features and structures.

- If the text is narrative: What do I know about the characters? What are the problems? Where and when is the story happening? How are problems being resolved? What themes are emerging?
- If the text is expository: How is it organized (e.g., sequential, cause/effect, comparison)?
- If the text is non-verbal: What stands out? How does the text feel? Why?
- Overall: What are the important details and features? How are they related to the big ideas I'm finding and creating?

Incubate. Take time out.

- How can I take a break so I can review and reconsider from a fresh perspective?

Synthesize. Pull big ideas together.

- What are the most important concepts, themes or generalizations, and conclusions?
- What big idea statements are most important?

AFTER *Reading, viewing, or listening to a text*

Organize and shape. Transform the big ideas.

- How can I best show my understanding of the most important big ideas?

Reflect and revise. Think about the comprehension product.

- What works or makes sense? What doesn't work?
- How can I better show my comprehension?

Publish. Make your comprehension public.

- How can I share my comprehension "product"? With whom? When? Where?

Sources: Baker & Brown, 1984; Block & Pressley, 2007; Cordón & Day, 1996; National Reading Panel, 2000; Pearson & Dole, 1987; Pearson & Fielding, 1991; Pressley & Afflerbach, 1995; Pressley et al., 1989; RAND, 2002)

At this point, it will be useful to see CPS in action in a classroom context. The following snapshot features a teacher who has been teaching CPS since September. It is now the middle of October. Notice how Emma Corbett uses the prompts "my turn" and "your turn" to engage students in problem solving that integrates multiple strategies. Boldface words indicate important concepts and general teaching strategies, including ones particular to teaching CPS.

classroom snapshot

COMPREHENSION PROBLEM SOLVING

Oh the thinks you can think up if only you try.   —DR. SEUSS

Emma's third graders are partnered on a large rug. On the wall to Emma's left is a chart of the CPS process. (See Ready Resource 2.1.)

"Echo me!" Emma whispers. "Think left."

"Think left," the students echo softly.

"Think right," Emma says in a high pitch.

"Think right," the class squeaks.

"Oh the thinks you can think up if only you try!" she says, emphasizing *thinks* and stretching out *only you try.*

The class echoes. Emma repeats the line, with even more expression, twice more, pausing for students to imitate. She then stops. The classroom is quiet. She slowly slides a chart from behind her containing the poem they've been chanting, and she props it on the chalk tray.

Lesson Introduction

"Who do you think wrote this?" she smiles.

"You?" a boy asks.

"Thanks, Andrew, but no. It is a writer and artist whose name begins with *doctor*."

Immediately hands go up, and Emma calls on a girl.

"Dr. Seuss!" says Tamika.

"Yes! **How did you know?**"

"Well, the *doctor* clue, but it sounds like him, especially saying 'thinks' instead of 'things.'"

"Why do you say that, Tamika?" Emma asks.

"Because he writes different ideas and uses strange words. But I like it."

"Me too, especially *Green Eggs and Ham*," says a boy.

Emma smiles again. "Dr. Seuss is a writer and artist who has published lots of books. **What do you think he is saying in this poem? Take a minute to think."**

After about ten seconds she asks for **thumbs-up** and calls on several students.

"To think different ways."

"He could say think up and think down!" suggests a boy.

"To just keep thinking and new thinks will happen *if only you try!*" a girl says, imitating Emma's expression.

"Those are all important ideas," Emma says. "Look at our CPS chart. **How does this poem tell us about comprehension?**" Emma waits. "**This is a think question, so it is good to take some time.**" The class stares at the chart.

Finally a girl volunteers, "Comprehension starts with a problem and under *DURING* you have to keep trying to think of . . . of . . . thinks . . . yes, that's it, thinks to say what the book or story is really about." She finishes in a rush.

"Wow, that was a mouthful, Cheree! **What are some thinks from the rest of you?**"

"I agree with Cheree. Good readers make meaning in their heads—new thinks, that is the reading problem," explains a boy.

Lesson Development

"You are so right, Jonah. We've talked a lot about **good readers** and the *Before/During/After* **thinks** they use to solve the meaning-making problem. Today our focus is going to be on these **strategies.**" She points under *During* to **INFER CONCLUSIONS** and *DETERMINE IMPORTANT IDEAS*. **The students automatically choral read each phrase.**

"I'm going to start with *infer,*" Emma explains. "*Infer* means to use clues to make sense. The answer is not right in the words. **Let me show you.** Watch and listen to me think as I pull three items from my **Mystery Bag.** Then it will be **your turn.**"

She takes out a table knife. "I'm inferring from the knife that something will be cut," she says. Next she pulls out a piece of bread. "I'm now inferring the knife is for cutting the bread," she says. She then pulls out the last item, a jar of peanut butter. "Oh, now I'm inferring the knife is to spread the peanut butter. I don't think it is for cutting, because I only have one piece of bread, so I can just fold it over."

"Like on that grandpa commercial!" a boy says.

"Yes, Ash, just like," Emma smiles. "Now, it's **your turn** to do the thinks," she says. "After each item I'll pause for thirty seconds for you to partner talk."

This time Emma pulls out a check, a bill, and finally a stamped envelope. After each item she stops for the pairs to talk. Then she asks for volunteers to tell about their thinks.

One pair explains, "At first we said it was about going shopping, because my mom always takes checks. But when you held up the phone bill we said you were going to use the check to pay the bill. Last was the stamped envelope. It was a clue that you were going to mail the bill."

"**I noticed you connected the items to change your inference,**" says Emma. "What did the rest of you notice?"

"The objects gave us **evidence to think.**"

"I felt sort of sad about the bill, because it was so much!" explains a girl.

"**You inferred a feeling,** not just a think," says Emma.

"It was good you had a check to pay!" explains the girl.

Emma nods her head and asks, "**What else helped you to infer?**"

"I just thought how it all fit. **The problem was to make sense.** Sending a check to pay the bill made sense," says a boy.

"Well said. But, **how did you make sense when the answer was sort of invisible?**" Emma presses.

"Because of the **clues,**" says a girl. "It's like if you smelled smoke you would conclude there was a fire."

"I think you have it. Now, it works the same with reading as it does with the objects. You put the clues together to *infer* conclusions. *Determine importance* is the other strategy. Not every clue or every word is important."

"Like *to, a, the!*" says a girl as she points to a High Frequency Word Wall.

"Right, the high frequency words are needed, but they don't usually give us the best clues to meaning.

"Let's try inferring conclusions *and* determining important ideas with words. I'll use just the first sentence from a fable. The book is *Fables,* written and illustrated by Arnold Lobel," she says as she opens to the title page and points to his name.

"We've read and talked about Aesop's fables before, but these are newer fables. **I'm not going to show you the picture.** Just think about the sentence I read, and I'll demonstrate how I infer clues. **Listen to my thinking.**"

Emma reads, "The Camel had her heart set on becoming a ballet dancer." She then does a **think aloud** to model:

"**I'm inferring** the Camel really wants to dance **because of the clue words** 'heart set on.'"

When she finishes speaking children immediately put thumbs up, but she says, "**Talk with your partner** about conclusions you can infer. I'll set the **timer.**" After thirty seconds she asks for volunteers.

"We infer the Camel is willing to work hard, because she has her heart set," a girl explains. Emma calls on several pairs, who all focus on the same words.

"Let me **think aloud again** using different clues. I infer that the Camel has seen or heard about ballet dancers before because of the word 'becoming.' I infer she had some kind of experience with ballet to think of this goal."

"I infer she is going to have trouble, because she is a camel!" a boy immediately says. "**Why do you think that,** John?"

"Because camels have four legs and I infer it would be hard to get up on your toes and jump with so many legs and all that hump weight." The class laughs.

"Hey, this is like prediction!" another boy says.

"**Good connecting and noticing detail,**" she responds. "The thinks in CPS do overlap!" Emma then continues.

"Your **inferring is based on evidence,** so it is right on," Emma says. "Let's practice the second strategy. Remember, good readers use several strategies at once, but we're trying these two right now. **My turn.** I think the words camel, heart set, and ballet dancer are **important because** they helped me create a picture in my head. Take thirty seconds to talk with your partner about your brain pictures." Emma sets the timer, and when it buzzes she calls on volunteers.

"We both had an image of a brownish camel with a beating red heart and wearing pink ballet slippers."

"Our CPS chart says **visualize,** not image," a boy points out. The children all look at *Visualize* on the chart.

"Good point, Sam. *Visualize* means picture in your head. It is one way to use your imagination or make images. **How does visualizing help** you decide what is important?"

"Well, we've talked and talked about that you can't do any of CPS without visualizing," a girl responds.

"I can't think without visualizing!" says another girl.

"I'm visualizing my lunch," comments a boy and the class laughs. So does Emma.

Emma then refocuses the group and reads the rest of "The Camel Dances," **stopping at three more points** to do a think aloud and have students **partner talk** about inferring from clues and determining which ideas are most important. The students continue to focus on images they visualize but add character actions and things they say to judge what is important. They also **notice the similarities between prediction and inference.**

Emma asks for ideas to **create a chart** using the three categories of Important Ideas, Why?, and Inferences. Student examples appear in Ready Resource 2.2.

Lesson Conclusion

Right before lunch Emma asks her students to think about their inferences and answer these questions: What was the fable "The Camel Dances" *really* about? **What is the big idea the author wants to tell us?**

Comprehension is thinking, which is invisible. Making comprehension visible is key to assessment. After lunch, Emma asked her students to write for five minutes, answering the question, "What was the biggest idea for you in the fable?" The students then met in groups of three to five to discuss their ideas. Each group chose one big idea and planned a drama called a *tableau* (a frozen picture using their bodies) to show their big idea.

Making comprehension visible. The next day each group performed its tableau for the class, and the audience gave feedback. Most of the groups created tableaux where each member showed something he or she loved to do, such as skateboard, dance, draw, or swim. In a variation, Emma invited volunteers to perform again, setting the tableau in motion. What emerged was moving pantomimes of the students' interests, with faces and bodies that radiated concentration and joy. Keep Emma's lesson in mind as you read the rest of the chapter. In particular, think about:

1. What seemed most important in the lesson? Why?
2. What teaching strategies seemed most important to developing students' comprehension?
3. What do Emma's students think comprehension is? Why?

READY RESOURCE **2.2**

Inference chart for "The Camel Dances."

IMPORTANT IDEAS	WHY?	INFERENCE?
■ feet blistered	■ shows hard work	■ she won't give up
■ no applause	■ feels sad and mean	■ tests the camel's heart
■ dance for myself	■ shows her heart is set	■ she never had any more audiences, but it didn't matter

Defining Problem Solving and Inquiry

C PS is all about problem solving and inquiry. Both of these concepts are labels used universally to describe thinking processes employed by intelligent people. The scientific community continues to grapple with differences between the two, as we do in literacy (Fetters, Beller & Hickman, 2003; National Research Council, 2000). What is indisputable is that in all disciplinary fields inquiry and problem solving are prized. National professional associations in science (National Science Teachers Association), social studies (National Council for the Social Studies), and math (National Council of Teachers of Mathematics) have called for all instruction to be "inquiry based." Such instruction focuses on teaching students to be skilled problem solvers.

Inquiry and problem solving both involve questioning, in a search for information and pursuit of meaning (Ebenezer & Connor, 1998). Inquiry, however, is generally acknowledged to be an elevated form of problem solving, during which the learner is more self-directed (Chiapetta & Koballa, 2002; Fetters, Beller, & Hickman, 2003). Problem solving is taken to the inquiry level when a person increases his or her intensity of thinking and degree of commitment. In other words, inquiry is ardent problem solving with deep personal investment. It is self-motivating, since it springs from interest, curiosity, and wonderment (Sunal & Sunal, 2003).

Inquiry is engaged when an individual *chooses* to pursue solutions. The person adopts a "questioning stance" and seeks a range of possible meanings or solutions. Good readers use this stance in approaching texts, so it makes sense to place inquiry at the center of any instructional design for comprehension.

An inquiry approach focuses on teaching students to view texts as sources to solve their problems. For this approach to succeed, an important condition must be met. *If* students are to achieve the inquiry state of mind, they must learn to consider texts, including the Internet and multimedia, as problem-solving tasks from the beginning. In addition, they have to put the goal of comprehension (meaning making) first. To reach that goal, students need to know how to employ a repertoire of problem-solving strategies, and they must believe this is the route to making sense. There is no shortcut around thinking for yourself when the goal is successful comprehension.

The Teacher Tap Web site includes links to articles that make distinctions among project-, problem-, and inquiry-based learning.

> **Project-, Problem-, and Inquiry-Based Learning**
>
> http://eduscapes.com/tap/topic43.htm
>
> ONLINE RESOURCE
> WWW

Why Teach an Inquiry-Based Problem-Solving Approach to Comprehension?

 R ecently I met a first grader in a rural South Carolina school who was wearing a rope around his waist.

"Great belt," I said.

He smiled. "It ain't a belt, ma'am. My pants were comin' down. This here is my sister's jump rope."

I was told later that the boy was a "title" child and was having trouble learning to read. It was clear to me he wasn't having trouble problem solving.

The compulsion to problem solve is inborn. Our success as a species is predicated on the human urge to solve problems, often in novel ways. Children don't go a day without problem solving, even those who are growing up in the worst possible circumstances. So-called "disadvantaged" children have to be resourceful. Kids who face problems with food, clothing, shelter, and safety have developed strategies for survival that teachers can tap. Inquiry-based comprehension activities challenge students to develop their innate problem-solving tools further and apply them to the task of making sense from diverse texts.

Although problem solving has not led literacy headlines, it has received high-level endorsements. For example, the National Reading Panel used the phrase *"problem solving"* to summarize how readers derive meaning (2000, p. 14). National language arts standards and position statements also reference problem solving (IRA/NCTE, 1996; NCTE, 2004). These documents focus on both critical reading across genres and creating diverse products. Critical thinking and the invention of novel products are integral to problem solving.

Research Supporting CPS

CPS coordinates thinking for the purpose of making sense of texts during reading, viewing, and listening. Research supports teaching a repertoire of thinking strategies that parallels how mature readers think. Capable readers use an integrated toolkit of problem-solving strategies; they do not use one strategy at a time. They fluidly coordinate multiple strategies to make sense of text (Pressley, 2006; Reutzel, 2007).

Plenty of folks achieve high levels of comprehension, so it is reasonable to look to them for instructional insight. Researchers have done so for decades, and the resulting body of work is called the "good reader research." Comprehension Problem Solving draws on that research.

Interviews and observations confirm that good readers are mentally active. They use a set of strategies that increases their engagement with the text (Block & Pressley, 2007). Making sense is paramount, even though good readers are not always conscious of that expectation. Good readers do quickly become aware when any part of a text does not make sense, and they proceed to take action to create sense. They read aloud, reread, read ahead, and so forth. They realize when a text isn't making sense because they continually ask themselves questions (often without knowing it), such as "What does this mean? Where is this going? How does this relate?" They do not expect or want pat answers. They want meaning.

All of these behaviors create the inquiry orientation to comprehension that teachers desire for all students. Why do we desire it? Because this orientation is inherently motivating, and it leads students to view themselves as competent and unique. The ultimate result is satisfying and successful learning and living.

CPS is based on thirty years of research that have yielded more than two dozen comprehension processes (e.g., see Baker & Brown, 1984; Block & Pressley, 2002; Block & Pressley, 2007; Dole et al., 1991; Pearson & Fielding, 1991; Pearson et al., 1992; Pressley, 2000; Pressley, 2004; Pressley & Afflerbach, 1995). CPS draws on research undertaken to create comprehension strategy groupings such as those listed in Ready Resource 2.3. Early on, the focus on grouping strategies resulted in several flexible approaches. Reciprocal Teaching (Palinscar & Brown, 1984), which was one of the first models, targets four thinking strategies: Predict, Question, Clarify, and Summarize. A more recent package is transactional strategies instruction (TSI) (Pressley et al., 1992), which the National Reading Panel cited as exemplary (2000). Newer programs, such as Guthrie's (2004) Concept Oriented Reading Instruction (CORI), address the important role motivation plays in comprehension and incorporate strategies to process content (e.g., CORI uses science concepts/big ideas).

Comprehension strategy groupings.

The following models are examples of efforts to organize comprehension strategies. These are just some examples of the many models that have been developed over the past thirty years to teach students how to make meaning from text, with the goal of independent strategy use by students.

1 Reciprocal Teaching: Predict, Question, Clarify, Summarize (Palincsar & Brown, 1984)

2 KWL: Know, Want to Know, Learned (Ogle, 1986)

3 QAR: Question Answer Relationship (Raphael, Au, & Highfield, 2006)

4 Imagery Training: Making Mental Art (e.g., see www.vue.org) (Housen & Yenawine, 2000)

5 TSI/SAIL: Transactional Strategy Instruction (Pressley et al., 1992)

6 CORI: Concept Oriented Reading Instruction (Guthrie et al., 1998)

7 QtA: Questioning the Author (Beck & McKeown, 2006)

8 Direct Explanation (Duffy et al., 1987)

9 Informed Strategy Training (Paris, Cross & Lipson, 1984)

10 Cognitive Apprenticeships (Collins, Brown & Newman, 1989)

11 CSR: Collaborative Strategic Reading (Klinger & Vaughn, 1999)

12 Reason to Read (Block, Mangieri, & Fowkes, 1997)

13 REQUEST (Manzo, 1969)

14 Thinking Themes (Cunningham & Smith, 2008)

15 Web Quests: Problem solving with hypertext (http://webquest.org)

16 CPM: Comprehension Process Motions (Block, Paris, & Whiteley, 2008)

17 START: Strategy Teaching + Active Response Tasks (Scharlach, 2008)

18 CPS: Comprehension Problem Solving (Cornett, 2010)

READY RESOURCE **2.3**

The CPS Process

The promise of the "comprehension first" proposal described in this book can be realized only if *qualitative* changes are made in the teaching of comprehension. It is not enough just to increase time spent on traditional "comprehension" activities, such as answering questions at the end of a text.

Qualitative instructional change should be built on the foundation laid by decades of research that has increasingly revealed details of how comprehension happens. Comprehension is a multifaceted process that relies on many thinking strategies, which have sometimes been referred to as problem solving. The premise put forth in this book is that comprehension is *always* about problem solving.

The Comprehension Problem Solving process stands on the shoulders of its thinking strategy ancestors. It goes further, however, to stress the importance of teaching students *how to* use the full range of problem-solving strategies purposefully and intentionally. The purpose of comprehension is presented as unequivocal: to make sense of the many forms of texts found in today's world. The essence of CPS is its inquiry orientation. Inquiry is directed by questions individuals generate in their search for meaning, i.e., comprehension. The goal is a comprehension product made of important big ideas found in and created from texts.

The CPS process organizes thinking strategies into *before, during,* and *after* (BDA) stages, but successful comprehenders use the process flexibly. Good readers frequently skip around and move back and forth in their use of thinking strategies. Capable comprehenders return to and revise their purposes and predictions as they process more text, in a "review and add to" manner. The amount of time that a reader spends using any single problem-solving strategy depends on the nature of the reader, the specific task at hand, the peculiarities of the text, and the context or place of text use, as well as available teaching support. In this way the Five Factors introduced in Chapter 1 and shown in Ready Resource 1.2 are revisited.

Throughout the BDA stages, readers construct comprehension by continually questioning, both intentionally and intuitively. Of course, mature readers, listeners, and viewers are not often conscious that they are using problem-solving strategies. A mark of comprehension maturity is the automatic, unconscious use of strategies, analogous to an experienced driver's coordination of the myriad skills involved in driving a car to a destination. Hence, one of the challenges for teachers is a personal one: teachers must become aware of their own thinking. This means slowing down their own personal comprehension problem solving and reflecting on how it happens, so that they can explain and model the process for students. Without such clarity in instruction, some students will not progress in their comprehension development.

Following is a more detailed explanation of the CPS process. Questions that propel the CPS process forward are included with each strategy.

BEFORE Reading, Viewing, or Listening to a Text

The stage is set for comprehension when learners start thinking prior to actual use of a text. Students need to understand why and how the text addresses their needs.

Purpose-set: Create motivation by focusing on the goal of comprehension

- *What's the problem?*
- *Why am I using this text?*

Purpose is integral to motivation. Human beings are wired to want to know why, and they seek texts that connect to their needs. Successful comprehension is more likely when text use begins with the reader's general purpose of expecting to make sense. The reader then couples this general purpose with specific reasons for using the text at hand. The question "Why am I using this text?" sets problem solving in motion.

Louise Rosenblatt (1978) theorized that readers have different purposes for reading. She divided these purposes into two categories: (1) efferent, involving seeking for information or facts, which may produce a more narrow interpretation of a text, and (2) aesthetic, where the emphasis is on "experiencing" the text, with more attention to the emotions and feelings the text provokes. When I want to read a good story in order to escape and relax, this is a different problem from learning something, but it is still a problem. I will make sense differently, because my purpose is different. For example, I may read faster to get the gist of the plot. Of course, any text may be read for a combination of purposes: I might read a poem for information or a recipe for aesthetic understanding (e.g., appreciation of the creative use of ingredients or even the sound of words like "arugula").

Let's say I want to understand illegal immigration better. My problem can be stated as "How can I make sense of or learn more about illegal immigration, using particular texts?" My problem or purpose will determine not just why I read, but how: I'll be looking for credible facts, so I will skim, scan, and slow down to study certain sections. I might read a narrative like *Esperanza Rising* (a fictionalized biography of the author's Mexican grandmother) along with consulting a government Web site. I can experience both texts aesthetically and efferently, proportionally to my purposes and the nature of each text. In the case of the narrative, I can't help but enjoy the author's artful chapter titles, which use Spanish names for fruits and vegetables. At the same time, I am also aware that I am learning many facts about immigrant experiences that help me better understand why people take risks and break United States laws.

Readers who begin by focusing on a problem understand that they must both find and make meaning by thinking about text clues. Problem solving requires mental action, not passive absorption of facts or pronunciation of words. A problem focus triggers motivation to inquire and activates a "can do, will do, want to do" attitude. The more the text relates to the reader's problems and interests, the more motivated the reader will be.

Predict and connect: Overview the text to activate prior knowledge

- *What is the text like, and how is the text organized?*
- *What do I already know about this problem or topic?*
- *What information or experiences do I predict this text will provide?*

An overview of a text activates areas of the brain, called *schemata*, that store prior knowledge. The overview (or preview/survey) generates questions related to what the text will be about and how it is organized. This helps the reader make connections to personal experiences (text to self). As a result, the reader can make predictions about how much the text may contribute to solving the initial problem, be it acquiring information, gaining pleasure, or both. The reader can also make connections between the present text and other texts he or she has read, heard, or seen (text to text) and then compare and contrast these texts, judging the attributes of each. The reader can make additional links between the current text and what he or she knows about the world in general (text to world). In the predict and connect step, the reader links the text to his or her own experiences (text to self), to other texts (text to text), and to what he or she knows about the world (text to the world) (Fountas & Pinnell, 2001).

Capable comprehenders begin to brainstorm and hypothesize during and after a text overview. For example, a reader of this book might predict that I am going to present research to support specific comprehension instructional practices. The reader hypothesizes by thinking, "I think this is going to be about . . . and I wonder if . . . ." This kind of engagement with text lays the foundation for successful comprehension.

DURING Reading, Viewing, or Listening to a Text: Data Gathering by Taking and Making Meaning

Once the reader, listener, or viewer is engaged with a text, he or she may use the following thinking strategies to engage in further problem solving. Each strategy is both discrete (useful on its own) and connected to the other thinking strategies.

Determine important concepts: Use text clues as evidence

- *What does the author want me to think? Why?*
- *What do I think are key concepts or topics that might lead to big ideas?*
- *What facts or details (evidence) make me think these concepts or topics are key?*

Mature comprehenders realize authors write with their own purposes in mind, so they think about the author's motives and purposes as they consider topics or concepts that may lead to big ideas. Even a novel that is read for pleasure requires the reader to focus on important plot events, character traits, and where the story is going (i.e., themes) in order to make sense of it. Emma Corbett scaffolded thinking about important ideas by directing students to notice strong images in the fable.

Infer conclusions: Use previous evidence to decide

- *What do I predict so far?*

To infer is to draw conclusions, using facts and details as evidence for decisions. Inferring and predicting are related. A reader, listener, or viewer repeatedly infers and predicts as she or he proceeds through a text. Readers use recursive (back and forth) and spiraling (building up from evidence) thinking. For example, I might learn statistics about illegal immigration and use those facts to start generating inferences about potential effects on the economy. Readers also continually discard irrelevant details, depending on their purposes.

Reading rate changes depending on the reader's purpose. For example, readers read faster when they skim or use selective scanning to locate details (e.g., sections of an expository text) and read more slowly when their intention is to study or savor.

Image: Use your imagination to think about the text

- *What visual images can I make in my head?*
- *What feelings, smells, tastes, and sounds do I connect to the text?*

"Image" is the root of the word "imagination." Without imagination, we cannot think about the past or envision the future. People image as they read, view, or listen to any text, and images may arise from any of our senses. There is particularly strong evidence for the influence of visual images on comprehension (Gambrell & Koskinen, 2002; RAND, 2002; Sadoski & Paivio, 2001).

An argument can be made that visualization is the basis for most thinking. Humans have thirty times more visual nerve fibers than auditory, and 30 percent of the brain's cortex is devoted to visual processing (compared to 3 percent for hearing) (Lindstrom, 1999). Written communication had its origins in visual images called pictographs. This history is apparent in Egyptian hieroglyphics and Chinese characters in which certain symbols retain a likeness to the thing represented. Our English alphabet, a much more recent invention, uses "abstract" symbols that are phonetic rather than image-based.

Einstein claimed he did all his thinking by visualizing, and most capable readers are able to generate visual images from texts almost effortlessly, which accounts for some of the enjoyment in reading. Of course, visual images may result from processing any text form. For example, music and songs frequently stimulate visual memories and can stir the imagination to produce emotions and other images, as well.

Question and wonder: Speculate by questioning

- *Ask the Five W + H questions (who, what, when, where, why, and how)*
- *What predictions about important ideas are confirmed? Which ones should be rejected?*
- *What new predictions can I make about what is most important in the text?*
- *What new connections can I make (text-to-self, text-to-text, text-to-world)?*

Questioning occurs throughout the problem-solving process, but here it is addressed separately, because of its importance. Without questioning there is no inquiry.

The basic Five W + H question stems enable readers to group and re-group ideas continually in order to speculate on meaning, even as it is created. Some predictions about what is important may be confirmed by text evidence, while other predictions must be rejected. New predictions result from the constant questioning that the search for meaning provokes. Of course, all of this questioning should connect back to the reader's original purposes for using the text.

Monitor: Check whether you are making sense

- *Am I understanding? If not . . .*
- *Which Comprehension or Word Fix-Ups should I use?*

People are "homo sapiens *sapiens.*" That means we are a species capable of thinking about our own thinking. Over thirty years ago Flavell coined the term "metacognition" to label this process (1977). Successful comprehension depends on the expectation that texts will make sense, and successful comprehenders think continually about the extent to which sense is being made. For example, mature readers are aware when a word, sentence, paragraph, or section isn't making sense, and they take action when this occurs. Ready Resources 5.5 (Chapter 5) and 8.11 (Chapter 8) show common actions readers take to fix problems at the word level and deal with general comprehension issues.

Analyze/critique: Zoom in—zoom out using text features and structures

- *If the text is narrative: What do I know about the characters? What are the problems? Where and when is the story happening? How are problems being resolved? What themes are emerging?*
- *If the text is expository: How is it organized (e.g., sequential, cause/effect, comparison)?*
- *If the text is non-verbal or non-print: What stands out? How does the text feel? Why?*
- *Overall: What are the important details and features? How are they related to the big ideas I'm finding and creating?*

Comprehension evolves as the reader's thinking moves back and forth between the big picture and the details. The reader zooms in on text features and structures (e.g., story elements and paragraph structures) and zooms back out to see how the details relate to developing big ideas. Topics, concepts, facts, themes, and details begin to organize into big ideas that will eventually take the form of theme statements and generalizations. These big ideas are more than main ideas in paragraphs, because they take the full text into account. The reader arrives at these big ideas through a process of deciding what is important to include and discarding the rest. Through continually judging what to keep and what to throw away (depending on the reader's purposes for using the text), the reader constructs meaning. This "critical thinking" is essential to meaning making (Gambrell, Malloy, & Mazzoni, 2007).

Incubate: Take time out

- *How can I take a break so I can review and reconsider from a fresh perspective?*

An incubation period is a pause that allows the reader's mind time to process significant details—to stir them around, group and regroup them in creative ways. This process is essential to creating new big ideas. Often reported examples of the power of incubation have to do with going to sleep and waking up with a solution to a problem. Incubation time may range from a few minutes to a few days, and it may take various forms. Artists and writers play or listen to music, exercise, and engage in other activities to promote incubation. They know incubation increases connections among prior knowledge, other texts, and world knowledge to yield a fresh perspective and the possibility of an "ah-ha" (creative insight) experience (Cornett, 2011; Duke, 2001).

Synthesize: Pull big ideas together

- *What are the most important concepts, themes or generalizations, and conclusions?*
- *What big idea statements are most important?*

As a person nears the end of reading, viewing, or listening to a text, its parts and pieces should start coming together to create "sense." The reader synthesizes in order to pull the ideas together to address the original purpose for using the text. Creative combinations of significant details can result in "insight"—a highly rewarding new view of how small ideas fit together to make big ideas. For example, in hopes of gaining insight in my pursuit of understanding about illegal immigration, toward the end of my reading I would synthesize the most important big ideas I had found or created.

AFTER Reading, Viewing, or Listening to a Text

At this stage, learners are taking the information and experience of the text further by responding in various ways. Some of the activities of this stage may result in "publication" of original ideas.

Organize and shape: Transform the big ideas

- *How can I best show my understanding of the most important big ideas?*

The comprehension product is revealed when the reader gives shape to big ideas that have been extracted and constructed. For example, the reader might create a text summary, which is more than a retelling. The summary need not take the conventional form common in schools. I might create a summary that explains my more informed stance on an issue like illegal immigration and present my point of view to the local Rotary Club. Alternatively, I might hone in on the texts themselves. I may have come to conclusions related to my general satisfaction or dissatisfaction with the texts I used, leading me to recommend or not recommend them. A recommendation reflects the organization and shaping of my conclusions.

Note that it is common for the shaping of big ideas to result in the creation of new texts. If I decide to discuss illegal immigration with a group of friends, I will shape my ideas differently than if I plan to speak at the local Rotary Club (for which I might create a more formal PowerPoint presentation). I might choose to write a song, create a painting, or design a model that shapes and expresses my personally constructed insights. All of these forms are texts.

Reflect and revise: Think about the comprehension product

- *What works or makes sense? What doesn't work?*
- *How can I better show my comprehension?*

Once big ideas have taken shape to solve the initial problem, it is time to step back and evaluate the comprehension product. Revision involves making both big changes (e.g., changing the point of view in a written piece or adding graphics or music for a multimedia product) and small changes (e.g., correcting spelling). Reflection and revision may result in a different concrete product, or they may lead to invisible changes, such as the reader's reevaluation of conclusions about what the most important big ideas really are.

Publish: Make your comprehension public

- *How can I share my comprehension "product"? With whom? When? Where?*

To publish means to "make public." No one immediately makes their comprehension of every text public, but all texts that are used purposefully will become part of who we are and what we know, believe, and do. Of course in school, teachers often require visible comprehension products when learners undertake a reading, listening, or viewing task. Unfortunately, school products are too often unlike the products of comprehension created in real life. Outside of school, comprehension is made visible in discussions, blogs, Internet postings, poems, songs, paintings, dances, playwriting, and other communication vehicles. In life beyond school, multiple-choice tests are not the most common way folks demonstrate and share personal understanding.

Special Features of the CPS Process

 he prominent features of the Comprehension Problem Solving process are summarized below. These features distinguish it from other groupings, supporting its use as the centerpiece of comprehension instruction.

FOCUSES ON PROBLEM SOLVING

The CPS process addresses the need for learners to have a full toolkit of problem-solving strategies. No one tries to build a house with only a hammer, wrench, and saw. Drills, screwdrivers, and levels are necessary. For too long, many teachers have tried to build the house of comprehension with an inadequate toolkit. The before, during, and after strategies in CPS provide a full set of problem-solving tools that can be used with a variety of texts, including non-verbal, non-print, and multimedia texts such as paintings, songs, films, and Internet sites. You will see that Ready Resource 3.1 (Chapter 3) gives an example of using the CPS process to make sense of a Cheerios box!

CPS pushes problem solving to the big idea level, which entails making sense of full texts, not just paragraphs or sections; however, it acknowledges that problem solving must also occur at the word and sentence levels. For example, during the monitoring step of CPS, good readers omit words, skip around, and reread words and sentences in their efforts to make sense. Readers also problem-solve paragraphs and then integrate them into whole texts (Block & Pressley, 2007).

ENCOURAGES INQUIRY

An important premise of this book is that literacy educators should take problem solving to the inquiry level. How? One effective way is by asking important questions, especially ones that begin with "why," "how," and "what if." Look back at the snapshot of Emma teaching the CPS process to see how she encourages students with open questions that both model good questioning and invite students to wonder and become more interested. The objective, however, is for students to initiate their own questions, which is a chief goal in the comprehension first approach.

Another teaching strategy that promotes an inquiry stance is to offer choices to students, such as which texts to use and where and how they can demonstrate comprehension in alternative ways. Emma does this with a form of drama, called tableau, that results in an arts-based text that can be "read" in its own right. Later chapters discuss further the use of choices and response options to increase comprehension.

IS USED IN CONTEXT

The strategies in the CPS process were selected because they occur frequently in many strategy groupings (see Ready Resource 2.3) and because they are important to solving the sense-making problem. CPS organizes thinking in a problem-solving format that parallels life outside of school. In daily life, we just don't go around predicting or summarizing in isolation and without a purpose. We must think to solve any problem, whether it is figuring out what to wear, what to cook, or what career path to choose. Problems come in all sizes and cannot be solved with "an unintegrated set of encapsulated strategies" (Reutzel, Smith, & Fawson, 2005).

Remember that Emma's students seemed to be familiar with the *whole* CPS process, even though, in this lesson, she focused on inferring and determining importance. Students need to see the entire CPS process from the outset so they have the big picture of comprehension processes. Emma made this process clear by posting a full chart. Over time, she then selected strategies to teach explicitly, and she integrated new strategies with familiar strategies in a review and add-to manner. Single strategies are important, but comprehension depends on choosing and coordinating *multiple* strategies when they are needed to make sense. For example, I don't need to zoom in and analyze particular details in a text unless I perceive a need to do so. If I do zoom in on details, it is often for the purpose of connecting discrete ideas to overall emerging big ideas. These "pieces" become evidence for conclusions I am drawing about what is important. I may also zoom in because I don't know a word in the text and need to use word-solving strategies to make sense. (Ready Resource 8.11 in Chapter 8 lists Word Fix-Ups.) Then again, I might analyze specific words or phrases simply because I enjoy their look, sound, or meaning, that is, for aesthetic purposes.

EMPHASIZES STRATEGIES VERSUS SKILLS

The word *skill* tends to evoke images of drill and practice. Practice is important, but drilling skills outside of meaningful problem-solving contexts deflates motivation, because it lacks authentic purpose. Motivation is the engine for any learning and for comprehension in particular. Students' motivation depends on a sense that schoolwork has worth beyond getting a grade or pleasing a teacher.

Strategies are bundles of skills used purposefully and flexibly to solve problems. Think of the skill of hammering a nail. That skill is really a skill-set (a set of actions) that becomes a strategy when it is used to solve problems ranging from hanging a picture to building a house. The use of comprehension strategies depends on the ability to use skills such as sequencing, comparing/contrasting, determining causes and effects, skimming, and so forth. However, having students practice these skills without connecting them to their use in problem-solving texts stalls motivation and will not result in deep comprehension.

Teachers have spent far too long teaching skills using isolated drills and worksheets. Even if skills are practiced with complete texts, they do not automatically add up to comprehension. For example, I can put all the events in the story of the "Three Little Pigs" in order, but that will not mean I have made sense of the big ideas. I might also be skilled at picking main ideas out of paragraphs, but main ideas are not the same as big ideas. "The Three Little Pigs" is not about pigs and wolves. One of the big ideas is that a house can easily fall if it is built with weak materials. Comprehension will also continue to be weak if we build it by dwelling on skills. Comprehension depends on the tactical use of problem-solving strategies to make sense of full texts. CPS teaches that.

PARALLELS PROCESSES IN OTHER DISCIPLINES

The CPS process involves orchestrating mental processes that accomplished thinkers routinely use across many contexts and disciplines. For example, it is parallel to the writing composition process (e.g., the sequence of plan/draft/

revise). Both begin with a problem focus and proceed using much the same thinking. Consider that composition (written, visual art, music, or dance) is *expressed* meaning that is first created mentally, just as in comprehension. Interestingly, comprehension is sometimes called "composed meaning." The CPS process also parallels scientific problem solving, historical reasoning, and the creative problem solving used in the creation of arts products and aesthetic understanding (Cornett, 2011).

IS EVIDENCE BASED

Recall how Emma pressed her students for evidence with questions like *"Why do you think that?"* Central to teaching the CPS process is what John Dewey called the "grounding of belief." Predictions, inferences, summaries, and conclusions have integrity only when they are supported with evidence, such as details from a credible text. Sense is not created without clues, cues, and supportive evidence.

REVOLVES AROUND IMPORTANT QUESTIONS

Integral to the CPS process are important questions that ratchet the process forward. Students learn to generate important questions and to expect questions to have a range of possible answers, not one right answer. Students learn to use the CPS process to arrive at big ideas by continually asking important questions (e.g., how? why? what if?). Teachers can scaffold the learning of how to generate questions by posting question stems and examples of provocative questions. Emma put hers on a window roller shade in her classroom to maximize space. See more question examples in Chapter 7.

LEADS TO BIG IDEAS

Remember that comprehension is both process (i.e., problem-solving strategies) and product. The product is made of the ideas that the reader extracts and creates through interacting with texts. The purpose of the CPS process is to help students coordinate multiple strategies to find and create big ideas using any text, be it verbal or non-verbal, print or non-print. Process when connected to content is given purpose and meaning. This happens when comprehension strategies are used as tools for understanding. A big idea focus improves comprehension of texts used during instruction, with the goal of comprehension transfer to new texts (RAND, 2002).

IS MOTIVATING

The CPS process taps into innate propensities to make sense. Making sense is highly self-motivating, especially when readers are inquiring into interests and personal questions. The exuberance of Emma's students gives testimony to this effect. I heard them say things like, "I can just see that camel dancing for the fun of it and that makes me so happy" and "I predict that the other animals are just jealous and won't like the show."

In sum, the CPS process makes sense because it coordinates thinking processes for solving problems. It is more comprehensive than other models, and it transcends the school context and a narrow focus on traditional print texts. The strategies of CPS are to be used as capable comprehenders use them: to derive understanding from texts. Of course, essential questions about *when* and *where* to use CPS strategies, as well as *why*, must be modeled by teachers and discussed with students in order for them to gain full use of the process. Without understandings about *when*, *where*, and *why*, CPS strategy lessons are reduced to mere academic exercises. With its big idea focus, the CPS process acknowledges that the comprehension process must yield a product—created understanding. Comprehension is the communication part of reading, listening, and viewing; text, alone, is simply a source, both "important and insufficient" (RAND, 2002, p. 11).

Big Ideas: What? and Why?

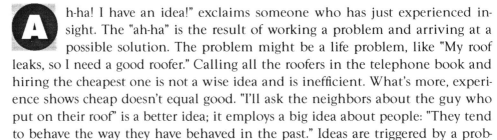 h-ha! I have an idea!" exclaims someone who has just experienced insight. The "ah-ha" is the result of working a problem and arriving at a possible solution. The problem might be a life problem, like "My roof leaks, so I need a good roofer." Calling all the roofers in the telephone book and hiring the cheapest one is not a wise idea and is inefficient. What's more, experience shows cheap doesn't equal good. "I'll ask the neighbors about the guy who put on their roof" is a better idea; it employs a big idea about people: "They tend to behave the way they have behaved in the past." Ideas are triggered by a problem-solving stance—trying to figure something out or make sense of a situation.

Kids learn early to ask, "What's the big idea?" when someone says or does something incomprehensible. People want to understand big ideas. That is why CPS focuses on teaching students how to find and create big ideas.

BIG IDEAS DEFINED

The concept of a big idea is analogous to many other concepts, including thesis, contention, argument, proposition, claim, premise, assumption, hypothesis, postulation, supposition, theme statement, enduring understanding, generalization, and universal truth (Costa & Kallick, 2000; Edelsky, Altwerger, & Flores, 1991; Perkins, 2004; Wiggins & McTighe, 2005). Literary big ideas can be formulated by converting themes into full sentences. For example, "death" is a theme, but "Death is a natural part of life" is a big idea theme statement. These are "generalized understandings," not "the many details that led to those understandings" (Pressley, 2007, p. 397).

Big ideas are more than isolated concepts or topics; they are greater than the main idea of a paragraph, as well. Big ideas are important understandings about people and the world. *Concepts* and *topics* like seasons, friends, community, and cycles are key to the development of big umbrella ideas. For example, after seeing the musical *Cinderella* (an arts/language arts text) at the Flat Rock Playhouse in North Carolina, students said the story was about "imagination." Coached with the question, "What about 'imagination'?" they said, "Using your imagination to escape a bad life" and "Using your imagination to give yourself hope." Additional coaching with open questions (e.g., How was hope created?) yielded these big ideas: (1) If you imagine or dream something, it gives you a goal to work for and (2) Sometimes you can live in your imagination and think about possibilities. That can make you feel happy.

In life we learn big ideas from many "texts," including life experiences and people we respect, such as our parents. "Think before you speak," "Sleep on it before deciding," and "Don't judge a book by its cover" are examples. Thinkers collect big ideas and use them to form assumptions or premises for theories and models. Major professional associations for literacy, science, social studies, math, and the arts have set out guidelines related to standards to help professionals focus on big ideas. See Ready Resource 3.6.

WHY BIG IDEAS?

We need content to "fuel comprehension and composition" (Gambrell, Malloy, & Mazzoni, 2007, p. 44). It is rare to think about nothing, even when we sleep. The fuel for thinking is, first, a natural desire to make sense (to inquire) and, second, something worthwhile to think about. That something is content. Content is made of ideas humans have categorized into disciplines such as science, social studies, literature, math, and the arts. Big ideas resist pigeonholing, however, so they often overlap: Where do you put "Life is made of cycles"? Is it science or literature? How about cycles in relationships? Hmmm—that seems to be social studies, but it is also a common big idea in literature, drama/theatre, music, and dance.

Today we are bombarded with content; it grows exponentially, as the Internet and television demonstrate daily. However, covering lots of content quickly and indiscriminately results in poor content learning (Torgesen, 2006). A curriculum that is an inch deep and a mile wide does not produce knowledgeable and thoughtful students. Nor does this kind of curriculum produce a satisfying learning experience. Long-term comprehension improvement just doesn't happen unless the focus of learning is on "critical content" (Duke, 2007; Torgesen, 2006, p. 30). Big ideas are critical content.

Students who are oriented to find and construct big ideas related to content texts have a motivational advantage over students who are geared to focus on learning for external reasons like grades (Guthrie, 2004). Big ideas have inherent interest, because they explain real life. Seeking big ideas involves problem solving and being "creatively flexible," which are also intrinsically motivating activities (pp. 386–387). Conversely, students who are urged to learn in order to perform well on tests become "procedural and anxious," which serves to remind us that *test* is a four-letter word (p. 386).

In summary, big ideas . . .

- Kick thinking up a notch, going beyond paragraphs to the meaning of full texts.
- Relate to students' lives, because big ideas are relevant to real-life problem solving and can be transferred to new situations.
- Prioritize the vast amount of material that makes up the world's content.

- Help teachers budget instructional time, so that the most time is spent on the most important ideas, as opposed to superficial covering of topics.
- Cut across disciplines, so interdisciplinary relationships can be explored. As a result, teaching can be integrated to economize on time (e.g., a unit on "Life is made of cycles and patterns").

snapshot revisited

In the thousands of hours I've spent observing hundreds of teachers, I have seen quite a few like Emma Corbett. She represents teachers who question convention and embrace research while maintaining personal style. Emma teaches in an integrated arts school, so she does have an advantage—she is surrounded by colleagues who are eager to experiment with hands-on, minds-on, hearts-on learning (Cornett, 2011). Did you notice how she . . .

- used charts to reinforce the poem and the CPS process visually?
- engaged students with a chant she improvised from a poem?
- showed enthusiasm and humor with smiles and comments that showed how much she enjoyed hearing the students' ideas?
- used a modern fable to give an authentic context and text for her strategy lesson?
- used motivational and engagement strategies, like the Mystery Bag?
- used explicit teaching, including labeling strategies and doing think alouds to model how to think?
- scaffolded students to success by coaching them to try strategies in pairs?
- used open questions that had a range of right answers?
- asked for evidence when students gave conclusions?
- used writing and drama as vehicles for students to continue problem solving and synthesize big ideas?
- gave options for making comprehension visible?

Emma's students seem to think comprehension means using the CPS strategies she has taught them to make sense. They refer to the chart, and they connect strategies like visualization (imaging) with the day's target strategies. The comprehension products they created (e.g., tableau) show they know how to focus on big ideas and not get distracted by trivial ones. Emma gets the "comprehension first" seal of approval.

Conclusion

This chapter described the Comprehension Problem Solving process. The CPS process is a comprehensive and authentic model of how people make sense of both verbal and non-verbal texts, print and non-print texts, including real-world texts like those found on the Internet. It organizes thinking strategies mature comprehenders use into flexible *before*, *during*, and *after* stages.

The chapter presented the CPS process as part of an inquiry-based approach that targets helping students find and construct big ideas from diverse texts. The motivational properties of inquiry-based problem solving were presented, including how inquiry is connected to life in the 21st century. When students are taught to use inquiry-based CPS, they tap innate problem-solving capacities to investigate real-life questions. That's where big ideas come in.

Comprehension is not just about process. While CPS outlines *comprehending processes*, the comprehension *product* results from intentional use of the strategies to find and create understanding of the most important ideas in any text. These are the big ideas. The section on big ideas explained what they are and why they are important in comprehension instruction.

CHAPTER 2 big ideas

The following are examples of big ideas from this chapter. Use the list to jump-start synthesis of your own priority big ideas.

1. The Comprehension Problem Solving process describes how people make sense of diverse texts in real life.
2. CPS relies on important questions to propel meaning making forward.
3. Comprehension skills are different from strategies, in that strategies focus on coordinated use of skills to solve specific problems.
4. Inquiry-based problem solving is inherently motivating and is used across disciplines and throughout life to make sense of texts.
5. Big ideas answer the question, "Comprehend what?"

a look ahead

The next chapter puts the teaching of inquiry-based CPS in the context of best practices for teaching the *task* of comprehension. Chapter 3 also further develops the comprehension task product, big ideas. The focus on big ideas and the teaching of inquiry-based problem solving top the list of nine best practices that make up the comprehension first proposal. Chapter 3 introduces all nine practices, along with two preconditions for their implementation.

2 response options

Responding to text shapes comprehension by further engaging problem solving to make sense. Use the following options in a group setting, when possible.

1. Create your own list of big ideas from this chapter and compare it with those of other readers. Explain reasons why the lists are different.

2. Check your understanding using the Important Questions that opened the chapter. Note questions that you would like to discuss further, and list additional questions.

3. Refine your definition of comprehension using information from this chapter. Design strategies for teaching the definition to children. Consider songs, chants, and artwork as vehicles. *Note:* You may want to review the definition from Chapter 1.

4. Evaluate your own use of the CPS process described in this chapter. Set goals for increasing your strategy use.

5. Practice using the CPS with your own reading. Start with the "before" strategies and just one or two of the "during" strategies. Continue to add strategies until you are aware of using the whole process to problem solve for meaning. Try using CPS with non-verbal texts, such as a piece of art, or alternative print texts, such as song lyrics.

6. Create a CPS chart to use with students. Consider using symbols and icons or hand signs to make the strategies more concrete. Choose one of the strategies and partner with a peer to think aloud about how to use the strategy with a text.

7. List several questions you now have about CPS, inquiry, or big ideas after reading this chapter.

8. Read a classic picture book such as *Where the Wild Things Are* (Sendak) or *Millions of Cats* (Gag). List topics/themes found in the book and then take the topics to the big idea level by turning them into full-sentence statements.

9. List concepts that are puzzling to you from this chapter or questions you have. Discuss your questions with a partner or a group.

10. Create a two-minute oral argument for a target audience (e.g., PTA, school faculty) for adopting an inquiry-based approach to comprehension that uses CPS strategies to derive big ideas.

CHILDREN'S LITERATURE CITED

Gag, W. (1928). *Millions of cats.* New York: Coward-McCann.

Lobel, A. (1980). *Fables.* New York: Harper & Row.

Munoz-Ryan, P. (2002). *Esperanza rising.* New York: Blue Sky Press.

Sendak, M. (1983). *Where the wild things are.* New York: Harper & Row.

Teachers, Context, and the Comprehension Task

preview

This chapter continues the development of the comprehension first proposal by zeroing in on comprehension best practices. The bulk of the chapter outlines how best practices are linked to the five comprehension factors introduced in Chapter 1: learners, teachers (and teaching), tasks, texts, and context (look back to Ready Resource 1.2). Two of these factors—supportive *teachers* who create supportive classroom *contexts*—are discussed as "preconditions" that set the stage for successful implementation of nine comprehension best practices.

All nine comprehension best practices are then introduced and two previously introduced practices are discussed in more detail. Those two practices are: (1) Teach the inquiry-based Comprehension Problem Solving process and (2) focus on big ideas (comprehension product). The remaining seven best practices are the subjects of subsequent chapters.

important questions

1. What are best practices, and where do they come from? How are they important to comprehension instruction?

2. How can knowing the five factors that influence comprehension help teachers plan and use best practices?

3. How do a teacher's personal knowledge and beliefs support or hamper implementation of best practices and subsequent student achievement?

4. Why is creating a supportive classroom a precondition for implementation of best practices?

5. How do big ideas and the CPS process relate to the task of comprehension?

6. What are ways to teach for big ideas?

7. What are instructional ideas for teaching the CPS process?

Introduction

Our chief want of life is somebody who shall make us do what we can.

RALPH WALDO EMERSON

The concept of best practice has its roots in "Progressive Education," envisioned by John Dewey, Maria Montessori, and Jean Piaget. Today, *best* practices are research-based curriculum and instructional design recommendations backed by evidence that shows they are likely to increase student achievement. They are also drawn from accumulated professional wisdom about instruction that achieves results (Allington, 2005b). Professional associations routinely endorse best practices and include them in standards documents (Daniels & Bizar, 2005). Identification of best comprehension practices that "generate long-term improvement . . . and thus promote learning across content areas" is "one of the nation's highest priorities" (RAND, 2002, p. xvi).

The idea of best practices is not without controversy. Reinking (2007) argues that the superlative "best" creates an obstacle, because it implies an absolute. I chose to use the label as it is generally understood. Best practices are the best ways we know to teach comprehension, *given our current knowledge base.* They are not written in stone. As famed economist John Maynard Keynes explained, "When the facts change, I change my mind. What do you do?" As the research base about "what works" to increase comprehension grows, educators should follow Keynes' lead: they should accordingly change what is considered "best."

Many educators claim to use literacy reform models that include best practices. However, all too often schools and teachers may still rely on practices that hold little potential to increase comprehension (Cuban, 1993; Taylor et al., 1999). For example, in many schools the basal reader series still dominates instruction. The problem with these commercial sets of student books and teacher manuals is that they are published for mass consumption, not for particular students. Furthermore, manuals do not teach; they outline procedures. Only a skilled teacher can creatively design and implement differentiated comprehension instruction tailored to individual strengths and needs. This is the instruction that produces comprehension success and what best practices are intended to achieve.

The International Reading Association (IRA), the best-known professional literacy organization in the world, used numerous large-scale research studies to craft a position statement on best practices. The statement should serve as an important guide for every school's comprehension curriculum and each teacher's instruction. It begins with, "We believe that there is no single method or single combination of methods that can successfully teach all children to read" and calls the search for one best way "futile." IRA recommends that teachers possess a "wide range of instructional methods and have strong knowledge of the children in their classrooms" (unpaged). IRA further recommends that teachers be in charge of deciding which methods to use and have the flexibility to modify instruction to meet specific student needs. (View the full IRA statement at their website.) Teachers caught in the web of scripted curricula and pacing guides should look for opportunities to share this and other important documents with administrators who may not have had the benefit of this information.

Using Multiple Methods of Beginning Reading Instruction

http://reading.org/General/ AboutIRA/PositionStatements/ MultipleMethodsPosition.aspx

ONLINE RESOURCE

WWW

Artful Implementation of Best Practices

Many books have been written on the topic of best practices, but a single definition has yet to emerge. What's more, a definitive list of what will result in comprehension success for all children does not exist. We do, however, know about practices that promise high impact on comprehension. This book focuses on nine practices that reflect a consensus of opinion about what is most likely to cause changes in student achievement.

The comprehension practices recommended in this book are the antithesis of instruction that "stays inside the lines." As Tomlinson points out, approaches that equate teaching with following a script "fail teachers because they confuse technical expedience with artistry" (2000, p. 6). Students may "confuse compliance with thoughtful engagement" (p. 6). In contrast, practices such as teaching inquiry-based problem solving have the potential to provoke intense student thinking.

Some of the best practices described in the pages of this book reflect long-called-for changes. For example, response options congruent with 21st-century life are recommended as replacements for worksheets. Instead of writing out answers to literal-level questions at the ends of chapters it is recommended that students be involved in genuine conversations and discussions, and long-term projects that culminate in performances and exhibits that reflect comprehension. These practices hold strong prospects for deeply engaging students (Allington, 2002b, 2005b). Teachers are urged to substitute informed instructional improvisation for scripted lessons and to motivate students by tapping their innate desire to understand rather than by using extrinsic rewards such as grades, points, and coupons (Guthrie, 2004).

The word *artful* has to do with creating unique designs. Artful best practice results when teachers tap research, assessment data, and professional wisdom to solve instructional problems in unique ways that make sense for their particular students. Excellent teachers are always artful. They don't apply best practices in a uniform fashion, because doing so doesn't consider learner diversity. They design comprehension instruction creatively, on the basis of professional knowledge and skill, responding to all the factors that influence instruction (RAND, 2002).

Creative instructional design focuses on adjusting to the strengths and needs of individual students. In the following snapshot, teacher George Darcy is applying best practices research. As you observe his lesson, notice how he crafts an artful implementation, drawing on his own personality. Key teaching strategies he uses are highlighted in boldface.

classroom snapshot

GEORGE DARCY TEACHES CPS

George Darcy has been teaching fourth grade for seven years and implementing best practices research for three. He is interested in the expanded concept of *text* because he sees his students increasingly using technology-based communication. In an age of "new literacies" and "multi-literacies," he feels he needs to demonstrate how to make meaning of texts that reflect the real worlds of his students (Lotherington & Chow, 2006).

It is the second week of school, and today George is introducing the Comprehension Problem Solving process. Notice the impact of George's definition of comprehension and his personal teaching style. Some of the best practices George uses are

- engagement/motivational strategies.
- use of alternative texts.
- explicit modeling of thinking processes.
- use of response options for students to show understanding.

Before the Lesson

George is well aware of the role of engagement in motivation and the important impact of motivation on comprehension. That is why he begins the day with **warm-ups** that engage "head, heart, and hands" for learning. Today he is using a **group sing** strategy, with students standing in a circle. George is famous at his school for how he gets students to write songs, and today he is using songs written by last year's students to motivate his new class.

"See if you recognize the melody. It's from an old commercial. **Echo me,**" directs George. He sings, "I'm a reader. You're a reader. He's a reader. She's a reader. Wouldn't you like to be a reader, too? Be a reader. Oooh, what a reader!" He stops after each line and waits for the echo. He also uses hand motions, pointing at himself and at different students. On the last line he throws up his hands and waves. Students imitate his actions. By the end they are smiling and laughing.

"Does anyone know the tune?" George asks.

"It sounds sorta familiar," a boy says.

"Well, it is a pretty old jingle. It's for soda—Dr Pepper," George explains.

"I've heard it," a girl says excitedly. "I'm a pepper. You're a pepper. He's a pepper. She's a pepper," she sings, and several other kids nod their heads in agreement.

"That's right, Julia," George grins. "Let's sing it again!" And they do, two more times with all the motions. George then explains that writing songs is a great way to pull your thinking together and that this song was written by a student from last year to express his thoughts about reading.

"Wow!" exclaims a boy. "I think I know him, because he did it with some other guys for our class."

"That's right," George says. "I forgot they went on tour! It's not hard to write songs. Maybe you'll want to go on tour, too." He smiles, but some students widen their eyes and grimace.

Lesson Introduction

"The important thing is to start with **something to write about.** Today I'm going to show you something that is very important about reading that we'll be using the whole year. You may be motivated to write a song about this special information. It's about how to comprehend or understand just about anything. In fact, this is a 'secret of the universe'!"

"What's a secret of the universe?" a girl asks.

"Well, secrets of the universe are **big ideas** about people and nature that are the most important things to know. That's why we'll be studying lots of secrets of the universe in science and social studies this year," explains George.

"That's awesome," another girl says. "How did you learn all the secrets?"

"I don't know all of them. I'm still learning, just like you. I love to keep finding more big ideas to teach my students. That is why I was so excited to learn about **the way good readers think.** I just learned it a few years ago, and I changed my teaching because of it," George confesses.

"Cool," says a boy.

"What is it?" asks another boy.

"Yeah! Tell us," says a girl.

Lesson Development

"Okay. Everyone take a seat, pretzel style," George says. "I'm going to show you how to read any text. *Text* is a word that means anything from which a person can get ideas. We can read paintings, music, and, yes, books."

"What about YouTube?" asks a boy.

"Yes, you can view videos and read any other type of information on the Internet using the process I'm going to show you," George explains. "Here is the thing. To understand any text, you have to **start with a purpose.** You have to really want to understand or make sense. This is the secret—good readers think every text is a problem to be solved, and they use a problem-solving process that you already know."

"We already know it?" a girl responds skeptically.

"Yes, you do this kind of thinking every day of your life. Let me just show you what I'm talking about," George says as he reaches around to grab an object covered with a black towel.

"What do you think is under the towel?" George asks.

"It looks like a box because of the shape," a boy says.

"It looks like a box of cereal," says another boy.

"You are absolutely right, Ricky!" George says. He pulls off the towel to expose a large box of Cheerios. "I'm going to **show you the most important ways readers think** when they read, and I'm going to do it by problem solving this text—the cereal box. It's like I'm letting you listen in on my brain."

"No way!" says a boy.

"I want to hear this," says another.

"Okay, here goes. **Any reading begins with a problem** or purpose. My problem is I'm worried about being healthy and eating better. I also need to lose a few inches," George says as he pinches his waist. "So, I went to the grocery and I started reading the *'texts'* in the cereal aisle."

"You mean you read the cereal boxes?" a girl asks.

"That's exactly what I did. **Cereal boxes are texts** that contain lots of information," George explains. **"Listen as I ask myself questions.** I'll click the **PowerPoint** so you can see the questions under 'Before, During, and After' as I read the box. I'm going to do the whole thing so you can see what you'll be learning to do this year." George uses a remote to bring up the first slide, and he begins to talk through his reading of the Cheerios box. Ready Resource 3.1 shows his whole presentation, which takes about five minutes.

Using CPS with alternative texts: Cheerios box.

BEFORE *Reading and viewing*

Purpose-set. Motivate with clear goals.

ASK MYSELF:

- What's the problem? Why am I reading this? *I want to find out if it is healthy so I can decide whether to buy it.*

Predict and connect (self, other texts, world). Overview the text and activate prior knowledge.

ASK MYSELF:

- What is the box like? How is it organized? *Bright color. Big title and brief information on front with more on back and most facts on side panel.*

- What do I already know about this problem or topic? *I've been hearing that Cheerios can reduce cholesterol. I've eaten them before, and I like the cereal. I'm thinking it will be fewer calories and carbs than the granola I've been eating.*

- What information might the box provide? *I'm expecting all the facts I need, but I expect there will be marketing hype, so I'll have to read the details carefully.*

DURING *Data gathering by taking and making meaning*

Determine important concepts. Use clues.

ASK MYSELF:

- What does the author want me to think? Why? *General Mills wants me to buy Cheerios, and they know "whole grains" are currently being hyped, so they put that right on the front. The company wants me to think Cheerios are good for my health, so there is a heart-shaped bowl on the front.*

- What do I think are key concepts or topics that may lead to big ideas? *Whole grain, lower cholesterol, happy heart, guaranteed, nutrition facts in four places.*

READY RESOURCE **3.1**

Continued.

- What evidence supports these ideas (facts or details)? *A serving of Cheerios has only 100 calories and 20 grams of carbohydrates. That is half the calories and more than half the carbs of my granola. I also see a cup has 25 percent of daily calcium, which I need for my bone problem.*

Infer conclusions. Use previous evidence to decide.

ASK MYSELF:

- What do I predict so far? *I'm inferring that I should buy and regularly eat the Cheerios. That should cause me to lose weight and be healthier.*

Image. Use your imagination to think about the text.

- What visual images can I make in my head? *I can see the little oat circles floating in white milk in my green bowl on the sunroom table.*

- What feelings, smells, tastes, and sounds am I connecting to the text? *I start to salivate and taste the crunch of the Cheerios, the soft bananas, and the creamy milk.*

Question and wonder. Ask yourself the 5 W + H questions.

ASK MYSELF:

- What predictions are confirmed? Rejected? What are new predictions and connections? *Cheerios does seem to be a better buy for my health, as I predicted. However, I'm wondering if it will taste as good as my granola.*

Monitor. Check whether it is all making sense.

ASK MYSELF:

- Is this making sense? If not, how can I make it make sense? *I'm not sure what all the ingredients are. What is "tripotassium phosphate"? I can use my Word Fix-Ups: I see the prefix tri, which I know means three, like in tricycle. I can pronounce both words. However, I don't know the meaning just because I can say them. OK, I'll try my computer pocket dictionary, but, nope, neither word is in it. I'll check the Internet when I get home, or I'm thinking Cheerios has a good reputation, so I'll probably just trust that this ingredient is a good thing.*

Analyze/critique. Zoom in–Zoom out. Notice text features and structures.

ASK MYSELF:

- If the text is narrative: What do you know about the characters? What are the problems? Where and when is the story happening? How are problems being resolved? What themes are emerging? *The Cheerios box is not a story, for sure!*

- If the text is expository: How is it organized (e.g., sequential, cause-effect, comparison)? *It is expository, because it gives information about lots of causes and effects if you eat Cheerios.*

- If the text is non-verbal: What stands out? How does the text feel? Why? *There is a lot of visual art— color, the design, photographs, the heart shape of the bowl.*

- Overall, ask, "What are the important details and features? How are they related to the big ideas I'm finding and creating?" *The idea that Cheerios is whole grain is repeated many times on the box and highlighted with a big check mark. I also notice that lots of vitamins have been added, but that may be true of my granola. I'll have to check. I do notice the front of the box is dominated by an ad for a free*

(continued)

3.1 READY RESOURCE

Using CPS with alternative texts, continued.

cereal bowl shaped like a speed racer. This annoys me, because I know this will cause kids to nag their parents into sending for this. I do like the familiar yellow box, which has a sunny feel overall.

Incubate. Take time out.

ASK MYSELF:

- How can I take a break so I can review and reconsider from a fresh perspective? *I decide to go get my canned goods and have a cup of coffee. Then I'll come back for the cereal if I still want it. I do still have lots of granola left at home.*

Synthesize. Pull big ideas together.

ASK MYSELF:

- What are the most important concepts, themes or generalizations, and conclusions? *I'm concluding that buying a whole grain low-calorie food is a good choice.*

- What big idea statements are most important? *I decide I really do need to lose ten pounds, so I should buy the healthy Cheerios and get into a routine of eating healthy foods.*

AFTER *Reading and viewing*

Organize and shape. Transform the big ideas.

ASK MYSELF:

- How can I best show my understanding of the most important big ideas? *I put two boxes in my cart, because I see they are on a buy-one-get-one-free sale.*

Reflect and revise. Think about the comprehension product.

ASK MYSELF:

- What works or makes sense? What doesn't work?

- How can I make it better? *I'm happy with my decision, and I look forward to telling my wife.*

Publish. Make comprehension visible.

ASK MYSELF:

- How can I share my comprehension "product"? With whom? When? Where? *I'll surprise my wife with my diet plan, using Cheerios in the morning.*

The students look astounded.

"What did you notice?" George asks after he finishes going through the PowerPoint presentation.

"It is a lot to think about," whispers a girl.

"It is, but you do this kind of thinking all the time," George explains.

"We do?" asks a boy.

"Yes. It is problem solving to make sense of printed texts that have words and also what are called non-verbal texts. It's all about active thinking," George explains.

"There are a **lot of questions**," observes a girl.

Lesson Conclusion

"There are. I'm going to put up a chart in the room that shows all the questions in the Power-Point. I have a **bookmark** for each of you with the same questions," George says as he reaches in a bag and pulls out a handful of bookmarks.

"When do we get them?" asks a girl.

"Well, right now!" says George. "But, one thing. I want you to know we'll be working on this all year, every day with every text. We'll study each of these kinds of thinking and the questions until everyone can do the problem solving well."

"I want a red one," says a girl.

"Look, they are coated with plastic," says a boy as George hands them out.

"So we can wipe them off when you sneeze," giggles a girl.

George laughs and then says, "We'll start right after recess with the BEFORE strategies."

"What are strategies?" asks a boy.

"Secrets of the universe?" asks another boy.

"Great questions, boys," George says. "I'll answer them right after recess, too."

Postscript: George is as good as his word. He not only explains that strategies are ways people solve problems, but he shows his students *how* to use the CPS strategies with verbal and non-verbal, print and non-print texts related to science, social studies, math, and literature. It does indeed take the entire year, but George's students become adept at using the strategies to think about big ideas in content units and in their own lives. They also write lots of songs. Many are about the CPS process and are taken on the road and performed for other classes, the PTO, and the local Rotary Club. Ready Resource 3.2 gives an example of a student rap.

Example student rap.

The CPS Rap

Purpose-set/Motivate, Predict/Connect, Cogitate
    Question Question Question Question
    What's the big idea?
Data Gather, Infer and Image, Check Predictions, Use Fix-Ups
    Question Question Question Question
    What's the big idea?
Zoom in, Zoom out, Incubate, Synthesize, Give It Shape
    Question Question Question Question
    What's the big idea?
Reflect/Revise, Make It Great, Show the Public, Celebrate!
    Question Question Question Question
    What's the big idea?

READY RESOURCE 3.2

The Five Factors and Best Practice Implementation

nterest in comprehension research has grown steadily in recent decades. A flood of studies has yielded a description of the cognitive actions and emotional responses that successful comprehenders use (see references in Chapter 2). George Darcy is among the teachers who now use research-based teaching practices that are considered to be the *best* path *at this time* to increasing comprehension. Acquiring a repertoire of best comprehension teaching practices is essential to a teacher's pre-service preparation as well as ongoing professional development (RAND, 2002).

Like his colleagues, George faces the task of implementing these findings in an actual classroom context where learners will have diverse needs (NRP, 2000). Research-based answers are not available for every variable in teaching comprehension, so practitioners have to be problem solvers. As John Guthrie explains, there are "points in history—and this is one of them—[when] the urgency of improving reading becomes too compelling to wait for researchers to catch up . . . practice must lead research" (2007, p. xx). George Darcy seems to relish the challenge of making the complex task of comprehension manageable and enjoyable.

Using categories helps to make it easier to understand the complexities of crafting the best comprehension instruction possible. Chapter 1 introduced five categories that most influence comprehension success. The Five Factors are the particular nature or characteristics of learners, tasks, texts, the context, and teachers/teaching. Based on each factor, we can generate questions to guide planning that results in differentiated instruction, which is key to making comprehension practices "best" for specific students. Here are examples of planning questions:

1. *Learners:* What strengths and needs do students have that may relate to comprehension?
2. *Tasks:* What does the act of comprehension require (process and product)? What outcomes can be expected if comprehension is successful?
3. *Texts:* What are the most appropriate materials to use to increase students' comprehension?
4. *Context:* When, where, and with whom will my students comprehend best? What classroom conditions support comprehending and comprehension?
5. *Teaching:* What instructional strategies are most likely to cause students to increase their comprehension? How should instruction be organized to foster comprehension?

We teachers join writers, scientists, and artists when we use this kind of questioning to set problem solving in motion to create a purposeful design. Notice that the lesson design process parallels the Comprehension Problem Solving process. When teachers use this process to address literacy needs (see Ready Resource 1.3), they do more than implement a fixed concept of "best" practice. Indeed, best practice is about custom design. As teachers, we need to reject rigid thinking and stale practices that have not worked. Inventional thinking is needed to meet 21st-century demands. It is ultimately the individual teacher who creates instruction for students. Whether that instruction is "best," "good," or even "bad" begins with the teacher. That is why the influence of teachers is a precondition for best practice implementation.

Preconditions for Best Practice Implementation

 his section examines two preconditions that set the stage for successful implementation of comprehension practices: *supportive teachers* and a *supportive learning context.*

PRECONDITION #1: SUPPORTIVE TEACHERS

You've got to be careful if you don't know where you're going, 'cause you might not get there.

YOGI BERRA

Knowledge and beliefs that support

A teacher's vision is a "deciding force" in comprehension (Gambrell, Malloy, & Mazzoni, 2007, p. 17). What a teacher knows and believes about literacy determines his or her instructional vision. Students need teachers who support a 21st-century view of literacy. The teacher who defines literacy as effective communication using a range of verbal (word-based) and non-verbal (wordless) texts makes instructional decisions based on that definition. Such a teacher is likely to teach students how to mine picture book art for meaning as readily as he coaches students to attend to words. The teacher who believes reading is synonymous with comprehension isn't satisfied with accurate and speedy pronunciation of words. He will budget time for work on vocabulary and fluency, but these sub-skills will not dominate the literacy block and will be clearly presented as tools to reach the goal of comprehension. Teachers who know how to teach problem-solving strategies for meaning making set the comprehension bar higher than teachers who rely on post-reading questions that ask only for recall of facts.

Teacher quality is center stage

Teachers are front and center in any intervention plan likely to change comprehension achievement (RAND, 2002). In an extensive review of research, Darling-Hammond (2000) found that teacher quality and expertise consistently and accurately predicted student achievement. As much as 43 percent of variance in student achievement can be attributed to teacher quality (Ferguson,

1991). Teacher knowledge and expertise is a "critical variable in student achievement" (RAND, 2002, p. 43). Since most students are in the regular classroom 80 to 85 percent of the day, generalist teachers are on the front line for learners who struggle. Unfortunately, paraprofessionals have been found to have "no positive effect on academic achievement" when they deliver interventions (Allington & Baker, 2007, p. 50).

Since students who receive "high quality teaching" can have a 40 percent achievement advantage over students who receive lower-quality instruction (Allington & Baker, 2007, p. 86), excellent instruction by well-trained teachers is the most promising means of increasing comprehension achievement and preventing comprehension problems (RAND, 2002). What does "quality" include? The following are teacher qualities that support students' comprehension development.

Style. All instruction is grounded in the vision, knowledge, personality, and experiences of individual teachers. Teaching practice should be both science and art. It starts with individual teachers who design instruction for specific students, using the best ideas research and professional wisdom currently have to offer. They twist and tweak, modify, combine, and elaborate on best practices information to suit their students' needs. Then they top it all off with an original implementation that reflects their own strengths. Such teachers have what writers and artists call "style." But, just like students, teachers also need skill and will. They need a solid knowledge base to support comprehension reforms, and they need to *want* to make change.

For example, teachers who present themselves as comprehension "masters" (e.g., those who use personal examples to demonstrate CPS) support student learning through example. These teachers walk the talk. Students choose to apprentice themselves to teachers who (1) show they have the "stuff" to support the learning needed to succeed outside of school and (2) use a unique teaching style to deliver substance. This combination of style and substance creates strong support for effective comprehension instruction. That is why teachers are center stage in a 21st-century design of comprehension and composition instruction (Gambrell, Malloy, & Mazzoni, 2007).

Personality. There is no substitute for enthusiasm, humor, and an optimistic orientation toward life when it comes to supporting comprehension best practices. Students know when a teacher enjoys helping them learn. While people cannot totally change their personalities, teachers can choose to be positive during the school day. At times, being positive simply demands good acting. So be it. If necessary, teachers can practice "method acting," artificially creating an emotion on the outside, which produces the emotion on the inside. Changing the outside works. Smiling engages facial muscles that trigger happy hormones (Cornett, 2002). As the sign says below a large mirror in the Toledo Board of Education building, "How would you like to look at yourself all day?"

Desire to learn. A teacher's personal desire to grow and learn is foundational to comprehension best practice implementation. The most effective teachers always say that they have more to learn. They seek out research that suggests more effective practices, and they delight in professional development opportunities. On the other hand, weaker teachers are often confident that they know it all and may even resist professional development (Pressley, 2006). This attitude does not support implementation of evolving conclusions about best practices.

Reflective strategic thinkers. A teacher's personal reading and learning habits do affect his or her instructional practice. For example, teachers who read a lot have experiences that allow them to explain and model strategic comprehension. The best teachers are practitioners; they can do well what they are employed to teach their students to do. In the case of comprehension, this means personal use of Comprehension Problem Solving strategies with diverse texts.

Teachers who consult their own reading, listening, and viewing habits have a profound advantage. No teacher can understand comprehension without reflecting on his or her own thinking, and an understanding of comprehension process and product is what teachers need in order to model CPS for students. Personal literacy expertise also frees teachers to deviate from the script. They can use teachable moments to share poignant personal, real-life examples of CPS use, ranging from trying to make sense of the directions for an iPod to trying to comprehend the big ideas in the ABBA song "Thank You for the Music."

Teachers who are skilled and enthusiastic learners are less dependent on teacher guides to chart the course of lessons, and no manual can ever respond to a learner's search for meaning in a picture book, novel, or historical event the way a real live teacher can. In particular, personal readership prepares teachers to fashion both personal growth plans and instructional designs that can revolutionize students' comprehension achievement. Like Charlotte in *Charlotte's Web*, each teacher can use her or his innate problem-solving capabilities to craft a comprehension magnum opus. Such a great work results from a continuing focus on big ideas and important questions related to literacy and learning.

Teachers as readers

We can't teach what we don't know or can't do. To help students comprehend texts, teachers need to know and personally use the set of strategies successful comprehenders use. By raising her self-awareness of how meaning is constructed, a teacher can gain important insights that inform instructional decisions. Successful comprehenders often are not *conscious* of their strategy use, but teachers don't have that luxury. Reflection on personal use of CPS strategies, with a focus on big ideas, helps the teacher make sense of the tangled web of research, teacher's manuals, standards, and tests. The perspective of ourselves as learners allows us to consider the logic of research implications. The Self-Assessment that follows is intended to raise awareness of personal strategy use.

CPS self-assessment. The self-assessment in Ready Resource 3.3 is based on the CPS process, as summarized in Chapter 2, Ready Resource 2.1. The purpose of the assessment is to scaffold reflections on how you personally problem solve to make meaning. As you respond to the questions, try to "think about yourself thinking." You may discover you use most of the strategies, but you may not have known you were doing so or even have known there are specific labels for all the different ways we think about text. Some questions will be easier, and these probably reflect strategies you'll be most comfortable modeling for students. Before teaching strategies that are less familiar, you can target them for personal study.

If this first self-assessment stretches you, take heart that successful comprehenders often are not conscious of strategy use. I suggest you think back to a recent experience with reading, listening, or viewing a text. You may also practice with a text as you move through the questions. The text can be this book, the Internet, a film, a radio program, a cartoon, a newspaper article, or even a soup can. After you complete the self-assessment, proceed to the next paragraph.

Comprehension self-assessment.

Use the following items to reflect on your use of CPS strategies and to set goals. To what degree do you . . .

1 Start with a clear purpose for using the text? (e.g., to derive pleasure or to get specific information)

2 Do an overview of the text to predict its content and organization, especially as it connects to your background and needs? (e.g., read the back cover, skim the table of contents)

3 Gather key ideas from the text by both *extracting* meaning and *constructing* your own sense? (e.g., zero in on stated themes, draw your own conclusions)

4 Infer the most important ideas by using text evidence? (i.e., use facts and details to draw conclusions about characters, events, issues, etc.)

5 Think about what the author wants you to think? (i.e., try to get inside the author's head to see his or her perspective)

6 Construct mental images related to the text? (i.e., visualize and use other senses to make the text come alive)

7 Periodically spiral back to recall your original purposes for using the text and to confirm, reject, or create predictions? (e.g., you may discontinue reading a book that isn't enjoyable, if enjoyment was your original purpose)

8 Monitor whether the text is making sense and then take specific actions if it is not? (e.g., use word-solving strategies to decode unknown words, use comprehension fix-ups such as rereading to repair misunderstanding)

9 Zoom in and zoom out to notice text features (e.g., graphs, pictures, headings) and structures (e.g., story elements and paragraph structures) that help you see what's most important?

10 Take breaks to review and reconsider what's most important in the text? (e.g., play music, eat a snack, or take a walk and then return with a fresh outlook)

11 Synthesize the most important ideas? (i.e., pull together what seems to percolate to the top, such as prominent emotions and messages)

12 Shape the most important text-based ideas to fit your purposes? (e.g., summarize relevant ideas in the form of a list of questions for a book discussion, a sketch, a poem, etc.)

13 Reflect on your comprehension product (from #12) and revise to make it better?

14 Share your big ideas from texts with others? (anything from a blog post to a formal presentation at a conference)

Post-assessment. You may want to repeat the self-assessment by thinking of a different text experience, such as a film, a painting, or a piece of music. This will help you understand how the text itself and the circumstances change your responses. Also, consider repeating the assessment periodically, noticing your changing awareness and focus on strategies.

The bookmark on the back cover of this book is another tool to increase your strategy awareness. You may want to cut it out and use the prompts periodically with any reading, including this text. Stopping to reflect on strategies during reading is an effective way to boost your consciousness of strategy use. You may find that focusing attention on strategy use distracts from comprehension, as is true during the learning of any new procedure. It can feel awkward. This activity provides insight into the task we are asking students to do and serves as a reminder that strategy use is not the end goal—comprehension of big ideas is the desired outcome.

The cause of comprehension instructional reform is a great one. It depends on teachers who can support student comprehension growth with their own personal knowledge and beliefs. The self-study of personal strategies is an important component of being a supportive teacher.

PRECONDITION #2: SUPPORTIVE LEARNING CONTEXT

The "place" of learning deeply affects learners and learning. John Dewey (1997) acknowledged this big idea when he recommended that classrooms be aesthetically stimulating. He even went further to point out that if classrooms are not "aesthetic," they must be the opposite: "anesthetic." Picture an anesthetic classroom that dulls the senses with stark walls and straight rows. Students hump over workbooks and slump at desks, all facing forward. Contrast this image with a room full of original student art and carpeted spaces where students gather in small groups for conversation and discussion. One environment seems to discourage, the other encourage. One environment numbs, the other excites and invites.

Implementation of comprehension best practices cannot be separated from the classroom ecology. The physical environment, the psychological impact, and the general culture of a place alter how we respond. Places can intimidate or liberate thoughts and feelings. Successful implementation of comprehension best practices depends on environments that support inquiry-based problem solving.

Supporting comprehension with an inviting culture

According to Vygotsky's (1978) socio-cultural theory, substantive learning is an active and constructive task very much influenced by the context. Instruction does not happen in a vacuum. Where and with whom one learns matters a great deal. For example, consider the influences on conversations in different locations (e.g., faculty lounge; college classroom; dorm room; church, synagogue, or mosque).

Each context has a culture that governs how people think, believe, and act while they are in it. Culture is basically a shared way of living, but it also means a medium for growing things. Both meanings have relevance as we think about creating classrooms that support comprehension best practice implementation.

The dominating influence in classroom culture is psychological and is controlled by the teacher's personal dispositions, rules, and relationships with students. Teachers have great power. Of course, they can humiliate and hurt, but these behaviors do not support student comprehension growth. A culture of respect and invitation is needed. Such a culture is marked by a climate that uplifts students by elevating learning to personal inquiry.

Physical features of classrooms are also key to an ecology that supports comprehension. For example, the physical space can support or inhibit dialogue, conversation, and discussion, which are key features in any comprehension instruction reform proposal (Graves, Juel, & Graves, 2007). I think of my grandmother's breakfast nook, where all manner of topics were discussed. To earn a place at that table became my ardent childhood desire. It is that feeling created by heads inclined toward each other in talk punctuated by laughter and sometimes tears that I envisioned each year as I set up my classroom.

Comprehension thrives in an aesthetic environment that stimulates the senses, causes students to want to be there, and motivates by offering support for taking risks, making choices, and responding to texts in diverse ways. Aesthetically stimulating schools and classrooms provide settings that provoke curiosity, surprise, and a sense of mystery. Murals line walls, clouds are painted on ceiling tiles, plants abound. A classroom should offer bright, carpeted areas, grouped desks, and comfortable places to sit. Soft background music sets mood and can create relaxed alertness. Unique art "texts" created by students should be displayed at their eye level and substituted for less interesting teacher-made or store-bought decorations. Boxes of children's books, organized by unit, genre, and level, often dot the room. Most important, a feeling of intensity emanates from the joy of discovery produced by an inquiry orientation. This means that classrooms buzz with activity as students move about. Teachers laugh, sing, and express delight as students take risks to make discoveries and experience how exhilarating comprehension can be.

Teachers have it within their power to create a positive, supportive context for comprehension development. Think about a classroom familiar to you:

- How does the physical environment contribute to or detract from support for comprehension? (e.g., desk arrangement, displays, organization of materials)
- How does the psychological climate contribute to or impede comprehension? Is the climate aesthetic (stimulating) or anesthetic (stultifying or threatening)?
- How does the teacher's disposition influence the climate?
- How do social relationships among students affect text comprehension? (e.g., influence of high-status students)

Based on their individual personalities and their beliefs about learning (philosophy), teachers can create an invitational climate that supports student construction of meaning. An invitational climate reflects a culture that celebrates differences, especially cultural and ethnic uniqueness. High-level comprehension blooms when students are immersed in a relationship of high expectations and mutual respect. Respect builds trust. Trust creates the comfort necessary for risk-taking and experimentation, which are essential for inquiry-based problem solving.

Making aesthetic changes to support comprehension

Classroom spaces can be arranged with attention to both function and form and consideration for order, balance, harmony, and color. Even little changes have large effects. Grouping desks implies that collaboration is expected. Open spaces indicate movement is part of the plan. Centers and stations with buckets of writing tools, baskets of books, and worktables indicate that hands-on learning is valued.

An inquiry-based classroom looks like a living room—a comfortable sanctuary and a pleasant place. Try featuring fresh flowers, bright curtains, and framed student artwork. Beautiful background music and light from lamps to illuminate reading areas are small but important additions. These simple changes make the environment more stimulating to the senses—more aesthetic.

Here are other important changes that can greatly impact the learning context of the classroom, and Ready Resource 3.4 includes a checklist to aid in designing a classroom that supports comprehension.

Visual references. A positive and reasonably strong correlation exists between the use of pictorial aids and comprehension (Gyselinck & Tardieu, 1999). It is important that teachers use wall space to display a CPS chart, questioning tools, word lists, and fix-up charts. Students should be frequently seen referring to interesting words on word walls and poem charts as they write and checking posted suggestions for how to fix comprehension problems during reading (see Ready Resource 5.5).

Peer artwork. Interesting art has the same benefits for schools that it does for homes and offices. In particular, framed *student* art enriches the classroom and gives honor and respect to student products. Teach students how to make museum labels to permit more informed browsing of the work of peers. Peer artwork can both challenge and inspire, stirring students' interest in experimenting with media, tools, styles, and subject matter that show comprehension.

Background music. At Hymera Elementary (Hymera, IN) a CD player sits right inside the front door of the school. As in many schools, background music fills classrooms, halls, and the cafeteria. Research shows that music stimulates brain activity that is distinct from responses to verbal communication. The elevated brain activity generated by music can boost learning (Cornett, 2011).

Student contributions. When students are invited to participate in making the classroom into a living room, they feel a sense of ownership. They become enthusiastic about the transformative power of aesthetic places. Children learn

Context: Classroom checklist.

WHAT YOU SEE . . .

Comfortable and organized

- [ ] Well ordered and clean
- [ ] Storage for independent reading books and ongoing projects
- [ ] Book crates and shelves with diverse genres and topics
- [ ] Share chair centrally located
- [ ] Folios available for students to monitor progress
- [ ] Management tools, such as jobs board and class rules, within easy view

Functional space arrangement

- [ ] Class meeting area: circle area for discussion (e.g., carpet on floor)
- [ ] Open space for movement
- [ ] Carpeted areas
- [ ] Desk arrangement: groups that facilitate collaboration
- [ ] Independent work: areas for students to work privately
- [ ] Conference area
- [ ] Centers: space for small and individual group work

- [ ] Noisy and quiet areas separated
- [ ] Easy for teacher to view entire room

Aesthetic contributions

- [ ] Plants
- [ ] Music
- [ ] Wall color
- [ ] Potpourri
- [ ] Changing displays

Print rich

- [ ] Displays of student work, including framed artwork
- [ ] Interactive word walls, including words chosen by students
- [ ] Reference charts (e.g., CPS and Fix-Ups)
- [ ] Poetry and song charts
- [ ] Pocket chart
- [ ] Multiple copies of texts
- [ ] Book baskets and crates
- [ ] Bookmarks
- [ ] Timer
- [ ] Index cards and sticky notes

READY RESOURCE 3.4

WHAT YOU FEEL . . .

- [ ] Welcomed
- [ ] Excitement
- [ ] Joy
- [ ] Intensity
- [ ] Involvement
- [ ] Curiosity
- [ ] Celebration
- [ ] Pride

Teacher's personality

- [ ] Positive and encouraging
- [ ] Teacher shows humor, smiles readily
- [ ] Expects quality and on-task work
- [ ] Aware of being looked upon as a literacy model

- [ ] Respectful of students
- [ ] Appearance of confidence and flexibility
- [ ] Integrity

Student-oriented

- [ ] Displays at kids' eye level
- [ ] Furniture that suits children's sizes
- [ ] Emphasis on student work and contributions instead of teacher displays (e.g., purchased cut-outs and posters)
- [ ] Students given genuine responsibilities
- [ ] Students asked for their thoughts
- [ ] Students expected to try to solve their own problems
- [ ] Students expected to ask questions

Sources consulted: Fountas & Pinnell, 1998, 2001, 2006

what they live. To paraphrase the well-known poem, if we want children to be curious, joyful, sensitive, courageous, and hopeful, we must structure environments that encourage those characteristics. Teachers who operate from an aesthetic frame of reference make senses-heightening a priority. Get ready for students to bring in plants, posters, and lots of CDs.

Best Teaching Practices

The previous sections described how the teacher and the classroom environment set the stage for implementing research-based conclusions about instruction called best practices. This section introduces nine best comprehension practices that reflect "a convergence of evidence" drawn from an array of research conducted in the past two decades (Gambrell, Malloy, & Mazzoni, 2007). In particular, studies have examined the Five Factors described in Chapter 1, with a focus on: the comprehension *task* (necessary cognitive processes for comprehension), *learner* variables, *text* influences, and specific *teaching* strategies.

As research uncovers differing conclusions about what works best, it behooves educators to make changes. For example, the view of comprehension as a leveled task (that is, literal, interpretive, and applied) has not been found to be helpful. It is recommended that this view be abandoned for two reasons: studies repeatedly show that skilled readers do not think in this manner, and instruction based on this view of comprehension has not yielded comprehension gains (Block & Pressley, 2007).

BRIEFLY, WHAT WORKS?

Among the best practices supported by experts is teaching students to use a coordinated strategy repertoire, such as the CPS process, to make meaning, with emphasis on instruction in how to repair misunderstanding using "fix-up" tools such as rereading, reading aloud, visualizing, and reviewing purposes (NRP, 2000). Such comprehension strategy instruction must be accompanied by

1. ample time for students to read and discuss.
2. attention to word study, including decoding for meaning.
3. significant work with a variety of text types, including technology-based texts and texts used in content areas.

These practices are among the nine featured in this book (see Ready Resource 3.5).

WHAT DOESN'T WORK?

Examples are crucial for understanding, but "non-examples" are important, too. This chapter introduces *best* practices—what *to* do. But there also are practices that should be avoided—what *not* to do. Appendix E includes both a Best Practices Self-Assessment and a list of teaching methods that are *not* recommended.

Nine recommended comprehension best practices.

PRECONDITIONS: To implement the following instructional practices, teachers must

(a) *support comprehension reform with their knowledge and beliefs,* and

(b) *create supportive classroom contexts.*

Note: Chapter references indicate where the practice is discussed first and in the most detail. As the book progresses, all of these practices become increasingly integrated with one another in a spiraling fashion.

1 Focus on big ideas (comprehension product).
(Chapters 2 and 3)

2 Teach inquiry-based problem solving (CPS process).
(Chapters 2 and 3)

3 Use varied assessments to plan differentiated instruction.
(Chapter 4)

4 Explicitly teach comprehension problem solving and key literacy concepts, including text characteristics.
(Chapter 5)

5 Use motivation strategies to engage comprehension.
(Chapter 6)

6 Use and teach questioning to promote "high-level" conversations and discussions.
(Chapter 7)

7 Teach vocabulary and fluency for comprehension.
(Chapter 8)

8 Teach diverse response options to show comprehension: written, arts-based, and digital texts.
(Chapter 9)

9 Embed best comprehension practices in literacy main events and content teaching.
(Chapter 10)

- Opening and closing literacy routines
- Interactive read aloud (IRA)
- Daily engaged independent reading (DEIR)
- Small group and independent work (e.g., centers)
- Writing workshop
- Content units: science, social studies, and math
- Performances and exhibits

READY RESOURCE
3.5

Main sources consulted: Anderson, Evertson, & Brophy, 1979; Barr & Dreeban, 1991; Block & Mangieri, 2003; Center for the Improvement of Early Reading Achievement (undated); Hoffman, 1991; Ladson-Billings, 1994; National Council of Teachers of English, 2004; National Reading Panel, 2000; Pressley, 2000; Pressley, Rankin, & Yokoi, 1996; Pressley et al., 2001; Taylor et al., 2003; Wharton-MacDonald, Pressley, & Hampston, 1998.

BEST COMPREHENSION PRACTICES IN THIS TEXT

Nine practices that have high-impact potential for comprehension achievement are summarized in Ready Resource 3.5. Two of the practices were discussed in Chapter 2 and are reviewed next. The remaining practices are discussed separately in subsequent chapters. The full concept of how to implement a comprehension first approach is brought together in Chapter 10, which describes how all the practices may be integrated into an instructional framework. The inquiry-based CPS is placed prominently in the daily literacy time block and embedded in content area blocks.

Best practice: Focus on big ideas

Thinking strategies such as those in CPS are not ends, they are means. Strategies should be viewed and used as purposeful tools to locate and construct big ideas. Big ideas are the desired products—the focus—of the comprehension process.

A big idea focus is about always expecting texts to embody meaning and about understanding that the meaning may be found at a surface level or may be hidden. Big ideas may be explicitly stated (e.g., morals in fables) and located right in the text. Other times, big ideas are implicit. This means the reader needs to notice hints or clues and synthesize them into big ideas. For example, in literature the seeds of big ideas are found in themes like friendship, dreams, and cycles. When the themes are stretched, they can become big ideas that represent truths worth understanding. For example, the big idea "Good friends stick by you when the going gets rough" is implicit (not directly stated) in White's *Charlotte's Web*.

Big ideas are more than the main ideas in paragraphs. They reflect meanings from whole stories, book chapters, plays, pieces of art, or films, not just parts of them (Walmsley, 2006). Even children's poems and songs, like "The Itsy Bitsy Spider," contain big ideas, but they are not directly stated. Instead, the reader must construct them, using story details and personal background knowledge engaged by the CPS process. Eventually, problem solving for meaning uncovers an unmistakable big idea in this familiar tale: "If you don't succeed, try, try again." But the text never explicitly says that (Walmsley, 2006, p. 283). This story, like all worthwhile texts, is a vehicle for truth. True ideas don't end thought—they extend it. Truth activates thinking, with the power to raise questions and generate learning (McTighe & Wiggins, 2004).

Teaching for big ideas. Teaching students to focus on big ideas happens through

1. explaining what a big idea is.
2. sharing examples and non-examples.
3. questioning, especially to cause students to focus and elaborate.

Big ideas can be found and created from any text, including literary texts, science and social studies materials, visual art, and music.

Fables are a good place to begin teaching about big ideas, because they are short and are sure to contain at least one explicit big idea (the fable's moral). Arnold Lobel's Caldecott-winning collection *Fables* works well for illustration.

Start by reading one fable aloud, such as "The Mouse at the Seashore." Ask students to listen to find what the fable is about. Don't read the moral at the end. After reading, ask, "What was it about?" Students will typically respond with ideas like "a mouse" or "leaving home." List their ideas and then ask for elaboration with questions such as "What about the mouse?" and "What did you learn about leaving home?" Eventually students can be coached to create "truth" statements that are bigger than any particular story or fable. An example big idea truth from the mouse fable is, "You have to take risks to achieve your dreams."

It is helpful to start a chart to accumulate examples of big ideas. Ask students for examples from their own lives, based on wisdom passed down by parents and grandparents. Common ones include "Treat other people as you'd like to be treated," "Every trip begins with a single step," and "Think before you talk." Statements like these are often called *aphorisms*, and you can use the Internet to find more, as well as buy collections of such wisdom.

Responding to big ideas. Any text that is read, viewed, or heard can also be an example of a form of text in which students might choose to respond. Comprehension response options are the subject of Chapter 9, but an example is showing students how to write their own fables by working backwards from a moral (big idea). Students can also write original fables based on a personally created big idea.

Judith Stark's book *Don't Cross Your Bridge Before You Pay the Toll* (1985) is a collection of drawings to go with big idea aphorisms written by first graders based on familiar stems. Ready Resource 3.6 gives examples of big ideas and sources for constructing big ideas from professional organizations for science and social studies.

Refer to the Snapshot of Emma Corbett at the beginning of Chapter 2 and the discussion of big ideas in Chapter 2 for additional examples.

Big ideas: Sources and examples.

Big ideas are core truths about people and the world. They represent the life lessons and deep understandings readers, listeners, and viewers take from verbal and non-verbal texts. More than main ideas in paragraphs, big ideas are associated with whole texts (Walmsley, 2006). They are the main points—the morals and themes—of books, plays, and films. Here are sources that will help you generate big ideas that cut across disciplines. Example big ideas follow each source.

THE NATIONAL SCIENCE TEACHERS ASSOCIATION (WWW.NSTA.ORG)

UNIFYING CONCEPTS AND PROCESSES: (1) Systems, order, organization; (2) Evidence, models, explanations; (3) Constancy, change, measurement; (4) Evolution and equilibrium; (5) Form and function

Example big idea for #5: The form or shape of something usually reflects its intended use. Discipline connection: architecture

(continued)

Continued.

NATIONAL COUNCIL OF SOCIAL STUDIES (WWW.SOCIALSTUDIES.ORG)

(1) Individual development and identity; (2) Individuals, groups, and institutions; (3) People, places, and environments; (4) Culture; (5) Global connections; (6) Civic ideals and practices; (7) Production, distribution, and consumption; (8) Science, technology, and society; (9) Power, authority, and governance; (10) Time, continuity, and change

Example big idea for #4: Culture is a shared way of living that bonds people. Discipline connections: music, visual art, and dance

Additional big idea examples are listed in this chart.

TOPICS/THEMES	BIG IDEA EXAMPLES
Beauty	Beauty is in the eye of the beholder.
Beliefs	People's beliefs determine their actions.
Chaos	The natural direction is toward disorder.
Community	People who have common needs bond together.
Courage	To show courage, you first have to be afraid.
Customs	People develop common ways of behaving, based on needs (e.g., celebrations, dress, housing).
Cycles	There are repeated patterns in life, like the seasons and life and death.
Freedom	Freedom isn't free.
Friendship	Misfortune tests the depth of friendship.
Happiness	You are as happy as you decide to be.
Humor	The source of humor is problems, not happiness.
Justice	Fair is not equal.
Order	It takes a lot of work to keep things in order.
Patterns	Looking for repetition in anything helps with understanding.
Persistence	Hard work leads to a measure of success.
Place	Where people live affects how they live.
Power	Knowledge is power.
Relationships	To sustain good relationships among people takes continual work.
Responsibility	You learn to be responsible by being given responsibilities.
Sacrifice	Most people will give up something for a cause they believe in.

Sources consulted: Perkins, 2004; Perkins & Blythe, 1994; Wiggins & McTighe, 2005.

Best practice: Teach inquiry-based problem solving

A problem can be anything from a dilemma or question to a puzzle, paradox, enigma, task, stimulus, phenomenon, discrepancy, or need. A problem can come in the form of a person, an issue, or a matter. Problems come in all sizes, from small irritations to life-threatening situations. Unfortunately, problems have a bad reputation. We think of problems as, well, problems—bad things. But problems truly are opportunities that provide significant motivation for learning. Problems are pervasive, and they reflect daily needs and purposes. Problems are so integral to human existence that no one goes a day without encountering and solving them. Rather than try to avoid problems—which is futile—it is both satisfying and effective, from a comprehension viewpoint, to embrace them and the universal process humans use to solve them.

Teaching the Comprehension Problem Solving process. People respond to problems with differing types and degrees of intelligent behavior. Best comprehension practices are intended to help students act more intelligently as they process texts. In this chapter's Snapshot, George Darcy used explicit instruction in the CPS process to do just that for his fourth graders. His teaching strategies for the CPS process provide a useful how-to checklist. Do you do the following?

- ☐ Use warm-ups to engage "head, heart, and hands"
- ☐ Engage the students with your own enthusiasm and humor
- ☐ Motivate with important goals
- ☐ Provide examples
- ☐ Use visuals
- ☐ Model with a think aloud
- ☐ Share an alternative real-life text (Cheerios box)
- ☐ Scaffold (bookmark)
- ☐ Ask thoughtful questions
- ☐ Forecast a commitment to working on CPS strategies the entire year (providing instruction and practice over time)

To achieve comprehension of big ideas, students must be challenged to create meaning by using problem-solving strategies such as the CPS set. Effective comprehension instruction shows students how to produce knowledge (make meaning), not merely reproduce it (locate information).

Encouraging inquiry. Inquiry is in-depth problem solving motivated by personal interest. Inquiry-based instruction is about creating interest, teaching to interests, and giving choices. Anything teachers do to increase involvement and engagement has the potential to trigger an inquiry stance. Starting lessons with intriguing questions, presenting "mystery" objects for investigation, and offering real-life dilemmas can stimulate inquiry. This kind of instruction is about creating the desire to know and find out. Curiosity is a powerful motivator for learning; it is responsible for human inventions and discoveries ranging from the paper clip and Velcro to the Internet. It was Philo Farnsworth's curiosity, wonder, and interest that set his problem-solving process in motion and gave us the gift of television.

The wondrous products of inquiry-oriented problem solving depend on many "ifs." Among the *ifs* are school-based preconditions, especially the two previously discussed: the nature of the teacher and the learning climate. Problem solving happens in all classrooms. How problem solving becomes inquiry is all about particulars. A particular person must want to solve a particular problem using particular texts in a particular time and place. When a person has the ability to coordinate problem solving strategies, given these particular circumstances, then comprehension is likely to be elevated to the level of inquiry.

snapshot revisited

Teacher George Darcy is in the process of implementing research-based best practices. He understands that comprehension strategies have to be presented as a set of problem-solving tools that students can use flexibly to understand all sorts of texts, even cereal boxes. The use of environmental print that combines visual art messages with informational and persuasive language is a credit to his goal of making CPS relevant to students' lives. He does a thorough job of modeling the self-questioning needed to construct big ideas about his problem from such a nonlinear text.

George realizes he needs powerful engagement strategies to gain and keep his students' attention for a very substantive think-aloud modeling of CPS. His use of a warm-up in a circle, PowerPoint slides, and bookmarks contributes to motivating his students. Although not all teachers are comfortable singing with students, George is. His voice isn't particularly beautiful, but his enthusiasm for using songs and songwriting to engage students and give them alternative ways to show comprehension is commendable. George's lesson provides examples of many best teaching practices considered key to pushing comprehension into first place in the literacy curriculum.

Conclusion

The best comprehension practices introduced in this chapter will be the subject of the chapters that follow. They form a strong framework for comprehension curriculum development and for instruction that addresses the Five Factors that most significantly influence comprehension. The nine best practices support an inquiry-based approach to comprehension that moves students toward problem-solving independence with a content orientation.

Two best practices previewed in Chapter 2 were further examined in this chapter. Both relate to teaching the *task* of comprehension: a focus on big ideas (comprehension product) and inquiry-based problem solving using CPS. This chapter also discussed two preconditions for best practices implementation: a supportive teacher and a supportive context for learning.

Pre-service teachers may have an advantage when it comes to acquiring and using a repertoire of best practices, since they begin with a clean slate. They are not saddled with a repertoire of traditional and conventional practices that veteran teachers sometimes have difficulty surrendering. Practicing teachers, however, have the benefit of experience, which gives them confidence and flexibility. Both novice and veteran teachers should take heart that the cause is great. A teacher may need up to thirty rehearsals to incorporate a new routine successfully into his or her repertoire, but it is worth the work (Joyce & Showers, 1996). Comprehension best practices have the power to transform learning. They are the tools we need to accomplish the mission we have chosen—to help our students be all they can be.

CHAPTER 3 big ideas

The following are examples of big ideas from this chapter. Use the list as a tool to generate your own priority big ideas that will guide your decisions about comprehension instruction.

1. Best comprehension practices are drawn from research, amassed professional wisdom, and other sources.
2. Conclusions about practices considered "best" should change as facts change.
3. The Five Factors that influence comprehension are important organizers for crafting best practice implementation.
4. Two preconditions for successful implementation of best practices are (1) teachers who can support comprehension reform with their knowledge and beliefs and (2) a classroom culture that supports active meaning making by students.
5. Comprehension is heavily influenced by when, where, and with whom a text is used.
6. Teachers who operate with outdated definitions of comprehension limit the learning experiences of their students.
7. Big ideas and the CPS process are core aspects of the *task* of comprehension.
8. Two recommended practices for comprehension instruction are (1) focus on big ideas and (2) teach inquiry-based CPS.

a look ahead

The next chapter describes the best practice of assessing to differentiate instruction and outlines a range of new views of assessment purposes, types, and guidelines. I introduce informal assessment tools that teachers can use to gather information about students' comprehension needs and strengths. A particular focus of the chapter is examining diversity among learners, which makes assessing to differentiate instruction an imperative for comprehension achievement.

CHAPTER 3 response options

Use these response options to increase your comprehension of this chapter. Each response calls for the use of CPS strategies.

1. Use big ideas from the chapter to write three to five if–then statements about teaching implications. For example, "If big ideas and the CPS process are core aspects of comprehension, then . . ." (What should you do? Be as specific as possible.)

2. Return to the questions at the start of the chapter and answer them to evaluate your comprehension. List additional questions you have about comprehension best practices associated with the nature of teachers, the context of text use, and the task of comprehension.

3. In a small group, discuss points from the text that make sense or don't make sense related to the two preconditions for implementing best practices.

4. Select a short picture book to analyze for big ideas. These titles would be available at most libraries: *The Big Orange Splot, Millions of Cats, Crow Boy,* and *Mirette on the High Wire.*

5. Review the list of best comprehension practices in Ready Resource 3.5. Rate how much you know about each, using a plus, check, or minus sign.

6. Look at the list of practices that are *not* recommended (Appendix E). Which practices are you surprised to find on the list? What would you add to this list? Why?

7. Observe a classroom and evaluate the environment using the checklist provided in Ready Resource 3.4.

8. Review the Snapshot describing George's lesson. List strategies he used that you would like to try.

9. What are you wondering most about (with regard to comprehension) at this point in the book? Email your thoughts to another student or educator who would be interested, or to me at ccornett@wittenberg.edu.

CHILDREN'S LITERATURE CITED

Gag, W. (1928). *Millions of cats.* New York: Coward-McCann.

McCully, E. A. (1992). *Mirette on the high wire.* New York: Putnam.

Pinkwater, D. (1993). *The big orange splot.* New York: Scholastic.

White, E. B. (1952). *Charlotte's web.* New York: Harper & Row.

Yasima, T. (1955). *Crow boy.* New York: Viking.

Assessing to Differentiate Instruction

preview

This chapter presents assessment as integral to the problem-solving process teachers use to gather data about factors that influence students' comprehension success. Assessment should be used to uncover both student strengths and needs (versus weaknesses). Such information is essential for teachers to craft comprehension instruction that is customized to the diverse needs of today's students. The chapter discusses this kind of instruction, called "differentiated instruction," in relation to the characteristics of a variety of learners, including English learners and low-performing students.

The chapter also highlights an additional purpose of assessment: to motivate students to learn. Assessment FOR learning holds promise for improving students' comprehension development.

The chapter explains examples of informal assessment tools, as well as guidelines for conducting and using assessment information. Assessment tools are also featured in the appendices.

important questions

1. What is assessment and why is it important?

2. What guidelines are important for judging assessment?

3. How are learner strengths and needs linked to assessment?

4. What different types of assessment exist, and which types are recommended for comprehension? Why?

5. What do the Five Factors have to do with assessment?

6. What is assessment *for* learning (AfL)?

7. What is differentiated instruction? Why is it needed?

8. How can teachers differentiate instruction for diverse learners?

Introduction

Isn't it ironic, the state doesn't test what really makes us special. They don't even know how.

T. ROBERTS, 2004

Teaching students to use the Comprehension Problem Solving (CPS) process to find and create big ideas is an important piece of the comprehension puzzle. More pieces are needed, however, to complete the picture. One is assessment. Effective teachers assess what makes learners special, along with other factors. They gather assessment information about the most influential factors that determine comprehension success. The goal is not just to collect scores and track student progress. Assessment data should be used to change instruction—to teach differently, because students are different. In this process, teachers use problem solving to design instruction likely to increase success. Teaching, like comprehension, involves inquiry.

Currently, widely used comprehension assessments focus on a few tasks and thus limit the literacy curriculum to the teaching of those few tasks. It is tempting to test what is easiest to measure, such as word pronunciation and fact knowledge. As Albert Einstein cautioned, however, what is easiest to count may not count the most.

Good comprehension assessment is expansive. It considers the product or outcomes of comprehension (i.e., learning content), the processes that create understanding, and much more. Effective comprehension assessment targets all of the Five Factors that influence success. The goal is differentiated instruction. This is the antithesis of the destructive practice of "handing a pacing guide to teachers and giving them no say in its development and no choice about implementing it" (Knight, 2009, p. 512).

Using the Five Factors for Assessment

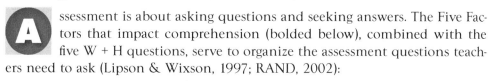

Assessment is about asking questions and seeking answers. The Five Factors that impact comprehension (bolded below), combined with the five W + H questions, serve to organize the assessment questions teachers need to ask (Lipson & Wixson, 1997; RAND, 2002):

- WHO am I teaching? (specific **learner** characteristics)
- WHAT am I teaching? (critical literacy **tasks,** such as CPS)
- WHY am I teaching the task? (student needs and the importance of the literacy **task**)
- WHAT materials are best? (variety of content-rich **texts**)
- WHERE should I teach? (learning **context** that is supportive)
- WHEN should I teach a particular concept or skill? (**learner** readiness to learn and district course of study)
- HOW should I instruct students? (differentiated **teaching** practices based on identified student strengths and needs)

Many aspects of the Five Factors are *external and visible*, which makes them easier to assess (Fountas & Pinnell, 2006). Observable factors include (1) the organization and format of texts, (2) aspects of the comprehension task, (3) the context in which the text is used (where and with whom), and (4) teaching methods. *Internal invisible* comprehension factors have to do with the learner's cognition and emotions. Teachers need tools to uncover and reveal specifics about each student's motivation, background, knowledge of, and ability to use comprehension strategies within the CPS process.

No single assessment tool yields a perfect picture of these factors. Assessment is always about estimating, so multiple tools are needed and assessment must be continuous. Continuous monitoring of the Five Factors enables teachers to approach planning flexibly and make good instructional choices moment by moment, day by day, and week by week, using assessment data as a guide.

The complexity of the comprehension task and variability in learner characteristics, texts, and learning contexts make effective assessment complex. Add individual teacher variables and assessment can seem daunting. Nonetheless, evidence is necessary for informed decision making and central to how effective teachers approach instruction. Assessment allows teachers to know where to start and how to stay on track.

Using Assessment to Plan Instruction

Contemporary assessment is correlated with national, state, and local standards created by professional organizations, such as the International Reading Association and National Council of Teachers of English. *Standards* are goals that describe what students should *know, do,* and *be* related to tasks such as comprehension (Drake & Burns, 2004). Good assessment gives students multiple ways to show what they know and can do in relation to comprehension. This information gives clues to the kinds of readers, listeners, and viewers they are becoming.

Assessment is a part of instructional problem solving used to craft appropriate instruction (Pressley, 2007). It involves collecting and using data. If assessment information is not used as the basis of instructional planning, collecting that information is a waste of time and money. The entire planning process can be summarized with the acronym APIE: assess, plan, implement, and evaluate (Stephens, 1970).

A **Assess.** The first step in planning instruction is to gather information about the Five Factors, as discussed previously.

P **Plan.** Assessment should result in a flexible plan to differentiate instruction using whole-group, small-group, and individual teaching formats embedded with the other best comprehension practices that were listed in Ready Resource 3.5.

I **Implement.** Once the instructional plan is implemented, teachers monitor student responses, re-assess, and revise instruction with success for all students in mind.

E **Evaluate.** Teachers continually evaluate the effectiveness of the plan, based on student improvement and long-term comprehension gains. Genuine effectiveness results in long-term gains, not fleeting success with a lone strategy or short-term retention of isolated facts.

The goal is for students to do what good readers do: take an inquiry stance to texts and use a problem-solving repertoire to extract and construct big ideas. Excellent comprehension instruction seeks a deep change in *how* students think and *what* they think.

We gather assessment data to answer the questions "What's going on now?" and "What should happen next?" For example, teachers need to know where each student is in the development of self-regulated use of problem-solving strategies. Does the student start text use with clear purposes? Does the student generate questions about connections between the text and his or her background and immediate purposes? To what degree does the student initiate such strategies? Appendices A and B contain example checklists to record student acquisition of CPS strategies over time. This kind of informal assessment data is used to plan instructional experiences, including regular conferencing, to motivate students to work toward the goal of effective strategy use.

Assessment *for* Learning (AfL)

W e assess in order to inform instructional planning and to monitor student progress. But there is another purpose: to motivate learning.

Assessment *for* learning (AfL) is an approach to assessment that promotes comprehension achievement by putting student motivation at the center of thinking about texts. Of particular importance is sharing assessment results with students so they can set comprehension goals, which then will direct future learning efforts. Coupled with ongoing feedback on progress toward specific goals, AfL has proved a strong influence on motivation and learning (Stiggins, 2004). It rivals one-on-one tutoring in effectiveness, especially with low-performing students, because assessment is FOR learning, not just OF learning. AfL changes *how* students comprehend; it does not just measure *what* they comprehend. It is formative—it involves doing observation and giving feedback as students practice strategies like inferring or imagining. AfL can be summative, too, when it describes achievement results.

In AfL, comprehension goals are made clear through teacher think alouds, work samples, rubrics, and checklists. Assessment results detail where students stand in comparison to progress points toward top comprehension goals. These top comprehension goals include (1) understanding of big ideas (products) and (2) use of the CPS process. Students become assessors themselves: they self-measure by using varied informal tools, such as checklists and rubrics, which are central in clarifying literacy goals. Students track their own progress and make changes, using feedback, which in turn increase the quality of their work.

In sum, teachers who use assessment *for* learning

1. determine criteria for success at the outset.
2. create fluid assessment criteria.
3. give continuous, specific feedback.

DETERMINING CRITERIA FOR SUCCESS AT THE OUTSET

Specific aspects of the comprehension task need to be made clear to students in advance of text use (refer to Ready Resource 4.1). This "front loading" engages the students' motivation to learn and unites students and teachers in pursuit of excellent work. Students come to understand that feedback is meant to increase comprehension, not grade it.

Comprehension criteria or goals are best developed when teachers work *with* students, explaining what high-level comprehension is and modeling how it is achieved through CPS strategies. Teachers provide both examples and non-examples so students can observe what to do and what not to do. Students are asked to identify good and poor examples of comprehension strategy use, and they should immediately practice strategies modeled in the context of continuous text, rather than practicing with isolated sentences or words.

CREATING FLUID ASSESSMENT CRITERIA

Although goals need to be specified, room should be left for the unexpected. No teacher can anticipate all the possible manifestations of something as complex as the comprehension process or the products students may create to show understanding. Teachers have to be ready to embrace novel evidence. For example, a student may offer an answer that doesn't seem to show the CPS process of inference. The teacher should follow up with questions like, "How are you thinking that answer is an inference?" Questions like this one seek more information (assessment) and allow the teacher either to re-teach inferring (e.g., define it, give examples, or model again) or agree that the student's answer made sense.

Criteria for creating a comprehension rubric.

Comprehension is both a process and a product. The comprehension *product* has two main features: immediate understanding and long-term knowledge gain (RAND, 2002). Top- and bottom-level descriptors for a Comprehension Task Rubric are provided below. To use the rubric, simply add two or more gradients between these levels for both the product and the process. Note that there is overlap between product and process criteria.

Description: Use a problem-solving repertoire of strategies to construct meaning or create solutions that feature big ideas. Big ideas are the complete thoughts that a reader, listener, or viewer can draw from any text.

TOP LEVEL: COMPREHENSION *PRODUCT*

Students should be able to . . .

- Find and shape *explicit* big ideas (complete thoughts) from texts.

- Construct summaries and synthesize products that demonstrate comprehension of high-value big ideas.

- Justify conclusions (big ideas) using text evidence and background knowledge.

- Construct *original* big ideas (complete thoughts) from texts using text evidence and background knowledge to support these conclusions.

- Explain that the goal of comprehension is to *make* sense by using problem-solving strategies to find and construct big ideas using text evidence and background knowledge.

TOP LEVEL: COMPREHENSION *PROCESS*

Students should be able to . . .

- Persist in problem solving until the comprehension task is accomplished.

- Concentrate, focus, and sustain text engagement until the comprehension task is accomplished.

- Independently, flexibly, and purposefully use a complete set of comprehension problem-solving strategies to find and construct big ideas derived from text evidence and relevant background knowledge.

- Adjust strategies to text characteristics that reflect the author's or artist's purposes.

- Make unusual connections among concepts, topics, and themes.

- Explain the comprehension strategies they used to derive big ideas.

- Explain their choices and provide evidence to support their big ideas (details and patterns).

- Judge, use, and respond creatively to diverse texts, including electronic and multimedia texts.

- Work collaboratively, including listening and giving suggestions, to make sense of texts.

- Use written, technology-based, and artistic forms to show comprehension (product).

Continued.

LOW LEVEL: COMPREHENSION *PRODUCT*

Students should be able to . . .

- Find key concepts, topics, and explicit main ideas in paragraphs.
- Construct paragraph-level main ideas from relevant details, with coaching.
- Construct big ideas from above, with coaching.
- Retell key information, such as narrative elements.
- Say that the goal of comprehension is to make sense of texts, without necessarily being able to explain or give examples of what this means.

LOW LEVEL: COMPREHENSION *PROCESS*

Students should be able to . . .

- Complete the comprehension task with scaffolding.
- Concentrate on the text, when supervised.
- Name a few comprehension strategies, when prompted.
- Predict, image, and make personal connections to texts, when prompted.
- Connect the text with background knowledge, although the connections may be tangential or irrelevant.
- Explain and give examples of basic differences between nonfiction and fiction and between stories and informational materials.
- Use and respond to diverse texts, including electronic and multimedia texts, by following directions.
- Work collaboratively, including listening and giving suggestions, to make sense of texts, under the direction of a teacher.
- Use oral, written, technology-based, and artistic forms to show comprehension (product), when these forms are highly structured.

READY RESOURCE 4.1

GIVING CONSTRUCTIVE FEEDBACK

Students are more likely to sustain motivation and meet goals when they receive specific guidance. Constructive or descriptive feedback provides this guidance. That's why athletic coaches routinely use constructive feedback to describe what they see athletes doing that is working or not working.

Constructive feedback is more than praise. For the purpose of comprehension, it focuses on the teacher describing what and how students seem to be thinking and on scaffolding so students think more deeply. For example, "You seem to be inferring that the spider was dumb. What in the song makes you think that?"

Constructive feedback often involves questioning, followed by feedback. Questions like, "What are you thinking?" and "Why?" can help students describe their ideas so teachers can then respond. Other questions, like, "What is working?" "What do you need to do?" and "How can I help?" ensure that students comprehend the purpose of feedback and understand they are expected to participate in solving their own problems.

The most meaningful feedback is not one-shot. Feedback should be ongoing, and it can come from sources besides teachers. For example, students can self-assess their own thinking strategies by using a checklist of CPS strategies and then give themselves feedback. Peers should also be taught how to give constructive feedback that is specific and useful.

Principles of Assessment

 even important principles guide the selection, construction, administration, and use of assessment tools.

1. FOCUS ON STRENGTHS AND NEEDS

Although it is common to assess what students don't know and can't do, it is more effective to identify their strengths. Student needs can then be addressed through their strengths. For example, CPS strategies can be practiced with any text, so why not use texts of high interest? To do so, teachers use tools such as interviews and interest surveys early in the year. If a student knows a lot about raccoons, teach him strategies by using texts about raccoons. These can be fiction, nonfiction, or even texts the student generates by writing or through dictation to the teacher. Students may end up reading different books during independent reading time and reading some common texts (e.g., ones on animals) during small-group work.

2. ASSESS AUTHENTICALLY

When information about comprehension is gathered in a context and a manner that reveal what students really know and can do, it is called "authentic." Paper-and-pencil tests are inauthentic when they fail to capture complex thinking, such as CPS. An example of authentic assessment is coaching students to explain their thinking about a text at the moment of use. This kind of coached conversation should take place frequently, and it provides valuable information to gauge progress. The CPS Checklist (Appendix B.2) can be used to guide observation and coaching.

3. ASSESS HUMANELY AND REALISTICALLY

Assessment must be humane and doable. The process has to uplift, not discourage students. Sitting side by side doing an interview or going over a checklist can be socially rewarding and enjoyable. Students should feel proud of their gains and motivated by clear goals that are made concrete in progress folders (see the discussion of portfolios later in this chapter). The challenge is to create assessment tools and procedures as creative and dimensional as comprehension itself. Note: If you sit with your dominant hand away from the child, you can make notes with less distraction. Kids may ask what you are writing, and there is no reason not to show them.

4. MAKE ASSESSMENT MULTIFACTORED

No single checklist or collection of anecdotal notes can create a full portrait of a learner's comprehension (Pressley, 2007). All assessment results are samples that merely provide estimates. Multiple and varied assessments reveal a more complete picture of a student's thinking about comprehension. In addition, use of several different kinds of assessment gives breadth of information to document comprehension process and product growth more accurately over time.

Culminating projects (presentations, performances, and exhibits) and portfolios may be combined with traditional tests to show the ultimate comprehension product—the big ideas that make up content or subject matter. The opportunity to choose *how* to show comprehension motivates students, especially those who have a track record of failure with traditional tests. Writing in diverse forms, participating in discussions, and creating arts products are important response options for students and assessment opportunities for teachers. These alternatives result in observable products that make comprehension visible. Chapter 9 explains more about response options.

5. USE ONGOING ASSESSMENT

Assessment data should be collected in many ways and from a variety of sources in an ongoing manner. Parent and student interviews, student self-reflection on goals, teacher observation, and peer feedback are important. Every lesson should include assessment opportunities. For example, teachers can punctuate lessons with time to discuss strategies that are working or not working and how to make strategy use more effective. Written drafts and work samples can be collected to help the teacher lay out concrete progress (e.g., use of more details to support big ideas constructed from texts).

6. MAKE ASSESSMENT TRANSPARENT

Daily observation of students working in real time on real comprehension tasks is the bulwark of comprehension assessment. Teachers can use sticky notes on a clipboard to jot down what a student is doing and what might be needed. These notes can easily be transferred to individual folders, which students should be able to access. Imagine a bin of folders students examine daily because they want to know about their own progress. Imagine students eager to see the latest note posted by the teacher, and students noting evidence of their own. Imagine them *requesting* conferences to discuss progress. Imagine first graders asking the teacher to include evidence they provide about their own strategy use. Vision can become reality when basic assessment principles guide common practice.

7. ASSESS TECHNOLOGICAL CAPABILITIES

Electronic texts are now common reading, listening, and viewing (Casey, 2008). Educators need to teach and assess digital text knowledge and skills, especially online reading capabilities. Educational Testing Service, among other groups, is developing models for assessing online digital literacy, and the State Educational Technology Directors Association offers frameworks for assessing technology literacy (Coiro, 2003a, 2003b). Unfortunately, state reading assessments do not currently measure the strategies needed to navigate and comprehend text online (Leu et al., 2004). Chapter 5 includes guidelines for teaching Internet use, Chapter 6 addresses motivational properties of digital texts, and Chapter 9 examines how students can create texts, including written, arts-based, and computer-generated texts, to show comprehension.

Types of Assessment

Comprehension assessment should identify specific needs that must be addressed if students are to be put on a successful path. It is inadequate to confine assessment to sub-skills, such as word recognition fluency and decoding, since comprehension is not merely the consequence of adding up phonic skills and accumulating new words. Children may have adequate word-level skills but lack key comprehension assets, especially problem-solving skills and relevant background knowledge (RAND, 2002). Effective comprehension assessment should reveal how students

- are motivated, especially through interests and goals.
- think about themselves as readers and comprehenders, especially their views on good readers and the role of meaning making in reading.
- use problem-solving strategies—which ones, when, how, and for what reasons.
- use information from texts to solve problems in their own lives or the world.
- change and build knowledge (big ideas), including how they respond to "what if" and "I wonder why" questions.
- think about texts, including their structure, format, accuracy, and artistry.
- respond emotionally and aesthetically to texts.

As a result of the need to identify so many different factors, effective assessment takes a variety of forms, including external evaluation, benchmark assessments, and classroom assessments.

1. *External evaluation* is a process of using standardized tests to make decisions at the school and district level. Student achievement is compared to state and national norms, and data are used to cite individual schools for excellence or lack of adequate yearly progress. Program assessment is not addressed in this book.

2. *Benchmark assessments* are used to gauge student progress toward curricular goals and standards. Teachers use these tests for instructional

planning, especially grouping for needs and communication with students and parents.

3. *Classroom assessments* aid teachers in planning differentiated instruction. These assessments are informal tools that zero in on specific comprehension needs and strengths. This form of assessment is the focus of this chapter.

ASSESSMENT VERSUS EVALUATION

I keep this quote posted near my desk: "*A grade is an inadequate report of an inaccurate judgment by a biased and variable judge of the extent to which a student has attained an undefined level of mastery of an indefinite amount of material*" (Dressel, 1983, p. 10). The terms *assessment* and *evaluation* are often used interchangeably, but assessment is distinct from evaluation and grading. Evaluation focuses on judging goodness (i.e., placing a value judgment on progress), while assessment focuses on gathering evidence, particularly through teacher observation.

SUMMATIVE VERSUS FORMATIVE

External evaluation (versus student self-evaluation), including grading, is a reality in the schools. It occurs after instruction and summarizes learning, hence the label *summative.* Assessment that begins before teaching and continues during the learning process to inform and form teaching and learning is *formative* assessment. Formative assessment should be embedded in all lessons and should include both teachers and students. Teachers need to observe student responses continually and modify their teaching based on that feedback. For example, teachers may ask more questions, give additional examples, change the pace, and so on. Students also need to do self-assessment to help "form" their own learning. For example, they can track their use of targeted CPS strategies during independent reading. Self-assessment boosts ownership of comprehension, because the learner decides what is working and not working. Goal setting should follow and should focus on personal improvement, not just grades.

FORMAL VERSUS INFORMAL

Formal tools (i.e., standardized tests) are mostly used to obtain summative data on student performance for program evaluation. With analysis, standardized tests can reveal specific needs (e.g., problems with inferring), but the analysis process is labor intensive and of limited use, since how students arrived at their answers remains unknown.

Informal tools yield specific information about comprehension, not just percentiles or grades. They give teachers what they need: specifics to teach (Reutzel, 2007). Students can also use these tools to set goals.

Common informal assessment tools, such as informal reading inventories (e.g., Leslie & Caldwell, 2006), and running records assess some aspects of comprehension. These tools allow teachers to observe students reading orally, which can be telling. However, using these tools alone is inadequate for assessing comprehension, and every tool has flaws. For example, oral reading of texts can make visible, to an extent, how students think. However, the act of oral reading changes how readers comprehend, since they must pay attention to aspects of oral performance, which can inhibit understanding. Another problem is that comprehension is more complicated than just thinking about words. Oral word fluency reflects thinking, but it gives a limited picture. Also, traditional informal reading inventories often are based on an assumption that comprehension is about levels of thinking, and they focus on immediate recall, such as retelling after oral and silent reading. But good readers don't think about texts using levels like "literal" or "critical–creative." Nor do they start at the bottom of a taxonomy of thinking and move up from memory to interpretation, analysis, and so forth, as in Benjamin Bloom's model (1956; Krathwohl, 2002). Retelling what is remembered is about extracting facts and may not involve constructing meaning at all.

Finally, assessments of listening comprehension and oral language production, both of which are closely connected to reading comprehension, tend to be rare (RAND, 2002, p. 54-56). Note: Most informal reading inventories describe an option of reading *to* students, followed by student retelling and/or answering questions. This variation can provide an estimate of the "listening level," which shows comprehension capabilities when students are not restricted by print fluency.

Assessment Tools

Today a veritable cornucopia of formal and informal assessment tools is available. However, not all are congruent with constructivist philosophy, which positions personal meaning making at the center of comprehension. Fill-in-the-blank and multiple-choice tests cannot show comprehension strategy use or reveal the big ideas students construct in the way writing, discussion, and arts-based projects can. Retelling and oral reading fluency tests also fall short. A compendium of informal comprehension assessment tools is included in the appendices. The following are basic tools.

INTERVIEWS

Interviewing is not the most common assessment tool associated with comprehension, but it can be very effective in providing information about a variety of factors that affect comprehension. Gary Fife, the teacher in the following snapshot, is well aware that the background, interests, and preferences of his students loom large in their comprehension development. He uses beginning-of-the-year assessments to reveal the invisible and internal knowledge, skills/strategies, and dispositions his students will bring to texts and comprehension tasks. Gary uses many types of assessment tools during the year, including informal and formal ones. This snapshot, in the form of a Q&A, is about an informal tool: comprehension interviews.

As Gary Fife explains, interviews accomplish many purposes. Ready Resource 4.2 offers some guidelines for conducting student interviews.

Quick tips for student interviews.

- Focus on establishing a relaxed conversational atmosphere.
- Begin by explaining that the purpose of the interview is to help plan teaching.
- Let the child ask you questions to clarify the interview process.
- Jot down notes, using a form as a guide.
- Explain that the notes will help you remember what the student has told you.

READY RESOURCE 4.2

classroom snapshot

GARY FIFE'S COMPREHENSION INTERVIEWS

It is August, and Gary Fife is getting ready to start another year. Gary has taught grades one through five and says he is the first to volunteer when the principal asks for someone to change grades. "Change keeps me fresh," he explains. "It really helps me keep curricular articulation in mind. I like having experience with the full map of content and skills our district has outlined."

A high priority for Gary is gathering assessment data on his students. Since interviews are one of his favorite forms of assessment, I decided to interview him about interviews.

CC: What kinds of interviews do you use?

Gary: I try to interview every parent before school starts. I call four to five parents each day. It takes about five minutes per call. I introduce myself and then ask about the interests and strengths of the child. I like to start with positives. I then basically ask them to tell me about anything they think will help me help their child learn. If the parent has a lot of concerns, we make an appointment for a conference to take the discussion further.

CC: What is the main purpose of the parent interview?

Gary: More than anything, I want to touch base, to meet them before there are any problems. Parents are often surprised by the call. They think there already is a problem, even though school hasn't started! I want to build a relationship so when there are concerns, I can contact them and they remember I was the guy who cared enough to call before school started.

CC: How do the interviews help you teach comprehension?

Gary: Well, I do ask a few questions directly related to reading, like, "How much does your child read?" and I explain that I will be teaching my class about comprehension strategies. I actually use those terms with the kids, so I want parents to know what is going on. I can't give the parent a whole course in reading methods on the phone, but I do tell them I'll email them the strategies, and I always put an article in our monthly class newsletter about comprehension. I also give the parents a heads-up that the kids have Literacy Folios, and I track things like their strategy use. I make notes when parents tell me about hobbies and interests of their kids, and I use that information to help kids select books for independent reading. I also encourage students to become "experts" in something. They start with an interest and do Internet and library research.

CC: So, all your students become experts?

Gary: Yes, every one of them. Some become experts in many things—everything from matchbooks to musicians. Some will get going on an interest and that draws in other kids. Often the interests connect with science or social studies units or something in the news, like an election.

CC: What problems do you run into with the phone interviews?

Gary: Not too many. If both parents work or there is a single working parent, I call in the evening. I leave a message during the day that I'll be calling back, or I invite them to call me at school. Occasionally a family doesn't have a phone, so I just stop by. This is a small town, so that can work well. Most of the time I get invited in for sweet tea. I'm careful to ask if they have time to talk and explain that I can come back. Oh, I've had ones who really bent my ear, usually about their own problems. Now I tell them up front that I only have a few minutes to talk, but if we need to talk more, we can make an appointment for them to come to school. That works pretty well.

CC: How do you use interviews with your students?

Gary: I enjoy those interviews. The kids tell me the most interesting things. I interview all students by the end of the first week of school. Actually, I try to interview each student before school starts, but some are farm kids and live way out.

CC: What do you ask the students?

Gary: The first interview is a general background interview about interests, hobbies, their computer background, where they have traveled, and so on. I ask them about favorite foods and colors. I had a boy last year who told me his favorite color was puce! He was serious, too. He was a great artist and was really into shades and tints and such.

CC: Are there comprehension items on that interview?

Gary: Not directly. Again, I'm trying to build a relationship and find out strengths and interests I can build on. Interests set the stage for comprehension, in my opinion. Later I do another interview that is specific to comprehension.

CC: What is it like?

Gary: I call it my Good Reader Interview. It is my bread and butter to get started with comprehension instruction. I ask all sorts of questions about reading: "What happens in your head," "Who do you know that is a good reader," even "What do you think reading is?" Kids can be so confused. They think good readers have to know all the words and always follow along when other kids are reading out loud. That tells me a lot. I don't use round robin reading, but I've had plenty of students who came from first grades where it is alive and well.

> ### Good Reader Interview
>
> What happens in your head when you read?
>
> Who do you know who is a good reader?
>
> What do you think reading is?

CC: How do you use information from the Good Reader Interview?

Gary: As I said, it is where I start. So many kids don't really have a clue that the goal is understanding. They aren't going to become good readers until they have the goal straight. Then there are kids who are right on target. They talk about picturing in their heads, being so into a book they don't want to go to sleep. Some still use flashlights under the blankets.

CC: How long does that interview take?

Gary: It is longer. About twenty, sometimes thirty minutes. I like to eat lunch with the kids occasionally, and I combine lunch with that interview, for some kids. I try to get one a day in, during lunch, after school, whenever I can work it in. I post a sign-up sheet so kids know where they are on the list. They actually remind me when their interview is coming up, and some will volunteer to give up recess. They like the attention.

CC: Isn't that a lot of interviewing during the first month?

Gary: It's about forty-five minutes, total, per child. It's so worth it. Information is power, and I get so much information about my students. They start to think interviews are cool. I think some watch Oprah and other interviews on TV. Some decide to do their own interviews. When I get done telling them how much I like interviewing them and they enjoy my interviews, they want to get in on the fun. Whatever we are studying, there's always the possibility of an interview. Kids interview their friends and relatives, each other, the principal. It's my favorite kind of assessment, and it has become an integral teaching tool.

Note: Appendices A and B include:

- Student Background and Interest Inventory
- Parent Interview
- Comprehension Strategies (CPS) Interview

INVENTORIES AND SURVEYS

Interest inventories are based on the premise that people learn faster and better when they are interested in the subject matter. The interest inventory focuses on strengths, so it is a pleasant assessment—a kind of "getting to know you." It is a good one to start with and can be conducted in a variety of ways. One is to ask students to fold a piece of paper in half and write the heading "Interests and Talents" on the left and "Problems and Questions" on the right. Typically students list sports, games, favorite books, music, and other arts in the left column. Problems and questions will range from general concerns, like getting good grades and having too much homework, to specific issues students are facing in their lives, like bullying or worry over a parent serving in the military. Teachers can expect to be surprised by the information students share. The two-column inventory may also be used to help students find topics for writing and art making.

Inventories can be done through discussion or by the student independently. Students should be encouraged to respond in a number of ways. For example, create question cards and invite students to draw sketches in response. An interest inventory that uses movement is called Step In. Ask students to stand in a circle and then ask them to step in (or twist, slide, etc.) in response to categories you name (Cornett, 2011). For example, say, "Step in if you play a sport." Ask for information from those who have moved, and make notes on a clipboard.

Interest inventories may be conducted as interviews, especially if a child has limited writing skills. Focus on establishing a relaxed conversational atmosphere. Begin by explaining that the interview's purpose is to help you plan teaching. Use the guidelines presented in Ready Resource 4.2, but also take time to share a few interests of your own, and let the child ask you questions to clarify the interview process. Most children enjoy talking about what they like to do and things they know about, as long as they feel the teacher wants to listen. Jot down ideas, using a form as a guide. Explain that your notes will help you remember what the student has told you. Appendices A and B offer ideas for questions and categories, including a background inventory that asks about interests.

CHECKLISTS AND RUBRICS

Checklists may be used to track strategies, concepts, and skills. The CPS Strategies Checklist in Appendix B involves students in tracking their own progress.

Rubrics are more elaborate checklists organized in a hierarchy to show a gradient of performance, such as the degree to which a strategy is used. There are many types of rubrics, but all use a rating scale (e.g., 1 through 4), and some include weighting. School districts often write rubrics to help make grading criteria understandable. Rubrics and checklists should focus on key comprehension strategies and big ideas. The Online Resource box below provides links to some useful websites.

BENCHMARKS

Benchmarks are like rubrics, in that they use rank ordering. Create benchmarks by "attaching quality to a small, rank-ordered body of work samples and then using them for comparison in making judgments about a larger body of work" (Baker et al., 2004, p. 29). Without research-based benchmarks that describe adequate progress in comprehension, we "risk aiming far too low in our expectations for student learning" (RAND, 2002, xix). The comprehension rubric given in Ready Resource 4.1 can be used to help rank work samples to serve as benchmarks.

Collaborative discussions about benchmarks can dramatically change your view of assessment tools (Baker et al., 2004). To establish comprehension benchmarks, discuss several possible text responses with your students (as I'll discuss in Chapter 9) and then order them collaboratively with your students. Be sure to use high-level criteria. For example, have students collect anecdotes about people

Useful websites for rubrics and checklists

- www.school.discovery.com/schrockguide/assess.html
- www.eduscapes.com/tap/topic53.htm
- www.4teachers.org/projectbased/checklists.html
- www.teach-nology.com

using comprehension strategies. Then coach students to rank-order these behaviors according to their importance to comprehension. (As an example, retelling the plot of "The Three Little Pigs" would be ranked lower than listing themes such as "making good decisions" and "planning ahead." At the highest level would be concluding that the story explains big ideas like "Taking short cuts can lead to long-term problems.") On a simpler level, write the CPS strategies on separate index cards and ask students to work in teams to sort them into "before," "during," and "after" categories.

STUDENT SELF-ASSESSMENT

By reflecting on comprehension criteria, students can get a sense of how the real world operates. From HVAC technicians to dentists, workers are expected to examine their own performance continually and make necessary adjustments. Students can examine successive drafts of their own work to monitor change. Ready Resource 4.3 presents examples that teachers should use daily for discussion or writing prompts.

PEER FEEDBACK

Students need to be taught *why* and *how* to respond to presentations, performances, and exhibits intended to demonstrate comprehension. The art of noticing must be taught and practiced so students learn to make evidence-based comments about what they see and hear. Direct them to use specific words, concepts, and feelings in their descriptions: "It made me feel ____." "I wonder ____." You may also use the learn–wonder–like (LWL) strategy, instructing students to make three columns with these labels and jot down responses in each column (look ahead to Ready Resource 7.11 in Chapter 7). Teach students that asking questions is another form of feedback.

Role-playing giving and receiving feedback is a useful activity. Have students take turns giving each other specific ideas about what is working or not working. Help students develop empathy by discussing the effects of both positive feedback and negative remarks.

Example questions for student self-assessment.

1. What strategies are you trying?
2. What big ideas did you find or construct?
3. Where is the evidence for your big ideas?
4. Why did you do what you did?
5. What did you try that you have not tried before?
6. How can you use _____ (strategy) in another subject?
7. What was most difficult? Why?
8. What worked? What will you do next?
9. What did you learn most?
10. What did you like best? Why?
11. How did this compare with other comprehension tasks?

READY RESOURCE 4.3

OBSERVATION

The famous baseball coach Yogi Berra advised, "You can observe a lot by watching." Successful coaches can provide educators with useful assessment ideas, and this is one of them. No other assessment tool is as important as careful observation of students actually working with texts. Coupled with interviewing students about their thinking, observation permits real-time assessment of actual problem solving and moments of insight. Skilled observation may seem casual and effortless. It isn't. Fruitful observation is predicated on teacher knowledge. You have to know what to look for, including gradients of progress toward key comprehension goals. Refer to the CPS Checklist (Appendix B.2) and the comprehension rubric (Ready Resource 4.1) for suggestions of what indicators to look for. Personal literacy also informs observation and helps teachers understand when students are moving in the right direction toward processes like summarizing and products like big ideas.

RECORD KEEPING

Checklists and graphs are examples of concrete ways to track comprehension growth. These records can serve as powerful tools both to motivate students and to inform parents. Any growth record needs to be as simple as possible, focusing on what's most important. Have students participate as much as possible in documenting their own comprehension growth.

ANECDOTAL RECORDS

Make these informal notes as students work with texts and as you observe comprehension products. A clipboard works well for organizing notes on the fly. I label a square for each student with permanent marker and keep a small sticky note on each square. This helps me keep track of which students I observe. Colored-coded stickies help track days or particular strategies (e.g., pink for "before" strategies). Keep larger notepads handy for additional notes. When students know you will post stickies in their folders regularly, they are interested in what you write. Their interest reinforces the focus on assessment *for* learning.

PORTFOLIOS

Teachers have long used collected work to show students' capabilities and skills. Checklists, anecdotal notes, and work samples give evidence of progress toward comprehension criteria. These work samples may be stored in folders, in three-ring binders, or in electronic format. Written products and arts responses can be invaluable progress indicators if students create them on the basis of clear comprehension criteria and if these products are then examined based on those criteria. Today's "folios" and "e-folios" offer great flexibility; for example, even student-choreographed dances can be evidence of big idea understanding. Such products can be recorded so students can view them, reflect, and assess the degree of understanding they demonstrate. Some schools now use digital portfolios, especially in the upper grades.

Not every piece of work should be kept. Focus on work that shows something important, but keep a range of work samples, not just "good" work, so students can see progress over time. Date the work and connect items to specific goals. Revisit older work to celebrate progress and past successes.

Each child needs a container for keeping evidence of growth toward comprehension benchmarks. The evidence serves as a motivator. Store portfolios where students can access them and check their own progress. Students should also be able to add dated evidence.

A set of guidelines for portfolios appears in Ready Resource 4.4.

CONFERENCES

Personal conferences provide valuable insight into children's thinking and convey the message that you care about their work toward specific goals. Three- to five-minute conferences allow students to discuss their comprehension goals, note their

---

Guidelines for student portfolios.

ORGANIZATION

1 Encourage students to decorate the front cover.

2 List goals and benchmarks inside the front cover. Goals and benchmarks should include a target date, e.g., "By the end of the month/semester/year you should be able to . . . ." (Review the CPS Checklist in Appendix B.2 and the com-

prehension rubric in Ready Resource 4.1 for ideas for comprehensions goals and benchmarks.)

3 Include dated work examples that show progress toward benchmarks. Include only work that relates to the goals and benchmarks listed in the front cover.

SUGGESTIONS FOR MAINTAINING AND USING FOLIOS

1 Number portfolios so students can easily keep them in order.

2 Provide generic goals for students to glue to the inside of their folder. Each child should also have a choice about individual targets.

3 Tell the class that the goals and the folder will show how much they are learning. Explain that they need to be thinking all the time about the goals and how they can put evidence in their portfolios to show they are getting closer to the goals.

4 Take time to discuss comprehension goals and to teach explicitly the concept of com-

prehension as problem solving, as well as all CPS strategies. Continue to bring up the goals throughout the day. Students cannot achieve the goals if they do not know what they are and know ways to meet them.

5 Use the portfolios to motivate students' learning and to promote independence. Example: "I'll be looking for people who are concentrating during DEIR. I have my clipboard and sticky notes with your names. I'll give the sticky notes to you to add to your portfolio."

(continued)

READY RESOURCE **4.4**

Guidelines for student portfolios, continued.

6 Target four or five students per day for observation assessment (e.g., note concentration or focus and use of evidence during discussions). This may be done during small group work with observation checklists. See the CPS Checklist example in Appendix B.2.

7 Conduct one- to three-minute individual conferences to review students' portfolios. Use a kitchen timer to gauge your time. Try "doing lunch" with students to accomplish this.

8 Schedule regular "portfolio time" for students to look at their work and note progress. Students might work with partners, or the whole class can come together to share one thing added that shows growth.

9 At least once a month, ask students to look at their goals and think about where they are and what they can do to keep growing. This may be done in small groups or as a whole group, but it should be directed by the teacher, with the teacher giving examples of goals and ways to meet goals. For example, "Everyone has a goal to make images in your head during reading. We've talked about using the visual art elements to help. What would help you do this more often and better?"

10 Once a month, conduct portfolio presentations: Ask students to share their portfolios with a partner. Next, come together as a whole group for students to share what they learned from their partners.

11 Make the portfolios the focus of parent conferences. Have students show their portfolios, pointing out the goals and benchmarks to their parents and sharing evidence of their progress toward goals.

12 Tie grades to portfolio evidence. Create a rubric that indicates what should be documented in the folder to earn an A, B, and so forth. This can be done for each grading period, or you might use an end-of-the-year rubric along with progress points during the year, as long as students and parents are very clear about the nature of their progress in terms of meeting the end-of-the-year grade goal.

13 Let students keep their portfolios at the end of the year.

progress, and set new goals. (Use an egg timer to ensure students get equal time.) You might ask students to bring a text to demonstrate CPS strategy use. This is a good time to review checklists, notes, rubrics, and work samples. Weekly conferences are an important priority for motivating student work toward comprehension goals.

Assessment: Task, Context, and Teacher/Teaching

The previous sections of this chapter addressed assessment factors involving the learner. This section looks at three other comprehension factors: the task, the context, and the teacher/teaching. The following section then discusses the final factor: the text.

COMPREHENSION TASK

Literacy involves many tasks, including all the sub-skills that make listening, speaking, viewing, reading, and writing possible. The task of comprehending written texts depends on readers having a solid foundation in sub-skills such as decoding and word fluency—and these sub-skills also have sub-skills, such as phonemic awareness and alphabetic principle. These sub-skills are means to the comprehension goal, and that goal is twofold: immediate understanding and long-term knowledge gain (RAND, 2002). To achieve both aspects of comprehension, readers must become increasingly adept at using thinking strategies to find and synthesize important big ideas from texts.

Assessment should reflect the ultimate goals of comprehension—increased knowledge and use of that knowledge to solve real-life problems—but, unfortunately, widely used comprehension assessments focus heavily on only a few tasks: immediate recall/retelling, extracting ideas, and word meaning (RAND, 2002). The assessment tools described in the preceding section reflect an expanded view of the comprehension task. (Chapter 1 and Chapter 2, in particular, describe the comprehension task in detail.)

The comprehension rubric in Ready Resource 4.1 is based on an expanded view of comprehension, using specific descriptors for the "top" level of both the comprehension product and the comprehension process. Teachers can use this tool to create a full four-level comprehension rubric to give students a clearer picture of comprehension goals.

CONTEXT

The *place* of text use (i.e., where and with whom the learner is encountering the text) was discussed in Chapter 3. Any environment, including a classroom, can encourage a culture of acceptance and encouragement or be a place that threatens and discourages. To facilitate comprehension, the classroom should be stimulating physically and psychologically. Look back to Ready Resource 3.4 in Chapter 3 for a checklist to use in assessing the classroom context for its potential to facilitate comprehension and to identify ways the classroom may inhibit comprehension.

TEACHERS/TEACHING

The effect of a teacher's personal knowledge and beliefs on comprehension was discussed in Chapter 3. The self-assessment in Ready Resource 3.3 can yield important information about a teacher's knowledge of comprehension strategies.

Although the comprehension task is often determined by the teacher, the ultimate goal is student self-determination. The thread of establishing student independence by increasing responsibility incrementally runs through comprehension best practices. You can informally self-assess your knowledge about best practices by using Ready Resource 3.5 and by studying the descriptions of effective and ineffective practices provided in Appendices D and E. You might consider to what extent you are encouraging independence and how to do so more effectively. For example, you might set a goal to have students increasingly generate their own questions for discussions so they become less dependent on yours.

Text Assessment

Texts—and whether they meet the needs and goals of the learner—are the fifth comprehension factor considered in assessment. Chapter 1 introduced a contemporary concept of text that includes verbal (word-based), non-verbal, print, non-print, digital, and arts-based materials. The characteristics of a text (e.g., its organization, content, and format) have a tremendous effect on how readers process the information it contains, and whether the reader even continues to use the text. For example, we readily flip to another television channel or click to another website if a show or site doesn't suit our needs and interests. Interest inventories help match students and texts. However, in addition to interest, we must consider several other factors when assessing texts for students, including accessibility, readability, and reading level.

INTEREST LEVEL

The sophistication and maturity level of a text's content, ideas, and themes affect how interesting it will be for a reader. These are not the only factors that influence interest. A text's format and organization can provide interest, especially if the form is new to the reader. For example, pop-up books and interactive Internet sites attract certain readers because of the texts' kinesthetic nature. Certain genres and authors may be of more interest than others.

ACCESSIBILITY

Texts must be accessible. Teachers should consider whether students have the background and emotional and cognitive maturity for the content of a text, be it a video on YouTube, a song, or a book. Judging a text's content appropriateness and the potential for a student to make sense of it can be complex. In the case of word-based print texts, students not only need the background and thinking strategies to comprehend its meaning, they also need to be able to recognize a large percentage of the words and attach appropriate meanings to those words.

READABILITY

For more than fifty years, readability formulas have helped teachers match students with books. Formulas such as the Fry and Fog estimate text difficulty based on variables such as average sentence length and number of multisyllabic words in several hundred-word samples. The resulting text levels indicate whether readers of a certain proficiency can be expected to comprehend the material. This is important because reading improvement comes from regular reading of texts that are not too difficult or too easy.

Advances in technology and statistical analysis have led to improvements in readability science. Lexiles is an example of the computer-based measures now available that rely on full scans of texts. Using more than a text sample aids accuracy, but with computer-based measures the criteria used must be computer friendly. Word counts and sorts, along with sentence length and complexity, are still used. Appendix C.3 gives Lexiles for familiar titles.

In truth, a text's actual readability is more complex than what a computer can recognize. Whether a text is readable has much to do with the reader's prior knowledge or background about the text topic, interest in the topic, and capability to use comprehension strategies. There are many text characteristics that readability formulas do not consider, such as suitability of content for a specific child. Indeed, interest in a topic can trump a text's difficulty. What's more, there are no definitive criteria to judge literary merit or artistic excellence, either. Decisions about these matters are left to informed educators and parents. Recommended criteria for assessing texts appear in Appendix C along with a correlation among Lexiles, grade levels, and other popular text levelers.

READING LEVEL

While *readability* applies to text difficulty, *reading level* is about the reader. Teachers use estimates of students' reading (comprehension) levels to help select appropriate texts. It cannot be emphasized enough that reading levels, like text levels, are abstract constructs created by people. They are not absolutes. A child's reading level is always an estimate. No test perfectly determines which texts are right for all students. There are too many variables (e.g., the Five Factors). Reading level is influenced by the test maker's definition of comprehension, and the test items.

Different assessment tools yield different reading levels. For example, one standardized test may report a grade level estimate of 5.5. That result may indicate the level of text a student can be expected to comprehend independently, or it may suggest a text level that could be used if the student has instructional support. The Lexile level is based on the assumption that the reader needs 90 percent word accuracy and 75 percent comprehension to read a text successfully. That is considered an "instructional level." But what does it mean to comprehend three-quarters of a text? We need to remember that percentages and other quantifications of comprehension have ambiguous meanings that we should question and cross-reference with other assessment information.

Instruments use categories, based on limited criteria, to define reading levels. Tests such as informal reading inventories determine these levels for individual students. In general, a person's independent level will be the lowest numerical level and frustration the highest. For example, a child's independent level may be 2.0, instructional 2.5, and frustration 3.0. The listening level may equal the frustration level, or it may be higher. The percentages cited below vary greatly depending on the test and the Five Factors.

- *Independent* (easy). Reader can read the text with few word identification problems and high comprehension. Standards vary from 95 to 99 percent for word accuracy and achieve better than 90 percent comprehension of text.

- *Instructional* (challenging). Word accuracy is 90 to 95+ percent and comprehension 75+ percent. A student needs help using texts at this level. At minimum, the teacher needs to introduce important words and phrases, do a guided walk-through, and supply relevant background knowledge to help the reader understand the text content.

- *Frustration* (difficult). The reader achieves less than 90 percent word accuracy and less than 50 percent comprehension. A text at this level is too hard for the learner. However, a student with a lot of background relevant to the topic and a high interest in the text can succeed, with teacher or computer support (e.g., CD-ROM to assist with word pronunciation and explanation).

- *Listening.* The listening level estimates comprehension potential, removing the limitations of print decoding. At the listening level, the student can understand 75+ percent of the key concepts and big ideas if the text is read to him or her.

Learners benefit from texts matched to their personal characteristics and reading goals. Texts should be selected that are not too difficult but nonetheless present some challenge, and that are suited to the maturity, background, and interests of particular students.

Effective Differentiated Instruction

A central purpose of assessment is to gather information in order to design instruction that is appropriate for the particular needs and strengths of students. Villegas and Lucas (2007) contend that "teachers have an ethical obligation to help all students learn" (p. 32). That is lofty talk, but most teachers probably would concur. Walking the talk, however, is hard work, driven by assessment. Teacher Gary Fife starts with interviews, but, like all effective teachers, he draws from a "panoply of practices" to assess and create instruction that matches students' needs (NRP, 2000; Pressley et al., 2001). The matching process is currently called "differentiation."

The root of the word "differentiate" is *differ*, which means *vary*. Students vary. While people of all ages and stages share commonalities, each child is unlike any other. Differentiated instruction is teaching made different because students are different. This is not a 21st-century idea. Differentiated instruction has 20th-century roots in personalized, tailored, and individualized instruction. Labels change, but the beliefs that underpin the concept of differentiation have remained strong and consistent. Why? Because differentiation has a dramatic and positive effect on achievement. Given current technological advances, we have more possibilities than ever before to design instruction that not only responds to differences, but *encourages* differences.

Educators and parents have long known that children cannot be treated equally—that just isn't fair. All children need help with some tasks to succeed. All need challenge, as well. Most students become literate by following the general developmental path from simple to complex, but each child proceeds at his or her own speed and needs varying levels of support. While some go straight, others zigzag. One-size-fits-all instruction will not suitably outfit the diverse children traveling the literacy road (Reutzel, 2007). Assessment allows teachers to create instructional maps suited to individual needs and strengths.

LEARNER DIFFERENCES

The list of all the ways learners can be different would fill more than one book. Differences among and within students have a major impact on what they need to learn, the pace at which they can learn, and the support they need to learn well (Tomlinson, 2000). Teachers who successfully differentiate instruction understand that comprehension is inextricably linked to a larger socio-cultural context. Students represent diverse groups, each with a worldview very different from the others based on

- socio-cultural background, values, and customs
- ethnicity/race
- language(s) spoken
- economic status
- religious practices
- political views
- physical abilities

Of course, educators can address only those differences to which schools can reasonably respond. For example, family income predicts student test scores, but schools cannot have much effect on the economic circumstances of families. Schools do try to compensate for some realities of poverty by getting more books into the hands of poor children. Teachers tap students' strengths and interests and teach them how to use family traditions and stories as sources for writing and art. This strategy shows respect for students' background, and it parallels how adult writers use their personal background to create their products.

Students differ further in their *specific* cognitive, physical, and emotional development and in their background experiences and past learning opportunities. As teachers start each new year, they face the task of getting to know the individuals who make up the class. Some of the questions that teachers will ask are specific to comprehension, but others are general. Some are listed in Ready Resource 4.5. Additional questions that should shape assessment as well as differentiated instruction include:

- What is special about this child?
- What is the student's background (socio-cultural, economic, linguistic, etc.)?
- What values does the learner hold (e.g., cultural and religious)?
- What does the learner already know and what can she or he do?
- What are the student's strengths and general developmental needs?
- What about needs of the moment (e.g., a recent family death)?
- What particular experiences have shaped this student, including school successes or failures?

DIFFERENTIATION GOALS

Americans have a tradition of valuing diversity. Diversity is our heritage, and tendencies to experiment and take risks rewarded our ancestors. Stark differences among members make families, communities, and the nation interesting and strong; embracing difference increases our adaptability, heightens our empathy, and broadens our perspective. Creating cookie-cutter kids is not a justifiable

General questions: Beginning-of-the-year comprehension assessment, or "Getting to know your students."

READY RESOURCE 4.5

LEARNER

1 What is the learner interested in? How can interests be used to motivate the learner to use texts to make meaning?

2 How developed is the student's ability to attend, focus, concentrate, and persist in the face of problems?

3 What general literacy knowledge and skills does the student have?

4 What prior knowledge does the learner have about topics to be studied?

TASK

1 Is the child motivated to make sense actively by finding and constructing big ideas?

2 Does the student understand that the goal of reading is to make sense using prior knowledge and other thinking strategies in the problem-solving process?

3 What comprehension strategies does the child possess that would permit him or her to make sense of different texts?

4 How independent is the learner at the coordinated use of CPS strategies to make sense of texts? To what degree can the learner generate questions to propel problem solving forward, with a focus on finding and constructing big ideas?

5 How developed are the learner's vocabulary and fluency skills?

TEXT

1 What experiences has the student had with the types of texts to be used? What about technology (computer use)?

2 What does the learner think the purpose(s) for text use are? How does the learner's thinking align with profiles of good readers?

CONTEXT

1 What contexts for learning are likely to facilitate the student's success?

WHAT NEXT?

Two additional questions pull assessment information together to be acted upon:

1 What should the priority comprehension goals be for this student, and in what order should learning experiences happen?

2 How can assessment information about comprehension development, goals, and progress be shared in an ongoing manner with the student and her or his parents?

American educational goal. Teaching for conformity and uniformity prepare for the status quo. The future is all about change, and it beckons us to be more inventional than conventional. To achieve this goal, comprehension instruction must be differentiated in order to *promote* differences while ensuring that all of our students have basic knowledge and skills to solve problems in creative ways.

Differentiated instruction seeks to "maximize each student's growth" by starting at a student's current level and creating interventions to move her or him forward (Kiernan, 2000). In practice, differentiation results in instruction that varies in delivery, materials use, and activities. For example, the teacher modifies the difficulty level, instructional intensity, or amount of time each child spends with given texts. Ready Resource 4.6 lists ten areas where teachers might think about how to differentiate. The mnemonic "PARTICULAR" can help you remember them.

Ten ways to differentiate (PARTICULAR).

The goal of differentiated instruction is student success. The means is to differentiate tasks, texts, teaching, and context to fit each learner's unique profile. Differentiation is about changing *what* is taught, *how, when, where,* by or with *whom,* and with what *expectations* (product).

KEY QUESTIONS FOR TEACHERS:

- What do I know about the student's strengths and needs?

- What comprehension product (content/ideas/concepts) and processes (skills/strategies) are to be learned?

- Why is the lesson important to the learner?

- How might the comprehension product or process be adjusted for the student's strengths and needs (e.g., pre-test and then compact the content)?

- When would the student be most successful? Is the student ready for this lesson?

- Where would the student learn best? With whom?

- What materials are best suited to this student's needs?

- What options can I offer for the student to demonstrate comprehension (assessment)?

The acronym **PARTICULAR** can help you think more specifically about the above questions and address the particular needs of particular students (Cornett, 2011).

4.6

P PLACE: Change the physical location or aspects of the environment to create more supportive conditions. Students are more productive when classrooms and schools offer a sense of community in which students feel significant and respected.

A AMOUNT: Increase or decrease the amount of content to be studied or the amount of time allotted.

R RATE: Slow down or speed up. For more able learners, pre-test and compact the curriculum. Allow some students to skip some tasks.

T TARGET/TASK: Change the comprehension task (CPS process or product) by offering tiered choices: students may focus on fewer strategies or be expected to find and construct varying amounts of big ideas supported with evidence.

I INSTRUCTIONAL SUPPORT: Adapt high-priority best practices, including explicit teaching, scaffolding (coached practice with examples and feedback), high-level questions, and motivational strategies. Look back at Ready Resource 3.5 in Chapter 3 for a list of best practices.

C CURRICULAR MATERIALS: Select texts that the student can use successfully. Consider the student's interest and background, text difficulty and structure, and genre (e.g., fiction/nonfiction).

U UTENSILS: Select other media and tools as appropriate to student needs (e.g., computer software, art materials, writing implements and surfaces, music)

L LEVEL OF DIFFICULTY: Make the lesson somewhat challenging, using surprise, interest, and mystery to engage.

A ASSISTANCE: Consider who the student should work with and under what circumstances (e.g., alone or collaboratively, with a partner or group). Use flexible grouping.

R RESPONSE OPTIONS: Vary the ways students can show they understand by offering choices ranging from writing to creating visual art, drama, dance, and musical products. All responses should have clear criteria to ensure they are connected to the target task.

Fitting differentiation with standards

In the recent past, the curriculum of many schools has become constricted—time for science, social studies, and the arts has been cut. Teachers feel compelled to "cover" tested standards even though we know "covering" will not boost test scores. Teachers often feel powerless and are distressed by pressures to make every student competent at the same level with the same content using the same texts.

The standards movement has provoked a national conversation about what is most important to learn. Unfortunately, the discussion is often reduced to how to make education more predictable. Standards imply standardization, uniformity, and conformity—yet, ironically, teachers are concurrently admonished to respond to *diverse* student needs (Tomlinson, 2000). Standards imply there are to be no surprises. Differentiation and standards-based teaching have to coexist if the goal is success for all students, but Tomlinson (2002) proposes educators step back and ask questions like these:

- Do current standards represent the knowledge and skills valued most by experts in each discipline? Is revision in order?
- Are standards reflected in the curriculum, or have they *become* the curriculum?
- How can standards-based curricula be organized so that students have time to make sense of ideas and master skills rather than "race through material to meet benchmarks"?

Misinterpretation of the purpose of standards and misunderstanding of how to use them can erode teachers' morale, eviscerate the curriculum, and cripple teacher efforts to customize instruction for student needs. Standards are one source for curriculum development: they are meant to offer guidance about *what* to teach. Differentiation, on the other hand, is process oriented, focusing on *how* to teach (Tomlinson, 2000). Differentiation is not a recipe. On the contrary, it is part of the instructional problem solving that is initiated by the kind of assessment discussed in this chapter. Teachers collect assessment data so that they can differentiate instruction that targets standards, making student success more likely. Ready Resource 4.7 summarizes what differentiation is and is not.

Assuming a differentiation orientation

Children learn differently as a result of both genetics and upbringing. General developmental human growth patterns can guide teachers' expectations of how children might respond to instruction, but nature and nurture interact to cause each child to become one of a kind. Universal student success is impossible unless teachers respond to the diverse characteristics each student possesses. Of course, some children need more responsive instruction—instruction that is differentiated for their particular needs and interests. The following ideas offer a "differentiation orientation" to help teachers implement best comprehension practices. In particular, teachers need to guard against *contributing* to

What differentiation is and is not.

DIFFERENTIATION INVOLVES . . .

- Engaging every teacher in problem solving to craft appropriate instruction that predicts what, where, when, how, and with whom students will learn best.

- Making changes within classrooms, not moving students out.

- Using ongoing assessment data to plan instruction suited to each learner's profile of needs, interests, and preferences (e.g., multiple intelligences).

- Delivering high-end curriculum for all students, using varied approaches, including flexible groups.

- Getting all students to work toward understanding rich content with varying degrees of complexity.

- Scaffolding to support students so they can achieve at a higher level than would be possible without differentiation (see Chapter 5).

- Creating a context of mutual respect and shared responsibility between teachers and students.

- Giving students choices, balanced with teacher decisions about curriculum and instruction.

DIFFERENTIATION IS . . .

- Necessary for all students to reach goals and standards regarding what they should know, be, and do.

- NOT a recipe. There are an infinite number of ways to differentiate.

- NOT just changing amount. Struggling learners don't need "less of what they don't understand, and advanced learners don't need more of what they already know" (Tomlinson, Brimijoin, & Narvaez, 2008).

- NOT creating a different lesson plan for each student. There are times when whole-group instruction is appropriate for meeting individual needs, while at other times one-on-one instruction is needed.

comprehension problems and, instead, make adjustments to increase students' comprehension, especially for low-performing students (RAND, 2002).

Embrace diversity. Teachers need to believe that difference can be an asset and not necessarily a liability. Socio-culturally conscious teachers know that their personal worldview is not universal and that it may not match that of their students. A person's worldview is profoundly influenced by his or her "life experiences, as mediated by a variety of factors, including race, ethnicity, gender and social class" (Villegas & Lucas, 2007, p. 31). For example, some cultures subordinate the value of individuals to that of the group, an attitude that conflicts with American culture. Some students from these cultures may be uncomfortable with individual attention and praise (Villegas & Lucas). Teacher should be sensitive to this fact and not use any teaching tool uniformly.

Eliminate low expectations. Hundreds of studies document the influence of teacher expectations on student achievement. This effect is known as the "self-fulfilling prophecy." Abundant research demonstrates that children live up to high or low expectations communicated in verbal and non-verbal ways. For example, teachers may tend to touch and stand closer to students who are achievers. They smile at them more, give them more chances, and affirm their efforts more often (Tauber, 1997). Teachers need to guard against creating a culture of low expectations for children who are disadvantaged by poverty or background. It does happen. McDermott and Varenne (1995) found that teachers working with high achievers focused on higher-order thinking about texts and reading for understanding. The same teachers, when working with low achievers, focused on low-level factual reading, interrupted children's reading more frequently, and talked little about comprehension as the goal.

A "culture of low expectations" is manifested when teachers give students from low-status groups unwarranted amounts of drill, practice, and rote learning activities. Children suffer when teachers focus on words and facts and neglect challenging work marked by "what if and I wonder why" questions (Gambrell, Malloy, & Mazzoni, 2007, p. 35; Villegas & Lucas, 2007, p. 32). The accompanying box offers additional tips for supporting students and guarding against expressing low expectations.

Make quantitative and qualitative changes. Best comprehension practices are appropriate for all learners, but they should be adjusted to fit specific students. The kinds of and amounts of coaching, questions, and options for responding to texts all matter when it comes to differentiating comprehension instruction (Taylor et al., 1999). Some students need more think alouds to master CPS strategies, while others need different examples from different people, including peers. Some students need individual tutoring, while others need a teacher

Self-Fulfilling Prophecy (SFP): Ways to Show Belief in Students

Be courteous	Speak respectfully to students.
Listen	Listen actively to students. Respond verbally and non-verbally.
Be close	Stand near students. Use touch judiciously, such as touching an arm with two fingers.
Show interest	Ask about students' interests.
Give chances	Make sure everyone has an opportunity to respond.
Offer help	Give individual assistance.
Wait	Give three to five seconds for a student to respond.
Give feedback	Describe exactly what the student is doing that is working and not working.
Ask high-level questions	Ask students why, how, what If, and what do you think questions.
Clarify	Ask students to explain their thinking to reach better understanding.
Discipline	Remain calm and make clear your behavioral expectations.

who will alter the work itself. For example, a student may become adept at predicting or summarizing using a non-verbal text (e.g., a piece of art) when she or he has failed at applying those thinking strategies to a word-based text. Once a student masters a strategy with one kind of text, the teacher can help the student transfer the strategy to another kind of text.

A student's ability to negotiate various texts may be affected by the range of individual characteristics previously discussed. Background knowledge and socio-cultural factors seem to advantage Euro-American students, because discourse forms in most school texts more closely match their language background (RAND, 2002). Teachers can facilitate student comprehension by using specific learner factors to select texts. For example, English learners read culturally familiar material faster, recall it more accurately, and make fewer comprehension errors.

Take the student's point of view. Teachers are well served by periodically sitting in students' desks, both figuratively and literally. It is easy to forget the obstacles words can put up. For example, by fourth grade students may lack the strategies to comprehend large chunks of text that must be read in relatively short periods of time. Inadequate background knowledge and lack of special vocabularies to comprehend content texts are common problems. This pattern of difficulties persists, even though educators have known the important role of vocabulary in content comprehension for over seventy-five years (RAND, 2002 citing Whipple, 1925). Chapter 8 describes vocabulary learning strategies, including a set of word-solving tools, that help students achieve increasing independence in constructing meaning.

Today's students may even reject "school literacy" as irrelevant compared to popular technologically dominated communication. Teachers can provide important bridges that make texts accessible to students. For example, explicit teaching of CPS strategies using alternative texts, including digital texts, is crucial to establishing relevancy.

Look for similarities as well as differences. The array of differences and difficulties that operate in the lives of majority monolingual students are also present in the lives of minority students and English learners. Despite differences, students have much in common. Certainly, they exhibit similar symptoms when they have comprehension difficulties. Differentiation principles should guide instructional adjustments, but best practices are appropriate for all.

Avoiding detrimental differentiation

Not all differentiated instruction is helpful. Uninformed teachers can make mistakes. For example, when teachers react negatively to students' dialects, this differentiated response has a more adverse effect on reading comprehension than the students' *use* of dialect (RAND, 2002). A dismal image has emerged from observations of teachers working with children from poor families and non–Euro-American English learners (Allington, 1983; Allington & McGill-Franzen, 1989; Duke, 2000). These students tend to receive harmful forms of differentiation such as the following:

- Lower-quality literacy activities, with more focus on skills and less focus on text interpretation, especially discussion to promote higher-order thinking and expecting students to use more developed language to respond.

- Placement in the lowest reading groups and lowest tracks, where isolated-skill instruction dominates and best practices are neglected.

- More teacher-dominated instruction that expects passive student response.

- More assignments to read and write single words and brief texts rather than lengthy texts.

- Provision of few or no computers, or computers that have only low-level practice-oriented software.

High-stakes tests that measure limited low-level competencies, require little inferring, and use forced-choice questions cause teachers to de-emphasize higher comprehension. If teachers expect low achievement, they often get what they expect.

Also troubling is the pattern found with students who have a history of reading problems in early grades. These students are likely to have had teachers who underestimate their capabilities by

- asking mostly low-level factual questions.

- correcting oral reading more frequently than is justified.

- rarely focusing on comprehension as the goal of reading.

- defining comprehension as getting or taking meaning rather than *making or constructing* meaning.

Students taught in this way come to dislike reading. They then read less, so they get less practice and accrue less knowledge to bring to reading. They simply never catch up (Allington, 2002a).

Positive differentiation is necessary to meet the needs of all students and is the key to comprehension success for English learners and students disadvantaged by background. Comprehension instruction that includes explicit teaching of strategies and self-monitoring has shown promise with these types of students (RAND, 2002).

DIFFERENTIATING FOR SUCCESS: STUDENTS WHO ARE LOW PERFORMING

Assessment information allows teachers to artfully select, adapt, and use best comprehension practices with low-performing students (Reutzel, 2007). The following examples fall within best practices that embrace the explicit teaching of comprehension problem solving for the purpose of constructing meaning. These modifications provide the sort of comprehension scaffolding learners need. They are organized using the before/during/after categories that align with the CPS process. Many rely on additional diagnostic testing, especially for Tier 2 and 3 students in Response to Intervention (RtI) programs. More information on RtI is provided in the box at right.

BEFORE reading, viewing, or listening

- *Activate prior knowledge:* Use extended discussions to call up background experiences relevant for the upcoming text.

- *Frontload:* Teach essential background knowledge, key concepts, and vocabulary related to the text. Use a pre-test or pre-reading discussion to determine content or vocabulary gaps.

- *Cue strategy use:* Remind students to use multiple comprehension strategies to increase understanding. Use a visual to review strategies about which students have questions.

- *Writing:* Use pre-reading and post-reading writing and discussion to increase student engagement with ideas and response to text. For example, engage students in freewriting, listing, webbing, brainstorming, or word association related to a topic.

- *Use visuals:* Use story maps, graphic organizers, and other visuals to help students structure their thinking. For example, create a form for students to record narrative literary elements during reading: characters, setting, problems, plot events, resolution, and themes or big ideas.

DURING and AFTER reading, viewing, or listening

- *Monitor:* Coach students to stop periodically and self-assess whether comprehension is happening. Teach them to ask, "What have I learned? What relates to my purpose or problem? What makes sense?"

- *Inference scaffold:* Ask students to restate information from the text during reading.

- *Assign projects:* Embed new ideas and skills in projects that are interesting and have clear meaning in students' lives.

- *Use hands-on activities:* Teach in ways that connect to students' lives (e.g., teach poetry using "rhythm and poetry" [RAP] music).

It is recommended that diverse texts be used, including primary texts, fiction and nonfiction, and verbal and non-verbal texts, including Internet texts. In particular, songs permit many students to practice CPS strategies, even those

Response to Intervention (RtI)

The Individuals with Disabilities Education Improvement Act of 2004 included a problem-solving mechanism that links special education with regular education to help struggling students more quickly. IDEA did not provide states or districts with a prescribed method of implementing RtI. Some states and districts have implemented a three-tier plan; for example, Tier 1 (all children), Tier 2 (students need more assessment to diagnose and provide more intense intervention), and Tier 3 (students receive additional assessment and the most intense intervention, including one-on-one tutoring). Other states use a five- or six-tier plan. For more information about RtI, visit http://idea.ed.gov/download/statute.html.

who do not have print fluency. For example, students can listen to songs to find and create big ideas using all the CPS strategies. Of course, most will need explicit teaching before attempting this independently.

DIFFERENTIATING FOR SUCCESS: ENGLISH LEARNERS

Ready Resource 4.8 provides a profile of the growing population of English learners (EL) and lists influences on English learning.

Profile: English learners (EL).

NCELA (2006) reports the following statistics:

- There are approximately 4.7 million EL students in the United States.
- This represents a 95 percent increase since 1991.
- 16 states have experienced an increase in EL population that exceeds 200 percent since 1991.
- ELs make up 19 percent of the total school population.
- 79 percent of ELs are Spanish speakers.
- Less than 2 percent of ELs are Vietnamese, Hmong, and Cantonese, and the rest represent 380 different language groups.

Characteristics: English learners are not homogeneous. Students differ in age, country of origin, mother tongue, socioeconomic status, and access to formal schooling.

- Compared with monolingual English speakers, English learners typically
  - have less background for topics in English texts or tests.
  - know less English vocabulary.
  - have difficulty with questions that rely on background. (e.g., García, 1991)
- Literacy development is affected by home and school environments. Important factors are
  - the age at which second-language learning is initiated.
  - the language in which exposure to print and early literacy instruction is initiated.
  - the child's degree of proficiency in a first or second language.
  - the child's proficiency in the language in which print exposure and literacy instruction begins.
  - the degree of support for first- and second-language learning and literacy development. (RAND, 2002; Snow, Burns, & Griffin, 1998)
- When ELs are immersed in second-language learning, learning in the first language and in English may be impeded.
- Limited English oral language does impede learning to read English, but a student who can read in a native language is more likely to learn to read a second language. Carlo concludes, "a 12-year-old who can read in first language needs different instruction from a 16-year-old who never went to school—who can't read at all" (2007, p. 104).

READY RESOURCE 4.8

Sources: Carlo, 2007; Gersten & Baker, 2000; RAND, 2002; Snow, Burns, & Griffin, 1998.

Studies of English learners who read well reveal strategies that can be taught to all English learners. For example, successful second-language readers use strategies and knowledge acquired in a first language to approach reading in the second language. They also use bilingual strategies, such as drawing upon cognates, paraphrased translating, code mixing, and switching (RAND, 2002). Less successful learners tend not to transfer strategies across languages, and some think they have to keep languages separate to prevent confusion.

Comprehension success for students from varied cultural and linguistic backgrounds depends on implementing the best practices described in this book, including use of assessment to construct learner profiles and differentiate instruction for their needs, interests, and preferences. Learner profiles intersect with the task of comprehension. This necessitates the teaching of words, decoding, and fluency alongside explicit instruction in comprehension strategies that permit access to big ideas. English learners need time to engage in extended reading of diverse texts, just as any other student does, and they benefit from choices in how to respond to texts, including written, arts-based, and computer options. English learners need to learn how to use technology and multimedia to support content learning, as well. All of these recommendations fall within the best practices framework that culminates in student participation in main literacy events and the embedding of content lessons with comprehension strategies. Ready Resource 4.9 includes further recommendations.

English learners: What works?

The following conclusions, which relate to the Five Factors that influence comprehension, should guide work with students whose first language is not English.

EL needs: In addition to the same needs all learners have, ELs need

- respect for their native languages. Teachers need to see the mother language as an asset.
- freedom to use their native language to (1) understand difficult concepts, including translation of test directions, (2) validate the worth of the first language, and (3) form relationships.

Task needs: In addition to general guidelines about CPS and inquiry into big ideas using important questions, ELs need

- teachers who understand that people only need to learn to read and write once. If a student is already literate in one language, the teacher should build on this ability to teach English and should not be overly concerned about pronunciation (Au, 2002).
- familiar content. They have the conceptual background for lessons, even though they may not know the English words that label these concepts.

(continued)

4.9 READY RESOURCE

English learners: What works?, continued

- discussions in which they can participate, first with short answers and then with increasingly longer responses.
- study guides that define relevant vocabulary and outline key concepts in English, using simplified language.
- correction of language when appropriate (e.g., grammar and formal usage) and with sensitivity.

Text needs: ELs need content-rich, diverse texts, including

- bilingual dictionaries.
- texts in their native language.
- dual-language texts (written in both languages).
- texts with strong visual supports, e.g., pictures.
- assistive technology (e.g., CD-ROMs that allow students to click on words for pronunciation or meaning, and speech synthesizer software for spelling support).
- texts about universal experiences, such as being a newcomer.

Context: ELs need comfortable and psychologically supportive and stimulating learning environments.

Teachers: ELs need teachers who

1. believe being bilingual is not detrimental to academic learning. Every study comparing English-only and bilingual teaching confirms this conclusion (Carlo, 2007).
2. know learning to read builds on oral language. Students need to hear lots of English (e.g., read alouds, discussion).
3. have a whole-child focus and celebrate diversity.

Teaching: All nine best comprehension practices apply (review Ready Resource 3.5 in Chapter 3). The following are examples of student needs:

- Comprehension assessment in the native language (e.g., interest inventory, comprehension strategies)
- A multisensory approach (visual, auditory/oral, kinesthetic, tactile [VAKT]) that uses "real things"—items that can be touched, seen, heard, and so forth. Examples are videos, virtual fields trips, models, and artifacts. The Internet is a rich source.
- Opportunities for informal and formal oral language use
- Vocabulary development and word-solving strategies to anchor comprehension. For example, teach cognates that are shared among languages and point out similar words.
- Arts-based teaching that allows non-verbal responses
- Visuals for vocabulary and concept understanding. For example, post key words (e.g., directions, high-frequency environmental words like "exit" and "entrance") with pictures.

 READY RESOURCE 4.9

Sources: Au, 2004; Fitzgerald & Graves, 2004; Gersten & Baker 2000.

Conclusion

omprehension is influenced by who is using the text, what text is being used, and where, how, and why the text is being used. When a person reads matters, too. Some folks read to put themselves to sleep at night; others can't imagine starting the day without the newspaper. This chapter addressed these topics as they relate to assessment.

The chapter described assessment as integral to instructional problem solving. It discussed the Five Factors that influence comprehension as a way to organize assessment for the purpose of collecting data and shaping differentiated instruction. The Five Factors are infinitely variable, making each act of comprehension like live theatre, never to be replicated. Think about yourself reading this text or using another text under different circumstances. How does the context (e.g., whom you are with) change both your reaction to a text and your subsequent understanding of it? Perhaps you can think of a film you have seen with friends or a song you heard at a concert. In particular, think about how your emotions are affected by the context of using a text. The Five-Factor model implies that teachers must respond to these influences.

The latter part of the chapter examined underserved students, such as English learners and students from disadvantaged backgrounds. Recommendations were made for differentiating instruction to facilitate comprehension success.

CHAPTER

4 big ideas

The following are examples of big ideas from this chapter. Use the list to synthesize your own list of priority big ideas related to assessing to differentiate comprehension instruction.

1. Assessment is the data-gathering part of instructional problem solving.

2. A major goal of assessment should be to motivate learners.

3. Teachers need multiple informal assessment tools to gather information about learners, the comprehension task, texts, learning contexts, and their own teaching.

4. A key instructional goal is to *increase* differences among students.

5. Assessment results allow teachers to differentiate instruction, with a focus on learners' strengths and needs.

6. When the task of comprehending is reduced to test taking, student thinking and motivation are diminished.

7. A growing body of research-based strategies helps teachers differentiate for diverse learners, including English learners and low-performing students.

8. Differentiation can be both detrimental and helpful to learning.

a look ahead

Next, Chapter 5 discusses the best practice of teaching the CPS process and text characteristics. The concept of *explicit* teaching is discussed in relation to its value in making visible the invisible act of comprehension.

CHAPTER **4** response options

1. Use the list of Chapter Big Ideas and rate your agreement with each statement from 5 (high) to 1 (low). Explain the reasons for your ratings.

2. Choose a big idea of particular interest and write an "I believe . . ." statement elaborating on it.

3. Return to the Important Questions at the beginning of the chapter to assess your own comprehension. Choose the ones you most want to discuss, and add other questions you have about assessment and differentiation related to comprehension.

4. Interview a student, parent, or colleague using one of the interviews provided in the assessment kit in Appendix A.

5. Choose a student or peer to study using the questions about English learner characteristics in Ready Resource 4.8. Summarize your most important findings based on likely routes to comprehension success.

6. Evaluate a text using the criteria in Appendix C.

7. Examine samples of how comprehension is assessed in any state test. Check Internet sites for state departments of education (DOE) or departments of instruction. Ohio, South Carolina, North Carolina, Tennessee, and Maryland all provide sample test items.

8. List the most surprising ideas from this chapter. Partner to share ideas and reasons why certain ideas surprised you.

9. Make a bookmark for yourself with differentiation ideas you want to remember.

10. Construct your own comprehension assessment kit by modifying the tools in Appendix A and B. Add checklists for context and teacher(ing) factors included in Chapter 3.

Explicit Teaching of Comprehension Strategies and Text Characteristics

preview

This chapter discusses in detail why and how the CPS process and the unique characteristics of diverse texts should be taught explicitly. It provides strategies for integrating the CPS process into daily classroom life, and looks at how text characteristics and structures can affect comprehension.

important questions

1. What are the key features of explicit teaching?

2. Why is explicit teaching recommended for key comprehension components such as CPS strategies and text characteristics?

3. Why is thinking aloud sometimes difficult for teachers and students?

4. How can using the 5 W and H questions help teachers and students construct clear explanations?

5. What are age and stage recommendations for teaching comprehension strategies?

6. How can explicit instruction be adapted to meet the needs of learners?

7. What are high-priority comprehension strategies that even primary students can learn to use independently?

8. What are examples of text characteristics that should be explicitly taught? Why?

9. How can students be helped to navigate the complex texts that characterize Internet reading?

10. How can explicit teaching be reconciled with inquiry, which emphasizes questioning and problem solving by the student?

Introduction

Traditional measures of intelligence are not highly correlated with basic reading sub-skills, such as word identification and letter–sound decoding (phonics), but IQ scores do tend to distinguish between children who are skilled comprehenders and those who are less skilled (Vellutino et al., 1996, 2000). Comprehension is thinking, and thinking is a cognitive process. Does teaching comprehension strategies make children more intelligent? When the operating definition for intelligence targets strategic problem solving, logic leads to an affirmative answer.

Comprehension relies heavily on thinking, especially coordinated and purposeful thinking orchestrated to solve the problem of how to make sense of texts—for example, the Comprehension Problem Solving (CPS) process. Teaching this kind of thinking requires more than talking about it. We as teachers must be able to demonstrate the process to students through very clear instruction that includes modeling *how* to coordinate the use of problem-solving strategies (Duke & Pearson, 2002). This kind of instruction has been labeled "direct" or "explicit" (Cambourne, 2002; Williams, 2002); the term "explicit" is used in this text.

Explicit instruction may be used to teach nearly any skills, from plastering walls to figuring out unknown words (Tompkins, 2003). In this chapter, the focus is on explicitly teaching the concept of CPS, the full range of strategies used in CPS, and the special characteristics of different texts. Most students benefit from explicit instruction that targets the *coordination* of strategies in the before, during, and after stages of the CPS process, as well as how to make mental adjustments to different text structures and forms. For struggling learners, such explicit instruction is required.

Explicit Teaching

Watch me do it" is very different from "Listen to me tell you how to do it" (Wiggins, 2007). Students need more than someone simply telling them *about* comprehension or giving them labels for comprehension strategies. Learners who do not naturally activate innate problem-solving capabilities to understand texts simply don't figure out how to make meaning without explicit teaching. When it comes to comprehension strategies, it is best to assume all students need some degree of being shown how.

Explicit means clear, detailed, and obvious. The antonym of explicit is *implicit*, which means implied or hidden. There are explicit and implicit themes in literature and explicit and implicit messages in speeches, advertisements, music, and art. Explicit teaching of key literacy concepts and processes, including Comprehension Problem Solving, uncovers the hidden and makes the invisible visible.

classroom snapshot

JANE WASKEIWITZ USES EXPLICIT TEACHING

In earlier snapshots, Emma Corbett (Chapter 2) and George Darcy (Chapter 3) used explicit teaching. The snapshot of George is a good one to review for an example of how to *introduce* the full CPS concept. Emma showed how to teach two strategies and integrate previously learned strategies using a fable. Both teachers clearly connected strategies to making meaning of texts, including a cereal box.

The following snapshot features Jane Waskeiwitz. She has previously taught her first graders several before/during/after CPS strategies. In this lesson, she is explicitly teaching another CPS strategy, which students will learn how to coordinate. The new strategy is imaging. Imaging includes making pictures in your head (visualizing), but it also includes the generation of other types of images (e.g., aural, tactile, olfactory). The text she eventually uses is the very first picture book published in the United States, *Millions of Cats* by Wanda Gag.

Jane's first graders are seated on the floor. Behind her is a blue pocket chart with cards that read BEFORE, DURING, and AFTER. Remember that key teaching strategies are boldfaced to draw attention to how Jane puts the whole lesson together.

Warm-Up: Attention Getter and Review/Add To

Jane holds up her hands and quickly shows five fingers, then six, seven, and eight. The students know the routine and **chant** with her:

"Five, six, seven, eight, pay attention, concentrate, focus!" They use hand signs for each step, ending with placing their hands beside their heads like horse blinders for focus.

"You are getting good at **concentration and focus**," Jane says, smiling. She points to the **chart** behind her. "What's this first word?"

"Before," they answer chorally.

"**Thumbs up** if you know one strategy a good reader uses before reading." Nearly all respond. She calls on a small boy.

"Predict?" he whispers.

"Yes!" Jane exclaims, and places a card with that word under BEFORE.

"Okay. The next word is . . ."

"DURING," the class responds.

"Thumbs up for one thing good readers do during reading." Again, most all of the children stick up their thumbs.

"On the count of three. One, two, three!" she says, and they call out, "Connect." She pulls out a card with this word and places it under DURING.

"What's the last step? **Whisper it this time**," she says as she points to the last card.

"AFTER," the class whispers.

"And one thing good readers do after reading is . . . Say it in a **deep papa bear voice**."

"SHARE," the first graders growl.

"Okay, let's **sing the song**," Jane says. And they do:

> "We're good readers, yes we are.
> We're good readers, we'll go far.
> Predicting before we read, what might happen in the story.
> Connecting as we read, what we know with what we see.
> Sharing, afterward, what we've learned about the world.
> Yes, we're good readers, yes we are.
> We're good readers, we'll go far!"

I recognize the familiar army cadence. It is obvious they have rehearsed the song many times. I resist applauding, but the children are smiling and looking back at me. I give them a big round of applause. A small girl nearby immediately says, **"We wrote it!"** I'm very impressed, of course, but I try to become wallpaper again so Jane can continue.

Explicit Teaching Begins

"Today we are going to learn another way readers think DURING reading. It is called 'image.'" Jane places a **card** under DURING, right beside *Connect*. "Good readers make images in their heads when they read words. *Image* starts just like a word you know . . . *imagination*. Good readers use their imaginations during reading, and that is one reason reading is fun."

"We went to the Magic Kingdom," blurts out a boy.

"Magic sort of sounds like imagination," Jane says. "Let's all say imagination." And they do.

"One way good readers image during reading is **to make pictures in their heads**," she continues. **"I'm going to show you** how, and then it will be your turn. I'll start with one word."

Jane pulls out a card with the word *dog* printed on it and places it beside the word *image* in the pocket chart. Jane then begins her **think aloud**.

"I know this is the word *dog*. When I read *dog*, I can make an image in my head of a dog. The dog I see has reddish fur that is long and silky. He is about this big (she holds her hand about three feet from the floor). He has floppy ears and brown eyes. I also have a smell image, because this dog needs a bath!" The kids giggle, and several put their thumbs up.

"Jerry, **what are you thinking?**" she asks.

"I guessed it is Chester," he says.

"Me, too," says a girl with her thumb up.

"You are right. I was thinking about my dog," Jane says.

"He's a Golden Retriever," a boy turns to tell me.

"But this isn't a guessing game," Jane explains. "**I want you to notice HOW I was thinking about the word *dog*.**" The students seem puzzled. Jane points across the room to a **chart** that reads VISUAL ART ELEMENTS (see Ready Resource 5.1). "**What were the *visual* images I made in my head?**" she **coaches**.

"You said he was reddish and had brown eyes," a boy responds to the category of color.

"I did have that in my brain image," Jane says. "What else?"

"You said he was silky. That is texture," explains a girl.

"Size! You showed us how big he is," exclaims a boy.

"You could have showed us his shape," adds another boy.

"You are absolutely right, Joshua," Jane says. They are on a roll, and now there are thumbs up all over. Jane takes another minute to allow students to share and then proceeds.

"Okay, I did the image making in my head, and **now it is your turn.** I have a new word to read. When I show the card, just read it in your mind, not out loud." Jane shows a card that has the word *cat*.

Scaffolded Practice

"You can close your eyes, if you like. **I'll give you suggestions, and you try to make the image in your head.** First, make a picture of a cat. Imagine it any color you want." Jane pauses. "Now

Jane's "visual art elements" chart.

VISUAL ART ELEMENTS

Element	Words that Describe
color	bright, dark, intense, pale, playful, serious
line	thin, thick, smooth, rough, messy, neat
shape	round, square, irregular, simple, complex
size	microscopic, tiny, little, medium, big, huge, gigantic, tall, short
texture	smooth, rough, bumpy, silky, velvety, hard, soft

READY RESOURCE 5.1

think the shape of the cat. In your head draw a line around its body like we do with shapes in art prints." She pauses again. "Now image how the cat's fur feels, the texture."

Some children are squinting. Others have covered their eyes with their hands. Some are looking up.

"This is our first try. Let's see how you did. Find your **Study Buddy** and tell each other about your images. Start with whoever is A for this week, and I'll cue you for Person B. Begin."

Most of the children seem to be seated next to a Study Buddy, so only a few move. The room is quickly alive with talk. I listen in on a pair of boys near me.

"Boris is a calico cat, so he isn't just one color. Even his eyes are different colors," explains a boy in a plaid shirt.

"Really?" asks his partner.

"Yeah. He eats a lot, so he is fat. My mom is always trying to put him on a diet! He's a fat cat." They laugh.

Jane **shakes a tambourine** and announces, "Okay, Person B, share your image." **Jane circulates** around the room to listen in. After a couple of minutes she shakes the tambourine again and all is quiet.

Debriefing

"How did it go?" she asks. Thumbs go up. She calls on students, who make comments like, "It was fun" and "I liked it."

"I'm glad you enjoyed making images from words, because that is one reason reading is fun. It's like you make your own movie in your head. But I have another question for you. Did anyone have the exact same cat image as his or her Study Buddy?" The children look at each other and then most shake their heads no.

"Why do you think everybody had a different image when you all read the same word, *cat?"* she asks.

"Cause we all have different cats!" a girl with at least ten bows in her hair says.

"I don't have a cat," says another girl.

"So, how did you make an image if you don't have a cat?" Jane asks.

"Well, I've seen lots of cats," she says.

"We all have seen lots of cats. There are cats all over our neighborhood. My mom says they are noos ants," a boy adds. Jane looks puzzled and then gets it.

"Too many cats can be a nuisance. What a great word!" she says. "But all those annoying cats do help you make images in your head."

"Mrs. W., is **that like using our background to predict** and **connect?"** a tall girl asks.

"That's exactly right, Becky. I'm so glad you remembered. Now, **you'll be using your background to make images** in your head when you read words. Let's try it with a whole sentence from the picture book I'm going to read to you today. I'll go first and **think aloud,** and then you can do the next sentence in your heads and share with your buddy. Here goes."

Text Use and Independent Practice

Jane takes the book *Millions of Cats* from the chalk tray and reads aloud the first sentence. She then does a think aloud to model her image making. The children then have a go at it and share with their partners. Jane then continues reading without showing any of the pictures, stopping several times for students to share their own mental pictures. These include specifics about the setting, characters (an old man and woman), and more cats.

There is a recess break, and when the children return Jane asks them **why they think making images in their heads would help them be good readers.** The children reiterate how it is fun and add how it makes them think more. One says it would help them remember ideas. Jane writes down the children's comments on sentence strips and adds them to an ongoing **bulletin board** entitled "**What Good Readers Do.**" Now it is time for Daily Engaged Independent Reading (DEIR), and Jane **reminds students to use all their good reader strategies,** and to use a **sticky note** to mark one place in their books where they try imaging. They'll be able to share during **Debriefing** after DEIR.

Postscript

Jane's classroom is a treasure trove of ways to teach CPS strategies. In addition to the "What Good Readers Do" bulletin board, I saw a massive collage on the back wall made of magazine pictures. The kids explained it was the **Reasons to Read collage** they had been working on since August. Each student also had his or her own **Good Reader wallpaper bound book** with pages labeled BEFORE, DURING, and AFTER, with *Predict, Connect,* and *Share* under the headings. The children had drawn and pasted pictures and written about each strategy. On the first page was the class **Good Reader song**, and another page listed **names of good readers**, obviously family members and friends. Jane explained that "image" would be added to the book and somehow written into the song. She was confident her class would think of a way.

Reflection

Take a few moments to think about how Jane made her teaching of imaging explicit. Find three things she did to make it clear to her students what they were to do, when, and why.

WHY USE EXPLICIT TEACHING?

Support for explicit instruction comes from two different kinds of empirical studies: (1) experiments showing the effects of learning strategies on comprehension and (2) case studies of exemplary teachers who use explicit instruction (Cambourne, 2002; Pressley et al., 2001; RAND, 2002; Williams, 2002). Explicit teaching has proven to be the most successful procedure for teaching comprehension strategies to date (Pressley, 2000).

Of course, implicit or inductive teaching is highly valued in literacy instruction and throughout every area of the curriculum. This kind of teaching involves students in exploration that encourages divergent pursuits and discovery of ideas. However, there are certain processes and ideas that are so important that they need to be taught up front. Explicit teaching of CPS focuses on foundational inquiry-based strategies that prepare students to pursue interests and find and create big ideas from all manner of texts in every discipline (Pearson, Harvey, & Goudis, 2005). Explicit teaching develops students' capacity to work with implicit ideas—to become independent constructers of their own meaning.

EXPLICIT INSTRUCTION GUIDELINES

Explicit instruction involves demonstration accompanied by a clear explanation of the purpose of the task. While this may sound easy, one must acquire the skill of explaining thought processes clearly. The following are key guidelines for effective explicit instruction. Ready Resource 5.2 provides a summary.

Plan teaching time and focus

Because explicit teaching demands attention and concentration, it should not last for more than five to ten minutes. Jane's lesson lasted about twenty minutes, but that time included the warm-up with the song (five minutes), which was fun and served to put the upcoming new strategy into context. Students were actively engaged in generating and sharing their own examples by ten minutes into the lesson, and these activities continued throughout the read aloud.

Explicit teaching leaves no doubt about what to do and think. It is an intense form of teaching that should be reserved for key concepts, strategies, and processes of such consequence that we cannot leave mastery to discovery. CPS meets this criterion, because it is central to meaning making, and meaning making is central to literacy.

In addition to teaching the concept of CPS and the before, during, and after strategies, teachers may explicitly teach other key literacy processes. For example, teachers should provide individual, small group, and whole group explicit instruction as needed to show students how to problem solve unknown words (look ahead to Ready Resource 8.11 in Chapter 8) and repair comprehension breakdowns (see Ready Resource 5.5 in this chapter), as well as help them acquire essential learning skills, such as how to concentrate. Indeed, many students who have difficulties with comprehension sorely need explicit teaching about how to attend, concentrate, and focus. Obviously, it is nearly impossible for a student to comprehend a text if she or he is not focused on it. Concentration and focus can be taught using the basic sequence of explicit teaching outlined in this chapter. In addition, warm-ups used in drama and dance that target control of body, mind, and voice can be helpful (Cornett, 2011). Examples are described in Appendix H, or you can search the Internet for "warm ups" and consult school dance, physical education, or drama teachers.

Guidelines for explicit teaching.

- Plan short periods of time (five to ten minutes)
- Identify the teaching focus (key concepts and processes)
- Model thinking by talking out loud ("think aloud" strategy)
- Provide scaffolded or coached practice
- Use an "I do, We do, You do, Re do" sequence

Model thinking

The think aloud is a teaching strategy that makes thinking obvious by making it audible. In the case of CPS, teachers talk out loud to make clear how they are making sense of a specific text. Jane did a think aloud to demonstrate imaging. When it comes to developing students' CPS repertoire, there is no substitute for modeling how to think about an actual text as students listen in. Although it often takes many rehearsals for a teacher to become adept at demonstrating thinking in this way, it is well worth the effort (RAND, 2002).

Initially, students may be confused about what you are doing and why, so it is helpful to explain what think alouds are and why you will use them. Props, such as a large thought bubble to hold up during think alouds, provide good signals. Student think alouds are also an essential part of successful explicit teaching. Recall that Jane quickly involved the children in doing think alouds with a buddy. Like teachers, students will not be as comfortable and as articulate during their first tries as they will be after they have several weeks of experience. It takes daily use! Strategy teaching should not be confined to narrative texts or happen exclusively during the literacy block—in fact, strategy teaching is most effective when it is integrated with science, social studies, and math texts.

Provide scaffolded practice

Explicit lessons will not succeed without time for students to practice with scaffolding. In the general lexicon, a scaffold is a temporary framework used as a support, usually during a building process. We've all seen masons standing on metal scaffolding to lay brick and window washers and painters using scaffolds to do their work. We as teachers also need to use scaffolds to support the building of literacy knowledge and skills.

To understand scaffolding, recall how you learned to ride a bicycle. First you had to want to do it (motivation), which came from seeing someone else do it (model). Next came the training wheels, along with demonstration and explanation, as needed. This is scaffolding. Note that Jane used scaffolding—the image of the cat—in the snapshot as she taught her students about imaging. Scaffolded practice includes support in the form of encouragement, asking questions, giving cues, providing feedback, and so forth. Scaffolding also includes coaching. When you were learning to ride a bike and the training wheels came off, it was helpful to have someone steady the bike and run along beside as you practiced. Eventually, Mom, Dad, or a friend let go and you were able to ride independently for a short distance. There was celebration (more scaffolding), and you continued to ride, sometimes with some falls, until you got better and better and became independent.

Scaffolding is a logical way to increase learning by challenging students to think slightly beyond their present level (Vygotsky, 1978). For example, when students are practicing individual and coordinated CPS strategy use, you can create a think stop, or a pause during reading for reflection. During this pause, students can be paired to share potential big ideas and strategies they used to arrive at their conclusions. The job of the teacher is to circulate, ask questions, and cue students to check visuals like the CPS chart. Of particular importance is making it clear to students that the goal is for them to eventually use strategies without prompting. The goal is self-regulated use during normal reading, rather than depending on cues from the teacher.

Scaffolding allows students to do something, with help, that they couldn't do alone. It gives the helping hand we all need at different points in life, as long as we continue to learn.

Use an "I do, We do, You do, Re do" sequence

There is no one definitive model for explicit teaching, but all models share common components (Duke, 2001; Gaskins, 2003). The general teaching sequence can be easily remembered as "I do, We do, You do, Re do" (Deshler & Schumaker, 1990), with the teacher being the "I," teacher and students the "we," and students working independently as the "you." Teachers also use the phrases "my turn" and "your turn" to alert students to their roles as, first, observers/listeners, then as unison responders, and finally as individual responders. In the examples that follow, notice the use of the Five W + H questions to make the explanations clear.

Explanation (I do). The teacher names the strategy or concept and briefly explains WHAT to do, WHY, and WHEN and WHERE it should be used. Example: "Today I'm going to teach you how to image. (Teacher points to image on CPS chart.) It is important to create images or pictures in your head when you are reading anything—books, magazines, even text messages. Imaging can double your comprehension." In the snapshot, Jane could have added a bit more to her explanation, but since she planned to work with imaging over time she did not need to explain everything in her introduction.

Modeling (I do). The teacher then models (provides a brief demonstration) of the skill, usually using a think aloud of HOW to use the thinking or concept in a real-world context. For example, Mr. Darcy in the snapshot in Chapter 3 used the Cheerios box as the text and situated his modeling of the whole CPS concept within the problem of finding more healthy food to eat. The text and the context increased the relevancy of the lesson, because they connected to literacy outside of school. Jane used familiar and easy words that tapped a pleasant image, her Golden Retriever, Chester, whom she'd brought to class many times.

Scaffolded or coached group practice (We do). Students all simultaneously practice, and the teacher coaches them. Students may be directed to practice in pairs or small groups, with the teacher listening in to offer suggestions, ask questions, cue, give more examples, demonstrate again, and encourage with descriptive feedback. Consider the following example of Jane preparing her students for coached group practice:

> "Now I'm going to ask you each to make images in your head. Here is a sentence. Let's read it together. Now each of you think about exactly what you see—the colors, shapes, sizes. You can also create images of what you smell and the textures you can feel, and your emotions. [PAUSE] Turn to your partner and tell about your images. I'll come around and listen to your ideas and help you."

Note that Jane used an art elements chart (see Ready Resource 5.1) to help coach her students to think about aspects of imaging. This worked well, since imagining is essentially mental art, and made an excellent connection to another area of the curriculum. While such scaffolds are not possible with all strategies, visual imaging has obvious transfer possibilities. Conversations with the art teacher about additional ideas and opportunities for imaging to be reinforced in art class would be worth pursuing.

Coached or scaffolded independent practice (You do). Students now try the strategy individually, with the teacher giving less and less help as students show progress. This is called "gradual release of responsibility" (Pearson & Gallagher, 1983). For example, to introduce her students to coached independent practice of imaging, Jane tells them:

> "Here is a paragraph [shown on the overhead]. Read it silently and create images in your head. Remember you are problem solving to make meaning. [PAUSE] How did it go? What questions do you have? Let's hear some examples. Who would like to volunteer to tell about his or her images?"

As students share, the teacher once again can coach with feedback and questions (e.g., ask for colors, sizes, shape, textures, emotions to elaborate on images—if that is the strategy being taught) or give another demonstration.

Cued independent use/debriefing (Re do). Finally, the teacher reminds students to use the strategy during independent reading time, during science and social studies class, and while reading math problems. In this example, the teacher is cuing students by telling them ahead of time what will happen, so they can prepare. She also provides stickies as concrete cues or reminders.

> "After Independent Reading, I'll ask each of you to share some of your images. I've given each of you three stickies to mark places in your books where you made images in your head. If you need more, let me know. I'll do it, too."

After reading, students partner to share one example, and volunteers are asked to share examples with the whole class (debriefing). The teacher again coaches to clarify aspects of the image making and asks for questions.

Explicit Teaching of Comprehension Strategies

No one grouping of comprehension strategies, or any single definitive order, has been found to be superior for all students. It makes sense, however, to teach the general *concept* of the before/during/after CPS sequence and then to target individual strategies within that structure in a "review and add to" manner. In this section, important issues related to explicit teaching of comprehension strategies are discussed, including where to start, how to monitor student progress, and how to differentiate instruction.

TEACH HIGH-PRIORITY COMPREHENSION STRATEGIES

Explicit teaching of high-priority strategies is recommended, beginning with primary students. Ready Resource 5.3 provides brief definitions of high-priority strategies; these definitions can be a good start for planning clear language for think alouds. In the following discussions, six of these strategies are highlighted as part of the CPS process.

Predict

Prediction includes recalling and using prior knowledge or background experience to anticipate or hypothesize about what will happen next or the purpose of something. Prediction is about generating expectations and narrowing possibilities related to actions, events, and outcomes. In CPS, prediction occurs early and continues throughout the during and after phases as the reader gathers more information, confirms or rejects early predictions, and makes new predictions. Predicting is key to ratcheting CPS forward, as well as keeping it honest.

Key questions include:

- What will this be about?
- What do you think will happen?
- Why do you think so (evidence)?

Connect

Our brains organize knowledge by grouping like ideas together. The brain seeks connections between new information and (Fountas & Pinnell, 2001)

1. current personal background knowledge (text-to-self knowledge).
2. other texts (text-to-text knowledge).
3. information about the world (text-to-world knowledge).

Connections result from related brain schemata (categories) being activated and new information being assimilated into the structure of the brain. When new schemata have to be created, the process is called *accommodation* (Piaget & Inhelder, 2000), which is usually more difficult.

Key questions include:

- How is this like something in your own life?
- How is this text like or different from _____ (another text)?
- What do you know in the world that relates to this text?

Infer

Inference is a thought process of using text information, in combination with background knowledge, to make an interpretation or draw a conclusion. Inferring involves thinking about what is not stated but is cued by the text. It is the problem-solving type of thinking associated with detectives, and it includes drawing implications or creating theories from clues and evidence. Inferring is about searching for big ideas or deeper meaning by "reading between the lines."

Comprehension thinking strategies: Brief definitions.

Use these definitions to plan think alouds and to help clarify thinking for students.

Predict: Recall and use prior knowledge or background experience to anticipate or hypothesize about what will happen next or the purpose of something.

> *Other ideas:* Generate expectations, narrow possibilities

Connect: Link text to other texts (TT), to yourself (TS), to your personal knowledge and feelings, or to what you know about the world (TW) (Fountas & Pinnell, 2001).

> *Other ideas:* Relate or search for relationships

Infer: Use text information combined with what you already know to make an interpretation or draw a conclusion.

> *Other ideas:* Think about what is not stated; consider implications; make theories from clues and evidence, like a detective. Focus on the search for big ideas or deeper meaning by reading between the lines.

Determine importance: Decide what are the big ideas or themes based on evidence (facts and details) and your own experiences, including your preferences and values.

> *Other ideas:* Think about the significance or relevance of information.

Question: Generate your own questions about the text in order to make sense.

> *Other ideas:* Use the Five W + H stems.

Analyze/critique: Zoom in to examine parts or pieces closely to see how everything fits together to make sense.

> *Other ideas:* Notice literary or artistic elements and what they contribute or signal; notice text structure, composition, or design features and think about their emotional and cognitive effects; integrate details with the whole.

Image: Use any of the five senses and your emotions to create meaning.

> *Other ideas:* Make mental pictures, visualize, hear sounds, and so forth.

Monitor: Ask yourself continually if the text is making sense, and use comprehension fix-ups if it is not. *Note:* Word Fix-Ups should be used if the problem is an unknown word. Refer to Ready Resource 8.11 in Chapter 8.

> *Other ideas:* Confirm or reject predictions and make new ones; assimilate and accommodate new ideas.

Synthesize: Combine pieces of information to arrive at unique or new ideas, especially a problem solution. The focus is on overall meaning (big ideas) that pull the whole text together versus the inferences made during reading.

> *Other ideas:* Reorganize or transform your thinking; use creative thinking; seek insight and integration of ideas.

Summarize: Paraphrase only the most important information. *Note:* Retelling is different from paraphrasing—retelling involves a complete recounting, whereas paraphrasing is condensing by selecting what is most important.

> *Other ideas:* Synthesize or pull together important concepts.

Transform: Organize and change; redesign; shape.

> *Other ideas:* Create a new representation.

Evaluate: Determine the worthiness, the rightness or wrongness, or the goodness or badness of an idea based on evidence and criteria.

> *Other ideas:* Make logical or aesthetic judgments; form a supportable opinion.

Reflect: Take time to review, re-experience, reconsider, redirect, and revise ideas.

> *Other ideas:* Introspect or examine your own thinking.

READY RESOURCE

5.3

Key questions include:

- What details seem to be important? Why?
- What does this mean? Why?
- What conclusions can be drawn from these clues?

Question

Although teacher questions often dominate classrooms, mature comprehenders learn to generate their own questions. Question generation stems from the inclination to make sense—to problem solve texts for meaning. The Five W + H stems are useful in teaching students to generate questions. For example, create a pie chart with *Who? What? When? Where? How?* and *Why?* written in each of the sections, and attach a spinner. Ask students to work in small groups and use the pie chart as a discussion prompt after reading, listening, or viewing a text. Students should be encouraged to interpret the Five W + H questions in diverse ways. Ready Resource 5.4 presents examples of ways the stems might be elaborated.

Monitor

Capable comprehenders know when they need to exert more mental effort, because they constantly monitor whether or not they understand the text. They continually ask themselves, "Is this making sense?" If the answer is yes, they keep going. If the answer is no, they use a variety of tools to repair the problem. This happens at different levels. For example, successful readers know they need to use additional decoding strategies when "sounding out" does not result in a word that makes sense in a specific context (Isakson & Miller, 1976). Good readers often repair word-level comprehension problems by rereading the unknown

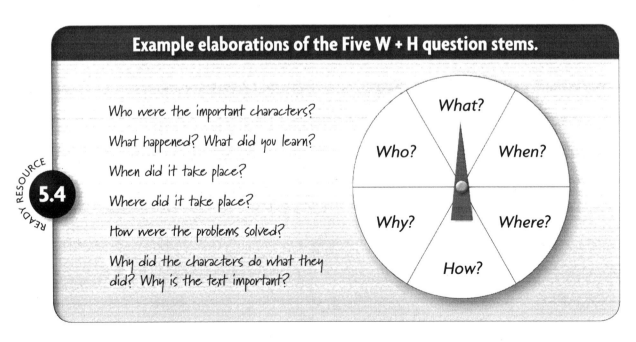

Example elaborations of the Five W + H question stems.

READY RESOURCE 5.4

Who were the important characters?

What happened? What did you learn?

When did it take place?

Where did it take place?

How were the problems solved?

Why did the characters do what they did? Why is the text important?

What? Who? When? Why? Where? How?

word in context, which may provide possible synonyms that might fit and can be synchronized with the grapho-phonic (spelling pattern–sound) information. Young readers can be taught to monitor and repair word-level comprehension problems through explicit teaching of Word Fix-Up strategies (see Ready Resource 8.11 in Chapter 8). Good readers are also aware when the comprehension problem is broader or when they are confused about the meaning of sections of a text (Baker & Brown, 1984). At this point, the reader must activate a greater range of fix-ups to solve the problem.

Most strategy packages include both comprehension monitoring and general fix-up strategies. Reciprocal teaching (Palincsar & Brown, 1984), which focuses on four comprehension strategies, includes clarification: readers are taught to seek clarification of meaning, often through rereading. Transactional strategies instruction (TSI) (Pressley et al., 1995) includes comprehension monitoring in the form of teaching students to ask, "Is what I am reading making sense?" Children are explicitly taught that they can do something when the answer is no. CPS includes a range of options for solving comprehension problems, called Comprehension Fix-Ups and listed in Ready Resource 5.5.

Monitoring depends on self-questioning during reading. Key questions include:

- Does this make sense? Why not?
- What can I do to make it make sense?

Comprehension Fix-Ups.

If you don't understand what you are reading, use these strategies:

- **Read on.** Keep going to get more information.

- **Reread.** Find ideas you may have missed.

- **Read it aloud.** Hearing the words can help.

- **Change your speed.** Try faster or slower.

- **Stop and think.** Take time to reflect. Give your brain some time to process. Take a short break.

- **Image.** Picture in your head what's going on. Use other senses as well (smell, taste, touch/texture, sounds).

- **Consider emotions.** Think about how the text makes you feel and why.

- **Ask yourself questions.** Use the Five W + H questions: Who is this about? What is the problem? Where is this happening? When is this happening? Why are the events happening? How can the problem be solved?

- **Review the reasons.** Remember why you are using the text, and adjust your thinking based on those purposes. For example, focus on key details.

- **Check questions.** Go back to your purpose-setting questions to see which ones are about finding information in the text and which expect you to use your background alongside text information to answer.

- **Think about the structure** (for example, the 3 Cs + S are compare–contrast, cause–effect, classification, and sequence). This tells you how the writer or creator of the text was thinking. By thinking in the same way, you can understand more.

- **Summarize or retell what you DO know.** Review to establish a foundation you can add to.

READY RESOURCE

5.5

Summarize

Summarizing is different from retelling. A summary is a distillation of important information—the big ideas. In order to summarize, readers must choose the most important information, based on their purposes for text use. The five W + H questions may help the reader organize information from fiction and nonfiction texts for the purpose of summarizing. As a part of explicit teaching of summarizing, it is a good idea to have students read examples of good summaries, such as short book reviews found on the Internet.

Key questions include:

- What is it mostly about?
- What are the three to five ideas that are most important, based on text evidence?

TEACH STRATEGIES AT ALL AGES AND STAGES

The tendency has been to view the primary grades as the time to hone word-recognition skills and to postpone genuine comprehension instruction to third grade and later. However, this view is now widely rejected (e.g., Institute for Education Sciences, 2008; Moats, 1999). Growing numbers of examples show comprehension interventions proving successful with primary students. For example, Block and Pressley (2007) report that first and second graders who were taught to use more than one comprehension strategy scored significantly higher on a standardized comprehension test, enjoyed reading more, were more skilled at comparing texts, and drew more conclusions from nonfiction than control groups. Third graders who were taught strategies demonstrated more skill at using nonfiction text clues to guide comprehension and by fifth grade were more skilled at predicting from nonfiction. Block and Pressley also describe a multiyear study in which students were taught three to fifteen strategies and at the end of eight weeks used more strategies continually than a control group. In this study, K–2 students applied an average of 4.5 comprehension processes without prompting as they read a full book. Students in grades three through five were able to successfully use 4.5 comprehension strategies with nonfiction texts after eight weeks.

It is difficult to find justifiable reasons to postpone strategy instruction. Strategy instruction can happen concurrently with the teaching of reading sub-skills such as phonemic awareness, phonics, basic vocabulary, and fluency. Strategies may be taught during discussions of a wide variety of texts, both narrative and expository, fiction and nonfiction, and with non-verbal texts such as pieces of visual art. All students can use CPS to make sense of a painting, a sculpture, or an illustration in a picture book. Of course, explicit teaching of *how* to do this is needed before teachers expect students to use strategies.

Primary children predict, image, infer, and evaluate in their daily lives and can be taught to use high-level thinking with texts (Block & Pressley, 2007). Postponing comprehension instruction risks loss of student motivation to learn and is thought to be the cause of the Reading First program's failure (Walker, 2009; Whitehurst, 2008). With expert teaching, most students can be expected to execute most CPS strategies, to some extent, by the end of third grade and to experience the intrinsic rewards of personal sense making. For this potential result, all strategy instruction must be presented so that students understand their roles as active meaning makers and that the purpose of comprehension is to find and construct big ideas.

TEACH A REPERTOIRE OF STRATEGIES

There seems to be little doubt that teaching students to use a repertoire of comprehension strategies increases their comprehension (Block & Pressley, 2007; Brown et al., 1996; Palincsar & Brown, 1984). Explicit instruction often features tasks that are broken down into small steps. After the initial modeling, teachers coach students as they practice each step. In the case of comprehension strategy instruction, teachers have tried teaching one strategy at a time with some success (Keene & Zimmerman, 2007). Increasingly, however, experts have called for approaches that coordinate the use of multiple strategies in a manner that parallels the way good readers use them—to make sense and solve problems using real-world texts (NRP, 2000). A review of available data makes an overwhelming case for teaching a set of strategies (Pressley, 2006). Teaching a repertoire of comprehension strategies makes more sense than teaching single strategies, especially after teaching the first strategy (Pressley, 2006). Block and Pressley (2007) recommend a six-day plan for teaching strategies, similar to that in Ready Resource 5.6.

Of course, explicit instruction entails sharing lots of examples that only a literate teacher can generate (Gambrell, Malloy, & Mazzoni (2007). The snapshot at the beginning of Chapter 2 provides an example of explicit teaching of coordinated strategies.

It is the teacher's responsibility to make sure students understand that individual strategies are parts of the whole problem-solving process used to make

---

Guidelines for teaching comprehension strategies.

1 Introduce one strategy using a think aloud. Have students practice with coaching.

2 Ask students to partner and do think alouds using the strategy.

3 Re-teach as needed in small groups.

4 Cue students to use the strategy with texts and debrief about use.

5 When students are comfortable with first strategy, introduce a second one using previous steps.

6 Cue students to use both strategies during independent reading.

7 Debrief students regularly to assess strategy use. Keep records of progress and re-teach as needed.

READY RESOURCE 5.6

Source: Block & Pressley, 2007.

meaning with any text. Explicit teaching can make clear how good readers perform this inquiry by using self-questioning (Block & Pressley, 2007). Strategy *coordination* must be modeled in a way that illustrates examples of *how to* think. Moreover, teachers must explain why, when, where, and how to alter, adjust, and shift strategies until meaning is constructed and the problem is solved (NRP, 2000).

TEACH STRATEGY TRANSFER

Teachers report that learning to teach coordinated use of multiple strategies is not easy (Block & Pressley, 2007). But this hard work gives "consistent and striking benefits," with comprehension strategy instruction producing both strategy learning and transfer of strategy use to new texts (Pressley, 2000). Transfer depends on teachers cueing students to use the strategies they know in new circumstances. For example, for students who learned to use strategies with narrative texts, a teacher might say:

> How will you know what to do in your head to make sense of this section of your social studies text? Look on the CPS chart or your CPS bookmark and choose three strategies to focus on today. I'll say the names of strategies; if I name one you chose, stand up. After reading you can date the ones you used in your folder. You will have time to talk about one you used with a partner.

MONITOR PROGRESS

As discussed in Chapter 3, student folders provide a good way for teachers and students to monitor progress. As a start, teachers and students can mark a simple CPS checklist when a strategy is introduced and record the dates when the student uses it. In another column, teachers may record notes on quality of use (e.g., in an individual conference). See Ready Resource 5.7.

TEACH STRATEGIES OVER TIME

It usually takes longer to develop automaticity in comprehension than in decoding. However, the time required to develop full independence at comprehension problem solving has yet to be established (Block & Pressley, 2007). The length of time it takes for students to learn to initiate and then sustain strategy use depends, as would be expected, on individual learner characteristics. It is clear that the teaching of comprehension strategies has to be conceived as a long-term developmental process, with instruction embedded throughout the school day, not just in the literacy block (Pressley, 2000). Students will likely maintain initial comprehension gains only if strategy instruction becomes mainstream, with students experiencing strategy teaching over years in various contexts.

DIFFERENTIATE STRATEGY INSTRUCTION

A strong case can be made that explicit teaching of a targeted repertoire of strategies will improve comprehension for students with learning difficulties (RAND,

Sample progress chart for monitoring comprehension strategy use.

NAME:

STRATEGY	DATE INTRODUCED	DATES USED	NOTES
Predicting	9/26	9/27	listed characters, setting, and problem predicted from cover art
		9/30	gave clear evidence for predictions
		10/06	rejected prediction b/c of conflicting evidence
Connecting	10/15	10/15	gave text connections to own life
		10/16	connections between 3 texts!
Inferencing	11/09	11/12	inferred an implicit big idea from themes
Imaging	9/11	9/11	explained detailed visual images based on expository texts
		10/15	drew detailed visual about photosynthesis
		11/19	wrote poem about sounds, smell, and textures related to news article on urban farming

READY RESOURCE 5.7

2002). Explicit teaching demands active responses from students and triggers the use of strategies that passive learners may possess but do not normally use. Comprehension success for struggling students does depend on teachers making "skillful adjustments to learner characteristics" and causing students to maintain focus on reading purposes (p. 34). Visual aids, such as charts and bookmarks, and extra cues to remember to use more than one comprehension strategy are important ways to differentiate instruction (Block & Pressley, 2007; Block et al., 2008).

While explicit instruction is necessary for low-performing students, it may not be so crucial for other students. Of course, there are degrees of explicitness. Some students just need more examples or practice with increased scaffolding. A particular student may need some combination of explanation, more think alouds, more practice time, assistance from peers or parents, and a visual scaffold. For example, a student may be helped to think further about a strategy

CPS strategy: IMAGE.

Text:	news article on urban farming
What did you see?	Flowers, corn stalks, tomato plants along highways and by tall buildings
Colors?	Many, but lots of green and there is red dirt because this is Georgia
Shapes?	Many, but lots of pointed leaves and curved flower blooms
Sizes?	Tall straight corn, tiny berries
Lines?	Straight rows in gardens
Textures?	Firm plump veggies; delicate blooms
How did you feel about the images?	Hopeful, happy. I want to have an urban garden patch.

READY RESOURCE
5.8

such as imaging by writing about it. A simple form, along with several spaced-out stop and write points, can help scaffold the student's thinking. The student will need enough stops for reflection (e.g., three), but not so many that they become distracting and the student loses focus on constructing big ideas from the text. Ready Resource 5.8 provides an example form.

Explicit Teaching of Text Characteristics

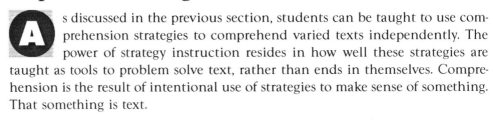

As discussed in the previous section, students can be taught to use comprehension strategies to comprehend varied texts independently. The power of strategy instruction resides in how well these strategies are taught as tools to problem solve text, rather than ends in themselves. Comprehension is the result of intentional use of strategies to make sense of something. That something is text.

TEXT DEFINITION AND PURPOSES

Over thirty years ago, Louise Rosenblatt envisioned the "transaction between the reader and the text" as the core of comprehension. She postulated a reader-response theory using this premise and predicted a range of interpretations and responses to any given text. She argued that a person's primary purpose for text use was highly influential in determining subsequent comprehension (1978). She identified two main purposes: (1) an *efferent stance*, which focuses on information or facts, produces a more narrow range of interpretation, and (2) an *aesthetic stance* results in a text experience that broadens the response to include attitudes, emotions, and feelings the text elicits. What about the text itself? Don't different texts have different properties that change the nature of the transaction? The answer is yes. The intersection among text factors and other comprehension factors is the subject of this section.

Technological advances have permanently altered how we communicate. Film, television, the Internet, CDs, MP3 players, PDAs, and multifaceted telephones are common ways we receive and express thoughts and feelings. As discussed in Chapter 1, a contemporary definition of text has to acknowledge innovative communication technologies as well as consider how the power of ancient text forms has been wrapped into modern life. I am referring here to the significant roles the arts play in 21st-century communication, including technology. Today, *text* is broadly used to refer to print and non-print, verbal and non-verbal sources that may be read, viewed, or listened to for the purpose of finding and constructing meaning (IRA/NCTE, 1996). While communication choices have become vast, the purposes for text use are much the same regardless of the medium: to experience pleasure and to gain information. Both of these purposes are rooted in sense making.

Teachers need to be explicit about basic literacy concepts, as well as processes, that are integral to comprehension. One such concept is that different texts have different organizational formats and features created for specific purposes. Good readers survey text characteristics before reading to determine the text's main purpose. They use text structure and format signals to predict how well the text might suit their purposes and how accessible it is. Teachers should also be aware of how they are presenting certain types of texts and the consequent associations students will attach to them. In the past, some teachers have misused texts, such as poetry, causing generations of students to associate memorization and line-by-line analysis with this genre. This perspective should frame our thinking about the explicit teaching of text characteristics and the creation of criteria for appropriate text use.

Text characteristics (e.g., the answer to, What is fiction?) are concepts, and teaching concepts is somewhat different from teaching strategies. Clear explanations should be provided alongside open-ended discussion and invitations for students to examine and generate examples and non-examples. These methods make text feature concepts such as headings, summaries, and indices understandable (i.e., more explicit). Children can be taught to self-question to tap into text structure and identify the information they need to construct big ideas. This teaching should include the 5 W & H questions.

Most students need more than exposure to diverse texts to understand their purposes and organization. Some explicit instruction about specific text characteristics is warranted, including the concept of genres, text content, and format, as well as the peculiarities of multimedia and digital texts (see Ready Resource 5.9). In particular, students should be taught how the organization of a text reflects the author's purpose, and that the purpose can range from telling a story to providing information to persuading. Understanding the author's intent prevents misunderstanding, too (Armbruster & Armstrong, 1993).

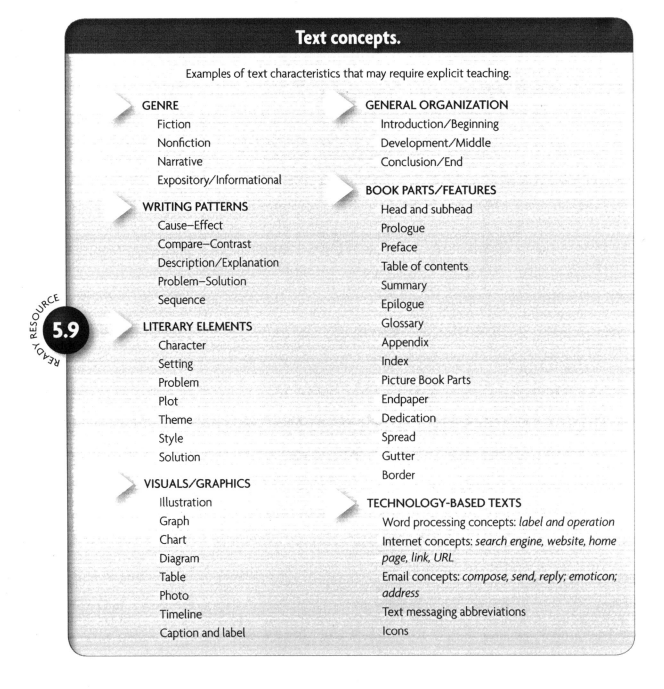

Text concepts.

Examples of text characteristics that may require explicit teaching.

READY RESOURCE 5.9

GENRE
Fiction
Nonfiction
Narrative
Expository/Informational

WRITING PATTERNS
Cause–Effect
Compare–Contrast
Description/Explanation
Problem–Solution
Sequence

LITERARY ELEMENTS
Character
Setting
Problem
Plot
Theme
Style
Solution

VISUALS/GRAPHICS
Illustration
Graph
Chart
Diagram
Table
Photo
Timeline
Caption and label

GENERAL ORGANIZATION
Introduction/Beginning
Development/Middle
Conclusion/End

BOOK PARTS/FEATURES
Head and subhead
Prologue
Preface
Table of contents
Summary
Epilogue
Glossary
Appendix
Index
Picture Book Parts
Endpaper
Dedication
Spread
Gutter
Border

TECHNOLOGY-BASED TEXTS
Word processing concepts: *label and operation*
Internet concepts: *search engine, website, home page, link, URL*
Email concepts: *compose, send, reply; emoticon; address*
Text messaging abbreviations
Icons

TEXT CHARACTERISTICS AFFECT COMPREHENSION

Good comprehenders attend to text characteristics more than poor comprehenders do. Students who read with an eye on the organizational patterns purposefully used by authors are better able to uncover embedded meaning clues (RAND, 2002). Immature and disadvantaged readers often are unaware of internal text structure. They do not understand that in order to comprehend the text they must think in the patterns the author used to create the text. Text-wise students know how to retrieve the basic structure or "grammar" of fiction and nonfiction. For example, when good readers encounter a narrative piece of fiction, they extract details by thinking in terms of story structure. They notice plot events, character traits, setting features, and themes that lead to big ideas. Knowledge of such genre features sets up expectations for how a text will unfold. For example, we expect mystery writers to weave in clues that allow us to participate in solving the case. A writer who does this well leaves the reader satisfied at the end. A lesser writer might spring the case resolution on the reader with little logic (called "deus ex machina"), causing the reader to be dissatisfied.

TEACH STUDENTS ABOUT GENRE

Texts are categorized using a dazzling set of labels. *Genre* is a French word that means type, form, sort, or kind. Libraries divide texts into two genres, fiction and nonfiction, with many subdivisions for each. For example, biography is a sub-genre of nonfiction. New genres do emerge; for example, science fiction appeared in the early 20th century, and new digital genres are now being created. Any topic can be treated using almost any genre: I can write a poem about cats, or create a blog about them, as long as I know and follow the specific conventions that govern the genre.

The traditional categories of fiction and nonfiction label the *content* as either true to facts or imaginary to some degree, and other categories label a text's organization or presentation, such as oral texts used by storytellers and digital texts ranging from television programs to Internet pages. Picture books and hypertext, for example, are labels for particular text *formats* that are enhanced with media. Picture books have transformed the teaching of reading in U.S. classrooms by giving countless children access to ideas through visual art. In the case of hypertext, the capability to access information through links has dramatically altered the concept of research.

Word-based genres are distinguished by the specific patterns writers use. For example, poets write in patterns ranging from diamante (unrhymed) to couplets (rhymed) and concrete (the poem looks like its topic). Writers use organizational patterns that allow them to tell stories (narrative), pass on information (expository), or persuade readers (rhetorical). Arts-based text structures range from paintings and dances to plays and musical pieces, which may include elements of both fiction and nonfiction, indicated by context-specific labels (e.g., realistic or representational visual art has aspects of nonfiction). Arts-based texts are discussed in more detail in Chapter 9. Ready Resource 5.10 lists common genres, each with its own conventions.

Text structures: Genres.

The term *text* is broadly used to refer to a print or non-print, verbal or non-verbal form used to communicate thoughts and feelings. Texts are structured in different ways to suit the purposes of their creators. These text forms are called genres. They intersect with formats, or the ways presented.

GENRES

Fiction/Narrative: Stories created or "imagined by" authors

EXAMPLES:

Traditional stories: folktales, parables, fables, myths and legends, tall tales

Fantasy: animal, toy, and tiny-being tales; modern folk and fairy tales; science fiction; high fantasy; time fantasy; horror

Realistic: contemporary stories about sports, animals, survival, school, and family; also includes historical fiction and mystery; often occur in a series

Nonfiction: Texts that present accurate information in a narrative or expository form

EXAMPLES:

Informational: expository or factual texts about the arts, science, math, history, geography, technology, and so on. Includes alphabet books, counting books, concept books.

Biography, and autobiography: Factual texts about real people

Poetry

EXAMPLES:

Couplet, limerick, concrete or shape, diamante, haiku, free verse

Humor

EXAMPLES:

Jokes, riddles, tongue twisters, spoonerisms, puns

Multicultural: texts that represent the characteristics of specific cultures, intersecting with other genres

EXAMPLES:

Folktales of various cultures

FORMATS

Books/Picture Books: May combine art and text, but can be wordless stories (all art)

Digital Technology: Television, video, photographs, and computer-based texts

Arts: Music, visual art, dance, and drama/theatre texts

TEACH STUDENTS ABOUT TEXT STRUCTURES

There is great diversity in text structures. Think about a how-to manual for a product as compared to a letter of complaint about the same product, or a political cartoon about a presidential candidate compared to a biography of that person. The text form changes to suit what is to be communicated, why, to whom, and even where the communication is to happen (e.g., a Facebook page). Text creators choose from a multitude of organizational and formatting conventions to influence how the reader will receive the message. For example, a narrative film might tell a story with a linear plot, or it might move back and forth among time periods in recounting events (IRA/NCTE, 1996). Students benefit from tuning in to text structure up front, because this helps them discern the purpose and organization of the text. This knowledge then directs and organizes their thinking.

Narrative text structure

Children who have heard many stories before starting school generally have a rudimentary sense of narrative structure. Beginning with "once upon a time" and ending with "they lived happily ever after," narratives such as folk and fairy tales have been staples in the literary lives of young children. In addition to fictional narratives, children often have heard many nonfictional narratives before they start school. For example, family stories about ancestors are common nonfiction stories told and retold to children. First texts used in school are often narratives, because their familiar structure is thought to make it easier for children to transition to learning to read independently.

At a basic level, narratives are texts that feature characters who confront problems, which set up the plot. Themes are revealed as problems are resolved. Ready Resource 5.11 describes these and more basic elements of narrative structure that should be explicitly taught. The Five W + H questions serve as prompts to cue students to think about these important organizational features of narratives.

Expository text structure

Reliance on narrative fiction and nonfiction in the primary grades has drawbacks. A falloff in comprehension achievement around fourth grade coincides with the introduction of more nonfictional expository texts that focus on giving information. These texts do not use the familiar storytelling pattern of characters solving problems in interesting settings.

Expository (explanatory) text is often loaded with new information and unfamiliar vocabulary. Students especially need instruction that shows them how to extract and synthesize important ideas from long passages with unfamiliar content and complex and varied structures (RAND, 2002). The procedures for the explicit teaching of narrative texts should also be used to teach students how to orient to expository texts and negotiate particularly troublesome features of expository material. For example, teachers should model how to chunk long sentences into meaningful phrases, use context clues (look ahead to Ready Resource 8.11 in Chapter 8), and turn to the text glossary to understand new vocabulary.

Over the past decade researchers have been building a case for earlier and increased use of expository texts. Since students are expected to read progressively longer and more complex chunks of nonfiction/expository material, especially in content areas, it makes sense to design comprehension instruction to meet this reality (Duke, 2000). Use of a greater range of texts, especially more nonfiction, in the primary grades would better prepare children for intermediate and middle grades, and the fourth-grade "slump" might be less steep. Teachers have responded enthusiastically to the increasing availability of quality expository texts for primary students. Beginning at pre-K, children are now introduced to texts that explain and give information, especially related to science, social studies, and math. It behooves teachers to instruct students about expository text characteristics. Explicit teaching is an important vehicle.

Elements of narrative text structure.

Purpose: Narrative texts, from books and films to radio and live storytelling, are meant to tell a story. Narratives may be fictional or nonfictional, as in letters, journals, and biographies.

Theme: the unifying truth or universal message in a work of literature. Theme topics may be developed into big idea statements

Key question: What is the text really about? What is most important about the story? (Go beyond a topic to a complete statement.)

- Explicit themes are directly stated messages.
- Implicit themes are indirectly stated messages, which the reader, listener, or viewer must use background experience to infer.

Character: any person, animal, or object taking a role (e.g., hero)

Key questions: Who is the story about? Who wants something? Who has a problem? By the end, who changes the most?

- Characters are revealed through: (1) description, (2) actions or behaviors, (3) speech and thoughts, (4) what other characters think and say about them.
- Character types: protagonist/antagonist, round or flat/stock, dynamic or static, foil, stereotype

Plot: the events set in motion by a problem or conflict and the order in which they take place

Key questions: What is the problem? What happened? Why? How was the problem solved?

- Types of conflict: between a character and (1) nature, (2) society, or (3) another character, or (4) within the character (internal)
- Plot patterns: (1) linear: introduction, development, and conclusion (includes climax and denouement), (2) cumulative: events build on one another, (3) episodic: mini stories tied together
- Plot variations: cliffhangers, flashbacks, foreshadowing

Setting: the time and place in which the story takes place

Key questions: When and where does the story happen?

- Types of settings: (1) scenery backdrop, (2) integral
- Aspects: (1) place or location, (2) time or time period, (3) weather
- The primary world is the real world.
- A secondary world is a created world used in fantasy.

Point of View: the vantage point from which a story is written

Key question: Who is telling the story? How?

- First person point of view uses "I" to tell the story.
- Omniscient or third person point of view has an all-knowing narrator and uses third person.
- Limited omniscient point of view has an omniscient narrator, but the narrator knows the thoughts of only a few characters.
- In the objective point of view, events are reported with no interpretation.

Stylistic or poetic elements: how words are used for artistic effect

Key question: How are words used in special ways?

- Figurative language is the non-literal use of words to stand for other things. It includes imagery, personification, metaphors, connotation and denotation, motifs, archetypes, symbols, and allusions.
- Mood is how the story feels. Mood is related to tone.
- Irony is saying or doing the opposite of what is meant.
- Humor is the simultaneous juxtaposition of sense and nonsense to produce a surprising result.
- Sound and musical features of style include rhyme, rhythm, repetition, alliteration, consonance, assonance, and onomatopoeia.

Ready Resource 5.12 describes organizational patterns common to expository texts. Refer back to Ready Resource 5.9 for a list of concepts students need to understand in order to navigate diverse texts. The accompanying Online Resource box presents a website about nonfiction features, including organizational and language features, and the ways that reading nonfiction differs from reading other types of texts.

Nonfiction

CreativeClassroomOnline
www.creativeclassroom.org

Expository text: Organizational patterns.

Nonfiction texts are meant to give accurate and current information: to explain, describe, persuade, and retell. Examples include recipes, experiments, reports, letters, email, interviews, and even cartoons and illustrations. Informational texts may include elements used in narrative texts, such as characters and settings, but usually focus on real people, places, and events. A social studies text is a good example of an expository text that includes narrative elements. Most often, expository texts employ "expositional" or explanatory writing and common thinking patterns that readers must uncover in order to achieve comprehension. Patterns to be taught include:

Compare–contrast: The author describes how things are alike or different.

Keywords: both, same as, different, in contrast, while

Example: Bridge and euchre are both card games, but they are very different. In bridge, only four people can play together, whereas six or eight can play euchre. Bridge is difficult to learn. In contrast, euchre can be learned quickly. Both games involve use of strategies.

Cause–effect: The author explains causes and the results or effects.

Keywords: so, because, therefore, if . . . then, reasons why

Example: Bridge involves playing with a partner, so you have to be able to communicate with each other. If your partner bids two hearts, you have to know what that means. Some partners play weak twos because that allows them to bid with fewer points.

Description/explanation: The author describes or explains a topic by listing its characteristics and giving examples.

Keywords: for example, words for characteristics or traits

Example: The game of bridge involves a lot of strategy and learning a special language to cue your partner. The object is to tell your partner how many points you hold and what suit would be best to win tricks. For example, if I have at least five spades and I have twelve or thirteen points, I would say, "one spade." It is a challenging game that can be played at increasingly complicated levels.

Sequence: The author writes about items or events using an order, such as numerical or chronological.

Keywords: first, second, third, next, then, finally

Example: In a game of bridge, the first thing that happens is all the cards are dealt to four players. Then the dealer bids her best suit. Next, the player to the left bids. The third bidder is the dealer's partner. Finally, the fourth person bids in response to the other bids.

Problem–solution: The author describes a problem or question and then presents solutions or answers.

Keywords: problem, question, solution, answer

Example: It is a big problem when you play bridge with someone who uses different cues than you do. Since you can't communicate with each other, you will probably lose, if you get the contract. One solution is to discuss the cues you are going to use before you start the game. This is important, because you can't discuss your cues during the game itself.

5.12

THE CPS PROCESS AND TEXT CHARACTERISTICS

It is important to keep in mind that, for purposes of comprehension, text characteristics are tools, and tools are to be used, not just labeled and explained. Good readers use their understanding of text characteristics in all three stages of the CPS process to increase comprehension. For example, in the before and during stages, text characteristics suggest text purposes and ways to access information. Think about how visual features such as a hard cover versus a soft cover and a thick versus a thin book stimulate your own predictions and influence your initial text selection.

In the "after" stage, students show comprehension by creating new texts in response to reading. Students need explicit teaching about how to synthesize big ideas from expository texts using diverse response forms such as written summaries. Often, expository texts include conclusions at the end (as in this book) that may be used as examples for summary making. As students gain knowledge of diverse text characteristics, they develop the background to shape their ideas in more diverse text forms, including PowerPoint presentations, websites, and songs. Chapter 9 discusses the ways teachers can expand response options for students to summarize their learning.

Technology-Based Texts

Although distinctions between comprehension of Web-based texts and comprehension of traditional texts have not been completely defined, it is clear that both require a problem-solving stance. Carr (2008) points out, however, that problem solving on the Internet is of a different sort and it may be "making us stupid" (p. 56). While the Web provides easy access to information, online reading is largely "staccato" in nature, with readers surfing and clicking for "capsule summaries" and "info-snippets" (p. 60). Carr worries that we may lose the capacity for making deep meaning that requires personal associations, analogies, and inferences to create our own ideas. Certainly, many students find themselves overwhelmed and distracted when reading on the Web, because Internet texts often break some of the most basic rules of reading, such as moving the eyes in a line from left to right. Learners may feel defeated by the amount and variety of information that is available and the numerous decisions they must make in order to navigate the Web successfully. The result can be decreased comprehension (Block & Pressley, 2002).

Hypertext, with its "uncensored, unedited maelstrom of anything and everything that is always available" (Richardson, 2009, p. 35), seems to demand more developed problem solving than conventional texts require. At the same time, hypertext has the potential to engage students deeply in an unprecedented level of inquiry.

UNDERSTANDING WEB-BASED TEXTS

Digital literacy includes understanding both the benefits and dangers of technology (Coiro, 2005; Wolf & Barzillai, 2009). Access to the wealth of information on the Internet requires students to be wary and discriminating, to know how to manipulate and organize information from many different sources, to be "mindful" (Langer, 1997). Some students are bound to have difficulty with non-linear multimedia sites where the user must make decisions about where to focus attention and how to select where to go next. Once at an online destination, students need strategies for choosing and summarizing information.

Recent studies show differences in students' degree of proficiency in reading online (Coiro & Dobler, 2007). Less skilled learners find online texts more complex than print texts, especially those learners who lack general background knowledge or do not understand that they must actively make sense from texts. These students depend on teachers who can provide explicit instruction in how to use CPS with the Internet.

CPS AND ONLINE READING

Online reading seems to require even more intensive problem solving as choices expand and time collapses in the click-and-go frenzy. The flexible and coordinated use of CPS strategies is more important than ever in an online environment. Badke recommends students be taught to think of information gathered from the Internet "as a tool to solve a problem rather than the goal of research" (2009, p. 56). Teachers should show students how to use CPS during actual Internet work. The box below offers suggestions for teaching each stage of CPS for online texts.

The Internet is a fabulous tool for inquiry, but Internet use is complex. Readers must bring problem-solving processes to bear on search engines and websites. Internet texts demand that the reader engage in continual inference, prediction, and comprehension monitoring strategies to stay focused on the task at hand.

Applying CPS to Online Texts

BEFORE READING

Start with a clear **purpose**. The problem to be investigated has to be defined. It is not enough for a student to want information about animals. Specifics are necessary, or the student will be overwhelmed by the thousands of sites displayed by a search engine.

DURING READING

Gather data. Choose sites that are accurate, trustworthy, and objective and that have information that is useful in meeting the purpose or solving the problem. Sites with URLs that have the suffix .edu are school sponsored, while the suffix .gov indicates sites sponsored by government agencies. URLs that end in .org may be published by any type of organization, and .com indicates a site published by a business (Coiro & Dobler, 2007; Harris, 2007).

Use high-priority thinking strategies. Once the reader selects a page to study, she or he must go back and forth, investigating links and returning to the page, with the problem kept in mind.

AFTER READING

Summarize important ideas by deleting any information that is unrelated to the original purpose.

EXPLICIT TEACHING: SEARCH, NAVIGATE, EVALUATE ONLINE

To teach students how to get beyond the random clicking and superficial skimming that characterizes much online reading, teachers should explicitly teach how to choose links, navigate within websites, and determine if the information is trustworthy. Coiro (2005) recommends directly addressing obstacles that block students' progress toward becoming savvy users of online texts.

Choosing links

Problem: How to choose strategically from a long list of search results

Solution: Model how to *stop, think, link* using the following steps:

- Use an example Internet search and think aloud to show students how to predict which websites are best for exploring.
- Examine each entry, noting the significance of the website addresses, annotations, and file extensions.
- Make inferences about each site's topic, purpose, creator, and audience.
- Point out the problem with broad searches that yield thousands or millions of results.
- Explain additional clues in the URL, such as "AOL," which indicates it is a link on America Online and probably a personal Web page (Coiro & Dobler, 2004).
- Next, assign small groups to use structured questions to repeat the task, using another search list.
- Coach as they work.
- Debrief by asking each group to explain their answers and their Internet navigation strategies.
- Ask, What did you do? Why? What did you find? How do you know it is accurate and trustworthy information?

Navigating within a website

Problem: Deciding what to attend to at a site (Coiro, 2005)

Solution: Demonstrate how to preview a homepage using the following steps:

- Explain that homepages share many of the characteristics of print texts: they may have titles, subheads, charts, and boldface words that help organize the reader's thinking.
- Point out that Web pages can contain text conventions that befuddle even tech-savvy people.
- Show students the ineffectiveness of trying to skim by rapidly paging through large sections of text.
- Explain the need to preview multiple levels of a site, keeping in mind specific purposes, and demonstrate how to do this.

- Use think alouds to demonstrate: (1) how to find important information about a website's content, (2) how to evaluate information on a page and monitor the pathways within and between sites, and (3) how to stay on task and avoid becoming confused by irrelevant pathways.

A specific set of steps for teaching how to navigate within a website might be:

1. Point out the title of the page and the title of the website in the margin at the top of the window.

2. Think aloud to model how to scan menu choices. Hold the mouse over the navigational menus that often appear down the left-hand frame or across the top of the window, but do not click on them. Get a big picture of the information within the site.

3. Predict where each of the major links may lead, and anticipate a link's path through multiple website levels.

4. Explore interactive images, such as animations, images that change as the mouse is held over them, pop-up menus, and scroll bars, that may provide additional levels of information within the site.

5. Check the website's author and date. Identify who created the site and when it was last updated. Click on a homepage button labeled "About This Site" to get this information. If it is not available, consider what this indicates about the site (Coiro, 2005).

6. Try out any electronic supports, such as an organizational site map or internal search engine.

7. Decide whether information you need will be found at the site, and, if so, explore further. If not, return to the search results.

8. If you stay, rank-order the areas to explore first.

Determining if the information is trustworthy

Problem: Evaluating credibility of information

Solution: Model website evaluation using the questions in Ready Resource 5.13. Many Internet texts are not carefully edited, link to vast amounts of related information, or are designed to deceive or persuade readers (Coiro, 2003a, 2003b; Harris, 2007). Many hoax sites may be found on the Internet. Students must learn to evaluate the credibility of what they find and approach Internet texts with informed skepticism (Leu, Leu, & Coiro, 2004).

One method of teaching students to evaluate websites is to model answering the questions listed in Ready Resource 5.13. Coiro (2005) recommends finding a "hoax site" for this activity, such as the ones listed at right.

Hoax Sites

Growing a crop of Velcro, www.umbachconsulting.com/miscellany/velcro.html

Pacific Northwest Tree Octopus site, http://zapatopi.net/treeoctopus

Sample questions for modeling website evaluation.

- *Does the information make sense?* Compare with other texts and your background knowledge.
- *Where can I check the accuracy of the information?* Consider searching keywords to see what sites come up. Use an online dictionary or encyclopedia.
- *Who created the website and why?* Click on "About this Site" to get this information.
- *How objective is the information?* Google the author's name and check his or her credentials.
- *Is there a way to contact the site?* Look for an email address for a contact person, a phone number, or a mailing address.
- *Who is linking to this site?* Search the site to find links to similar websites and make judgments about the associations.

READY RESOURCE 5.13

Don't Overdo It

Explicit teaching of comprehension strategies, text characteristics, and other literacy concepts and skills can be essential, especially for low achievers. But explicit teaching may be unnecessary for some students. The amount and frequency should match student needs. What's more, explicit teaching does not guarantee transfer of the concepts to a new text or context. Transfer must be explicitly addressed when texts are introduced in other contexts and content areas. Sometimes it is enough to ask students about strategies previously learned and how they might be flexibly applied to this new situation. Students usually benefit from refresher demonstrations and coaching during new text use.

Teaching Comprehension of Technology-Based Texts

Classroom 2.0 Wiki, http://wiki.classroom20.com
How to use Web 2.0, including podcasts, blogs, webcasts, Voicethread, and Google Earth

Route 21, www.21stcenturyskills.org/route21
A resource portal provided by the Partnership for 21st Century Skills

Edutopia, www.edutopia.org
Archives best teaching practices

Apple Learning Interchange, http://edcommunity.apple.com/ali
Lessons, teaching ideas, and opportunities for collaboration

National Educational Technology Standards for Students,
www.iste.org/AM/Template.cfm?Section=NETS
Standards for Digital Age knowledge, skills, and attitudes

ONLINE RESOURCES WWW

Of course, explicit instruction is not the only tool in the box for increasing comprehension. Students need to spend most of their school time interacting with texts. Explicit teaching can increase the quality of this interaction, but so does skilled questioning by teachers and self-questioning by students, along with lots of discussion about what works and doesn't work. Another useful tool is WebQuests, inquiry-based Internet studies that may be found or created and may be lightly or heavily structured. WebQuest.Org offers 2,500 examples organized by topic, rubrics to evaluate sites' value, and an easy-to-use template.

snapshot revisited

Jane Waskeiwitz teaches first graders, but she does not underestimate their capacity to comprehend. She is both committed to and successful at compelling these young children to increase their comprehension strategy repertoires. It is not a secret why she succeeds. She has become skilled at explicit teaching of CPS, which she adapts for these young children. She also shows all of us that a teacher can remain artful while devoting segments of time each day to a kind of teaching that is very structured. Artistic teachers understand that their students need to master a problem-solving skill-set over time, if they are to become independent users of CPS to construct personal meaning.

All artistry demands discipline and skill, but teachers do not have to follow somebody else's script entirely. Rigidity is a mark of "mindlessness" (Langer, 1997). We need teachers who are fully aware of comprehension best practices and can carefully adapt them to "specific content, process, and context elements" (National Staff Development Council, 2001). Indeed, the influential and controversial National Reading Panel report recommended that teachers be expected to be decision makers, not simply direction followers (2000). Artistry is about using tools in diverse ways to create meaningful products. Explicit teaching is a tool that teachers may use in diverse ways to help students become creative meaning makers.

Conclusion

Explicit teaching lets students in on the purposes of lesson agendas at the outset. Most important, it unveils the ways good comprehenders think. Explicit teaching happens during mini-lessons that focus on the why of thinking (purposes); the what (actual content or skills, including labels); and the when, where, and how (including demonstration, with several examples). The mnemonic I Do (teacher purpose-sets, shows, and explains), We Do (teacher scaffolded students' practice and provides coaching), You Do (student practices, rehearses, and reflects independently) encapsulates the process (Deshler & Schumaker, 1990). A further Re-Do step allows students to revise based on feedback. To be effective, this sequence should be continually repeated with a variety of texts throughout every school day and in every content area. The goal is for students to become increasingly independent in initiating strategy use and to feel pride in successfully problem-solving texts.

To do explicit teaching, teachers must have personal competence and self-awareness. They can't teach what they don't know or can't do (Reutzel, 2007). Clear teaching of comprehension strategies is absolutely necessary and should be the responsibility of all teachers in all subject areas—not only during reading time. Teachers develop explicit instruction through hard work, and it sometimes takes a dozen practices to get the hang of talking about thought processes. Part of the reason is that most thinking is visual (non-verbal), and teachers need to use words to describe something that exists beyond words. Ready Resource 5.3 can help teachers compose brief explanations for their thinking strategies.

This chapter also explained how explicit teaching applies to text characteristics. It explained the step-by-step procedure and gave examples for how to use a seemingly rigid, but powerful routine in flexible ways to meet the needs of students of differing maturity. Experts agree that "teachers must teach comprehension explicitly, beginning in the primary grades and continuing through high school" (RAND, 2002, p. 10). Teacher expertise makes all the difference. Once again, teachers take center stage in the proposal to put comprehension first in literacy and content area curriculum and instruction.

CHAPTER 5 big ideas

The following are examples of big ideas from this chapter that you can use to synthesize your own high-priority list of big ideas for teaching comprehension strategies and text characteristics.

1. Explicit comprehension lessons work because they make thinking visible.

2. Explicit teaching is characterized by purposeful demonstration and explanation followed by scaffolding and coaching students' practice.

3. Explicit teaching might appear to be easy, but it takes practice to be clear and specific.

4. Less able learners and primary students are capable of learning to apply comprehension strategies and use text characteristics, with explicit instruction.

5. It is important to explicitly teach a coordinated set of comprehension strategies.

6. Use of comprehension monitoring and fix-ups is part of a high-priority set of strategies that should be taught explicitly.

7. The characteristics of diverse texts, especially their unique purposes and structures, should be taught explicitly.

8. Students should be taught explicitly how to apply CPS strategies to digital texts, especially for Internet inquiry.

a look ahead

Critical to successful comprehension is student motivation. The best practice of using motivation strategies to cause students to engage in Comprehension Problem Solving is the focus of the next chapter. The chapter explains key aspects of motivation, with attention to ways to help students experience *intrinsic* motivation.

CHAPTER 5 response options

Complete the following activities in small groups, if possible.

1. Discuss three to five of the big ideas from the chapter that you think are most important. Compare your list with those of your classmates.

2. Return to the questions at the start of the chapter to evaluate your comprehension. Choose the question that you most want to discuss or investigate further.

3. Choose a strategy other than "image/visualize" from the CPS process. Prepare a brief explanation and develop reasons to use the strategy. Present your thoughts to a group in an explicit five-minute lesson.

4. Recall a time when you provided scaffolding to someone or when someone scaffolded for you. Analyze all the aspects of that experience to hone in on why it helped.

5. If you have access to students, try the six-day plan for teaching comprehension strategies described in Ready Resource 5.6.

6. Explain why you think it takes more time for students to learn to comprehend than to decode words.

7. Locate examples of expository text characteristics mentioned in this chapter. See Ready Resource 5.12.

8. Make a "cue card" that summarizes key steps in explicit teaching. Choose a technological text and prepare an explicit lesson on how to use a specific characteristic effectively.

9. Create a WebQuest to help students learn about comprehension strategies or about text characteristics.

10. Visit one of the websites recommended to help teachers understand Web 2.0 technology. Share with your classmates one important idea for teaching comprehension that you find. Practice using the LWL response format: List big ideas you LEARNED, ideas you WONDER about, and teaching strategies you LIKE.

CHILDREN'S LITERATURE CITED

Gag, W. (1928). *Millions of cats.* New York: Coward-McCann.

Using Motivation Strategies to Engage Comprehension

This chapter focuses on the role motivation plays in causing students to engage in Comprehension Problem Solving. Once again, the Five Factors are used as organizers, this time to examine how to increase students' intrinsic motivation to comprehend. The chapter describes specific aspects of motivation that hold special promise for engaging students, including worthy goals, interest, choice, group work, feedback, and diverse texts, especially digital ones.

153

important questions

1. What is motivation? What does it have to do with engagement?
2. How are motivation and engagement connected to comprehension?
3. How can teachers adjust the Five Factors to increase students' motivation and engagement?
4. What are the differences between intrinsic and extrinsic motivation, and why are these differences important for comprehension instruction?
5. How can teachers use content goals, interest, choice, group work, and feedback to motivate students to engage in the work of comprehension?
6. What are examples of motivational practices that are questionable—not consistent with inquiry-based comprehension instruction aimed at problem solving for big ideas?
7. How can teachers use texts to engage students so that comprehension increases?
8. What makes electronic texts motivating, and how can teachers use them to increase comprehension?

Introduction

> Dad: Do you read for fun?
> Jake: No, I read for points now.
> Dad: Could you read for fun?
> Jake: Sorry, Dad, I don't read for fun anymore.
>
> R. VAN VALKENBURG

Although games, points, stamps, and snappy attention-getters may seem to engage students, their effects are temporary. Authentic engagement occurs only when students are cognitively involved and understanding is the focus. Unless students are increasing understanding, their engagement falters. Tools such as those just listed become entertaining gadgets. Moreover, evidence shows that traditional motivational tools such as grades, tracking, and competition actually have negative effects on *intrinsic* motivation to learn (see the work of John Guthrie and Alfie Kahn).

Intrinsic motivation works from the inside out. It is internal, coming from students' own will and desire to learn or do a task because they see inherent worth in the learning and doing. The opposite is *extrinsic* motivation, which focuses on doing something to get a reward that is outside oneself. External reinforcers, such as coupons and money, provide limited control over behavior; when they are removed, the behavior is likely to stop (Eisner, 2002a). The interchange between Jake and his dad illustrates the problem of imposing extrinsic reinforcers on good readers like Jake. Jake was already reading when he started school, but the school had purchased a commercial program that uses points to extrinsically motivate children to read. The goal became points, not comprehension.

Think about how long you would keep *working* if you didn't get paid. Now think about activities you do for *fun*. Fun activities are viewed as self-rewarding ones that you would do without pay, grades, or points. Reading should be fun. It should be taught so that students perceive it as enjoyable. The author of *The Read Aloud Handbook* (2006), Jim Trelease, explains, "Reading is an accrued skill. Humans are pleasure oriented. Children need to find more pleasure than pain in reading."

Understanding is essential for enjoyment. Comprehension is understanding achieved by problem solving that focuses on personal meaning. Comprehension frequently culminates in the "ah-ha" experience. This can happen in the final stages of the "during" part of CPS and in the "after" stage, when the reader is synthesizing, transforming, and shaping big ideas. When a person suddenly understands a concept or thinks of a problem solution, it is definitely pleasurable. This chapter addresses classroom conditions that set students up for the "ah-ha" or insight, which often stems from the "ha-ha" experience and results in the sensation of being in a good humor (Cornett, 2006; Koestler, 1964).

Again, as in previous chapters, the focus is on the Five Factors that influence comprehension: (1) learner characteristics, (2) how the comprehension task is defined, (3) the texts used, (4) the classroom context, and (5) best teaching practices. In particular, calls to expand the current concept of the literacy task beyond a few reading components often recommend motivation be included as an essential (Allington, 2005c; Gambrell, Malloy, & Mazzoni, 2007). It is indeed unimaginable that anyone could become a good reader, by any definition, without intrinsic motivation to learn. And "good" reading is all about comprehension. The conclusion: motivation is a foundation for comprehension. It is motivation that causes students to engage in problem solving to make meaning.

The setting for this chapter's snapshot is a reading center that serves struggling readers. The center's director has put comprehension first, and motivation strategies are primary building blocks of her effort. The goal is to help students like Justin, who came to the center with this perspective: "I'd rather clean my room than read. I just don't get it." Key motivational strategies are printed in boldface, along with ideas that reflect key motivational concepts.

classroom snapshot

MOTIVATING TO ENGAGE STRUGGLING LEARNERS

Over the door to the reading center is a big sign: "Come in to Laugh and Learn." Right inside on a table is a **Joke Box** that holds a half dozen or more joke books. Also on the table is a stack of blank **"funny bones."** (See Ready Resource 6.1.) A boy arrives and stops to put a funny bone in the box. His name is Brad.

"Want to try it out on me?" I ask.

"Sure!" He smiles broadly and unfolds the bone-shaped paper. "What happened when Batman and Robin got run over by a semi?" Brad stumbles over the word "happened," and I notice he says "truck" for the word "semi" written on his funny bone. He looks up at me with huge brown eyes and smiles even more broadly. I try to think of something that would make sense.

"Um, they had to go to the hospital for heroes?" I guess.

Brad's funny bone.

What happened when Batman and Robin got run over by a semi?

READY RESOURCE
6.1

"Well, that sorta makes sense," Brad responds, "but it's not very funny."

"Oh, it has to be a *funny* answer?" I say, and we both know I'm kidding. "Okay, I give up."

"Flatman and Ribbon!" Brad says proudly.

It is a pretty good answer, so I can genuinely laugh, and Brad is obviously pleased with himself.

"So, I thought this was a reading center. What's with the jokes and riddles?" I ask Brad.

"Well, I read the riddle," Brad explains, and I wait, because he seems to have more to say. **"You have to use problem solving to understand riddles,"** he says, and he points to a **big poster** that lists comprehension problem-solving strategies. Then he continues, "The answer comes from the clues in the question. **The answer has to make sense,**" he finishes.

"And nonsense!" I add.

"Yeah, it has to be funny," Brad says.

"So, what makes *funny?*" I ask, knowing I'm really pushing him, but I'm interested in what he is thinking. It is a hard question, but Brad responds quickly.

"It has to be a **new way of thinking,** you know, like bat rhymes with flat and ribbon sounds like robin, but it is how it would look that also makes it funny. Like they would both be squashed like paper, but still alive," Brad explains.

"Wow, so it is the sounds of words *and* the images in your brain that make it funny?" I ask.

"Yeah, it is funny sense," he says, and he begins to look around into the center. He sees his tutor, Dale.

"Gotta go," he says, and I'm dismissed.

Move at IT

More children start arriving, and many of them are wearing big **buttons with the letters IT** in the center. I approach three girls who all are wearing IT buttons.

"What's the IT?" I ask.

"Everybody's is different," one girl explains.

"What is an IT?" I press on.

"Something you want to learn about, like horses. I want to do dressage someday," a different girl explains.

"Is that like horse dancing?" I ask.

"Sorta. Yeah, I guess it is, but it takes a lot of work to train the horse to do it," she says.

"What about you?" I ask the girl who hasn't spoken.

"I want to be able to read a whole *Harry Potter* book," she says. "At least, that is my IT right now."

"Oh, so the **IT can change?**" I ask. All three nod their heads in the affirmative. "Why's that?"

"Well, **an IT is your goal right now.** When we come to the center, we read books or use the Internet to find more information about the IT we picked. But after a while you can pick a different thing you want to study," the girl whose IT is learning about dressage explains.

"Sounds interesting, but I thought this was a *reading* center," I say.

"It is, but we can read about stuff related to our IT, and that is more interesting. I used to hate reading. Actually, I still hate to fill out worksheets and write answers to questions back in my real class," one of the girls says. I realize I didn't ask about her IT, so I do.

"I love music," she says. "My IT is to write my own songs. I listen to CDs with Suzanne and she **shows me strategies** to think about the lyrics—that's the song's words," she explains.

"What do you mean, 'strategies'?" I ask, and all three turn to point at the same poster that Brad showed me, which displays comprehension problem-solving strategies.

"The chart is about problem solving," I say. "How is that related to 'strategies'?"

The girl who loves music explains, "We are all learning to use the problem-solving strategies to comprehend. Like see the 'purpose-set' under 'before'? The purpose is to figure out the meaning. That's the problem. I get to use song lyrics to practice the strategies."

"I think I understand," I say. "So, have you written any songs yet?" I ask.

"Yeah, three, want to see?" she says. "They're on the computer, and I'm learning how to use Garage Band to add a melody," she adds. She is so excited she takes my sleeve and tugs me toward the computer.

Of course, I'm delighted to be dragged along, and all four of us go together. Suzanne, a tutor, appears, and at the computer she coaches Cheree to get her files and show me her songs. The other two girls listen for a bit and then find their own tutors.

Later, I talk with Dale, Brad's tutor, and Suzanne about my conversations with the kids. I ask them about the effects of the riddles and the IT buttons.

"The riddles are wonderful tools to engage students in problem solving," Dale says. "They are small texts that are great places to start. They are the perfect setup, because there is a question, and the answer requires all kinds of meaning making, from inferring to imaging. Riddles are intrinsically motivating to the kids, because they make the kids feel smart when they share them. Of course, they find some real groaners."

"How is it going with the IT buttons?" I ask.

"The IT buttons and the IT books have really helped my children engage," Dale explains. "For example, Brad was nonresponsive at first. I think he thought we were just going to do flash cards and computer drills, like I observed his teacher using with the kids at a low level. He was not motivated and did not want to **engage.** But, when I showed him that the letters in "motivate" could be rearranged to spell "move at IT" and explained he could choose his own IT, he got interested. His IT is comic books, of course, and they are working great as texts for teaching him comprehension problem solving."

Suzanne seems to concur, because she nods several times and then jumps in. "Yeah, it really is incredible how letting the kids choose goals and focus on their interests has caused them to want to engage the problem-solving strategies. I mean, this kind of thinking is hard, even for me sometimes, and these are the kids in the low group, the ones we just see at the half-round teacher tables having to grind through those flimsy decodable books. Sure, they need more work with vocabulary and fluency, but take Cheree. She's in the fourth grade. She can think just fine, and it is a joy to see her inferring and synthesizing big ideas from songs. And some of the songs are pretty deep. You know, she wanted to work on "Hey Jude," the Beatles song, and I couldn't believe the big ideas. She is a smart girl. I'm so glad she gets to come to the center, where comprehension is put first."

The Motivation Problem

Motivation is a common problem of students struggling to learn to read. It is not unusual to hear them report some degree of dislike for the task of reading, and some say outright that they hate it. These are the students who can appear sulky, inattentive, and unengaged in regular classroom contexts. They can be passive and unresponsive to teacher questions. They rarely volunteer during discussions. Even worse, I've seen students who are low performers cover their face and tear up when forced to read aloud in front of peers.

Motivation is necessary for comprehension. Kids need to understand what comprehension is, if they are to head in that direction, but they also need to grasp the concept of motivation. How do you make the abstract concept of motivation clear to a six-year-old? At the reading center, motivation was explained in kid terms. In a moment of insight, it became clear that the letters in the word *motivate* could be rearranged to address the goal of motivation. Motivation does mean to "move at it"—to make an effort to reach an "it" or goal. So the IT buttons were invented, and the teachers and tutors devised strategies to help students set IT goals to work toward. Goals ranged from moving up to second grade to getting a driver's license. Comprehension instruction was then connected to these goals every day. For example, a booklet to prepare for the driver's licensing test became the main text for one 15-year-old.

Gathering Data About Motivation

Information about comprehension problems may be gathered in many ways and from many sources. Classroom observations and interviews are very valuable. (Appendices A and B include example tools.)

COMMON CHALLENGES

Over many years I have made dozens of observations of unsuccessful readers. Common patterns emerged: classroom context, texts used, and teaching practices reflected a narrow interpretation of the reading task that left comprehension out.

One unmotivating practice, round robin reading (cold, unprepared oral reading), is still used in classrooms, usually with small groups, but sometimes with whole classes. Oral reading can be unbearably painful for students—lots of huffing and puffing, spitting and sputtering as they attempt to "sound out" words. Struggling learners can experience humiliation because of a non-fluent reading performance in front of peers. Often, teachers end up just telling students unknown words. Other children may even be allowed to supply unknown words, which denies the opportunity to problem solve to those who need it. Unfortunately, it is still unusual to hear teachers cue students to use word solving tools such as "what's a part you know?" or "look at how it starts and think of what would make sense."

Teachers regularly ask struggling readers to read from decodable books (small paperbacks with a high percentage of phonetically regular words). Older students are often given similar material, without the small book format. Such special "reading" texts used with struggling students may offer little potential for discussion and simply are not interesting. It would be hard for the best reader to make much meaning of sentences along the lines of "Dan can fan a man." I recently met with a special education teacher in Knoxville to try to extract some potential from a set of such texts she was required to use. The content was so meager I couldn't get beyond a "topic" answer to the question, "What was the story about?" The kinds of big ideas that open up kids to "truths of the universe" were unavailable, so the "stories" were unmotivating.

Overall reading achievement scores are still used to group together kids who are experiencing the most problems. Some are left in the same group for a whole year or more. There they languish, receiving low-level instruction that focuses on pieces of reading. Comprehension is not put first, and when it is addressed, it is often about firing questions at students that ask for memory responses—extracting facts, not constructing meaning.

INTERVIEWS

As mentioned in previous chapters, assessment and interviews can yield telling information. Interviews were prominent in the assessment package for the reading center that was the setting for this chapter's snapshot. Teachers and parents can be the subjects of interviews, as well as students.

Teacher interviews

Appendix A.2 contains an example tool to use for teacher and parent interviews. Interviews conducted under the auspices of the reading center in the snapshot targeted the teachers of classrooms from which the center students came. The most common teacher responses to questions such as "What is the goal of reading instruction?" were comments like "to get students to grade level" or "to do well on end-of-year tests." Teachers talked about the need for students to acquire "sight words" (depending on the grade level), phonics skills, and fluency (word accuracy and rate targets by grade level), but few ever articulated a substantial focus on comprehension. Those who did mention comprehension described student retelling of literacy elements (emphasizing characters, setting, and plot); few talked about theme generation and big idea generalizations as goals. Teachers said they did not directly teach a concept of what reading is, nor a concept of what good readers do, and many seemed confused by follow-up questions related to meaning making and problem solving. Few could give examples of what their students were interested in, but they could list lots of problems, especially related to words and behavior (attention, concentration, and focus inadequacies).

Parent interviews

Interviews of parents were also a part of the reading center's assessment protocol. Parents seemed to be either anxious or passive. The anxious parents had tried everything from drilling their children daily with sight word cards to buying expensive computer software. Some of the software had interactive capability, allowing kids to click words for sound and meaning, and some used texts that did have significant content (e.g., traditional fairy tale stories). Passive parents just wanted somebody to fix their children. They seemed tired or at a loss and often said they didn't have time to read personally or read to their children because of work and home responsibilities.

Student interviews

Student interviews are valuable tools to gain insight into how learners think about comprehension (see Appendix A.1 for sample interview questions). Kids with reading problems often articulate some variation on the following misguided conclusions:

- Reading is pronouncing words correctly and fast.
- Good readers are fast readers who know all the words and can answer the teacher's questions.
- Reading is hard because knowing all the words is hard.
- Reading is not fun.
- I am not a good reader.

It is interesting that many students who think they aren't good readers still say they want a turn to read out loud in their classrooms. It seems that the need for attention and to be part of the group trumps the humiliation of poor oral reading performance.

Frontloading Motivation

he problems that students experience in learning to read are manifested in a range of symptoms (see Chapter 1). Lack of motivation to learn to read is a common problem, which implies that motivational needs have to be addressed. While developmental considerations affect the task of learning to read print (e.g., phonemic awareness is a foundation for phonics learning), motivation transcends ages and stages in all aspects of literacy development. Any plan to increase reading achievement has to have a substantial motivational component. Since the goal of reading is comprehension, this means using motivational strategies to engage comprehension problem-solving strategies.

Any teacher who has worked with students with reading difficulties has seen evidence of motivational problems. Students may have negative attitudes and misperceptions that block meaning-focused engagement with text. These are children who

- have learned to dislike reading. They don't want to read because of negative experiences, such as being laughed at when they have read aloud.
- lack sub-skills (e.g., phonics) and resist out-of-context drills with isolated letters/sounds and words. They perceive these as meaningless or of little purpose in their current worldview.
- don't find reading interesting. The texts used are not connected to personal interests, or the text formats are not interesting (e.g., all texts are traditional print texts).
- think reading is basically pronouncing words correctly, and they reject this goal because it seems unattainable or unimportant.

These students are telling us something important about reading: It isn't just about adding up sub-skills. It is first and foremost about wanting to understand, to make meaning that has a personal connection. Students have to have the will to gain the skill. It isn't that many students with difficulties *can't* read, it's just that they *won't*. A key question for educators is "How can we cause students to want to?"

The reading center described in the snapshot is not a research clinic, but it does boast dozens of success stories. Student folders are evidence of books read, projects created to show comprehension, words learned, CPS strategies mastered, and so forth. More gratifying, however, are the stories of children who came to the center who are now adults. One man I spoke with is now a married father in graduate school. He remembers making his Good Reader person by tracing his own body and adding CPS strategies to body parts as he learned them. Another former student is now an accountant. His father brought him to the reading center for two years. His father told me Justin still has his IT button.

Motivation and Comprehension

Teaching a boy how to scrub his neck is no guarantee he'll have a clean neck. . . . If he knows how but doesn't want to wash his neck, it's going to stay dirty. But when that boy meets the right girl, he'll have a clean neck—thus, you need the combination of know-how and motivation.

JIM TRELEASE

Motivation involves making a commitment to do a task that is perceived as important. It is about being willing to expend energy to reach a goal. Motivation is very much tied up with hopes and dreams, visions and aspirations. But aspirations have to be undergirded with skill. Inspiration is not enough to bring about achievement of goals. Desire to understand or comprehend seems to be innate, but there is no doubt that some children don't develop their innate problem-solving capacities or do not apply them to mainstream school texts. Comprehension is a highly cognitive task. Guthrie (2004) explains that even a "motivated reader is not likely to automatically gain complex cognitive competencies independently and an unmotivated reader is quite unlikely to gain these reading competencies at all" (p. 351).

Motivation is not an extra or add-on when it comes to comprehension. It is a "necessary part of a comprehensive plan for reading instruction that ensures growth in reading comprehension" (Guthrie, 2004, p. 351; Gambrell, Malloy, & Mazzoni, 2007). In other words, instruction that focuses on phonemic awareness, the alphabetic principle, phonics, vocabulary, and fluency, without regard for motivation, is not likely to produce deep comprehension gains. Witness the recent results from the Reading First program, which concentrated on reading sub-skills and did not put comprehension first (IES, 2008).

MOTIVATION AND THE FIVE FACTORS

Comprehension and motivation are integrally connected; you don't get one without the other (Duke, 2001). There is abundant evidence for substantial connections between motivation and comprehension. Students who lack knowledge, skills, or the will to understand are not likely to comprehend well (RAND, 2002). Studies of intrinsically motivated learners show these learners are

- more proficient readers (i.e., use comprehension strategies more effectively to make meaning) than less engaged and less intrinsically motivated children. This holds true for both advantaged and disadvantaged populations (e.g., Guthrie, Wigfield, & Von Secker, 2000; Strickland, 2001).
- more knowledgeable, and because they know more about subjects they are more likely to understand new texts, regardless of their general aptitude. The finding that both general knowledge and specific subject knowledge account for variability in comprehension achievement suggests it is very important to motivate students to build background knowledge (RAND, 2002).
- purposeful and goal-directed, and they become better comprehenders than less purposeful and less goal-directed readers.
- more likely to see learning as fun (DeMoss & Morris, 2002).
- willing to work hard because they see learning as a challenge (DeMoss & Morris, 2002).

With regard to comprehension, intrinsically motivated learners saw the task as purposeful. They were goal-directed and oriented toward understanding, not just accumulating facts (DeMoss & Morris, 2002). These learners received teaching at school and at home that responded to their interests, which is important because interest has a significant effect on comprehension. Intrinsically motivated learners had the advantage of growing up surrounded by high-interest texts that they could comfortably read at school and at home (RAND, 2002). Ready Resource 6.2 summarizes other motivational connections to comprehen-

Five Factors: Concepts for creating a motivation rubric.

1 MOTIVATED LEARNERS

- Interested: have preferences and favorites
- Inquiring: are curious and like to explore
- Independent: want choices-related texts, tasks, and contexts
- Ownership/control: know CPS strategies, including comprehension and Word Fix-Ups
- Capable: see self as competent, able to do things, find answers, and solve problems

2 MOTIVATING TASKS

- Worthy: viewed as important and useful
- Novel: different; involve using new media, tools, and technologies
- Creative: allow diverse solutions and surprising results
- Challenging: cause a degree of stretching
- Fun: open-ended, multisensory, exploratory

3 MOTIVATING TEXTS

- Useful: relevant
- Novel: unusual
- Content-rich: packed with important information

- Appropriate: well suited to students
- Artful: use words and images in creative ways
- Real-life: reflect the kinds of texts used outside of school—not worksheets and computer drills (Tompkins, 2003)

4 MOTIVATING TEACHER

- Enthusiastic: shows passion for learning and teaching
- Knowledgeable: is well versed in content and pedagogy
- Positive: shows good humor and likes students
- Flexible: changes perspectives and gears easily
- Creative problem solver: can generate diverse ways to meet student needs
- Uses best practices: employs strategies backed by research and professional wisdom

5 MOTIVATING CONTEXTS

- Aesthetic: stimulating, "living rooms" rich in communication opportunities
- Comfortable: physically and mentally
- Orderly, but not rigid
- Social: constructed to facilitate group work, performances, and audiences

READY RESOURCE 6.2

sion using the Five Factor model. Use them to create a rubric for motivation that promotes comprehension.

FULFILLING BASIC LEARNER NEEDS

Guthrie (2004) explains that while a motivated reader will not automatically gain complex cognitive competencies independently, an unmotivated reader is "quite unlikely to gain these reading competencies at all" (p. 351). Comprehension success for all learners thus depends on teaching practices, tasks, texts, and learning contexts that have motivational properties.

Motivation stems from common needs all learners possess. Abraham Maslow long ago envisioned a "hierarchy of needs" (1968) that incorporates the ABCs—the need for achievement, belonging, and control—that can help contribute to intrinsic motivation. For classroom purposes, use the ABCs to devise differentiated instruction that moves students toward learning for its own sake: intrinsic motivation to learn.

Achievement needs

When a task is perceived to increase knowledge and competence, students will be motivated to engage in the task to fulfill *achievement* needs. The task must be seen as important. For example, if students are shown how CPS strategies can help them become better readers, including more skilled users of computer-based texts, they lock on to this relevance to their lives. Activities that enable and encourage students to take responsibility can increase reading achievement, too. For example, when teachers provide somewhat challenging reading passages, students exert effort and persist to meet the challenge (RAND, 2002).

Belonging needs

Tasks that involve group work fulfill the *belonging* need. For example, class book clubs and small group text response projects allow students to feel part of a group. Teaching strategies and texts that cause students to feel isolated from the group create motivational problems. Students disengage or never engage in the first place (DeMoss & Morris, 2002).

Human beings are social animals. It is motivating to be a part of and make contributions to groups we perceive as important.

Control needs

As students mature, they increasingly feel the need to *control* their own lives. When teachers offer choices, students are motivated by this chance to fulfill control needs and become more independent. Teaching CPS puts students in control of how to solve the comprehension problem.

Ready Resource 6.2 lists "The Big C's," an alternative look at how motivational factors build on the needs for achievement, belonging, and control.

Teaching That Motivates Through Engagement

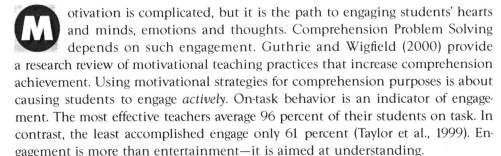otivation is complicated, but it is the path to engaging students' hearts and minds, emotions and thoughts. Comprehension Problem Solving depends on such engagement. Guthrie and Wigfield (2000) provide a research review of motivational teaching practices that increase comprehension achievement. Using motivational strategies for comprehension purposes is about causing students to engage *actively*. On-task behavior is an indicator of engagement. The most effective teachers average 96 percent of their students on task. In contrast, the least accomplished engage only 61 percent (Taylor et al., 1999). Engagement is more than entertainment—it is aimed at understanding.

Motivation: The big C's.

These motivational factors elaborate on basic learner needs. Teachers should design and implement practices that create or offer opportunities for students to

- commit to goals, hopes, and dreams.
- develop a comprehension problem-solving strategy repertoire.
- use comprehension (product) response options, including composition options.
- use creative problem-solving tools.
- develop communication skills, including the language arts and fine and performing arts.
- focus on constructing meaning.
- cognitively engage by first concentrating and focusing.
- develop compassion and empathy that allow extended viewpoints.
- have choices based on interests and preferences.

- develop competence through developed capabilities that build independence.
- find courage to take risks and experiment.
- take control over their own efforts.
- meet challenges to "stretch" thinking.
- build confidence because they believe success is possible.
- collaborate and cooperate with others.
- experience consequences that *naturally* reward efforts.
- learn in a classroom culture that is supportive.
- be part of communities to which they contribute.
- learn content that is substantive and important.

READY RESOURCE 6.3

Sources: Cornett, 2011; Turner & Paris, 1995.

The motivational practices addressed in the following sections have strong support in research for their ability to increase comprehension. These practices tap basic learner needs and enhance engagement because they (1) teach to interests, (2) offer choice, (3) focus on content goals, (4) use collaborative group work, and (5) give constructive feedback. The practices are interrelated; for example, use of group work and choice both increase interest.

To understand the power of these practices, consider the large effect sizes on comprehension and motivation for four of the practices (see Ready Resource 6.4). Contrast this information with Guthrie's (2004) finding that phonics instruction had an effect size of only .27 on reading achievement for grades 2 through 6.

TEACH TO INTERESTS

The first study of student interests took place over a hundred years ago, in 1897. Since then, more than five hundred studies have been conducted (Sebesta, 2003). Most of us know that becoming successful at almost anything requires becoming interested in the activity and feeling that doing it is enjoyable.

Interest has astounding effects on comprehension. It has been found to account for more than twenty-five percent of the variance in reading comprehension

Motivation practices and their effects.

How do factors like interest and choice affect comprehension and motivation? Guthrie (2004) reports the following effect sizes (ES) for several factors. ES is shown for comprehension and for motivation (in parentheses).

	COMPREHENSION	MOTIVATION
1. Using interest (e.g., interesting texts)	1.64	(1.15)
2. Giving students choices	N/A	(.95)
3. Focusing on understanding important content	.87	(.72)
4. Providing opportunities to work collaboratively	.48	(.52)

Note: The effect size for comprehension strategies instruction was .80.

0 = no difference

.20 = small effect
(move from 50th to 58th percentile)

.50 = moderate effect
(move from 50th to 69th percentile)

.80 = large effect
(move from 50th to 79th percentile)

1.00 = treatment's mean 1 SD higher than control

*The effect size (ES) is how much the mean of the experimental group exceeded that of the control group on the outcomes, measured in standard deviations (SD). The ES is valuable because it allows conversion of outcomes from very different studies to one metric so that average ES can be calculated and compared. ES is considered the "most essential information from studies because it allows a statement about the relative magnitude of study outcomes and can be combined across studies" (p. 114). Average effect size can be calculated by weighting sample sizes.

Source: Guthrie, 2004.

(Sebesta, 2003). That's not surprising, since interest is a driving force for inquiry. It is often the spark that lights the fire of problem solving. Unfortunately, in interviews with students about memorable school experiences, Starko did not find a single student who remembered being allowed to study a personal interest (1995). All lessons cannot be interest-based, but teachers can shift the balance and foster achievement that grows from motivation.

Early studies of student interest focused on how to alter interest and develop "taste." Since then, the focus has broadened to how to teach to student interests and help students develop new interests. Teachers do so through differentiated instruction. Here are examples:

1. **Assess.** Start the school year by using an interest inventory or doing interest interviews. For example, see the Background Inventory (Appendix A.1).

2. **Schedule time.** Give opportunities for students to read texts that interest them (e.g., daily independent reading time).

3. **Expand interests.** Introduce new texts about commonly interesting topics. Do book talks, display new texts, and read aloud challenging books that are too difficult for students to read independently but at their interest level. Most students are drawn to learning about animals, enjoy humor, and are curious about successful people in every facet of life, ranging from sportscaster to scientist.

4. **Integrate technology.** Set up ongoing opportunities for research on the Internet. For example, students may be encouraged to become "experts" on topics, people, places, or events. Students in the reading center were urged to start collections that provoked research. Students chose such foci as rocks, buttons, shells, and beer cans (with parent permission). The websites shown at right offer useful applications that can guide students through inquiry into personally interesting topics.

Research and Inquiry

Mindmanager, www.mindman.com

Mindjet, www.mindjet.com

Inspiration, www.strategictransitions.com

ONLINE RESOURCES

5. **Promote questioning.** Intriguing questions are intrinsically motivating and are key components of an inquiry-oriented approach to comprehension (Guthrie, 2004). Questions posed by students themselves are more powerful than teachers' questions when it comes to engaging complex thinking. Teachers can scaffold student question generation by posting generic questions and stems such as the Five W + H questions. Use a Question Box to invite students to contribute "I wonder about . . ." comments and questions for discussions.

6. **Integrate concrete activities.** Use engaging multisensory activities with texts. For example, precede text reading with drama activities related to the ideas to be found in the text content, to increase comprehension. After reading, use drama strategies to synthesize understanding, which can increase comprehension, too (Deasy, 2002; DeMoss & Morris, 2002).

7. **Discuss.** Plan regular time for students to engage in open-ended conversations about their interests. This may occur in small groups or with the whole group, as in the popular opening Circle Meeting used in many schools. Circle Meetings are more than show-and-tell times. They focus on students raising thoughtful questions and discussing substantive concerns about current issues in their lives. Teachers need to teach students explicitly how to participate meaningfully. See Chapter 7 for discussion guidelines.

8. **Combine factors.** Integrate interest with choice, content goals, group work, and feedback. The next section describes how to do this.

PROVIDE CHOICE

The power of choice has been made clear in many experiments. For example, when children were given puzzles to assemble or collage materials to use and were given the choice about how to do so, they had more intrinsic motivation to repeat the task. Students in the choice group were significantly more intrinsically motivated, even after a two-week lapse time, and they stuck with the task longer, as compared to no-choice students (Amabile, 1996). What's more, students in choice groups produced more creative products. Comprehension is much more than assembling puzzles, but it depends similarly on intrinsic motivation to engage students in problem solving. Choice plays a "crucial role in intrinsic motivation" (p. 169).

The idea of motivating students by giving them choice is not new. Decades ago, Daniel Fader's Hooked on Books program showed the power of choice in motivating recalcitrant boys to read (Fader & McNeil, 1976). Choice is credited with increasing the quantity of student reading and student adeptness in using comprehension strategies (Guthrie, 2004; RAND, 2002). Why? Choice activates intrinsic motivation, which causes students to be more engaged, so they put forth more effort.

Teachers can offer small choices that make big differences. Even limited but meaningful choices cause students to invest greater energy in learning than when the tasks are prescribed by the teacher (Turner & Paris, 1995). For example, students may be given a choice of topics, a choice whether to work alone or in a group, and options for showing comprehension. Of course, students like to be given a choice of books, and it is not surprising that they usually choose one that interests them. This practice engages the use of multiple strategies to make meaning. High interest, born of choice, leads to high comprehension. It is befuddling why more teachers do not rely on choice to boost motivation.

ORIENT TO CONTENT GOALS

Beginning in toddlerhood, humans have a strong motivation to ask "why?" The need to know arouses motivation driven by purpose. A classic study conducted by Ellen Langer in the 1970s and repeated in the 1980s drives home this point (1989; 1997). Confederates in the study approached people at a copy machine and asked to "cut in." People let cutters in some 60 percent of the time. But when the confederates added a reason, such as "I'm in a hurry," the allowance percentages increased to 95 percent. Interestingly, people were more willing to step aside even when confederates used a nonsensical reason like "because I need to make copies." Folks respond to reasons because we respect purposes and understand the need to try to reach goals.

Students want to learn important things and know why they are important. Big ideas in literature, science, social studies, math, and the arts are important things, because they give students access to truths about people and the world. When teachers direct students to find and construct big ideas, they are emphasizing content goals. Orienting students to content goals causes students to see learning itself as the reward and is likely to produce better comprehension (Guthrie, 2004). For example, instead of urging students in science class to work for grades, the teacher should focus students' attention on studying science to unravel the mysteries of the natural world; a history teacher should encourage students to learn about history to better understand how people's actions in the past have created the world of today. Students have a natural curiosity that teachers can tap to increase comprehension. Who wouldn't be interested in the inventor of the paper clip and the problem that motivated this creation? Or, better yet, the compelling story of Philo Farnsworth, the inventor of television. Teachers who direct students to work for better test performance as the goal and reward students with extrinsic incentives (e.g., points or grades) should actually expect lower achievement test scores.

Effective comprehenders have a sense of ownership about reading for meaning. They are clear on the goal of putting comprehension first, and they know how to use CPS strategies, including comprehension monitoring, to derive big ideas. They know what to do and believe they can do it. This is called *self-efficacy*. Self-efficacy causes students to self-initiate use of comprehension strategies, such as questioning (Alexander & Murphy, 1998). Students who spontaneously apply strategies, when it is sensible to do so, improve their comprehension. Content goals give purpose to learning and have been found especially important in increasing comprehension achievement for students with lower interests. Content goals engage students in the kind of comprehension strategy switching needed to make sense of texts, with the result that students will experience success and increase feelings of self-efficacy.

ENCOURAGE COLLABORATIVE GROUP WORK

People are social beings, so it is not surprising that group work motivates students. Working with others gives a positive feeling of being connected, boosts engagement, and stimulates thinking. Studies demonstrate that students who work in groups to complete a task choose to work longer than those working alone on the same task (DeMoss & Morris, 2002; Guthrie, 2004). It follows that longer engagement holds greater prospects for increasing comprehension. Motivation and comprehension also increase when students are given the chance to *teach* a group. Teachers who experience enjoyment from instructing students certainly understand how this works. For some, it is the satisfaction and pride that come from making a worthwhile contribution that are motivational. For others, it is the opportunity to "perform" before a group.

Group work guidelines

Group work succeeds best when students are supported with clear guidelines, are given specific roles and time limits, and have clear goals. Cooperative or collaborative work requires

- *interdependence:* understanding that the group will sink or swim together.
- *individual and group accountability:* each person must contribute, or the task can't be completed.
- *interpersonal skills:* problem solving depends on students listening to each other and sharing leadership.
- *reflection:* discussing what worked and brainstorming suggestions for improvement creates a better product.

Group work includes book clubs and teams that work on projects to show comprehension in science, social studies, or any area of the curriculum. Groups seem to work best when the size is small (three or four students) and when they are heterogeneous, with diversity of interests, perspectives, and abilities. Johnson and Johnson (2002) provide more information on setting up effective groups.

Audiences

An important motivational factor is the effect of audiences. When students know they will be presenting before an audience, surprising aspects of motivation are activated, including a greater desire to do well (Cornett, 2011; DeMoss & Morris, 2002). Award-winning teacher Rafe Esquith tells the story of a fifth grader who was part of a group given the opportunity to perform a history recitation before the Supreme Court. One boy memorized a letter written by a Civil War soldier to his wife. The group rehearsed many times, and the boy was fine. However, when he actually performed for the justices, he was literally transformed. Esquith shows a dramatic video of this young boy slowly "becoming" the soldier as he gets further into the letter. His voice begins to crack, his breathing begins to labor, and a tear rolls down his left cheek, as if on cue. It is mesmerizing evidence of the power of an audience to heighten engagement. Never had this boy become so emotional or "gotten into it" to this degree in rehearsal (Esquith, 2008).

The Hobart Shakespeareans

www.hobartshakespeareans.org

ONLINE RESOURCE

Of course, an audience can arouse a degree of nervousness, even for veteran teachers asked to speak before adult groups. Teachers can alleviate students' over-anxiousness by describing nervousness as a sign of caring about the audience. It helps to suggest they take the role of a good host and focus on the needs of the audience and not on themselves. Nervousness can boost energy and actually be a positive factor, if students feel they are well prepared to present and thoroughly understand the material. It helps some students to be part of a group presentation rather than going it solo. Groups who take risks together can form strong bonds, which can increase their willingness to share their efforts in public. Students are excited to share songs they co-write, enjoy presenting group tableaux (a drama strategy), and are proud of murals and other group art they create.

PROVIDE FEEDBACK

If we want students to sustain efforts to reach the goal of becoming independent, active meaning makers, certain conditions are critical for them.

■ *Students must be clear about the goal.* Use a CPS chart and explicit teaching to help solidify how comprehension happens and to reinforce that the goal is finding and constructing big ideas that make up academic content.

■ *Students must receive clear feedback about progress.* Students need to know how well they are doing in applying strategies. They need to know what they are doing that works and what isn't working. For example, a student may be activating prior knowledge, but it may not be relevant to the topic, so the student's predictions are not logically connected to the upcoming text. Constructive feedback can help refine the broad strategy of simply predicting. The teacher can explain and model how to back up predictions with evidence and then scaffold students' attempts to do the same. In order to focus and fine-tune comprehension efforts, students require more than ambiguous grades and vapid praise. They need to be told and shown exactly what they are doing that is on target, as well as how and why their efforts may be off base. Of course, this feedback should take place in a classroom climate characterized by help and support.

■ *Students must know the criteria for success.* Rubrics and checklists may be used to detail progress in CPS strategy use and acquisition of content understanding (big ideas). See Ready Resource 4.1 and Appendices B.2 and B.3 for examples and ideas. Motivation and comprehension increase when students are able to assess their own progress using these and other tools, and when they have opportunities to review work of peers (Guthrie, 2004).

Constructive feedback is more than praise. Praise uses value-laden words, such as "good" and "awesome," that are both fuzzy and controlling. We want our students to be clear about what makes for "good work," and that happens when we focus on descriptions of what is working. Statements that begin with "I see" or "I hear" can structure descriptive feedback. "I hear you making a prediction by using two clues—one from the cover art and one from the book's title" is an example of feedback that teaches. "That is a great idea!" may leave a student with an emotional rush, but when the emotions subside the student may be foggy about what exactly he did or said that was so great and will be left with little understanding of how to repeat the praised behavior.

Praise also can become an addictive extrinsic reinforcer. Students are not helped when they learn to seek increasing doses of praise. What *will* foster students' independence and self-efficacy is a focus on refining efforts. Teachers need to teach students to reflect on their own efforts and take pride in progress. Does this mean we can't ever use praise or celebrate students' efforts? Of course not! It just means the scale should be tipped in the direction of constructive comments. Praise can increase dependency and should be minimized, whereas self-efficacy can be a powerful motivator (see the box on p. 172). Ready Resource 6.5 summarizes practices that may be incorporated into classroom activities for daily engagement and motivation.

Texts and Technology Factors That Motivate

A seven-year study followed sixteen low-income students in kindergarten through grade six. Kids started carrying around *Harry Potter* books by second grade. By fifth or sixth grade, most had read them all. Interestingly, fourteen of the students achieved or surpassed benchmarks for reading level (Hallett, 1995, citing Barone).

The Roles of Independence and Self-Efficacy In Motivation

As children move from elementary grades to middle school, they experience a well-documented downward progression: a decrease in intrinsic motivation to read. Researchers attribute the decline to changes in instructional practices (e.g., a trend toward more teacher lecturing) and an increased focus on expository texts. But even adolescents with a history of reading difficulties can be motivated with strategies like those previously discussed, including a focus on clear content-oriented comprehension goals and a practice of giving students feedback on their progress in developing and using a strategy set.

Classic work in psychology has established two general divisions of human motivation that group people into either "origins" or "pawns" (deCharms, 1976). Pawns believe they succeed or fail because they are either lucky or unlucky. Pawns attribute success to being born smart or getting the right breaks.

On the other hand, origins believe success comes from hard work. They believe that effort is the key to success and that they can take action to make a difference in their own lives. They are problem solvers who continually add to their repertoire of ways to improve themselves.

Pawns are passive. They sit and wait for others to do for them. Origins are active problem solvers who are self-motivated because it feels good to be competent and independent. They feel proud of their efforts, even when the effort to use a strategy doesn't yield spectacular results. Their resiliency builds as they acquire additional problem-solving strategies and learn to apply them flexibly across situations.

Knowledgeable and caring teachers want their students to need them less as time goes by. Skilled use of motivational strategies causes students to become more self-disciplined and capable of self-initiating appropriate CPS strategy use. The goal is self-efficacy—to help more students become origins rather than pawns. Ready Resource 6.5 summarizes important motivation and engagement practices.

J. K. Rowling's *Harry Potter* novels are a literary phenomenon. At one point, this British author's first three books occupied three spots on the *New York Times* hardback fiction best-seller list. The sixth book in the series broke publishing records with an initial run in the United States of 10.8 million copies. Nearly 75 percent of kids ages 11 to 13 have read at least one of the books (Hallett, 2005).

What is it about these books that has turned many non-readers into readers and causes youngsters to carry Rowling's books around long before they could possibly read them? Why are certain texts so compelling, so motivating? These are important questions in light of the fact that students with a history of reading difficulties don't read much. They get less practice, are less engaged, and accrue less background knowledge to bring to new texts. Look ahead to Ready Resource 10.8 in Chapter 10 for a summary of the startling gaps in the amount of text read by high achievers and low achievers.

The nature of texts is described in Chapter 4, and Appendix C.1 describes key characteristics that may provide clues to the *Harry Potter* motivational effect. The fact that interest stands out is not surprising. One does not need a research study to know that interest is a key reason why we select texts when we are free to choose. Research does connect interest in a text's subject to comprehension (Morrow & Gambrell, 2001). But the subject matter of the *Harry Potter* books is hardly novel. Susan Cooper and many other writers of well-done, fanciful fic-

15 ways to promote active engagement and motivation to learn.

1 **Create a supportive invitational environment.** Relax students with your body language. Show respect for diversity and share classroom ownership. Show concern by listening and regularly conducting individual conferences.

2 **Engage using "heads on, hearts on, hands on" activities (mind, emotions, body).** Use humor, novelty, and surprise, as well as physical warm-ups and clear purpose-setting related to important goals.

3 **Teach attention, concentration, and focus.** Be explicit about how and why to control your mind, emphasizing the "high" that comes from concentrated attention or a "flow state." See the box on teaching concentration and focus in Chapter 10 for guidelines and Appendix H for example lessons.

4 **Make "important" goals clear.** Target CPS for understanding important content (e.g., big ideas). Connect texts to the real world. Go for depth versus coverage. Stress test performance less.

5 **Give descriptive feedback.** Give students specific information about their progress toward important goals such as individual and coordinated use of CPS strategies. Focus on students' efforts rather than luck. Minimize praise.

6 **Use interest.** Assess students' interests, teach to their interests, and help them develop new interests. Model your own interest in reading and use of alternative texts.

7 **Offer choice.** Even limited options engage motivation. Let students choose what, when, where, how, with whom, and why (purposes) to read, as much as possible. Teach them how to respond through all art forms and using diverse writing types.

8 **Harness social forces.** Use the group effect to engage students (e.g., collaborative work, where students teach each other). Use the power of audiences. Minimize competition.

9 **Use inquiry-based problem solving.** Stimulate students' curiosity with questions, suspense, mystery, paradoxes, and dilemmas.

10 **Challenge appropriately.** Stretch students with texts, open questions, wait time, and activities a bit beyond their reach.

11 **Use a multisensory approach.** Engage all the senses—visual, auditory, kinesthetic, and tactile—as well as the sense of humor to make abstract concepts more concrete. Give examples and show rather than tell.

12 **Increase independence.** Focus students' attention on people who are independent. Be explicit. Teach how to concentrate, attend, focus, and put forth effort. Scaffold and coach. Encourage risk taking. Teach strategies and ways to fix up problems, such as how to repair misunderstandings of text.

13 **Be a model.** Practice what you preach; walk the talk. Demonstrate what it means to be intrinsically motivated, and explain the joys of becoming more literate.

14 **Have fun.** Fun is fundamental to motivation and learning. Fun is not just fluff. When asked to define fun, students describe the first twelve motivators above.

15 **Start each day fresh.** Give students hope by giving them the choice to make a new beginning. Discuss this concept in conferences and with the whole class.

READY RESOURCE **6.5**

Sources consulted: Brophy, 1986; DeMoss & Morris, 2002; Guthrie, 2004; Pressley, 2007; Purkey & Novak, 1996.

tion will never come close to being billionaires. Certainly, the interest power of Rowling's books is not that these are tales of magical adventure. More likely, these books are examples of texts that manage to capture the compelling and complex power of art. Artful texts defy analysis, but they represent the kinds of materials most likely to turn around students who've been turned off to reading (DeMoss & Morris, 2002).

Not to be forgotten, of course, is the group effect. Adolescents are not alone in the high value they place on "what everyone else is doing." The *Harry Potter* novels were well marketed, no doubt, but at some point readership reached a critical mass, and it was marked by an elite group whose influence was stunning. Harry became hip.

TEXT/LEARNER INTERACTION

To understand the connection between a book's content and comprehension, we must understand the text/reader interaction. Texts are neither interesting nor boring in isolation. The reaction of a learner to a book, song, piece of art, or website has to do with how the learner characteristics discussed in previous chapters intersect with the text at the particular moment of use. For example, as a teenager I was never particularly interested in Harriet Beecher Stowe, and I found *Uncle Tom's Cabin* to be maudlin. However, when I agreed to play Ms. Stowe at a local history event, I reread the book and found it fascinating. The book hadn't changed, I had.

Every text has unique characteristics, with quantitative and qualitative dimensions that influence whether a student wants to use it and is able to do so. For example, long words and long sentences can make a text more difficult, and the complexity of navigating hypertext can be daunting. Qualitative text characteristics may or may not trigger interest, since interest draws on a host of individual learner characteristics, including background, needs of the moment, and peer group trends—just to name a few. What is boring to one student is exciting to another, within limits. Unnatural texts made for the purpose of decodability (where most words are phonetically regular), with little regard for content, may offer little to think about. Short-term boredom can produce long-term distaste for reading, which plays havoc with comprehension growth.

DIVERSE TEXTS

In the past it was common to limit student access to certain types of texts. For example, information-based texts were reserved for use with primary students only after a degree of print decoding was established. There is no longer support for a literacy curriculum that assumes children must learn to read and then read to learn—a sequence in which students learn to read by reading stories and then read to learn informational texts. Nonfiction texts are now recommended as core materials for primary students, who are quite capable of using these texts in sophisticated ways and often prefer them (Duke, 2001). Smolkin and Donovan (2002) even found that informational texts used in teacher read alouds could provoke more use of comprehension strategies than fictional texts. The challenging and provocative nature of nonfiction seems to provide a motivational trigger for some students to problem solve, which makes these texts rich in comprehension instructional potential.

It boils down to the need to use diverse texts from the start. This means drawing on good works of fiction and nonfiction, as well as integrating technology texts.

TECHNOLOGY-BASED TEXTS

Technology has all the features necessary to motivate students. It is novel, hands-on, and definitely hip. Technology is social, too. The popularity of instant messaging, blogs, and social websites dramatizes the social nature of literacy and the impact of mediated texts. Text messaging and email have been great motivators for many students to learn to read and write. Even book and film characters now text and twitter, create Facebook pages, and connect through computer matchmaking services.

Technology gives power. It makes us all more connected, and being connected is all about access to and control of communication. Students love the sense of control and access technology provides. No wonder skillful use of electronic texts boosts confidence. Suddenly a third grader knows much more than the teacher, because he knows how to get answers, fast. If comprehension is reduced to getting answers, the Internet can easily outpace any of us. The challenge is to teach students to do more than get answers from digital and multimedia texts. The goal is to use digital texts as sources for constructing meaning. This goal is no different from that for print texts. But the texts are different, and the need for teachers to teach students to apply problem-solving strategies to computer-based texts has never been greater.

Multimedia's motivation promise

In addition to increasing communication and giving a general sense of control, technology motivates because it provides interest and choices: anyone can now click and go on a virtual field trip to nearly any spot on earth, and beyond. Technological texts often employ multimedia images, animations, links, videos, and audio material, all of which can increase comprehension. Multimedia may be more memorable because it stimulates both visual and verbal processing by the brain (Mayer & Moreno, 1998). If this is so, hypertext holds great promise.

Hypertext is text that includes links to additional material. It is well suited to searching out information about personally interesting questions. However, hypertext comprehension demands "understanding of three-dimensional text" (Block, 2004, p. 185). It is nonlinear and non-sequential. Add to this the pictures, icons, and animations frequently accompanying hypertext, and students can find themselves drowning in choices. What does the research say about the value of hypertext for teaching comprehension? There are contrasting conclusions—some studies support hypertext use with students with low prior knowledge, and others find that it interferes with comprehension (Lawless & Kulikowich, 1996; Mayer, 1997). Children who have low background for a specific task may benefit from fewer options for hypertext navigation and browsing. The transient nature of multimedia poses additional issues for novices and students who have fragile comprehension strategies that are just being established with conventional print texts. Research findings reinforce the importance of maintaining a developmental perspective when choosing texts for their motivational properties. Too many choices can be detrimental.

Computers have opened up many avenues for motivating students. Many students are motivated by the novel capabilities of word processing programs that allow the creation of texts. For example, students with learning disabilities were found to experience fewer writing difficulties when they used word processing programs along with transcription software, spell checkers, speech synthesizers, multimedia applications, and semantic organizers (Tierney et al., 1997).

The following suggestions for computer-based teaching strategies further capitalize on interest, choice, group effect, and content learning.

1. Set up digital pen pals or e-pals with students from other locales.
2. Teach texting shorthand and emoticons as they relate to the concept of abbreviations and alternative ways people communicate thoughts and feelings.
3. Establish barrier-free universal access for special populations.
4. Use supportive electronic books (e-books) with digitized prompts for specific words to scaffold independent reading for struggling readers.
5. For students who are learning English, use e-books on CD-ROM in their home languages to allow them to listen as they follow the English text.
6. Use digitized video, dictionaries, glossaries, databases, electronic encyclopedias, and graphic organizers to expand students' reference capabilities.
7. Obtain speech synthesizer software to provide spelling support for students as they write.

Locating and Evaluating Software

Children's Software Revue, www.childrenssoftware.com (subscription)

Harmony Interactive, www.harmonyinteractive.org

Living Books, www.livingbooks.com

Broderbund, www.broderbund.com

Interactive e-books may be used flexibly. Students can simply listen to the story, read along with their eyes, echo read, read first and then listen, partner read, or play "I spy" to find words. Some companies have developed multimedia books that can aid in comprehension and motivate students to explore. Ready Resource 6.6 lists examples of interactive software. Detailed descriptions of each product may be found at the companies' websites.

Building student Internet skills

Because of their motivational potential, digital texts are an important part of differentiated instruction. However, motivation can collapse if students lack pre-

Software to motivate students to engage in comprehension.

- **Thinking Reader** by CAST (Center for Applied Special Technology) embeds within the text different levels of strategy support students can use to scaffold comprehension.

- **Discis Books** (Discis Knowledge Research) offer stories and poems that include animation and labeling of objects.

- **The Reader Rabbit series** (Learning Company) teaches prereading, writing, and language skills in a game environment.

- **Smart Books** (Scholastic) are arranged by topic.

- **Start-to-Finish** (Don Johnston, Inc.) library is suitable for older struggling learners.

- **Thinking Readers** (Scholastic) offers text to speech function, multimedia glossary, background knowledge links, and embedded strategy instruction to develop metacognition and increase comprehension with prompts.

- **Wiggle Works** (Scholastic) are leveled predictable books on CD-ROM.

Additional aids in writing, fluency, and vocabulary development:

- **WriteOutLoud** (Don Johnston) is a talking word processor and writing software.

- With **Illuminatus 4.5** (Digital Workshop), students can collaboratively create electronic talking books.

- **KidPix** teaches how to visualize concepts and label them using semantic maps, outlines, and diagrams. Drawing, writing, and voice recording software allows students to draw before they write but should be monitored to avoid distracting students from content focus.

- **Soliloquy Reading Assistant** is a sophisticated oral reading fluency practice and feedback package.

- *The Language Experience Approach* (LEA) is a time-honored strategy for teaching reading. Students dictate stories and other ideas, which the teacher transcribes. These "texts" are then used as reading material (Lee & Allen, 1963). LEA can be made digital with speech synthesizers, drawing tools, and imported video animations and sounds. Book reviews may be presented in a multimedia format, such as PowerPoint.

6.6 READY RESOURCE

requisite skills to navigate texts and mine them for information treasure. Chapter 5 gave suggestions for explicit instruction regarding Internet use. Additional ideas for explicit instruction include:

- *Computer concept teaching:* how to use the screen and keyboarding skills, as well as special vocabulary

- *Internet etiquette or "netiquette":* appropriate online behavior. Related to netiquette is appropriate computer use. McKenne and colleagues coined the term "mouse wars" to describe student arguments over mouse control (2007). Of course, there is much more to appropriate behavior than sharing the clicker.

- *Hypertext navigation:* how to approach so many choices strategically

- *Inquiry projects:* how to conduct Internet research and produce new texts to show comprehension

- *Copyright:* how to summarize and synthesize information from the Internet to avoid plagiarizing

Learning More About Web 2.0

ONLINE RESOURCES

Anime movie videos (www.AnimeMusicVideos.org): *create music videos by downloading clips and syncing with songs*

Blogger (www.blogger.com): *a hosting site for "web logging"*

Delicious (www.delicious.com): *a site that allows sharing of bookmarks*

Fanfiction (www.fanfiction.net): *allows collaborative writing and reviewing of literary works*

Flickr (www.flickr.com): *photo sharing service*

PBwiki (http://pbwikicom/academic.wiki): *a service for creating wikis*

Podomatic (http://podomatic.com): *a site that hosts podcasts*

Survey Monkey (www.surveymonkey.com): *service for conducting online surveys and compiling responses*

Note: Some of these sites offer RRS (Really Simple Syndication), another way of viewing a webpage. An RSS page viewed through a web browser gives the titles of recent articles in a list, with a brief note about content. If an RSS view is available for a website, a clickable orange RSS button appears in the address bar. Synonyms are feed, news feed, RSS feed, and XML feed.

ESPECIALLY FOR TEACHERS

ASCD Inservice Blog (www.ascd.org): *blog for educators regarding new research and best practices*

All Things PLC (www.allthingsplc.info): *information about learning communities*

NewLits.org (www.newlits.org): *a wiki that focuses on new literacies and use of digital technology*

snapshot revisited

IT buttons may not be every teacher's cup of tea, and motivation is much more complicated than "energy directed at a goal." But, if I were again in charge of a reading center, I would fire up my button maker again. Direction and goals are crucial to engagement. Interest can lead to a dead end, if it leads away from literacy, and we all know teenagers who have had that happen. If I had it to do over, I would spend more time helping students select and revise goals, with more attention to worthiness. The set of key concepts shown earlier in Ready Resource 6.2 can help, and may be used to create a rubric for motivation that promotes comprehension. The Five Factors that influence comprehension serve as organizers. Rubrics are particularly effective in helping students self-assess and then set goals for improvement.

Conclusion

This chapter offered an overview of what motivation is and how it relates to engaging comprehension strategy use. The chapter reviewed basic aspects of the complicated nature of motivation and mined them for teaching applications. In particular, the chapter focused on: (1) establishing clear learning content and strategy goals, (2) building and tapping interests, (3) offering choice, (4) emphasizing group work, and (5) providing feedback. The special role of diverse texts, including technology texts, was discussed as it relates to motivation and engagement.

All of the motivational factors align with the thesis of this book: that comprehension achievement for all students depends on putting inquiry-based problem solving that targets creating meaning at the forefront. Inquiry is embedded in interest, thrives in choice, is enriched by collaboration, and delights us with its consequences—the discovery of big ideas that make up content learning. The important questions examined in this chapter further drive the conclusion that there is real power in putting a reformed view of comprehension first on our curricular agendas.

CHAPTER 6 **big ideas**

The following are examples of big ideas from this chapter. Revise the list to create a better picture of your own comprehension.

1. Motivation is energy directed at a goal.

2. Motivation is more highly correlated with comprehension than phonics.

3. Student motivation is boosted by content learning goals, interesting texts, choice, and collaborative work.

4. Motivated students are more engaged with texts, so their comprehension is increased.

5. Intrinsic motivation is internal and lasting, while extrinsic motivation is external and temporal.

6. The problems with using extrinsic rewards, such as points, stamps, and coupons, to encourage reading are that they can diminish intrinsic motivation and they teach that learning is not its own reward.

7. Students experiencing comprehension difficulties often view the task of reading as uninteresting or irrelevant.

8. Successful people believe success comes from effort, while those who fail tend to believe success is all about luck.

9. Texts can be motivational powerhouses that turn non-readers into readers.

10. Technology-based texts have special motivational properties to engage students in inquiry-based problem solving.

a look ahead

Chapter 7 focuses on the best practice of using questioning to promote thoughtful conversations and discussions that engage CPS thinking. Since students are motivated by group work, a chapter on the use of discussions and conversations is an appropriate sequel to this one.

CHAPTER 6 response options

Work in pairs or with a small group to respond to the chapter using the following options.

1. Use the Chapter Big Ideas as examples to generate your own big ideas. Discuss one or two of the ideas you consider most important with another reader.

2. Use the questions at the start of the chapter to evaluate your comprehension. List at least two questions you would like to discuss or investigate further.

3. Reflect on the role extrinsic reinforcers, such as grades, points, or money, have played in your learning. List several positive and negative motivational effects you recall.

4. Explain the role of your own personal interests in your past and present learning.

5. Make a list of choice options you could offer to students, ranging from easy ones such as where to sit to more difficult ones related to selecting topics and problems to research over time.

6. Think of people you know who take the "pawn" perspective on life and others who are "origins." Create several ideas for encouraging your students to be origins (e.g., daily events, visual aids).

7. Prepare a five-minute argument for making motivation the sixth reading pillar (in addition to the five under NCLB).

8. Create a bookmark or other visual to help you remember key motivational factors.

9. Work with a group to prepare a panel presentation on the role of motivation in comprehension.

10. Pretend to be a technology advocate and create a short sales pitch on the importance of digital technology for increasing motivation.

11. Check out some of the technology mentioned in this chapter on the Internet and make a wish list of purchases.

12. Create a blog or wiki or use Skype to conduct a professional conversation with others about using technology to motivate students to use comprehension problem solving.

Using Questioning to Promote Discussion and Conversation

preview

This chapter continues the Comprehension Problem Solving emphasis on using important questions to arrive at big ideas. This time, the focus is directed to using conversations and discussions about texts to increase comprehension. The chapter provides specific guidelines for teaching both kinds of classroom talk as well as suggestions for using questioning to promote "high level" talk. Recommendations are given for ways to ask provocative questions, teach students how to generate good questions, and set up a variety of discussion formats. The overall goal is to make thoughtful discussions and conversations an integral part of the comprehension curriculum.

important questions

1. What roles can big ideas and important questions play in comprehension development, including Comprehension Problem Solving?

2. Why are certain questions better than others? What are examples of important questions?

3. How can students be taught to generate important questions that lead to big ideas?

4. Why are discussions and conversations so important to comprehension? How do they relate to CPS?

5. What are different types of discussions? What are the advantages of each?

6. What strategies cause students to prepare for discussions and learn to participate with a meaning-making orientation?

7. How can discussions and conversations be integrated into daily routines in literacy, science, social studies, and other areas?

8. How does the kind of questioning and discussing described in this chapter follow an inquiry orientation? How is inquiry linked to comprehension?

Introduction

I need to talk," says a friend. You both know you are about to discuss a problem. You listen and give information. You ask questions: "What do you mean? Why do you think that? What do you want to do?" Or you meet a new neighbor at a party. You ask, "Where are you from? Why did you move here? How's it going so far?" Your questions contribute to the conversation and are intended to solve many problems, ranging from making the newcomer more comfortable to finding common needs and interests. You expect the new neighbor to reciprocate with similar questions. When the questions stop, the conversation peters out.

Questioning is a necessary part of life. Questions are the currency of building relationships, both personal and business. They are a principal tool to access information. We start the day asking questions ("What's on for you today?") and end with questions ("How did it go?"). We are questioned by doctors and car mechanics; even the grocery bagger asks, "Paper or plastic?" It seems unimaginable to live a day without questions.

Everyone asks questions, so why does a teacher need to study them? The fact is, when it comes to comprehension, questions are the force that drives inquiry in general and CPS in particular. However, all questions are not created equal. Some are better than others as vehicles for understanding. How you ask and what you ask matter. The doctor asks, "Does it hurt here?" but neglects to go further and misses a diagnosis. The hairstylist asks, "Do you want a trim?" and faces an unhappy customer when he takes off too much. The parent asks, "Did you do your math homework?" and finds later it was social studies that wasn't getting done. These are all yes/no questions, a type teachers need to avoid. Notice the difference when the questions are *open* and elicit more information: "Where does it hurt?" "How do you want it cut?" "What homework do you have to do?" All of these open questions prevent and solve problems. "Why didn't you tell me you were having problems in social studies?" Dad asks later. "You never asked me about social studies," replies the son. Best comprehension practice demands that teachers not fall into such traps and learn to be expert questioners.

Humans are predisposed to question, but teachers need more than off-the-cuff thinking to generate questions that motivate students to dig for meaning. The main purpose of this book is to show how to teach Comprehension Problem Solving in a manner that will result in students extracting and constructing big ideas. Of particular emphasis is questioning that directs thinking toward informed conclusions about people and the world. Hence the subtitle, "Inquiry into big ideas using important questions." Important questions activate inquiry into the meaning of texts, which builds motivation to learn. Inquiry-based comprehension instruction is about *living* in a classroom where big ideas are the focus and good questions, both teacher- and student-generated, are deeply valued (Wolk, 2008).

Questions initiate both short conversations and long discussions, so they are key to extending focused classroom talk during the literacy block, as well as during science, social studies, math, art, music, drama, and dance classes. This chapter examines the role of questioning in creating the "high level" talk shown to increase text comprehension (Duke & Pearson, 2002). The chapter describes the role of questions in stimulating conversations and discussions about texts and explains the what, why, when, where, and how of discussions.

The opening snapshot shows how one teacher helps students generate their own discussion questions for a whole book in preparation for a teacher-led discussion. The goal is to cause students to become increasingly independent in their use of the inquiry-based CPS process.

classroom snapshot

JACK SANCHEZ AND *ESPERANZA RISING*

Jack Sanchez teaches fifth grade. It is now February, and he has taught many lessons on good questions, big ideas, and CPS strategies during the year. He now expects students to read independently and apply comprehension strategies to derive big ideas worth discussing. The students follow his "**Discussion Rules**" (provided in Ready Resource 7.6, p. 197), which they have learned to use in teacher-led whole-group and small peer group discussions.

Book Introduction

Jack previously chose the award-winning book *Esperanza Rising*, by Pam Muñoz Ryan, to accompany a current **social studies unit** on immigration. After he explains this connection to the students, he tells them they will be partner reading the chapters over the next two weeks. He is about to introduce the book by reading the first chapter aloud. First, he asks a **purpose-setting** question.

"We've talked before about how to start discussions. When we discuss this book it will be whole group, and this will be the first question: **'What does the title have to do with the book?'** I'm going to read the first chapter to you, and we'll talk about that question afterward. Questions?"

"Can we talk about that question with our partners?" a boy asks.

"Sure. That's a good idea. You'll be making your own questions, too. Just remember our Independent Reading rules about whispering and staying on task," Jack explains.

"Should we take notes?" another boy asks.

"Yes, this is like our other discussions. It will be **text-based,** so you need to have evidence from the book for your conclusions. I'm going to give you a special way to take notes after I read Chapter 1. Other questions?"

Seeing no hands, Jack shows the cover of the book. Right away a girl puts her hand up. He calls on her.

"I think it is cool that the girl is flying. That goes with 'rising' doesn't it?"

Jack smiles. "It sure does. You are already picking up **clues to meaning.** That's great. How about I give you some more to think about with Chapter 1?" The girl smiles and nods in agreement.

Jack explains that the medal on the cover is named for a Latina woman who was a librarian. He reads the dedication and the quotes in Spanish that precede the chapter and asks if anyone can translate them. A boy named Jose comes close, and Jack fills in the gaps. The class looks at Jose, obviously impressed.

Jack reads the place and date that start Chapter 1 and stops to pull down a map and show where Aquascalientes, Mexico, is. A girl quickly calculates they are about eight hundred miles from there, and the book took place eighty-five years ago. Jack then starts reading. He **changes his voice** for Papa and six-year-old Esperanza. A Spanish proverb appears on page 2, and once again Jose is able to translate it pretty well. The chapter is only three pages long. After the read aloud, the class wants to talk about their **clues** to the meaning from the title, and they make many predictions. They are excited about the idea of hearing the heartbeat of the earth and want to try it. Since it is nearly recess time, Jack takes the class outside, and, despite the chilly weather, they all lie on the grass and listen.

After recess Jack passes out paperback copies. He could only get twelve, so students will read in pairs. He shows them how to keep track of **(1) important ideas they find or create and (2) questions they want to discuss.** He demonstrates how to make a **T-chart** (see Ready Resource 7.1) with one side for a list of big ideas and the other for questions. He reminds students to note **page numbers** for ideas and questions. They all write his question about the title on their T-charts, and Jack gives the pairs a few minutes to talk about anything in Chapter 1 that gives a clue. He reminds them that it will take the whole book to answer the question and not to worry if they don't have a lot of text evidence yet. He also refers them to a chart about **"good questions"** to help them pose their own questions for each chapter (see Ready Resource 7.3 on p. 197).

Scaffolding Work

Students finish the book during daily independent reading over a two-week period. Jack does **30-second conferences** with each pair each week to check their progress and keep them on

T-chart example.

ESPERANZA RISING

QUESTIONS	BIG IDEAS
What does the title have to do with the book?	Your dreams give you a life goal.
Why did the author include the doll, roses, crocheting, and the birthday song?	Being rich can make you weak.
Why didn't the author tell what happened to Marta?	Hard times can make people strong.
Why does the author include all the signs and proverbs in the book?	You discover a lot about yourself during hard times.
Why did Esperanza have to go through so much hardship to become a good person?	Determined women can do just about anything.

7.1 READY RESOURCE

track. Some need more help with understanding what a big idea is and how to craft questions worth discussing in the upcoming book discussion. When students come up with single concepts, such as prejudice, immigrants, and hard times, Jack coaches them to expand their themes into big ideas with questions like these:

- What did you learn about _____?
- How can you say that in a whole sentence?
- What would you tell a friend was the most important thing you learned about _____?
- What will you remember most about _____?
- What do you see in your head when you think about _____?
- How does _____ make you feel? Why?

Esperanza Rising Discussion Day February 12!

The big date for the discussion is posted in a speech bubble right by the clock. The students know Jack has budgeted nearly an hour for the discussion, and the pairs seem excited to find ideas and questions to bring up in the discussion.

Discussion Day

When the day finally arrives for the discussion, the students sit on a large carpet in a circle. They are ready for Jack's starter question about the meaning of the title, and most have brought several T-charts with notes. Jack has asked them to **star the question and the big idea they most want to discuss.** Here are examples of their starred questions:

1. What do the chapter titles mean? For example, Chapter 2 is "Grapes" (p. 4), and Chapter 8 is "Onions" (p. 110).

2. What caused the stereotyping of the immigrants, and why is there still prejudice?

3. Why did the author include the doll, roses, crocheting, and the birthday song?

4. Why is "striking" such an issue among the migrants?

5. Why didn't the author tell what happened to Marta?

6. Why does the author include all the signs and proverbs in the book?

7. Why did Esperanza have to go through so much hardship to become a good person?

Some of their big ideas are:

1. Your dreams give you your life goals.

2. You discover a lot about yourself during hard times.

3. Determined women can do just about anything.

4. Being rich can make you weak.

5. Hard times can make people strong.

6. Fighting for a good cause is worth the struggle.

7. When you grow plants and respect the earth, it makes you feel uplifted.

8. Families and friends need to help one another to survive hard times.

Discussion Process

The discussion easily takes an hour. Jack is true to his word and begins with his one question, but the students quickly get involved in asking their questions and sharing big ideas. When the hour is nearly up, Jack asks students **to tell an important idea they learned from the discussion**—something they hadn't thought about before the discussion. He starts with a volunteer, who then calls on another student, and so on until nearly all have shared. Jack keeps track of which students didn't volunteer and asks them **what ideas they heard that made sense.** Using this strategy, all the students participate in the summing up. Ready Resources 7.7 and 7.13 later in this chapter show other strategies for facilitating discussions.

Become an Expert Questioner

High-level discussions don't happen without good questions. Teachers ask hundreds of questions per day—as many as 120 questions per hour (Vogler, 2008). Is asking lots of questions critical to comprehension? Marzano (2007) claims asking good questions yields a huge payoff in student achievement. "Good" has more to do with the quality of questions than quantity. Unfortunately, in a study of effective schools Taylor and colleagues found that few teachers asked the kind of thought-provoking questions that would advance the discovery and construction of big ideas. Only 16 percent of teachers in grades one through three were frequently observed asking higher-level, aesthetic response questions that invited students to express critical opinions and feelings. Little or no discussion occurred in these classrooms, and when discussions did happen, discussion of text facts dominated (1999). Despite these disappointing findings, some teachers showed that, with professional development, the picture could improve. These "most accomplished" teachers asked higher-order questions 31 percent of the time; teachers with less skill asked higher-order questions less than 9 percent of the time. The more accomplished teachers also asked questions that required text-based evidence 48 percent of the time, as compared to 46 percent for less accomplished teachers and 24 percent for the least accomplished.

Setting the bar at asking good questions at least 50 percent of the time seems like a reasonable goal, given these findings. Why not 90 or even 100 percent? Expert questioning is harder than it seems, but it is an art teachers need to master in order to make significant process in increasing comprehension achievement. In addition, teachers need to be models of expert questioning in order to mentor students in generating their own questions. And that is a serious goal. Students need to make progress toward question generation if they are to become increasingly independent problem solvers. Some of the strongest scientific evidence for boosting achievement was found for the practice of causing students to generate questions (NRP, 2000). This is not surprising, since self-questioning ratchets CPS toward the extraction and construction of big ideas; question finding and generation are at the heart of inquiry-based problem solving. The goal is for teachers to be able to ask students, "What questions do you have?" instead of using their own list or one from a teacher's guide.

KNOW PURPOSES OF QUESTIONS

Becoming an expert questioner involves knowing about the different purposes for questions. It would take a catalogue of every aspect of human inquiry to list all the reasons people ask questions. Some examples should suffice and are presented in Ready Resource 7.2.

Questions emanate from interest, confusion, curiosity, and our need to know. They are born of problems and set inquiry in motion. Some questions grow out of other questions, in a spiraling fashion. Teachers use questions to assess students' understanding, and good readers use questions to monitor whether they are making sense.

Example question purposes and types.

We ask questions to . . .

- learn and get information
- probe for more information
- clarify meaning
- speculate

- satisfy curiosity
- express confusion or wonder
- form relationships and friendships
- show concern and empathy

7.2 READY RESOURCE

To model generating questions for their students, teachers must first examine their own questioning behaviors and the reasons behind most of their questions. You can easily obtain good data by turning on an audio or video recorder during discussions and then tallying your question types, purposes, and frequency. If most of your questions relate to testing recall after text use, then a change is in order. We have known for decades that confining questions to after reading does not promote comprehension. Quality questions are needed before text use, and students should continue to generate them during reading. *When* questions are asked is important, but more important are the types of questions asked and the manner in which they are used, including how they are sequenced.

ASK QUALITY QUESTIONS

Engaging students with quality questions improves comprehension of texts read during instruction, and the benefit transfers to the comprehension of independently read texts (RAND, 2002). More isn't necessarily better when it comes to getting students to elaborate for comprehension purposes. Quality questions are necessary to grease cognition. Such questions lead to the big ideas that are both explicit and implicit in texts. Text evidence (facts and details) is important to deriving big ideas, but questions that ask for literal information have to be crafted carefully. Otherwise, questions that hone in on trivial bits of information can detract from comprehension. For example, asking the name of Jack's cow in *Jack and the Beanstalk* is a discussion stopper. It just doesn't have any relevance to the story's implicit or explicit big ideas. However, asking about what Jack traded the cow for and why does matter. If Jack had not received the beans, there would have been no beanstalk. So, quality isn't just about whether questions ask for students to recall or do higher-level thinking. Quality questions cause students to zero in on important evidence that can support conclusions about big ideas.

Timing is also important in questioning. Quality follow-up questions are necessary, or discussion falters. For example, it would be important to ask (not tell) students *why* the beans are important to the story to keep discussion going in the direction of big ideas.

Text comprehension has many doors through which a mind may enter. Ready Resource 7.3 summarizes criteria for good questions. Additional examples of quality questions and how to use them in discussions may be found in subsequent Ready Resources.

Asking open-ended ("fat") questions

Questions that provoke a range of answers are called open ended. They are also called "thick" or "fat," because they are rich in possibilities for activating substantive thought. Questions that lead to big ideas usually can't be answered with a simple yes or no or with one word. It is a problem when teachers are the only ones asking questions and the questions are thin and closed, eliciting

Criteria for good questions.

Good questions . . .

- are ones you really care about. They stem from problems or perplexing ideas and begin with "I wonder why . . ." or "What do you think about . . ."

- are ones for which you do not know the answer, but can find clues in the text.

- are open ended (fat) versus closed (thin). Such questions require more thinking, can't be answered with a yes or no, and don't start with words like *do, could, should,* and *would.* Open-ended questions begin with stems like *why, what if,* and *how.*

- lead to big ideas that are explicitly stated and implicit in texts. Such questions provoke students to find important facts and details to use as they infer what is important.

- are often follow-up or clarification questions that ask for evidence or examples. These grow out of careful listening to the thoughts of others.

- ask for aesthetic response: What did you like? Why?

- ask for summary of big ideas: What will you remember most?

READY RESOURCE 7.3

short right-or-wrong answers that close off connective and elaborative thinking. Questions that elicit a range of answers provoke deeper thinking. That doesn't mean there aren't wrong answers. For example, "What do you know about George Washington?" has a range of answers. "He freed the slaves" is not in the range, since Washington didn't even release his personal slaves, let alone those of the whole country. An example of an open question for almost any text is "What was it *really* about?" That question focuses thinking and sets the CPS process in motion to make meaning. Ready Resource 7.4 on page 191 lists numerous examples of open questions.

Asking questions for aesthetic understanding

Open questions allow a lot of room for individual sense making, and sense making should heighten enjoyment. Questions shouldn't dampen the aesthetic experience of a text; they should expand it. Aesthetic experience is about understanding. It focuses on using all the senses and triggers an emotional response. While conventional views separate aesthetic sense making from cognitive meaning making, a broader view of comprehension embraces both. Why wouldn't teachers want students to use all manner of processes to make meaning? Those who ascribe to "whole child" teaching should be able to see the logic in this perspective.

As an example I'll use an actual field trip to see the Rodgers and Hammerstein musical *Cinderella*. The goal for students was to make sense of the characters, plot, set, costumes, songs, and dances. I wanted them to experience the whole, in an aesthetic sense, integrated with cognitive thinking. The discussion problem, after seeing the play, was to distill the essence collaboratively and by doing so make the experience more than entertainment. The range of possible "right answers" was large for questions like "How did the play make you feel?" and "What was it really about?" Students talked about feeling hopeful and happy as they zeroed in on the themes of imagination, dreams, and hope drawn from the song lyrics, set, characters, and costumes. However, when a student said the play made him feel disgusted because it was about "pigs," the answer seemed wrong. But, wrong answers may not be so. When asked another important question, "Why do you say that?" (asking for evidence), the student replied, "The stepmother and the stepsisters were pigs. They wore gaudy clothes and were greedy for themselves. They tried to hog the stage and the prince, but they ended up with nothing. If you are a greedy pig you will end up losing." This student articulated a big idea no one else had considered, and he provided clear evidence for his conclusions. Everyone agreed his idea made sense, and it had enough heft to call it a big idea. Ready Resource 7.4 also gives examples of questions that stimulate an aesthetic response. The aims of these questions are identified in the parenthetical notations.

Using a line of questioning

Over the years, many taxonomies have been developed to categorize thinking in different levels. The most famous is Benjamin Bloom's taxonomy (1956), intended as a device for educators to categorize educational objectives from the low level to a high level (memory, interpretation, application, analysis, synthesis, evaluation). Teachers have used it for many years to become more aware of "higher order" questions needed to provoke analysis, synthesis, and evaluation. The concept of levels of thinking is important. Good readers, however, do not start with the facts (memory level) and proceed up a hypothetical mental ladder to interpretation, information use, and so forth until the pinnacle of evaluation is reached. Comprehension is much messier, with a great deal of recursive thinking for the purpose of making meaning. Herein lies a big problem: focusing on question levels in isolation, as taxonomies do, doesn't increase comprehension. Questions have to work together to lead somewhere, and the most important destination is big ideas. All levels of questions are needed to arrive at the goal.

The sequence in which questions are asked is important, too. Some teachers, like Jack Sanchez, start with broad questions like, "What is the significance of the title?" while others prefer to lead students through topic and theme identification in an effort to lay a base for big ideas. Questions that ask for personal connections are engaging, but the "How did the book relate to you?" type of questions can get discussions off on tangents quickly if the facilitator is not clear about connecting text-to-self responses to key big ideas. Teachers have to begin with the end in mind. When big ideas are the goal, questions should lead in that direction.

Text comprehension has many doors through which a mind may enter. The questions listed in Ready Resource 7.4 may be used to open doors for both fiction and nonfiction. The questions are organized in a before, during, and after sequence that can serve to scaffold reading, listening, or viewing a text. Note that there is no one set order for questions at each stage.

Questions to scaffold text use.

The questions demonstrate using a line of questioning. Also use these questions to create a reference chart to help students generate their own questions. Most of the questions may be adapted for narrative and expository, fiction and nonfiction, and non-verbal texts. The major concepts and types of thinking required follow each question in parentheses. Return to Ready Resource 5.11 in Chapter 5 for questions organized by literary elements.

BEFORE: Look at title and artwork, then ask . . .

- What do you think this is about? Who? When and where? (prediction/characters/setting)
- What might be the problems in a text with this title? (conflict/big ideas/themes)
- What does the cover art suggest? (prediction/hypothesizing)

DURING: Read, view, or listen a bit, then ask . . .

- What's the "big" question? How do you know? (conflict/plot/inference/big idea)
- What problems are being raised? How might they get solved? (conflict/theme/big idea)
- What are the main characters or people like? How do you know? (evidence/inference)
- What should the character do? Why? (critical thinking)
- What's happening? Why? (plot)
- What are the important things that have happened? (plot/inference)
- What did you notice so far that seems important? (inference/details)
- What will happen? Why? (prediction/evidence)
- What would you like to find out? (inquiry/aesthetic response)
- Whose POV (point of view) is this? How do you know?
- What do you notice in the artwork that seems important (color, texture, shape, line, perspective, etc.)? (critical analysis/inference)
- How does the art affect the text? (aesthetic response/evidence/inference)
- What is most interesting to you? Why? (aesthetic response/inquiry)

DURING: Read, listen, or view more, then repeat above or ask . . .

- What other texts does this one make you think of? Why? (compare–contrast/connect)
- How does this text connect to your life? (connect to prior experiences)
- What do you now know that you didn't know before? (data gathering)
- What questions got answered? (confirm/reject predictions)
- What is confusing? (clarification)
- What events, concepts, and details are important? How do you know? (critical thinking/inference)
- What words or language stands out? Why? (aesthetic response/style)
- How does the text make you feel so far? Why? (aesthetic response/mood)
- If there is dialogue, what does it show about characters or people? (inference)

AFTER completing the text, ask . . .

- What happened? Why? (plot/cause–effect)
- What was this text really about? (conclusion/themes/key concepts/big ideas)
- What did the title mean? (big ideas/themes)
- What were the problems? How were they solved? (data gathering/problem solving)
- What will you remember about this text next week? Next year? (conclusions/big ideas)
- What does the text tell you about people (e.g., how they behave)? (inference/big ideas)

(continued)

READY RESOURCE

7.4

Continued.

- Why did the characters or people do what they did? (inference)
- Did the story end the way you thought it would? Why or why not? (prediction/evidence)
- How did the characters or people change? Why? (characterization/themes)
- Was it right that _____? Why or why not? (critical thinking/evaluation)
- Was _____ a believable character? Why? (evaluation/aesthetic response)
- What was special or important about _____? (inference)
- What did _____ believe or value? (inference)
- How does this text change your thinking about other texts like it? (text connections/comparison)
- What was special or unusual about the illustrations? (aesthetic response)

Author or Artist Focus

- What is special about how the author writes (or this artist creates)? (aesthetic response/style/imagery/figurative language)
- How did the author or artist make it interesting? (aesthetic response/style)
- Why did the author or artist create the text? (inference)
- What did you notice about how the author or artist organized ideas? Why do you suppose this organization was used? (drawing conclusions/inference)
- What would you like to ask the author or artist? (question generation)

Personal Connections*

- What did you like? What were your favorite parts? Why? (critical/aesthetic thinking)
- What in this text was like something in your life? (connections/comparison)

*These questions can derail the focus on big ideas, so consider asking them later in the discussion—after the text has been thoroughly mined for big ideas, which then can be a focus for personal connections.

Teaching Students to Question

Young children are famous for their need to ask questions that begin with "why." Why is the sky blue? Why do I have to go to bed at 8:30? Why am I a girl? So why, despite this natural inclination to question, do some children become students who do not ask questions before, during, or after reading? Struggling readers can erroneously learn that question asking is restricted teacher territory. These students do not understand that generating questions is essential to comprehension. Posing questions causes readers to engage. Lack of questioning leads to passivity and superficial or incomplete comprehension that underlie many academic difficulties (Palincsar & Brown, 1984).

LEARNING FROM MATURE READERS

Teaching students to use the kind of self-questioning mature readers use enhances their comprehension of the immediate text and transfers to comprehension of new text (RAND, 2002). Mature readers ask copious questions before, during, and after reading, listening, or viewing a text. They ask why the author or artist created the material and how. They ask questions about the meaning of specific words and passages and, ultimately, what the whole text means. They also ask, "What does this have to do with me?" questions that generate connections between texts and themselves. Mature readers use questions to focus attention on what is most important so they can drill down to essential meaning. They also realize that answers to their questions may not be explicit in the text; while some answers are "right there," many demand that readers combine information from texts and background knowledge. Refer back to Chapter 2 for a complete discussion of questions good readers use during the CPS process.

All teachers want their students to comprehend what they read, listen to, and see, whether they teach first grade or college. Understanding is the key to learning. Understanding is the best kind of comprehension, and it is a result of meaning making activated by student questions. But what if students don't automatically raise questions? Unfortunately, just *asking* questions doesn't cause students to become questioners, especially if the teacher primarily uses questions as tools to assess whether assignments have been done. Students may associate questions with being monitored and graded, rather than seeing them as tools to initiate discussion and create understanding.

USING EXPLICIT TEACHING FOR QUESTION GENERATION

Students imitate respected teachers. Teachers who use inquiry-oriented questions are more likely to have students who also ask such questions. For all students to learn to generate questions to increase comprehension, explicit teaching is required, and teaching students to pose questions should be a priority.

When explicit teaching is successful, students learn the *why*, *what*, and *how* of question generation. This begins with helping students understand the many purposes of questions. A discussion that calls for students to reflect on reasons questions are used in life can provide a rich list that can be amplified with examples (see Ready Resource 7.2). For example, we ask questions to get information, such as "What exactly is a dongle?" Teachers can also invite students to examine teacher-generated questions to discover the range of purposes, and these questions can serve as examples. The questions in Ready Resource 7.4 may be used as a reference to create a brief chart to help students create their own questions. Many of those questions can be used with both narrative and expository texts. In addition, Ready Resource 5.11 in Chapter 5 lists questions related to literary elements.

Teachers also need to explain the criteria for "good questions" (Ready Resource 7.3) and demonstrate how to use those criteria before, during, and after reading, viewing, and listening to texts. Gradually students should be expected to generate more and more of their own questions, with coaching and scaffolding to support their growth. Refer to the steps for explicit teaching in Chapter 5 for specifics.

As teachers make an effort to pose more questions before reading, which set purpose and focus, some may go so far as to develop study guides with questions that lead students through a book or a chapter. These questions do not belong to students and if used too extensively can cause students to become reliant on the teacher for questions. Successful students learn to use these types of teacher questions as one source of purpose and focus, but know they must rely on their own questions. Struggling learners, on the other hand, may continue to view teacher questions as tasks to be completed, rather than scaffolds to increase their engagement and comprehension. Ready Resource 7.5 provides examples of ways to scaffold for students to ask more questions.

Teaching question generation.

READY RESOURCE 7.5

1 Emphasize the importance of inquiry-based problem solving in all learning by embedding question-generating lessons throughout the curriculum. Show how the scientific method is basically a series of questions, as is the writing process. Invite guests to talk about the questions they ask in their jobs, and have students prepare interview questions. TV and news reporters, doctors, and repair technicians are wonderful speakers for this topic, but nearly anyone can be tapped. Have students keep logs of their own questions, friends' questions, parents' questions, and teacher questions.

2 Teach the difference between open and closed questions using the explicit teaching guidelines offered in Chapter 5 (Ready Resource 5.2).

3 Post the Five W + H question words as stems to help students derive important details and create big ideas (see Ready Resource 5.4).

4 Assign students to watch cable news (or appropriate talk shows) and tally the number and types of questions. Advertisements may also be used. Have students chart the Five W + H questions, as well as open versus closed.

5 Post a CPS question chart and give students desktop cards or bookmarks with the same information. Refer back to Ready Resource 2.1 in Chapter 2.

6 Partner students to compose questions as they use a text. Suggest they create "before," "during," and "after" columns to list questions, and show them how to select the best questions to star.

7 Provide extended question frames, such as "What if _____?" "How is _____ like _____?" "Why did _____?" to scaffold question generation. Ready Resource 7.4 lists many questions that may be used to create frames.

8 Collaboratively set criteria for "most important" questions, such as: How does this make sense? What is it really about? What did I learn? How can I use this information?

9 Do a series of mini-lessons (with explicit teaching) on questions that uncover important text characteristics. Ready Resource 5.11 in Chapter 5 lists examples for narrative texts, which may also be used for expository texts.

10 Explicitly teach how to use questions to identify and solve comprehension problems. See the Comprehension Fix-Ups given in Ready Resource 5.5. "What is the problem?" and "How can I help myself understand?" are key questions in this process.

11 Collaboratively create questions based on art prints, photographs, and other visual texts that permit students without word decoding fluency to participate.

12 Show students how to keep a Question Log of personal questions they have. Use these for discussions, research (e.g., WebQuests), and writing.

Discussion and Conversation

It is important to understand that the difference between a discussion and a conversation is one of degree. *Discussions* are more formal, focus on problem solving, and may involve many people. *Conversations* are informal talks that focus on sharing stories, ideas, and opinions and may also be problem-based. They jump about and typically occur between two people or in a small group.

Certain myths surround questions and discussions. They include:

1. It is the job of teachers to ask the questions and students to answer them.
2. Questioning is a natural behavior, so it requires little teacher planning.
3. Young children can't answer high level open-ended questions.
4. Children have to be able to get the words right and the facts straight before they can engage in text-based discussions that target big ideas.
5. Quiet classrooms facilitate student comprehension.
6. Discussions are easy, because they are mostly about sharing personal experiences and opinions.
7. Since discussions are hard to assess, they are a low comprehension priority.

The goal of this section is to present logic supported by credible information in order to dispel these myths. The section also provides definitions to help clarify thinking.

THE BENEFITS OF TALK

Both discussions and conversations are important to thinking and language development. Experts propose that the fourth-grade slump is partly caused by the schools neglecting oral language development during earlier primary grades in favor of work on reading and writing mechanics (RAND, 2002). Allington (2005b) insists that even a little conversation can make a huge difference in children's language development and that it boosts motivation to learn. His conclusion is based on longitudinal studies of the amount of talk children hear.

Another study found a troubling "talk gap" among children. Those from poor families hear some 32 million fewer words than affluent children by the time they start school. This astounding data comes from tapes of conversations in professional versus working-class and poor families (Hart & Risley, 2003). By age four:

- children with professional parents had heard 45 million words.
- children with working-class parents had heard 26 million words.
- children from poor families had heard only 13 million words.

Children from professional families sometimes experienced as many as 4 million verbal interactions in a year, compared to about 250,000 for children in less-advantaged families. The quality of language interactions and language development during the preschool years predicted reading achievement six years later, with more language-advanced preschoolers becoming better readers.

Discussion, with its problem-solving orientation, does more than expose children to lots of words. A good discussion engages higher-order thinking to get to main points (big ideas). Discussion also engages interest under social circumstances, so it can be intrinsically motivating and can positively affect comprehension (Almasi, O'Flahavan, & Arva, 2001; Pearson, Harvey, & Goudis, 2005). Discussion also enhances comprehension by bringing together a variety of perspectives. It's the two-heads-are-better-than-one idea.

When text-based discussion is a regular classroom routine, students can learn to associate text use with social rewards. They can come to see texts as sources of information, as well as aesthetic experiences and means for deep understanding. Students expand their comprehension as they take on different roles in discussion, including critic, questioner, fact checker, and word expert. They can also take the roles of characters and proceed to discuss from that unique perspective.

INCREASING DAILY CONVERSATION

Short conversation times may be integrated throughout the school day to encourage focused talk about texts. Students can partner for one-minute conversations in Pair Share or Buddy Talk format. Here are more ways conversation can be integrated into the school day:

■ *Morning Meeting* is a brief time each morning for discussion. Teachers can write, "Let's talk about . . ." on the board and invite students to write in a topic as a focus of the Morning Meeting.

■ *Lunch Bunch* is an open invitation to talk about topics of interest during lunchtime. Conversation can be encouraged by labeling each table with a student-chosen topic. Students can sit with others who wish to talk about the topic.

■ *Buzz Groups* are built-in think stops during science and social studies or at the end of class. Three minutes is enough time for small groups to produce dozens of ideas, if they focus on the topic. For example, students might be prompted to talk about ways to decrease their carbon footprint after a lesson on going green.

■ *Four Corners* is a conversation activity that begins with labeling each corner of the room with a topic. Students choose a corner and then have two to three minutes to talk. When time is called, students move to a new corner. At any point the labels may be changed. Topics can target favorites, interests, birthdates, or experiences. For example, the north corner might be labeled for pets, south foods, east sports, and west toys. To connect the topics to a unit or a text, just change the categories. For a narrative text, you might use literary elements: characters, setting, plot, style, and themes. For an art text, use art elements such as color, lines, shapes, texture, composition, subject matter, style, media, and techniques.

Facilitating Discussions

Discussions that stretch thinking are laced with variety of meaning-making strategies. They are characterized by the use of good questions, active listening, and thoughtful comments that show participants are gleaning information and shaping ideas.

At the outset of the school year, teachers should work together with students to establish rules such as those described in Ready Resource 7.6. The goal is to create a climate where students can continue their individual Comprehension Problem Solving along with other students in the same pursuit of big ideas from texts. CPS thrives when everyone contributes and different viewpoints are welcomed and respected. The box on book discussion etiquette offers additional suggestions.

Discussions are meaningful and enjoyable when everyone is clear about the *how* and *why*. Generally, guidelines and specific discussion rules should be introduced and first used during teacher-led discussions. Teachers should be explicit about discussion guidelines and rules (e.g., explain and model each rule using a chart) and should follow up with scaffolded practice. Students will need coaching as they practice rules and guidelines. For example, ask students to role-play ways to show respect and listen actively. Students will need to be reminded about rules and guidelines *before* each discussion and debriefed about their use *after* discussions to solidify these behaviors into habits.

The goal is for students to be able to discuss independently in student-led groups. Imagine ideal discussions where students lean forward to listen, mull over questions raised by peers, pause after provocative comments to digest, and check texts to clarify

Discussion rules and guidelines.

1 **Prepare:** Come prepared. Use CPS with the text so you can participate. (Use preparation frameworks described later in this chapter in Ready Resources 7.9–7.12.)

2 **Plan new ideas:** Expect to learn big ideas you didn't think of on your own. The goal is to create meaning by problem solving together. Aim for new and different perspectives.

3 **Give evidence:** Your opinions and interpretations about big ideas should be supported with specific ideas from the text (i.e., page numbers where facts and details are found).

4 **Listen:** Listening is as important as talking during cooperative meaning making.

5 **Show *active* listening** with "body talk" and by responding to others with positive comments and questions.

6 **Respect:** To maintain a free flow of ideas, everyone must show respect for diverse interpretations. If you wish to present an opposite interpretation, it is respectful to restate the other person's idea first.

7 **Make it flow:** Try to link your ideas to those of previous speakers to continue the problem-solving spiral. Connecting ideas is essential to weaving the web of meaning.

8 **Take turns:** Use the agreed-upon way to get the floor. Don't talk when someone else is talking, and avoid monopolizing the discussion.

READY RESOURCE 7.6

Book Discussion Etiquette

"Before teaching others, we must teach ourselves," advised acclaimed New Zealand educator Sylvia Ashton Warner decades ago (1986). Her work motivated me to join my first book club so I could practice what I was preaching to my fifth graders. Now I can't imagine teaching without being a member of an adult group that regularly reads and discusses books. Teachers' personal experiences as readers and members of discussion groups help them understand and explain how and why in-class groups help students become increasingly literate. Critical "ah-ha"s about comprehension from my own discussion experiences and efforts with students include these:

- It is not interesting to listen to someone dwell on re-telling a story plot or expository text. A basic rule of participation in any discussion is that everyone uses CPS with the focus text and finishes before the discussion, whether they enjoyed the text or not. It simply is boring to hear a sequential literal retelling, and this does not help the group progress toward creating significant meaning from the text. Key events, facts, and details should be raised, as needed, to support conclusions about big ideas.

- Groups that expect the discussion to take a big idea focus *prepare* differently, in a way that will create a more provocative discussion. For example, a meaning-making orientation motivates people to ask themselves the question, "What is this really about?" from page one. Details become important because they are treated as clues or evidence for conclusions about big ideas.

- It is important to limit the discussion to the text everyone has read (or viewed or listened to) and avoid bringing up tangentially related experiences. Although making relevant connections is important to each person's own comprehension, personal stories frequently take the discussion away from discernment of big ideas. This doesn't mean folks can't share connections that may act as metaphors to aid text interpretation. The problem is extended personal stories that begin with something like, "That reminds me of the time . . ."

- The most important big ideas come from *whole texts*, not single paragraphs. Discussions should focus on synthesizing from the whole text, using the parts as evidence, and should not be allowed to stall on points raised in the beginning or middle of the text.

or elaborate on points that promise new big ideas. In such discussions everyone can expect that problem solving will yield new perspectives. This includes teachers, who will be surprised by the insights even young children are capable of producing.

DISCUSSION PROCEDURES

I feel fortunate to have had training from the Great Books Foundation early in my teaching career. This professional development is open to students, teachers, and anyone else who wants to learn how to ask questions and conduct a text-based discussion of high-quality literature. I adapted many of the ideas I learned from years of conducting Great Books interpretive discussions for this book and particularly for the sections that provide procedures to use before, during, and at the conclusion of a discussion. Ready Resource 7.7 provides an overview of these procedures. The goal is to conduct discussions in which everyone who participates comes away with new perspectives, including the teacher.

Great Books Foundation

www.greatbooks.org

ONLINE RESOURCE

Overview of the procedures to use before, during, and at the conclusion of a discussion.

Preparation Choices

- Ask individuals to write down questions or ideas they want to discuss, or pair students to generate questions. Collect and draw the ideas from a hat, or start with volunteers: Who has a question they are really interested in?

- Provide student note-taking frames, such as EPC, IQU, LWL, and T-charts.

- Prepare just one or two teacher questions to discuss in depth.

Discussion Starters

- Read aloud a section.

- Do a Write Right Away (WRA) about a question or the book's title.

During Discussions: Ask . . .

- *Meaningful questions* that provoke thought and lead to important big ideas. Even memory questions can be thick or thin. For "Little Red Riding Hood," ask, "What did Red do that started her troubles?" versus "What was in Red's basket for Grandma?"

- *Open/thick/fat questions.* These have many "right" answers that can be confirmed with the text. They require divergent thinking because these questions cannot be answered with a simple yes or no or with one word. Limit the use of questions that begin with "Do you," "Could you," "Would you," and "Should you."

- *"Why" questions that call for evidence:* "Why do you think that?" or "What evidence or examples can you give to support that?"

- *"What if" questions* to cause creative thinking.

During Discussions: Other Ideas

- *Connect and support.* Ask for connections among ideas shared, to the text, to other common texts, to the world, and so forth and for evidence that supports conclusions.

- *Use wait time.* Follow each question with a pause of three to five seconds to give students time to think and prepare more developed, higher-level answers. Wait time will also help more students participate.

- *Use every pupil response (EPR) to increase engagement.* Say, "When you have an idea, put your thumb up" (or some other agreed-upon action). Wait for most students to signal before calling on anyone.

- *Offer a pass option.* Allow students to control moments when they go blank. Conference with those who pass too often.

- *Randomly call on responders,* versus always taking the first volunteers. This ensures all genders, races, and abilities are included. Try numbering students and pulling numbers from a bowl. Tally student participation to minimize monopolizing and involve everyone.

- *Give signal options.* Offer ways students can get a turn besides raising their hands. For example, use an "I have the floor" object that is passed around.

- *Teach active listening.* Model and role-play paraphrasing, piggybacking on answers, and posing clarification questions such as "What do you mean by . . . ?" (See Ready Resource 7.13 for more ideas.)

Wrap Up

- Don't just stop. Bring the discussion to a conclusion.

- Ask for aesthetic responses: What did you like? Why?

- Ask for a summary of big ideas: What will you remember?

- Ask about the best points heard.

- Do a Tell One Thing activity around the circle, with a pass option.

7.7

READY RESOURCE

Before the discussion

Plan and prepare. Students must be taught how to discuss, and they need to be clear about the roles they will be playing. Teachers should provide mini-lessons on critical discussion components, such as how to ask and respond to thoughtful questions and how to listen actively.

Teach question generation. Growth in comprehension depends on students becoming increasingly independent in asking thoughtful questions. The following strategies will help them learn to pose their own questions:

- Display charts of CPS questions and generic questions to help students construct their own questions. Ready Resource 7.4 provides examples of discussion questions. Select from these and post them to help students create their own questions.
- Teach mini-lessons on good questions. Give examples of questions that create rich discussions.
- Emphasize that good questions are often ones for which we don't have answers. Inquiry is about searching for unknown answers.

Teach active listening. Listeners who are mentally engaged are called active listeners. Teach active listening by using the following strategies:

- Ask students to show what an active listener looks like. Say, "Use your body and facial expressions to make me believe. [PAUSE] Now show a passive listener."
- Ask students to describe the differences between active and passive listening and give reasons for active listening.
- Have students practice giving feedback, paraphrasing, and asking clarification questions in role plays. For example, write what-if questions on slips and have students draw them and practice in pairs. (See Ready Resource 7.8.)

Select a discussion format. How and where students sit and the roles they expect to play change the nature of any discussion. In general, everyone should be able to see each other's facial expressions and make eye contact. This helps

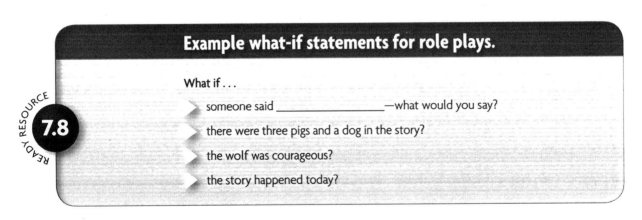

Example what-if statements for role plays.

READY RESOURCE
7.8

What if . . .

> someone said _____—what would you say?

> there were three pigs and a dog in the story?

> the wolf was courageous?

> the story happened today?

with listening and improves communication. Circle arrangements are desirable. Refer to the section on discussion types.

Provide a framework for preparation. Most students benefit from a scaffold that helps them plan for participation in a discussion. Preparation frames also help students take notes as they read.

Two- and three-column note-taking formats are useful. Jack Sanchez used a two-column T-chart that focused his students' thinking on important questions and big ideas. Another type of two-column chart is a bridge. Typically, the left-hand column of a bridge contains quotes or key ideas from the text, and the right-hand column is used as a bridge to personal experiences, where students write about their feelings or experiences that are connected to the text. Ready Resource 7.9 provides an example. Three-column formats or clusters may be organized around categories, such as Interesting Ideas, Questions, and Useful Information (IQU) or Learn, Wonder, Like (LWL). Of course, bubbles, clouds, and simple shapes can replace the columns. For example, an EPC chart consists of three circles on a piece of paper, labeled "Exciting," "Puzzling," and "Connecting." See Ready Resources 7.10, 7.11, and 7.12 for examples (Cornett, 2000). As students read a text, they note the parts (with page numbers) that

Tara's bridge.

BOOK: *When I Was Young in the Mountains* by Cynthia Rylant

KEY QUOTES/IDEAS FROM THE BOOK	BRIDGE
"When I was young in the mountains, I never wanted to go to the ocean."	When I was young I never wanted to go to the mountains. I only wanted to go to the beach! I still just want to go to the beach. I guess you just like to go where you have had good times in the past.
"Late in the middle of the night, she walked through the grass with me."	My grandma does that kind of thing. She always holds my hand when we go somewhere which some kids would be embarrassed. I'm not because I remember she even slept on the floor by the sofa with me when I stayed with her when my brother was born. It had to be a hard night for her.

READY RESOURCE 7.9

Charles' IQU chart.

Book: *When I Was Young in the Mountains*
Author: Cynthia Rylant
Artist: Diane Good

READY RESOURCE
7.10

QUESTIONS

1. Where were the parents?
2. Why did they drape the dead snake on them?
3. Why did they swim in a dark hole with snakes in it?
4. Why is it called a Johnny house?

INTERESTING

This was olden times so the family had to live without running water, an inside bathroom, and other modern conveniences. It seemed like it would be a hard life but they were happy in the pictures.

USEFUL

I think it would be a good way to live because it seemed more green than how we live today. I would like to try this simple life in the mountains if my mom and dad would agree.

---

fit into these categories and star one or two to discuss. Connections may relate to personal experiences, another book, or the world. These three categories tap into the CPS process at the "predict and connect" point.

Choose a discussion starter. It is important to plan how to begin the discussion. In the Write Right Away (aka Quickwrite) technique, students write about one question before discussing it. This causes everyone to focus and creates an atmosphere of thoughtfulness. The nature of the question is critical. It should be one the leader really cares about but cannot answer personally. For example, using the book *Charlotte's Web*, I might ask, "Why would the author give the book that title when the main character is Wilbur the pig?" After students write for three to five minutes, the discussion can begin, with volunteers who wish to share what they wrote. Alternatively, partners can share before starting the discussion. Students can also draw quick sketches instead of writing.

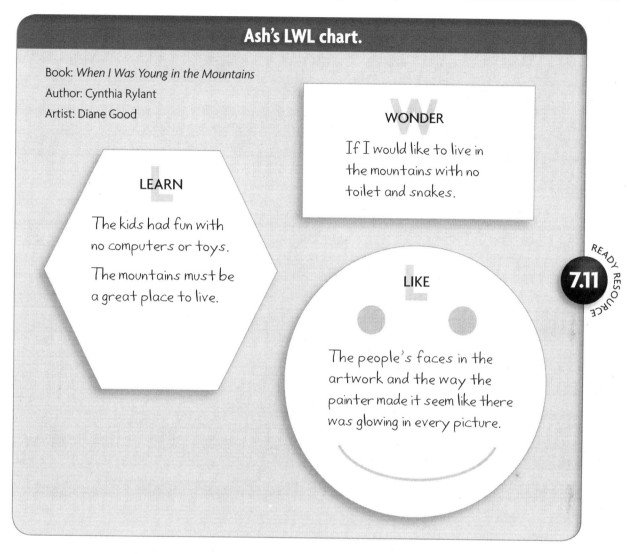

Ash's LWL chart.

Book: *When I Was Young in the Mountains*
Author: Cynthia Rylant
Artist: Diane Good

WONDER

If I would like to live in the mountains with no toilet and snakes.

LEARN

The kids had fun with no computers or toys.

The mountains must be a great place to live.

LIKE

The people's faces in the artwork and the way the painter made it seem like there was glowing in every picture.

7.11 READY RESOURCE

Although discussions often begin with a question, there are other possibilities. To start the discussion, students may choose part of the text to read aloud and explain why they chose it (e.g., important event, use of language, connected to their lives). Student read alouds should be rehearsed so that the reading is fluent. Guide students to select parts that contain a whole idea, and set a time limit of a minute or so to prevent monopolizing.

Discussion cards are also helpful for starting discussions. They may use similar categories to two- and three-column frames. Invite students to use index cards to jot down ideas they would like to discuss. Cards can be placed in a hat and drawn for discussion, or each student might choose one card from his or her stack. Categories include

- character actions that are noble, despicable, or curious.
- important events.

Kat's EPC chart.

READY RESOURCE 7.12

Book: *When I Was Young in the Mountains*
Author: Cynthia Rylant
Artist: Diane Good

PUZZLING

I didn't understand why she only wanted to be in the mountains because I like to go to the ocean and desert, too.

EXCITING

The family seemed poor, but they made their own fun, like swimming in the muddy hole and sitting on the porch at night.

It was exciting when Grandma killed the snake with a hoe to protect the family.

CONNECTING

We live in the mountains at Lake Toxaway in the summer. Our cabin is cozy like in the drawings and we have a cast iron stove like Grandmother, but it is green. We sit on our back deck and look at the Blue Ridge and grill food.

- puzzling things.
- surprising events.
- emotional parts.
- quotes or special words.
- theme topics that may be grown into big ideas.

If students have prepared a frame or chart (or bubbles, circles, etc.), then volunteers may be asked to open the discussion with one of their responses. A brief sharing around the circle will give everyone a chance to present an idea. The group may then choose which idea to discuss first in depth.

During the discussion

One important goal during a discussion is for everyone to participate. Everyone should be ready, because "be prepared" is the first rule of coming to a discussion circle. To make it more conversational, I have "no hands up" rule. Students can signal with a more subtle thumbs-up, if they wish.

During the discussion teachers can weave a more complex web of meaning by keeping in mind Tom Brokaw's observation that the best question comes from the last comment. Watch Jim Lehrer's interviews on the PBS *NewsHour* to see this advice expertly followed. Teachers can also go for depth, with questions such as the following:

- What do the rest of you think about Cindy's idea?
- Who had the same or a similar idea?
- Is this a new idea for anyone?
- Who has an opposite idea?
- What in the text is evidence for that idea?
- What's an idea that needs to be discussed, but no one has mentioned?

It is important to recap key ideas periodically. Although teachers can ask, "So far, what have been the most important ideas you've heard?" it is best if students take leadership. Pairing students to recap increases participation.

When students are reluctant to speak up during discussions, it is important to remember that adults can be shy as well, especially if they don't feel prepared or think their point of view will not be respected. Scaffolds that help students organize their thoughts can increase participation, because students feel more prepared, more confident, and less nervous.

When you observe that several students have not participated, make it easy for them to get involved. Ask everyone to think of an idea that someone has already shared. Ask for thumbs-up when they remember one idea, and call on students who haven't participated previously. Or ask: What have you heard that you agreed with? Disagreed with? Have a question about?

Ending the discussion

Discussions shouldn't just stop—they should be wrapped up, with a focus on synthesizing the most important ides. You might use Write Right Away again or ask students to share the most important points made, what made sense, what someone said that was a new idea, ideas that were similar to their own, and questions that may persist. This activity is called Tell One Thing (TOT). TOT is often done by going around the circle, giving everyone a chance to comment. I recommend a pass option be available for students who may need more incubation time. This is really a "pass and come back," since at the end of the sharing passers should expect to participate, at least by sharing an idea they heard. Refer to Chapter 9 for response options for extending discussions through written, arts-based, and technological text making.

FACILITATING A DISCUSSION WITH A BIG IDEA FOCUS

Discussions can be important vehicles for developing students' comprehension, but how the discussion is conducted determines its impact on students. Ready Resource 7.13 provides suggestions for facilitating a discussion with a big idea focus. These techniques

Techniques for facilitating a discussion with a big idea focus.

Model use of each technique, and teach how to use them. Remind students to use them before each discussion, and debrief afterward, asking students about techniques they noticed.

Invite: Ask others to comment on ideas

- What do the rest of you think about this?

Acknowledge: Accept a comment without agreeing or disagreeing

- I hear what you are saying.

Paraphrase: Repeat another's comment using your own words

- What's another way to say that?
- What do you think (student) means?

Clarify: Ask for explanation of someone's comment

- Are you saying that . . . ?
- What do you mean by . . . ?
- What questions does the group have about this?

Piggyback: Support and extend another's idea

- Who has a similar idea?
- If _____ is true, then _____?

Agree/disagree:

- I agree because . . .
- I disagree because . . .
- What do the rest of you think?
- What evidence is there for that idea?
- What other ways can we look at this idea?
- How does that make sense?

Elaborate: Extend discussion on certain points

- What are some other examples of that?

- What evidence is there for that idea?
- Provide evidence: give specifics to support conclusions
- What are examples of that?
- Where in the text did it say that?
- How did you come to that conclusion?

Re-focus: Bring discussion back to the original focus

- Let's get back to our focus.
- How does that idea connect to our focus?

Change direction: Open new avenues for discussion

- Who else has a new idea?
- What are some ideas that haven't been brought up?
- What are other important ideas we can discuss?
- What was surprising or puzzling?

Generate questions: Cause participants to raise questions

- What questions do you have?
- What do you still wonder about?
- What do you want to know?
- What would you ask the author (or a character)?

Wrap up: Bring discussion to a close

- What were the most important ideas you heard?
- What did you hear that you wouldn't have thought of on your own?
- What will you remember most from this discussion?
- What questions do you still have?

READY RESOURCE
7.13

- promote active listening and respectful responses.

- focus on extracting and constructing big ideas.

- increase participation by causing more thoughtful responses and involving more students in the discussion.

When presenting these techniques to students, model use of each and teach how to use it. Before discussions, remind students to use the techniques, and debrief their use of them afterward.

Types of Discussions

Many different types of discussions are available, and they may be further adapted for learner needs and the demands of curriculum standards. The popular designs described in this section are consistent with the focus of this book: putting comprehension first by engaging students in inquiry into big ideas using important questions. All of the discussion formats draw upon the facilitation guidelines and rules previously discussed.

For any type of discussions, teachers should select an appropriate variety of texts, including digital, arts-based, and multimedia. Over the course of the year students should learn to ask questions about and discuss any type of text. The discussion is intended to extend the meaning students made individually through the power of group problem solving. Texts that allow creative extrapolations by asking "what if?" and other provocative texts that generate interest are invaluable bases for meaningful and memorable discussions. The more layers of meaning in a text, the greater the discussion potential. Use diverse text formats and content, such as

- non-verbal texts: paintings, sculptures, songs, films, and videos

- texts connected to science, social studies, and math (informational books)

- short stories, poems, and magazine and newspaper articles

- live performances, such as dances and plays

- current events of high profile, such as the Olympics

- WebQuests (refer to Chapter 9) and online reading

- children's literature, including multicultural literature

Bibliographies of award-winning children's literature are available at the American Library Association's website. Information on censorship is available there as well, including bibliographies of censored books. It is well worth perusing the list to find some of the most famous and favored books of all time among the banned books (e.g., books by Mark Twain, Maurice Sendak, and Judy Bloom). These can serve as excellent texts for discussion.

American Library Association

www.ala.org

TEXT-BASED DISCUSSION

A powerful type of discussion, called text-based, engages participants in collaborative CPS to understand a text with which everyone has used CPS individually. Text-based discussions shift the focus from personal experiences that may be triggered by the text to focus on big ideas supported by evidence in the text. I first experienced a text-based discussion in a book club in South Carolina. The book was *Gone with the Wind*, and the discussion facilitator began with what has become one of my favorite starter questions: "What is the meaning of the title?" With teaching acumen, she had us do a quick-write about that question, which set the stage for an animated exchange.

Everyone participated, and I was surprised by the range of responses. Several talked about how war causes so much loss. Others brought up the allusion to the place, Tara, and how the earth is only loaned to us and cannot be owned by us. Some comments focused on the word *wind* and its various uses in general parlance, such as "winds of change"; wind as an uncontrollable act of nature; wind as an invisible force with potential to provide clean energy or create tornadic devastation. We were twenty minutes into this engaging discussion before we had finished squeezing the title for all we could.

Listening to the profound connections was exhilarating, and I realized I would never have thought of these on my own. I was hooked on the motivational and intellectually engaging power of this kind of group inquiry and the insightful discoveries that can result. I vowed to make this kind of discussion happen with first graders, fifth graders, and eventually with college students. The questioning and discussion guidelines and rules in this chapter, including all of the Ready Resources, reflect the influence of text-based discussions.

LITERATURE CIRCLES

Literature circles, now routine in many classrooms, are usually small, heterogeneous groups that meet to discuss a text in whole or part. Members may choose or be assigned different roles that direct their preparation for and participation in the discussion (Graves & Graves, 2007). Students may be assigned to groups, but it is recommended that students have as much choice as possible, to engage motivation. Often, the choice offered is the specific text to read.

Teachers usually do a short (twenty- to thirty-second) text talk (preview) for each text option, to guide student choice. Options may be offered that have similar content but offer a variety of difficulty levels to accommodate a range of students. For example, a teacher may assemble a set of texts around a topic or theme connected to a science or social studies unit. Author and artist studies are popular—different groups read, view, or listen to texts that are all by the same writer or artist. At times, students may all read the same text. Here are suggested procedures for using the literature circle format:

1. Choose four or five texts on a similar topic but at various reading difficulty levels.
2. Introduce the options by giving a brief talk about each.

3. Display the options and give students time to preview them (e.g., a day).

4. Provide slips for students to sign up for choices in 1, 2, 3 order. This allows teachers to adjust groups and text levels to meet learner needs.

5. Assign the students to groups based on the texts each group will read, view, or listen to.

6. Give students clear purposes for reading, using preparation frames and other strategies.

7. Establish a schedule so students know when the group will meet and where they need to be in the text. Shorter texts (e.g., picture books, articles, songs) may be discussed as a whole, others by chapter or section.

QUESTIONING THE AUTHOR

Although most discussions focus on the text itself, it is possible for a discussion to examine the author's background and perspective. This option is frequently one part of a text-based discussion, taking place toward the end of the discussion. However, Beck and McKeown outline a discussion format that targets discerning the author's intentions. It is called Questioning the Author or QtA (2006). Use the following procedures for a QtA discussion.

1. Open the discussion with broad questions such as
   - What is the author saying or talking about?
   - What is the author's main message?
   - What is the author thinking?
   - Why did the author write this?
   - That is what the author says, but . . .

2. During the discussion, make links with questions like
   - How does that connect with your life?
   - What information does the author give that fits in with . . . ?

3. Encourage discussants to clarify confusion with questions such as
   - Does that make sense? Why or why not?
   - Did the author explain that clearly? How?
   - What did the author leave out?

4. Encourage students to refer to the text to clarify, repair misunderstanding, and support inferences with evidence. Useful questions are
   - Where did the author say that?
   - How did you get that idea?
   - Is there another way of looking at it?

5. Conclude the discussion with questions like
   - What questions would you like to ask the author?
   - What have you learned about the author from this text?

DRAMA-BASED DISCUSSIONS

Drama can have a dramatic effect on comprehension (Cornett, 2007; Deasy, 2002). Comprehension depends on the ability to examine different perspectives, and drama—which is all about assuming roles—requires trying out different points of view.

Drama-based discussions, which may include acting out a text, ad-libbing in character, or discussing a dramatic text, are usually introduced in a teacher-led discussion and may lead to small student-led group discussions later. It is critical that students prepare for their roles, so that they know their roles before reading and use the role to direct their preparation for discussion.

Teachers will need to clarify for students what drama is (pretending using your mind, body, face, and voice—except in pantomime). Students need help learning to stay in role and can learn to do so over time with coaching from the teacher. Posting examples of roles and giving students time to practice appropriate role behaviors before using them will help them during discussions. Modeling, charts, and the use of headbands or role buttons are also helpful.

The following are examples of roles students may take. Multiple students can assume the same roles.

- *Leader:* starts the discussion with a fat question and keeps it going with fat questions
- *Word Weaver:* finds important and special words that may connect to big ideas
- *Reader:* chooses two or three important parts to read aloud and tells why they are important
- *Keep It Going (KIG):* asks questions and provides comments to keep the discussion moving
- *Artist:* creates or finds art related to important ideas and explains the connections
- *Connector:* finds ideas in the text that can be linked to common experiences; texts, and events, places, or people
- *Fact Checker:* clarifies facts when confusion arises
- *Puzzler or Devil's Advocate:* challenges the group with "what if" and "I wonder why" questions; offers a contrasting perspective
- *Elaborator:* asks others to give examples and tell more about key ideas
- *Closer:* summarizes key points from the discussion

Empathy roles

German scholar Theodore Lipps coined the term "empathy" at the turn of the 20th century to explain what audiences have to do to understand art. Empathy is more than sympathy—it is deliberately making meaning using one's imagination to see and feel as others do. To conduct a discussion based on empathy roles, use the following guidelines.

1. Start with students taking the role of a character, a real person, or the author, before reading, listening to, or viewing a text (Cornett, 2011).
2. During reading, students should make notes about
   - how the character looks, feels, and speaks
   - motives—what the character wants most
   - problems or obstacles to achieving those goals
   - likes and dislikes
   - relationships to other characters
3. Start the discussion with the question, "What happened?"
4. A volunteer responds, in character, and the discussion proceeds with other characters giving their perspective.
5. The leader should keep the discussion moving in the direction of discovering big ideas, using questions like, "What did you learn from that?" and "How did that help you or someone else?"

Discussions may be set up in a fishbowl arrangement (described on p. 215) with a surrounding audience who may participate at certain points by asking questions of characters. Empathy roles work well with literary texts and with social studies, science, or current event topics. For example, to discuss important big ideas about individuality versus conformity in Pinkwater's *The Big Orange Splot*, students can become Mr. Plumbean, different neighbors, the mayor, or a policeman. Just as easily, students may choose real-life people, such as historical figures featured in a social studies text, and discuss in character to reveal different perspectives on key events of the time.

STUDENT-LED DISCUSSIONS

Teacher-led discussions need to be balanced with student-led discussions to encourage independent meaning making. On the other hand, not all discussions can or should be student led. There is a place for teacher-led discussions that bring everyone together in a common experience around a common text or set of texts. Such community building helps students become comfortable with one another and learn to value different perspectives, and it lays the foundation for inquiry. However, carefully structured student-led discussion is associated with greater achievement and more positive social and motivational attitudes for all genders, levels, classes, and ethnicities, so it should be high on the agenda, too (Johnson & Johnson, 2002). Student-led discussions can take many forms, including QtA, empathy roles, literature circles, and other formats discussed previously. Student-led discussion groups can become clubs that meet after school.

When teachers divide students into small groups to discuss material without providing instruction about how to conduct discussions, problems can arise. Although the goal is eventually to have students lead small group discussions, this does not happen on the first day of school. It can be a reality by the end of the first month. Preparing students with explicit instruction is the key. Teachers will need to coach groups, using visuals to explain question possibilities, role definitions, discussion facilitation, how to give descriptive feedback on what is working, and so forth, especially during the first efforts. Once good discussion habits are established, teachers may still coach student discussions, but they should not participate as discussants.

Teaching student-led discussion behaviors

A particularly useful format for teaching discussion behaviors is the Fishbowl or Outside/Inside Circle. This format helps students learn all aspects of discussion.

1. Start by inviting volunteers into an inner circle to discuss a question while an outer circle (the rest of the students) listens in.

2. After a few minutes, stop and ask the outer circle to comment on what they saw and heard and to ask questions of the inner circle. For example, "I liked what Teresa said because I didn't remember how many Mexicans lost their land to America" (*Esperanza Rising*) or "I noticed Andrew showed active listening by following up on Sarah's idea."

3. Next, the circles exchange positions and the discussion is resumed.

Notice that comments may be about the content of the discussion or about the process.

Guidelines for student-led discussions

The following additional guidelines may be helpful in setting up student-led discussions:

- **Group size.** Use small groups of four to six students to encourage full participation. Groups should change composition on a weekly or monthly basis so everyone works with everyone else over time.

- **Seating.** Seat groups far enough apart so they do not disturb one another. Each group should sit in a circle so the members are face to face. They may sit on the floor, in chairs, or wherever it is comfortable.

- **Time limits.** Start with short discussions of five to ten minutes and work up to the goal of sustained discussion for thirty minutes. Use a kitchen timer, and cue students when they have five minutes left; cue again at one minute.

- **Wrap-up.** Teach students how to bring the discussion to a close with Tell One Thing. Choices are: you learned, what you were surprised about, what someone said that was the same as something you thought of, what is a question you still have. Students may also do one- to two-minute free-writes to wrap up.

- **Debriefing.** Assemble the whole group and ask, "What worked? What didn't work? What were the best ideas? Why? What can we do to make discussions better?"

- **Assessment.** Tape (audio or video) discussions so that students can observe themselves and set goals for learning. Ready Resource 7.14 provides a rubric to modify for student self-reflection on their discussion behaviors.

Example discussion rubric.

CRITERIA	LEVEL 4 (high)	LEVEL 3	LEVEL 2	LEVEL 1 (low)	POINT VALUE
PREPARATION:					
Questions	Many written open-ended questions, with text evidence	Several written open-ended questions, with text evidence	One or two written questions, with text evidence	At least one text-based question, but not open	15
Big ideas	Many written in statement form, based on text evidence; implicit and explicit big ideas	Several written in statement form, based on text evidence; at least one implicit big idea	One or two written big idea statements, based on text evidence; all are explicit	At least one text-based idea; may be explicit and not full statements (i.e., topics only)	15
Text-based knowledge	Thorough knowledge of relevant details, topics, main ideas, and themes	Shows knowledge of most important details	Partial knowledge of important details	Big gaps in knowledge of important details	15
DURING:					
Initiative	Often volunteers to ask questions and share ideas	Sometimes volunteers to ask questions and share ideas	Rarely volunteers to ask questions and share ideas	Never volunteers	10
Respect	Disagrees courteously, paraphrases, asks for clarification	Sometimes paraphrases others and asks for clarification	Rarely paraphrases or asks for clarification	Non-responsive to the comments of others	10
Listening	Uses active body language: eye contact, facial expressions, etc.	Some active listening behaviors	Inconsistent active listening behaviors	No eye contact or body/face indication that he or she is listening to others	10
Problem solving	Frequently points out clues to big ideas in text	Sometimes points out clues to big ideas in text	Occasionally points out clues to big ideas in text	Almost never points out clues to big ideas in text	20
WRAP-UP:					
Conclusions	Easily summarizes most important points and questions	Summarizes important points and questions with coaching	Provides important points if directly asked	Gives one-word answer to requests for big ideas learned	15

READY RESOURCE

7.14

Differentiating Discussions

Teachers can change discussions in a myriad of ways to make success for all likely. Ready Resource 7.15 gives "A–Z" options for differentiating discussions. The following are examples using the PARTICULAR acronym described in Chapter 4:

- **P**lace: Group can meet outside or in a carpeted nook to minimize distractions.
- **A**mount: A book may be broken down into chapters or sections for each discussion; discussion time may be shortened or lengthened.
- **R**ate: Give students more or less time to complete the reading, listening, or viewing.
- **T**ask/target: Change the roles students take to prepare for and participate in the discussion.
- **I**nstructional support: Repeat explicit instruction about discussion roles and use of CPS strategies. Use small group lessons or tutorials, as needed. Discussions may occur after a text is read aloud to the whole group, instead of after independent reading.
- **C**urricular materials: Change the texts. Use diverse text types and formats to accomplish similar purposes. For example, couple the reading of *Sarah, Plain and Tall* with viewing of the film version.
- **U**tensils: Allow use of CD-ROM interactive books or recorded versions of books.
- **L**evel of difficulty: Use easier texts or ones with more supports, such as pictures. Chapter 4 discusses readability levels.
- **A**ssistance: Allow students to buddy read. Bring in older students or adults to read with students or to help them prepare/rehearse their roles.
- **R**esponse options: Offer choices for how to show comprehension (e.g., writing, visual art, drama, PowerPoints).

Groups may be allowed to use discussion time to create a response to the text. For example, students may plan and create a mural that shows significant locations in a book like *Tuck Everlasting* by Natalie Babbitt. (Meaning is often linked to settings in literature, so visual art that uses place as subject matter can be an effective way to make the invisible act of comprehension visible.) These products may then be used to start discussions.

Discussion options from A to Z.

Discussions are informed conversations about texts centered on specific focal points. The following are ideas to prompt students' thinking about texts and offer diverse ways to prepare for and organize discussions. All of the following options should include giving text evidence to support conclusions.

- **Author Interview:** List questions you'd like to ask the author.

- **Before and After:** Discuss how characters changed and why.

- **Blitz:** Brainstorm, using categories such as adjectives to describe the main character, motives, emotions, or places.

- **Book Critic:** Find a part that does not make sense. Defend your choice.

- **Book Review:** Critique the book, rate it, and defend your decisions.

- **Book Dedication:** Say, "I dedicate the book to _____, because . . ."

- **Cliffhanger:** Read aloud and stop at a suspenseful point. Make and defend predictions using evidence.

- **Clubs:** Meet in a small group to choose and discuss books. Members rotate roles.

- **Current Events:** Choose a real event. Discuss facts and draw conclusions.

- **Decision Maker:** Brainstorm what would have happened if a character had made a different decision.

- **Demonstrate:** Show something you learned to do from the text.

- **Epilogue:** Explain what happened after the text ended.

- **Expert Interview:** Find real people (on the Internet or in the community) to speak on an important topic in the book.

- **Face-to-Face:** Sit in a circle. On round one, each person makes one comment (see prompts for Tell One Thing, given earlier). For round two, each student responds to a comment from round one. Continue on with more rounds as time permits.

- **Favorites:** Explain your favorite part, focusing on why you liked it.

- **Fishbowl (Outside/Inside Circle):** Two to four students sit in a small circle and discuss a text. The rest of the group stands on the outside, periodically giving observations and asking questions. Rotate into the inside by using various techniques, such as tapping individuals.

- **Fortune Teller:** Based on everything you know now in the story, what do you think will happen and why do you think that?

- **Friendship:** Discuss characters or people in the text you would like as friends.

- **Funny/Serious:** Tell about the funniest and most serious parts of the text.

- **Gab Fest:** Pick one big idea from the text and talk about it nonstop until you run out of steam.

- **Heinz 57:** Work with a group to describe the text in fifty-seven words.

- **Important Part:** Discuss the most important part.

- **Interesting Event:** Describe the most interesting event.

- **Jigsaw:** Organize into groups, each one with a specific focus (such as literacy elements, exciting/puzzling/connecting, questions, etc.). After a time, rotate so that new groups are formed. Individuals now share what they discussed in their previous group.

- **Keep Going:** Read another text with the same themes. Have a compare/contrast discussion.

- **Listen Up:** Listen to a CD of the book and compare it with reading the book.

7.15

READY RESOURCE

(continued)

Continued.

- **Make It Up:** Discuss titles for a sequel or "next text" that should follow this one.

- **Net Work:** Research the author or related topics and discuss how this information contributes to comprehension of the text.

- **Prompts:** Choose categories for making notes about a text, and use the notes as discussion starters. Categories might be: Interesting or intriguing things, Exciting parts, Puzzling or bothersome things, Confusing parts, Useful ideas, Novel or new ideas, Questions, Surprises, Connections to self, Connections to other texts, Connections to the world.

- **POV:** Explain how would it change the story if the point of view were changed (e.g., from first to third person).

- **Profile:** Describe characters as if you were an FBI agent.

- **Questions, Anyone?** List a certain number of questions about a character or an aspect of the text.

- **Rate It:** Decide how many stars you would give the text, and explain why.

- **Reporter:** One student is the reporter, and the others each choose a character. The reporter interviews the others with a plastic mike, asking "What happened?"

- **Second Chance:** Talk about how it would change the story if a character had made a different decision (e.g., what if Charlotte decided not to write in the web?).

- **7-up:** Describe important points in seven words, or make seven points.

- **Sound Off!** Play a video version of a book, but turn off the sound while you are watching it. Ask students to narrate, discuss, or write about what is happening, what the actors are revealing through their faces and gestures, and other topics.

- **Telephone:** Tell what you would say to a friend on the phone about the text if your battery was low.

- **Venn Diagram:** Watch a film inspired by a book (e.g., *Sarah, Plain and Tall; Harry Potter; Charlotte's Web*). Compare/contrast characters, setting, and plot between the book and the film using a Venn diagram. Variation: Compare and contrast two different texts.

- **Web:** Write a character's name or an important concept in a bubble in the middle of a large piece of paper and brainstorm associations. Write your ideas on legs coming from the bubble. Discuss the connections.

- **What If:** A volunteer proposes a "what if" that could have changed everything. The discussion proceeds until it is exhausted, and another "what if" is then proposed.

- **Why or Why Not?** Go around the circle with each person asking a "why" question about the text.

- **X:** Xerox a picture or another text that meaningfully connects to the original text in some way. Share in and explain how it connects.

- **Zero In:** Explain the absolutely most important thing you got from the text.

Conclusion

This chapter focused on the important role of questions in comprehension. In particular, it examined questions for their potential to engage students in substantive discussions that use "high level talk" (Duke & Pearson, 2002). It described the benefits and types of discussions and a process for making discussions integral to comprehension instruction, focusing on discussion as a form of collaborative inquiry into the big ideas in whole texts.

High-level discussions go beyond plot retellings, and that takes time. Where does this time come from? Teachers cannot expand the school day to implement inquiry-based comprehension instruction, so the use of time has to change. To paraphrase Barack Obama, we need to do what we can with what we have wherever we are. That means reforming comprehension instruction, changing how we teach—not just adding to the time budget.

Discussions can actually become timesavers. How? Discussion motivates students to engage in learning. Disciplining students is time consuming, and students who are meaningfully engaged do not require discipline or take time away from the comprehension task. Expert questions tap into students' goals and interests, and good discussions happen in a social context with a cooperative meaning-making focus. Using questions to promote conversations and discussions is a best comprehension practice that can yield quick observable results. Students studiously prepare, with their sticky notes and other notes, as they anticipate sharing with peers. They savor words and linger over pictures that provide clues to the meaning-making mystery. Students become animated as their energy is directed at the goal of making meaning. They work to present persuasive evidence for their big idea conclusions and consider the views of classmates who offer ideas no one else thought of. On this path to intrinsically motivated comprehension, students experience poignant moments. They "re-member"—become members again of the human family, as they discover big ideas embedded in common beliefs and history, concealed in the word-based and wordless texts people create. Students are thus disciples of learning instead of discipline problems.

Of course, students have to be taught to ask the kinds of questions that help them dig into texts and participate as valued contributors to discussions. They learn these skills from explicit teaching and from seeing how teachers lead discussions. Gradually the responsibility for leading is transferred to students. Small-group, student-led discussions become main events during the literacy block and during content blocks.

Discussions have unmatched potential to increase comprehension, because talking out thoughts and listening to others enriches the web of meaning and forges strong bonds that create a sense of community. Discussions with these results are not made of ping-pong question-and-answer sessions between teacher and students, or of dull plot retellings (Cornett, 1997). Putting comprehension first involves students in generating their own inquiry questions that lead to big ideas they share during "grand conversations" among people who are all know the plot and wish to seek meaning together (Peterson & Eeds, 1999).

7 big ideas

The following are examples of big ideas from this chapter. Use the list as a resource to generate your own priority list of big ideas related to questioning to promote discussion and conversation.

1. The desire to question is innate, but asking good questions that facilitate high-level talk is an art, informed by a skill-set.

2. High-level discussion requires many questioning and facilitation skills.

3. Open, fat, or thick questions generate more qualitative responses and thus more substantive comprehension.

4. Questions that promote discussion should be selected and sequenced to uncover big ideas from full texts.

5. Students should learn to do most of the questioning in discussions and conversations so they become more independent at problem solving to make meaning.

6. Students need to be taught explicitly how to discuss, including how to take different roles to expand perspectives for the group.

7. Classroom discussions should focus on inquiry into big ideas, with emphasis on using text evidence (and sometimes author information), along with personal background and world knowledge.

a look ahead

Chapter 8 describes how to teach words with a focus on comprehension. The chapter describes specific guidelines and teaching ideas for increasing students' vocabularies so they can more easily apply Comprehension Problem Solving strategies. Discussions and conversations are described as key strategies to develop vocabulary.

In particular, the chapter highlights ways to problem solve unknown words, along with ways to deepen understanding of words. One section of the chapter is devoted to increasing fluency with words so that students are freer to concentrate on meaning.

7 response options

Use these response options to continue your own comprehension problem solving. Work with a group, if possible.

1. Generate several big ideas of your own from this chapter that are not listed above. Choose one or two to discuss. Give reasons for your decision to describe them as big ideas.

2. Return to the chapter opening questions to examine their structure (e.g., open versus closed). Select several for discussion in terms of their structure and their content.

3. Try a text-based discussion using a short text (e.g., a folktale). Use one of the frames in the chapter (T-chart, EPC, IQU, LWL, etc.) to prepare.

4. Create a cue card for yourself that lists points to remember about asking good questions.

5. Make a chart of five to ten general discussion questions that students could use as a reference for small group discussions.

6. Assume the role of an expert on either the what, why, or how of discussions. Along with classmates who have prepared the same topic, take turns making your points. Then open the discussion up to the audience (the full class) for further questions and discussion.

7. Prepare an explicit lesson to teach students to ask questions or to prepare them for discussions.

8. Keep a log of all the questions you ask in a day and then sort them by purpose.

9. Make your own list of criteria for "best" questions, using information from the chapter. Observe a teacher's questioning and tally the numbers and types of questions (e.g., open or closed) and the length of wait time after questions. Evaluate the teacher's questioning in light of your data and your criteria.

10. Check out discussion resources on the Internet by exploring sites that review books and offer study guides that provide discussion questions for particular books.

11. Add missing ideas to the A–Z discussion options (Ready Resource 7.15). Missing are O and Y.

12. Research other ideas for building comprehension through discussion by consulting these authors and programs: Taffy Raphael, Harvey Daniels, Grand Conversations (Peterson & Eeds), Great Books Discussions, Instructional Conversations (Goldenburg & Saunders), Collaborative Reasoning (Anderson et al.), and Accountable Talk (Sarah Michaels).

13. Participate in a blackboard discussion forum about teacher questioning and its role in comprehension.

14. Use Question the Author (QtA) in a real way: Send me a question you have about this chapter or about the concept of comprehension first: ccornett@wittenberg.edu.

CHILDREN'S LITERATURE CITED

Babbit, Natalie. (2007). *Tuck everlasting.* New York City: Square Fish.
Muñoz-Ryan, P. (2002). *Esperanza rising.* New York: Blue Sky Press.
Pinkwater, D. (1997). *The big orange splot.* New York: Scholastic.

Teaching Vocabulary and Fluency for Comprehension

This chapter describes how to teach words, for the purpose of increasing comprehension. Specific guidelines and teaching ideas are described to increase students' vocabularies so they can more easily employ Comprehension Problem Solving (CPS) strategies. Ways to problem solve unknown words are highlighted, along with ways to deepen understanding of words. The chapter particularly emphasizes the need for teachers to distinguish between words as labels and words as concepts. One section is devoted to increasing fluency so students are freer to concentrate on meaning.

important questions

1. What are the differences among words, vocabulary, and concepts?
2. How are vocabulary and comprehension related?
3. How can students be taught to (1) enjoy words and word study, (2) develop larger vocabularies, and (3) use word strategies to increase comprehension?
4. How is fluency related to vocabulary and ultimately to comprehension?
5. What specific fluency strategies have been shown to increase comprehension?
6. How can vocabulary and fluency strategies help students use CPS to inquire into the meanings of texts?

Introduction

As I first drafted this chapter, Hurricane Ike was hitting Galveston, Texas. Weather Channel reporters were using words like *breach* and *overtop*. My husband was in Louisiana for the Red Cross. He called to tell me about the "ERV"s and "Refers." These recent experiences remind me that vocabulary development continues throughout life. Without continually acquiring new words, it would be hard to talk to anyone. Technology, in particular, spawns new words every day. Word processing has pushed words formerly reserved for the publishing industry into common usage: *font, header, footer, page layout.* Then there is the lexicon of texting—a whole language made of abbreviations, FWIW (for what it's worth). For some parents and teachers, this may be a RA (red alert) about the degeneration of youth, but IMO (in my opinion) it is a great indicator of interest in communication.

Literacy experts agree that vocabulary is essential to comprehension, but they are not of one mind about how to teach it (Gambrell, Malloy, & Mazzoni, 2007). There are deep divisions about how to teach vocabulary in a manner that leads to the goal of comprehension. On the one hand are staunch supporters of "words first" approaches that emphasize explicit teaching of spelling sound patterns (i.e., phonics rules) that accumulate to reach a threshold where students can practice with "decodable" texts. They take an additive part-to-whole stance. On the other side are folks who believe that reading a wide variety of rich, unregulated texts extends vocabulary and develops fluency—a whole-to-part philosophy.

A combination of these approaches is recommended in this chapter. The emphasis is on teaching students to access word meanings quickly and accurately and to be able to bring those words to life in oral reading using personal interpretation reflected in expression, pronunciation, and rate. Such fluency with words is necessary for comprehension. Short-term memory capacity limits how much we can think about consciously. We need word fluency so that we can devote our conscious thinking to comprehension purposes and not word decoding (LaBerge & Samuels, 1974).

How can students develop word fluency in ways other than traditional drill and practice? How can the learning of word meanings become inquiry-oriented, with comprehension the priority? How can vocabulary study become integral to daily literacy development and even become a highlight of the school day? The classroom snapshot profiles one teacher's efforts to integrate best practices into a daily word study routine that focuses on three basic word aspects: meaning, spelling, and sound (Pinnell & Fountas, 1998). General teaching strategies and strategies specific to teaching vocabulary are printed in boldface.

classroom snapshot

LISA LATROUBE'S WORDS ALIVE ROUTINE

Lisa LaTroube and her third graders are seated around the perimeter of a large braided rug. Spaces between students break the circle into three groups.

"Show me your teeth," Lisa says with a big smile. Twenty-two children look at her and smile widely.

"One, two, ready, begin," she says, pointing to one section of the circle. They start to **chant** "bub-bub-bub-bubblin'" over and over.

On Lisa's signal, the second group comes in singing, "Words words words are a bubblin' over, words words words bubble in my soul."

Another signal from Lisa brings the third section in, singing the same lyric as the second group. They sing the round three times, ending with the first group once again alone with their refrain. When they finish, the class shouts **"Words Alive!"**

"Monday people, hands up. Great. Here are your numbers: *uno, dos, tres, cuatro,"* Lisa says as she points to each student. "Terry is *primo,* so begin."

"My weather word is *hurricane,"* Terry says as he holds up a swirling-wind-shaped red card with that word printed on it. "A hurricane is a violent storm with winds over seventy-four miles per hour. Another name for hurricane is *cyclone.* The word *hurricane* came from a Spanish word. Okay, that's the meaning, **what do you see?"** Terry asks. Many hands go up, and he points to a girl.

"I see four vowels: *u, i, a,* and *e,"* she explains, and Terry then points to a boy.

"I see that there are two *r's,"* he says.

"Okay, what about the sound?" Terry asks, and again many hands go up. He calls on fellow students.

"The e is silent. It follows the vowel–consonant–silent *e* pattern," another girl responds.

"The *u* is r controlled, so it sounds like in *fur,"* another boy says.

"It rhymes with Lanacane, which my mom uses," observes a girl.

"I see something else. Can I tell it?" a boy asks, and Terry nods his head.

"It looks a lot like *hurry* except for the *y,"* he says.

"That makes sense, too, because the wind is in a hurry," another boy blurts out.

Terry waits and looks to Lisa, who rotates her hands to signal "wrap up."

"Okay, **what did you learn?"** he asks, and calls on a boy.

"A hurricane has winds over seventy-four miles per hour," he says.

"Gustav was 150 miles per hour," a girl says. "We had to evacuate to Baton Rouge."

"That's over two times seventy-four," Lisa responds.

"I didn't know *hurricane* was a Spanish word," a boy says.

"So, **what is a synonym?**" Terry asks. "Ready. 1–2–3."

On signal, most of the class says "cyclone."

Terry then gets up and takes his **word card** to a bulletin board that already has a dozen weather words on it. All the words are on **different shapes and colors** of paper. Terry uses a removable glue stick to post his word.

"**Why did you put it in the southeast corner?**" Lisa asks.

"Well, hurricanes mostly hit in the south, like Louisiana and Mississippi, but sometimes on the East Coast, like here in South Carolina," Terry explains.

"Wow, what a great reason," Lisa says.

"How about your shape and color?" a girl asks.

"It is supposed to look like on the Weather Channel when they use red to mean high wind going around in a circle with the hole in the center," Terry says.

"You forgot **your initials,**" a boy points out, and Terry looks at his posted word.

"Here's a marker," a girl offers. Terry takes it and draws a line under the word *hurricane* and writes TT below it.

"Okay, *numero dos,*" Lisa announces, and a girl holds up a card with the words *wind shear* printed on it. The **Words Alive** routine continues until four words have been "worked," as Lisa calls it. The routine concludes with a few minutes of "**I Spy,**" during which students look at the growing **collage of weather words** and tell things they spy about the meaning, spelling, or sound of the words. Lisa passes around a laser pointer, and students locate words by north, south, east, and west directions, which are labeled on the collage. They take about three minutes to share ideas related to words that have similar meanings (e.g., violent weather events like *tornado, hurricane,* and *ice storm*), as well as words that have spelling and sound similarities (e.g., *tornado* and *hurricane* both have three syllables).

Words Alive Routine

Each day, four or five students present their words, with every student doing a word each week. Words are chosen by the students and are usually connected to a science or social studies unit. Students have the option of choosing from a Word Box on Lisa's desk in which she places key words from the unit written on slips of paper.

Lisa says, "The students love Words Alive. It took a couple of weeks before they understood all the sharing options, but now they present in many creative ways. They are so motivated to perform their words for an audience. They know they need to share about the word's meanings, spelling, and sound, but how they do it is up to them. I've taught them how to write songs, create dances, and use drama. Some have created word raps, and one girl taught us an "earthquake" dance to present her word. They are taking more and more risks as the year goes on. They are also using more and more resources to find interesting information to share. All the students use MacBook's dictionary, but they also use online resources like Wikipedia. I have students begging to do extra words!"

Words Alive presentation options appear in Ready Resource 8.4 on pages 234–235.

Word Study for Comprehension

In the beginning was the Word . . . John 1:1

The Bible isn't the only place where words are put on a pedestal. The literacy community is in consensus about the importance of vocabulary for comprehension success. Words are fundamental components of thinking, and comprehension depends on thinking, especially the kind of strategic thinking represented in the Comprehension Problem Solving process. While there can be understanding without words, as in communication through music and visual art, the strength of a person's command of words (vocabulary) is a determiner of his or her comprehension capacity for all written and oral word-based communication.

Words are the building blocks of a person's vocabulary, or lexicon. There is more to words than how they look (spelling) and sound. Words are *labels* for concepts, and key concepts underlie big ideas. The existence of hundreds of languages means that many labels or names exist for the same concept, such as *madre* (Spanish), *mère* (French), and *mum* (British) for "mother." Sometimes the spelling and sound of a label helps us access the concept (e.g., *crash* sounds like a crash). Other times a label, such as *dongle*, is arbitrary. This common computer device simply needed a name, so someone invented one. Central to comprehension success is understanding the concepts behind words, not just pronouncing the words. You can undoubtedly pronounce *dongle*, but you may not have a clear concept of what it is. Keep reading!

We can think without labels, but we can't think without concepts. In addition, the relationship between words and comprehension involves more than labels and concepts. Vocabulary development and in turn comprehension are affected by background experiences, including cultural knowledge, and instructional opportunities (RAND, 2002). In particular, building new vocabulary depends on aspects of the Five Factors discussed in every chapter of this book. For example, vocabulary development is influenced by the nature of the *learner,* especially her or his background and interests, and by the type of *text.* Specific elements of the text that affect vocabulary understanding are

- its difficulty for the specific reader, which includes the proportion of unfamiliar words.

- roles of specific words in the text, such as multiple-meaning (polysemous) words.

- the learner's purposes for using the text, in particular the expected comprehension outcome.

INCREASING MULTIPLE VOCABULARIES

Further complicating the relationship between words and comprehension is the fact that individuals have various personal vocabularies. The listening vocabulary, the largest, includes words a person understands when he or she hears them. During youth, the speaking vocabulary—words used to communicate through talk—is usually next in size. The reading and writing vocabularies build on the foundation of the listening and speaking vocabularies. For most adults, the reading vocabulary eventually surpasses the speaking vocabulary. Throughout life, the writing vocabulary usually remains the smallest, since it depends on translating known words into written form using many skills, including spelling, handwriting, and keyboarding.

Strong comprehenders tend to have strong reading, writing, speaking, and listening vocabularies, but each person's profile has a unique design. For example, some of us have stronger listening vocabularies than speaking vocabularies. Vocabulary development, as measured by the number of words a person can read, is frequently used to predict IQ score. This, however, is primarily a *correlational* relationship—the two things tend to occur together. Having big feet also correlates with better comprehension, but stretching your feet won't increase your comprehension. Spending more time studying words won't automatically raise a person's IQ score, and it also won't automatically increase comprehension. When word study does improve comprehension, it is because of the instructional quality. How vocabulary instruction is delivered is the key. Isolated pronunciation drills won't catch kids up, if "catching up" means closing the comprehension gap. For this purpose, *thorough* multidimensional vocabulary instruction offers the most potential (Beck & McKeown, 2006).

THOROUGH VOCABULARY INSTRUCTION

What constitutes thorough? First, any quality instruction is informed by the fact that most words are learned *in context*, either in oral/aural interactions (e.g., high-level discussions and conversations) or in written forms—anything from a newspaper to a blog. Word meanings are learned through repeated exposure and deep processing, not just focus on spelling and sound (surface structure). For the purpose of increasing comprehension, word study must go beyond examining the spelling patterns that create the sounds of words (graphophonics). Teaching vocabulary for comprehension has to focus on diverse ways to build word *meaning*, and it has to be differentiated for learner needs and the four other factors that influence comprehension (Bear et al., 2006). Teaching and independent work with words should be integrated throughout the school day, not isolated in word study times. Isolated phonics and spelling lessons are certainly a part of word study, but they should be a small piece of the literacy instructional pie, even for immature readers. Thirty minutes or less is plenty, even for students who are low performing, which leaves plenty of time for work with word meanings during the literacy block and content area study.

Most of the Ready Resources in this chapter give examples of strategies that go beyond spelling and pronunciation. For example, the word ladder in Ready Resource 8.1 lists a series of questions to scaffold the concepts behind word labels. The example is a word most adults have heard and may use regularly but incorrectly.

Word ladder.

Hoi Polloi	
What is it a kind of? people	What are the kinds of it? clerks, mechanics, waiters, factory workers
What is it a part of? words that categorize people	What are the parts of it? categories of people who work for minimum wage
What is it a stage of? prosperity	What are the stages of it? accumulating wealth
What is it a product or result of? economic conditions	What are the results of it? having a large workforce
How does the word make you feel? thankful	What image can you make in your head related to the word? crowd of people in jeans in a public space

READY RESOURCE 8.1

Students who have heard a lot of language and a variety of words start school with a distinct literacy advantage, and that advantage persists (Hart & Risley, 2003). To level the literacy playing field, teachers should set up daily classroom opportunities for students to hear, speak, read, and write lots of words related to rich and interesting content. Comprehension is about problem solving with a focus on concepts and ideas that are usually represented by words. Students need immersion in language-rich contexts that engage them in using words for communication—the comprehension and expression of thoughts and feelings. The following are some key daily activities. Literacy events are discussed further in Chapter 10.

- daily read alouds, discussions, and conversations during which students hear new words used in meaningful oral contexts and participate in language use
- extensive reading, listening, and viewing of texts full of new words
- daily opportunities to write, create, and perform full texts
- explicit teaching of word meanings, including strategies to expand meanings
- explicit teaching of tools for solving unknown words

Optimally, these literacy main events are situated in a word-rich classroom environment that includes high-level talk directed toward discovery of big ideas. Printed words should surround students: word walls, word collages, poem charts, and other evidence of enjoyable language activity.

Students who learn in a classroom where words are celebrated as keys to meaning simply have a leg up on comprehension. Some fifty studies support the use of a variety of word study practices such as those described in this chapter (Baumann & Kameenui, 1991; Graves & Watts-Taffe, 2002). To bring vocabulary instruction fully in line with comprehension, the Five Factors that influence comprehension (characteristics of learners, texts, tasks, teaching practices, and context) must be addressed. Doing so produces differentiated vocabulary instruction. Foremost in teachers' minds as they plan such word study should be these questions:

1. How can tapping students' interests motivate them to become more conscious of words and engage in student-directed word study?

2. How should words be taught so that meaning is emphasized?

3. What strategies do learners need in order to gain independence with decoding unknown words and growing their vocabularies?

Creating Interest in Words

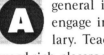 general interest in words can lead students to become motivated to engage in learning new words, which in turn increases their vocabulary. Teachers can encourage general interest in words by creating a word-rich classroom and encouraging word play. In addition, the motivational factors discussed in Chapter 6 apply to vocabulary learning. Vocabulary instruction should be connected to student interests, along with engaging students through clear purposes or goals, student choice, opportunity for group work, and feedback on progress. All of these motivational factors interact with one another.

WORD-RICH CLASSROOMS

As discussed in Chapter 3, physical and psychological aspects of the learning context influence students' comprehension. To help students develop vocabulary, a classroom needs to be word rich, with an atmosphere of excitement about finding and using interesting words. The physical space itself can become a key teaching tool when it is used to make vocabulary visual.

Word collages

Students can be charged with selecting important and interesting words related to units under study to contribute to a collage, as Lisa LaTroube did in the snapshot. They may write the words on colored paper of different shapes or find them in magazines or newspapers. Students initial each of their contributions and tell why they are positioning the word in a particular space on the collage. A word wall can take the form of a collage, instead of a list.

Word chains

Students can write words on long slips of paper and loop them into paper chains. Hang a chain above each student's desk by hooking it over a dropped ceiling bar, or suspend the chains from a class clothesline. Students may add words from content study, read alouds, and independent reading. An alternative is to hang a large fishing net and let students paper-clip words to it. Chains and nets give students concrete feedback on personal vocabulary growth.

Quote banners

Quotes inspire with their artful use of words. Quote banners are another way to create a word-rich environment, and they have the advantage of showing words in context. Studying artful word use helps students see how studying words can give them power in real-world settings, which provides motivation. Quotes may be taken from song lyrics, advertisements, and presidential speeches, among many other sources. Students should find and select the quotes themselves, using diverse sources.

Quotes

www.bartleby.com

http://en.wikiquote.org

www.quotes.net

ONLINE RESOURCES
www

Quote banners may be hung ceremoniously and changed periodically to accompany units of study. For social studies and science, the quotes may be from scientists and inventors. Quotes from authors and artists might accompany literary and arts-based units.

Poem charts

Poems are another way for students to encounter words in context and to experience the power of literary language. Students need to *see* poems that they have heard and performed. Poems posted on the classroom walls provide models for word patterns and inspiration for artful writing. In addition to Shel Silverstein's collections, check out poetry by Jeff Moss, Jack Prelutsky, Arnold Adoff, Ashley Bryan, Langston Hughes, and Byrd Baylor. All-time favorite poems and poets may be located through the Academy of Poets. Ready Resource 10.12 in Chapter 10 lists ideas for performing poetry.

Favorite Poems and Poets

Academy of Poets, www.poets.org

ONLINE RESOURCE
www

Forms of word play.

Echo bursts: How did the lion feel after he ate the pretty gladiator? Answer: Pretty glad he ate her.

Hink pinks: A rhymed pair that answers a riddle (What is an unhappy father? Sad dad.)

Palindrome: A word or phrase that is spelled the same forward and backward: madam, dad, tot

Sniglet: An invented combination: cinemuck (goo on cinema floors)

Tongue twister: A phrase that is difficult to pronounce: "bugs black blood"

Tom Swifty: A pun in the form of a quote and an attribution with an adverb: "I want a hot dog," he said frankly.

Twins and triplets: popcorn and peanuts; red, white, and blue

Rebus: 1/2 back = halfback

READY RESOURCE **8.2**

WORD PLAY

Teachers can foster students' interest in words by playing word games, doing word puzzles, and punning. Ready Resource 8.2 lists forms of word play. Warm-ups, riddle-a-day, and a funny word collection are especially fun and motivating.

Warm-ups

The Minister's Cat is an example of a warm-up or "sponge" activity. It is played as a circle game. The leader says, "The minister's cat is an _____ cat," plugging in an adjective beginning with "a." The whole class chants the sentence. The next person says "The minister's cat is a _____ cat," filling in an adjective starting with "b," and so on through the alphabet. To play this as a memory game, the class has to repeat all previous adjectives before each new one. For variations, change the stem. For example, "The minister's cat hates _____" could be used with Lisa's LeTroube's weather words.

Riddle-a-day

Riddle-a-day is a highly motivating routine that permits students to problem solve while focusing on important clue words and interesting words. To provide context, riddles should be related to content units and current events. Use the following steps:

1. Post a riddle with blanks for each letter of the answer.
2. Ask students to choral read the riddle and then suggest letters to fill the blanks.
3. Coach students to discuss meaning clues, along with spelling and sound clues.

4. Warn students not to call out answers.

5. Make this activity easier or harder by providing varying letter clues. Giving the first and last letters makes it easier.

Transfer the responsibility to the students for finding and conducting riddle-a-day, and connect the riddles to units when possible. Example:

What do you call a teacher who had a shark bite off her left arm and left leg?

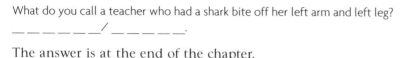

The answer is at the end of the chapter.

Funny word collection

Humor can both motivate and boost learning, because comprehending and producing humor involves problem solving that results in a flood of positive feelings (Cornett, 2002). Invite students to collect funny words and contribute them to word rings, collages, and class and individual books. The words might sound, look, or mean something humorous. Use categories such as funny names, places, foods, actions, sounds, animals, or events.

INTERESTING WORDS

A teacher's personal enthusiasm for words is contagious. When teachers place high value on expanding their own vocabulary, students are likely to follow suit. Teaching strategies that focus on learning interesting and important words every day can increase students' interest in words.

Word-a-day (WAD)

Popular calendars feature a word for each day, and online dictionaries frequently offer a word of the day. Start WAD by demonstrating how to present words to the class:

1. Say it.
2. Use it in context.
3. Tell why it was chosen.
4. Practice it as a class, using a variety of echo pronunciations, or tell or show the meaning to a partner.

Invite students to sign up once a month to present a word. This routine takes about two minutes. Add the words to a word wall or collage and to students' individual collections.

Word buttons

As an addition to the word-a-day activity, give students wipe-off buttons to write the word on. If you have a button maker, make up ones that read, "Ask me about ____" and have students write the word in the blank. These make great conversation starters inside and outside the classroom.

Beat the teacher

After the teacher introduces an interesting word, students and the teacher compete to use it *meaningfully* during the day. Uses may be tallied on the board. My fifth graders beat me 24 to 5 in one day using the word "canoodle"!

VISUAL PROGRESS RECORDS

Motivation depends on knowing one's goals and purposes and seeing progress toward accomplishing them. Students need to feel the excitement of learning new words and see that knowing more words boosts comprehension. The following activities make vocabulary growth concrete and provide student reference tools for reading and writing.

Word rings and boxes

As students accumulate words, inexpensive metal shower curtain rings provide a simple way to keep them organized. Recipe boxes have the advantage of alphabetized tabs, but rings don't spill. Either way, students can see their personal word caches grow. Of course, rings may be used in conjunction with boxes.

Students should be taught how to select and study new and interesting or important words, write them on index cards, and place them on the ring. Students' progress can be assessed during weekly mini conferences. Use a check system to indicate levels of knowledge. For example, ✓ = pronounces and spells the word, ✓✓ = explains its meaning, ✓✓✓ = uses it properly in a sentence. Write the checks on the word card. When a card gets three checks, it is moved from the ring to the student's word box.

Word collections

The appeal of searching out and adding to a collection motivates ongoing inquiry. Word collections may relate to physical collections students already have—anything from rocks to records. Students can also collect words in categories such as hink pinks, onomatopoeia, alliterative phrases, foreign words, funny words, and so on. Offer a choice of categories, and have students paste or write the words in a blank book or a computer file, with the category at the top of each page. Students may partner to share additions. Ready Resource 8.3 lists examples of word categories.

Student dictionaries

Like word rings and boxes, personal dictionaries provide visual evidence of learning and may serve as references. Each student will need a 26-page blank book with the pages marked A through Z. Words may be written or pasted in. Definitions should be synthesized from dictionaries, and the student should write one for each word in her or his own words. A sentence using the word in a meaningful way may be added to clarify meaning. Some teachers require students to list synonyms in the form of a thesaurus.

Word and phrase categories.

Words may be grouped in many ways. Grouping aids comprehension, because words are stored in the brain in categories. The more categories in which a word is stored, the more complex the thinking a person can engage in about the word. Use these categories to create charts, word books, and rings; to do word wall workouts (described in the classroom snapshot); and as the basis for collections.

Abbreviations: shortened forms of words, as in text messages or more traditional usage (e.g., is short for "exempli gratia," which means "for the sake of example")

Acronyms: words created from the first letters of other words (NEWS = north, east, west, south)

Anagrams: scrambled words (WENS for NEWS)

Animal names: porpoise = "pig fish" (Latin); *porcupine* = "pine-porker" (French)

Antonyms: words with opposite meanings (*up* and *down*)

Brands: labels for products (Kleenex, Xerox)

Clichés: overused words and phrases (busy as a bee)

Clipped: shortened words (taxicab for taxi cabriolet)

Coined: created words (*emoticon* for the emotion symbols typed in emails, such as the smiley face)

Collective nouns: words for groups of animals or things (herd, gaggle, pride, flock)

Colloquial words: words not used in formal speech or writing (*soda* or *pop* for "soft drink")

Compounds: combined words (playground, tarpaper)

Eponyms: words based on people's or place names (levi = Levi Strauss; teddy bear = Theodore Roosevelt; booze = E. G. Booze; jeans were named after Genoa, Italy, the city where they were first produced)

Flip flops: pairs of words where only one letter is different (ping pong, willy nilly)

Homographs/heteronyms: words that look the same (spelling) but have different sounds and meanings (I can *read.* I *read* it yesterday.)

Homonyms: words that have the same spelling and sound but different meanings, multiple-meaning words (swimming *pool, pool* your money, *pool* table). See *polysemous words.*

Homophones: words that sound the same (pear, pare, pair)

Multiple meaning words: includes both *polysemous words* and *homonyms.*

Oxymorons: conflicting couplets (jumbo shrimp)

Pleonasms: redundant word phrases (baby puppy, young baby)

Polysemous words: multiple-meaning words (pool, contact)

Portmanteaus: combined words (*smog* = smoke + fog)

Slang terms: very informal and often ephemeral usage (cool, neat, groovy)

Synonyms: words with similar meanings (*big* and *large*)

WORD CHARACTERISTICS

Assonance: repetition of vowel sounds (stiff, pick, lift)

Consonance: repetition of consonants (a fair field full of people)

PHRASES AND WORD USE

Analogy: comparison (*fork* is to *eat* as *shovel* is to *dig*)

Aphorism: wise saying (Early to bed and early to rise makes a person healthy, wealthy, and wise.)

Epitaph: inscription on a tomb or statement to memorialize a person

Euphemism: a more positive way of saying something negative ("went to his reward" instead of "died")

Hyperbole: exaggeration (I could eat a horse.)

Idiom: words or phrases used in a way that cannot be understood literally (in a pickle, frog in my throat, spill the beans)

Metaphors: comparisons (He is a walking time bomb.)

Onomatopoeia: words that sound like what they mean (zip, crack, bang)

Simile: comparison using *like* or *as* (soft as silk)

Synecdoche: use of a part to represent the whole (head of cattle)

READY RESOURCE

8.3

GROUP WORK

Collaborative word work in pairs or small groups is both motivating and effective. Students can work together on just about any vocabulary project. Ones that involve performance for the class go further to invoke the power of the audience to motivate.

Words Alive word wall workout

Lisa LaTroube used the Words Alive workout in the classroom snapshot. This is an easy, student-directed, whole-group routine. Assign four or five students to each day of the week. They have the responsibility of finding a word to add to the wall and teaching the word to the class. Demonstrate options for ways to present the meaning, spelling, and sound of each word. Use the activities listed in Ready Resource 8.4 during the Words Alive routine or during small-group or independent work.

Words Alive word wall workout activities.

PERFORM WORDS: MUSIC, DANCE/MOVEMENT

- Word choir: four to six students say the word or a synonym, as conducted by another student (e.g., fast, slow, loud, soft, repeated).
- Sing the word: the leader recites the word, changing pitch, tempo, rhythm, accent, and volume, and the audience echoes.
- Adapt song lyrics: use a familiar melody to write a song about the word.
- Dance or move: stamp, clap, or jump along with the spelling, sound, or meaning of the word.

ART

- Word cards: use a shape and color to suit the word.
- Illustrate the word.
- Write the word in a way to show its meaning.
- Create concrete poems: use words about the word to create a shape that symbolizes the word.
- Make word collages: find or write words that are all related in meaning.

DRAMA

- Improvise, using as many words as you can in two minutes.
- Pretend to be the word and talk about your life.
- Pantomime or do word charades.
- Be a one-minute expert: tell everything you know about the word's meaning, spelling, and sound.

I SPY

Ask students to find . . .

- Types of words, such as parts of speech or contractions.
- Phonics and spelling:
  - vowel patterns
  - syllables
  - consonant patterns
  - chunks, rimes, or phonograms
- Words that *look* alike.
- Affixed words (words with a suffix or prefix).
- Rhyming words.

(continued)

Continued.

WORD SORTS

Students categorize words using . . .

- Open sort: students choose categories to group words.
- Closed sorts: categories are given to students (e.g., nouns and verbs).

WRITING

Students use word wall words to write . . .

- A–Z writing forms (see Ready Resource 9.1).
- Poem patterns (see Ready Resource 9.5).
- Tongue twisters.
- One-liners (a sentence a person or character might say; e.g., *"Who said it?"*).
- Word riddles: give three clues, moving from general to specific. Example: (1) animal, (2) furry and four-legged, (3) purrs.
- Songs about words or using words.
- A story with a beginning, middle, and end (BME).

MAKE NEW WORDS

- Add affixes (prefixes and suffixes).
- Rearrange the letters. Example: *saw* reordered makes *was*.

- Combine words (e.g., make compounds or portmanteaus).

PLAY WITH WORDS

- Word pyramid: start with one short word at the top, add letters to make the next below it, and so on. Example: dog, dogs, doggy, dogged.
- Word stairs: start with a word, the next word steps down, using the last letter to start the new word.
- Web a word: brainstorm other words connected by meaning, spelling, or sound.
- List rhyming words.
- Acrostics: write a word vertically and write a phrase or word that relates in meaning, starting with each letter. Example:

C ommunicates by purring

A nimal with fur and four legs

T ail swooshes when mad

Many excellent word play books for children are available. I recommend Marving Terban's books, such as *Too Hot to Hoot,* and Willard Espy's *A Children's Almanac of Words at Play.*

8.4 READY RESOURCE

Word research

Groups can research the etymology (origin) of words using any dictionary, including computer dictionaries. This activity may be part of the word wall routine or may be connected to a science or social studies unit. Students enjoy researching their first names and surnames by conducting family interviews and consulting baby name books.

Songs

Songs convey thoughts and feelings. Many songs, such as the birthday song, are written for celebrations, and collaborative song writing to celebrate words builds students' interest. Lisa LaTroube's "Bubblin' Words Alive" song is an example of collaborative song writing by students. Ready Resource 8.5 presents another example, from one of my classes.

Words Alive Song.

This rap, written by sixth graders, is meant to be sung in five groups, with everyone singing the refrain.

Group 1:   Homophones / antonyms / homographs / homonyms

Refrain: VOCABULARY VOCABULARY VOCABULARY WORDS!

Group 2:   Synonyms / synecdoche / pleonasms / similes
            (Refrain)

Group 3:   Homographs / assonance / heteronyms / consonance
            (Refrain)

Group 4:   Metaphors / palindromes / alliteration / calindromes
            (Refrain)

Group 5:   Echo bursts / tongue twisters / hink pinks / lip blisters!
            (Refrain)

STUDENT CHOICE

Offering students choice enhances interest, motivation, and learning. Students should be expected to be continually learning new words, and many of those words should be self-selected. Encourage students to notice words in their reading, on television, in discussions, and so forth. Words may be chosen for their *meaning, spelling, sound,* or all three. Students can collect words in personal wordbooks, on rings, or just on a list on the computer. In particular, teachers should use strategies to encourage students to use the new words in writing and speaking. For example, I've used word collages (described previously) with every class I have ever taught, from primary grades through college, to emphasize personal choice. Of course, any strategy should connect as much as possible to content units under study or to students' personal projects. This enables students to see the place of vocabulary in problem solving oriented toward big ideas. For example, word collages may be themed by topic (e.g., friendship) and connected to units about commonalities and differences among people. A word collage based on a category such as "affixed words" will draw attention to aspects of words that affect meaning, and the meaning connection should be made prominent. In this case, students should be asked to find and generate affixed words in texts used in content units.

Group collages make word displays into art while serving as writing and speaking references. Their design extends problem solving into a visual dimension. Students also can make personal versions of collages and word walls, using file folders, boxes, or any surface on which to write or glue words.

Teaching Words for Comprehension

The question of how to teach vocabulary so that meaning making is prominent leads to the question, "What does it mean to know a word?" Certainly, there are degrees of knowing. On the low end are words that are totally unknown. In the middle are words that we know something about— perhaps we've heard them on occasion or seen them here and there. At the high end are words we truly know: we comprehend them easily, can explain their meanings, and use them in writing and talking. Obviously, words that we know thoroughly have a greater potential to affect our comprehension than words with which we have a passing acquaintance. The goal of vocabulary instruction is to cause students to move more and more words to the top of the knowing scale (Allen, 1999; Beck & McKeown, 1998).

Another questions is which words should be taught. It seems logical that if teachers had lists of words most students should have learned at certain mileposts, we could better catch up students who are behind (Biemiller, 2005). However, even the most ambitious vocabulary programs can directly teach only about a thousand words each year, and four hundred learned is considered a success (Biemiller & Boote, 2006). This adds up to a maximum of twelve thousand words by high school graduation, with a more likely estimate of five thousand. But *most* graduates actually know between fifteen and twenty thousand root words. At the rate of four hundred words per year, those with meager vocabularies could not be brought up to this par. Other means of accelerating vocabulary development must be used, along with direct or explicit instruction.

The following sections describe basic principles for vocabulary instruction that target knowing words well and are consistent with an inquiry-based approach to comprehension.

ENCOURAGE INCIDENTAL LEARNING

To reiterate a previous point, students' vocabulary sizes are far greater than one would predict from the number of words taught directly during thirteen years of schooling. Mature readers read some one million words per year. This implies that most words are learned by means other than isolated word teaching in school (Graves & Watts-Taffe, 2002). In fact, 90 percent of the words students learn annually are learned *incidentally*, in natural integrated contexts such as conversations, discussions, television, the Internet, and print texts (Carlisle & Katz, 2005). For example, you may have found yourself learning new words and phrases from this text (e.g., *word fix-ups*) before they were explicitly defined.

Indeed, most words are learned without explicit instruction (Stanovich, 1986). This doesn't mean words and word learning strategies shouldn't be explicitly taught; it means teachers are obliged to design instruction so that high-powered literacy events rich in words dominate the schedule. Interactive read alouds by teachers, daily engaged independent reading by students, and regular high-level discussions provide opportunities for students to learn vocabulary in incidental ways. Content texts and discussions during science, social studies, math, and arts lessons are especially fertile ground from which students harvest new words. Incidental word learning is not a panacea; it can, in fact, be flawed. Meanings derived from context can be incomplete or even wrong. Explicit teaching about words must accompany incidental learning. Many adults could benefit from explicit word instruction. For example, it is common to hear misuse of terms, such as *hoi polloi*, mispronunciation of words, such as *nuclear*, and misunderstanding of words, such as *niggardly*.

LINK NEW TO KNOWN

Research during the 1980s honed in on how the brain stores knowledge in categories (Rumelhart, 1982). These categories are called *schemata*. The brain acts like a computer, with schemata being the folders. Students need to learn how to put new words and ideas into existing folders—connecting new words to already known ideas and storing them in pre-existing brain schemata—and how to make new folders—the brain physically altering itself to create a new schema.

The greater the quality of and number of connections between new words and known words, the deeper the brain processing and the greater the comprehension. The following activities, if used regularly, will cause students to create mental webs of word meanings.

Maps and webs

Clustering related ideas around a new word helps to solidify its meaning. Demonstrate how to map associated words around a new word, using both think alouds and open-ended brainstorming. Webs and maps may be structured with legs or sections labeled to suggest connections. Categories for web legs or map sections include synonyms, antonyms, category the concept belongs to, cognate words (having the same root), examples, non-examples, and where the word might be found. Ready Resource 8.3 lists some word groupings that may suggest connections.

Cubing

Neeld (1986) used the idea of a cube to devise a strategy to expand words and concepts. "Cubing" is a way to generate ideas that can be used to develop vocabulary meanings. Cubing expands thinking by prompting one to look at a topic in six different ways. The basic strategy is to think of—or even actually make—a cube with a different action written on each face. Common actions include: (1) describe it (use adjectives), (2) analyze it (identify its parts), (3) associate feelings with it, (4) apply it (state what it can be used for), (5) argue for it (pro), and (6) argue against it (con). Other choices are compare/contrast it and give its causes or effects. To use the cube, perform all six actions in turn.

Students may work together in teams and may be given a time limit (e.g., one minute on each side) or, for in-depth work, they might concentrate on one side per day. See Ready Resource 8.6 for an example (and the definition of *dongle*).

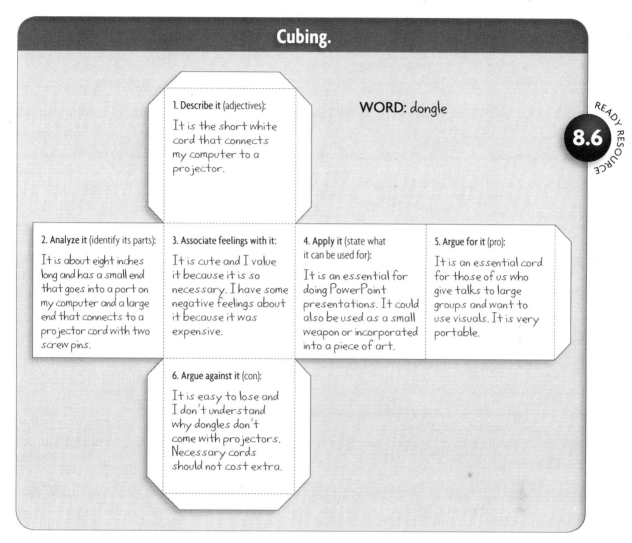

Cubing.

WORD: dongle

1. Describe it (adjectives):

It is the short white cord that connects my computer to a projector.

2. Analyze it (identify its parts):

It is about eight inches long and has a small end that goes into a port on my computer and a large end that connects to a projector cord with two screw pins.

3. Associate feelings with it:

It is cute and I value it because it is so necessary. I have some negative feelings about it because it was expensive.

4. Apply it (state what it can be used for):

It is an essential for doing PowerPoint presentations. It could also be used as a small weapon or incorporated into a piece of art.

5. Argue for it (pro):

It is an essential cord for those of us who give talks to large groups and want to use visuals. It is very portable.

6. Argue against it (con):

It is easy to lose and I don't understand why dongles don't come with projectors. Necessary cords should not cost extra.

READY RESOURCE 8.6

Word sorts

To do a sort, students group words in categories. Sorts may be open, with students creating their own groups, or closed, with assigned categories. An example of an open sort is to ask students to list interesting words they find while reading, listening to, or viewing a text. Use index cards. Afterward, students work collaboratively to categorize the words. An example of a closed sort is to present a list of words from a text *before* the students read it, and ask the students to sort the words into given categories, such as *characters, problems/plot, setting, style,* and *theme.* Choose categories appropriate to the content, such as *causes/effects,* or *important events,* and specific categories related to the material, such as *types of rock* or *kinds of weather.* This is good prediction exercise, because students must think of the meanings of the words and anticipate how they will relate to the content. Sorts may also be done as a whole group on an overhead or in a pocket chart.

PROVIDE MULTIPLE MEANING-ORIENTED EXPOSURES

Repetition solidifies any learning, and word learning is no exception. But the type of repetition matters. Learners are more likely to develop complex webs of meaning for words that are experienced multiple times in richly textured circumstances. This suggests teachers should focus on more than just allowing students to see and hear words; one can see and not understand and hear and not listen. The activities related to seeing and hearing—spelling and pronunciation—focus on surface-level word aspects that may have little or no connection to meaning. For example, students may spell sight words such as *was* and *to* repeatedly and learn to pronounce them instantly through repeated drills. But ask a student to explain the meaning of these words, and it becomes apparent that saying is not necessarily knowing. It is the words that are repeatedly experienced during discussions and read alouds and are used to write and speak thoughts that become known at a deep level.

The principle of providing multiple exposures to increase meaningful vocabulary knowledge is best implemented through literacy main events and embedded practices discussed later and examined in depth in Chapter 10. These main events include daily interactive read alouds, engaged independent reading, and discussions that involve direct vocabulary instruction, "on the spot" teaching, and incidental learning.

ENCOURAGE ACTIVE ENGAGEMENT

The quality, variety, and intensity of word work have much to do with the depth of word learning. Engagement means sustained involvement that focuses on understanding. Without understanding, engagement can stall and become mere entertainment. The following types of activities motivate meaning-oriented engagement, which has been found to increase word learning and improve comprehension (Graves & Watts-Taffe, 2002).

Discussions and conversations

Nothing is more important to word learning than engaging in literate talk with others where interesting words are used and heard. For detailed descriptions of ideas for ensuring that discussions and conversations are a meaningful part of the comprehension program, see Chapter 7.

Mental images

The root of the word *imagination* is *image*. Our brains are wired to create images, with 30 percent of the cortex devoted to visual processing (Lindstrom, 1999). While capable comprehenders readily generate images from verbal and non-verbal texts, many students need their teachers to model how to make mental pictures. With regard to vocabulary, word definitions may be imaged with the think-aloud concept that is integral to explicit teaching. Chapter 5 gave detailed guidelines for explicit teaching, including examples of teaching visual imaging.

To prepare, teachers should practice making "mental art." For example, make an image of a *dog*. Imagine how the dog looks, including its color, size, and shape, the texture of its fur, how it smells and sounds, and how you feel about the dog. This is the kind of practice that students enjoy and that benefits comprehension of individual words and concepts.

Pantomime/drama

Pantomime involves using your body, face, and gestures to communicate meaning. By miming, students can extend word meanings and "say" more than their speaking or writing vocabularies allow them to express. Pantomime is particularly helpful for primary children, English learners, and others with low reading and writing vocabularies. For example, a teacher might ask the class, "Show me how your face and body would look if you were really *concentrating*. On the count of three, add movement and a sound that shows concentration." There are dozens of ways to integrate drama with literacy (Cornett, 2011).

Sign language

Students who know signs for words can communicate concepts using an alternative symbol system. Hand signs allow students to learn to think about words in different ways. Sign language is fun to learn, because it is novel and engages movement, and is relevant because students can use it in many contexts. Riekehof's *Joy of Signing* (1987) is an excellent resource.

Writing

When students use words to make meaning through written composition, the process is the reverse of how words are used in comprehension. To write a word, the student must first retrieve the word from memory. The process of calling up words from brain schema for use in new contexts can provide powerful learning experiences. Writing should be a much richer activity than merely using words to create sentences. Writing experiences should target using words to *compose meaning*, resulting in texts that range from riddles to whole books. Chapter 9 describes many written response options teachers can show students how to use.

Computers and multimedia

Information on just about every subject, from the etymology of words to ways to animate them, is available on the computer desktop. One of the strengths of the computer is that it offers animations, whose multisensory nature has the potential to cause the brain to store meaning in many schemata. Word animation that focuses on meaning can be especially useful for English learners. Of course, a computer isn't essential—there is always a pencil or a crayon standing ready to motivate students to animate words for the purpose of deepening meaning.

USE EXPLICIT INSTRUCTION

Explicit teaching that targets both word pronunciation and meaningful use is key to teaching words for comprehension purposes. It can also be highly engaging. The modeling sequence "I Do," "We Do," "You Do," "Re Do," outlined in Chapter 5 may be adapted for teaching word meanings.

1. In the "I Do" modeling and explanation stage, the teacher chooses a word and follows these steps:
   - explains why he or she needs to know the word
   - provides an example of use in context
   - thinks aloud about clues from context
   - uses the spelling to try to arrive at pronunciation through spelling pattern cues
   - consults a current dictionary to find the meaning, if necessary
2. In the coached group practice "We Do" stage, students follow the same steps to solve another word, with the teacher coaching them.
3. In the coached independent practice "You Do" stage, students practice the strategy individually, with the teacher giving less and less help.
4. In the cued independent use "Re Do" stage, the teacher encourages students to adopt this problem-solving stance during all text use.

In general, explicit word teaching should be restricted to important concept words and content vocabulary that students need in order to comprehend subsequent reading. It is not necessary to teach explicitly all "unknown" words—just ones that are key to big ideas. Demonstrate how to draw on multiple sources of meaning around and inside words, such as context and meaningful word parts. The following sections describe additional ideas for regular explicit lessons related to word learning.

Etymology

Etymology is the study of the history of words. Words change in meaning over time, and often words migrate from one language to another. English, in particular, is full of unusual words that have been assimilated from other languages (see Ready Resource 8.7). For example, *enthusiasm* contains a derivative of the Latin root *theo*, which relates to god. Originally, an enthusiastic person was one who was "in god"—generally, an extremist or zealot. Today, when someone is called enthusiastic, it is taken as a compliment with nothing to do with one's religious persuasion. *Villain* is another word with an interesting etymology—originally, it meant someone who lived in a villa. Etymology is a naturally interesting subject and feeds students' desire to know *why*. Teachers can tap this motivational capacity by giving frequent explicit lessons about the histories of words, including student names (e.g., *Claudia* means "lame one").

Words derived from other languages.

African languages	*banjo, cola*
Arabic	*alcohol, zero, magazine*
Australia	*boomerang, kangaroo*
Chinese	*tea, wok*
Czech	*robot, pistol*
French	*ballet, beef, coup d'ètat, restaurant;* city names such as *Baton Rouge*
German	*dollar, kindergarten, noodle, pretzel, waltz*
Greek	*atom, chaos, giant, hero;* also many word parts, such as *-ology*
Hawaiian	*aloha, hula, luau*
Hebrew	*cherub, hallelujah, kosher, schmuck*
Hindi	*jungle, pajamas, shampoo*
Irish	*bog, shamrock*
Italian	*carnival, piano, pizza, umbrella, violin*
Mexican Spanish	*chocolate, taco, tomato*
Native American languages	*canoe, hammock, moose, raccoon, skunk, chipmunk;* many city and state names, such as *Ohio*
Persian	*orange, peach, sherbet*
Polynesian	*taboo, tattoo*
Portuguese	*coconut, molasses*
Russian	*tundra*
Scandinavian	*cozy, egg, husband, knife, rug, skate, skin, ugly*
Scottish	*gold, slogan*
Spanish	*alligator, guitar, hurricane, mosquito, potato*
Turkish	*caviar, kiosk, yogurt*
Welsh	*penguin*
Yiddish	*bagel, pastrami*

READY RESOURCE **8.7**

Word relationships

Graphic organizers, such as semantic or word meaning maps, may be used to show relationships between words, which increases comprehension. For example, a web for the word *settle* shows that many other words can be derived from it (see Ready Resource 8.8). Teachers should regularly demonstrate how knowing one word can be the foundation for knowing many related words. This concept is particularly valuable for students who are struggling with acquiring words. English learners benefit from webbing words for this purpose.

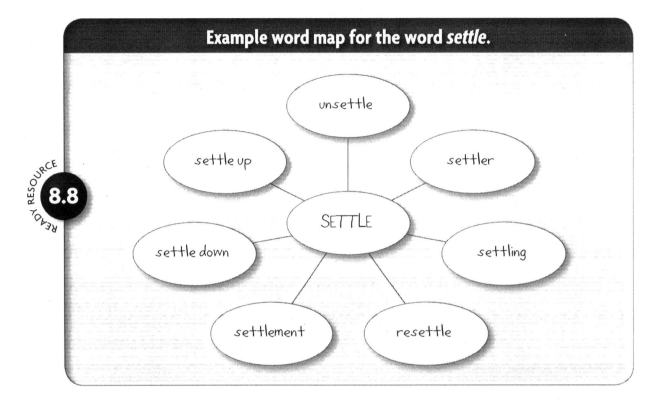

Example word map for the word *settle*.

Introduce important words

Explicit vocabulary instruction improves comprehension when it targets the *important* words in an upcoming text. Frequency should not be the criterion—a word might be very frequent, but not important to text meaning. Here are some suggestions for introducing important words:

1. Introduce only words that students can't figure out using Word Fix-Ups (refer to Ready Resource 8.11 on page 250) and words that represent ideas.

2. Don't assume . . .

   - all words are equally learnable.
   - words have only one meaning.
   - that "mentioning" a word is sufficient.
   - vocabulary instruction can come only during pre-reading.
   - that only those words that are taught are learned.
   - that pronunciation is the object of vocabulary instruction.

3. For words that represent key ideas, use deep processing activities such as word sorts, word ladders, examples/non-examples, and questions such as those in Ready Resource 8.9. You may post Ready Resource 8.9 and use it to generate questions that ratchet students through deep word learning practices. Drama, art, analogies (see Ready Resource 8.10), objects/pictures, and hands-on experiences are also helpful.

How to learn a word.

EXAMPLE: Hoi polloi

1. Place in a category: type of people
2. List synonyms or words with similar meaning: everyday people
3. List antonyms: upper class
4. Give examples: factory workers
5. List key attributes of the word: hoi is Greek for "the," so we shouldn't say THE hoi polloi.
6. Write a definition: Hoi polloi are the masses of people who are not rich, nor advantaged by education.
7. Write a sentence: The Queen of England is not a part of hoi polloi.

KEY QUESTIONS:

- What is it? Two words meaning "the" and "common working class people"
- What are its characteristics? From two Greek words
- How is it like or different from a word you already know? Sounds like "boy"; means something like "working class"
- What are examples of it? store clerks, factory workers, restaurant servers

OTHER IDEAS:

- Create images: sketch or just think of images associated with the word. Add action, proportion, and exaggeration (APE) to make the images more memorable.
- Say the word repeatedly and add musical elements: rhythm, dynamics, pitch.
- Say the word and add movement.
- Keep a list of words you want to use in your own writing.

READY RESOURCE 8.9

The Word Ladder, described earlier in this chapter, is an excellent strategy for introducing new words. The following example is for the word *canoodle*.

1. Category: loving action
2. Example/experience: (show hug)
3. Similar word/synonym: hug
4. Non-example: slap, shove
5. Important attributes: use of intertwining body parts to show affection
6. Own definition: a noun or verb meaning to cuddle or hug

Teaching analogies: Word relationships.

First, use explicit teaching to show students how to figure out relationships between words. Major types of relationships and examples are listed below.

RELATIONSHIP TYPES	EXAMPLE	RELATIONSHIP TYPES	EXAMPLE
1. Cause/effect	overeat : fat	8. Object/action	clock : wind
2. Purpose or use	fork : eat	9. Place	Olympics : Beijing
3. Synonym	yell : scream	10. Degree	raw : cooked
4. Antonym	cry : laugh	11. Characteristic	diabetes : obesity
5. Part/whole	foot : body	12. Grammar	eat : kick
6. Whole/part	clock : hands	13. Sequence	Monday : Tuesday
7. Action/object	wind : clock	14. Association	smiley face : happy

Next, give word pairs and ask students to figure out the relationships, using the above categories.

Finally, teach students how to solve and create Analogy Riddles by figuring out relationships to complete the riddle. Coach by asking, "How are the first two words related?" Point out that more than one relationship is possible and that the colon should be read as "is to."

EXAMPLE ANALOGY RIDDLES

fur : cat	as	hoof : _____	(relationship = part/whole)
Columbia : South Carolina	as	_____ : Maine	(relationship = _____)
giggle : dance	as	_____ : dig	(relationship = _____)
itch : scratch	as	_____ : berries	(relationship = _____)

USE WORD TYPES TO PLAN INSTRUCTION

Teachers have long categorized words for instruction into groups such as parts of speech. The science of word categories is in its infancy when it comes to identifying the words that are most important for boosting comprehension, but the dearth of science has not kept teachers from using word groupings, especially *high frequency words,* in literacy instruction. A perfect methodology for teaching high-frequency words has not been pinned down, either, although multisensory word introduction and repeated exposure are common methods. The search for a perfect methodology is complicated by the fact that high-frequency words are likely to have multiple meanings.

The 20th century saw many efforts to categorize words to facilitate vocabulary instruction that focused on pronunciation. The most well-known category is high-frequency words, also called "sight" or "instant" words because they occur so often that students need to know them instantly, as opposed to sounding them out. Automatic recognition of high-frequency words remains a component of fluency and is important because a relatively small number of words constitute the bulk of words in texts. Indeed, a mere ten words account for a significant percentage of what we read and write. Those are: *the, of, and, a, to, in, is, you, that, it.* Longer lists of high-frequency words are available online. (See the Online Resource Box on the next page for examples of word lists. Also see *The Reading Teacher's Book of Lists* [Fry & Kress, 2006].)

The Dolch Basic Sight Vocabulary, constructed by Edward Dolch, was one of the first lists of words in this category and was followed by many others (e.g., Edward Fry's list). Computer technology has refined these earlier lists, created by hand counts. Computer-generated lists are now popular. Word lists are typically divided into grade-level batches. Today, even kindergartners are expected to pronounce (not explain) as many as forty words correctly by the end of the year. However, as was previously discussed, pronunciation does not guarantee comprehension. For a stark illustration of this point, ask any primary student to explain the words in the Pledge of Allegiance.

Fortunately, high-frequency words are usually in most learners' listening/speaking vocabularies, so they may be taught as labels rather than as unfamiliar concepts. To teach a label involves teaching the spelling and sound; to teach a new concept requires significant instruction that develops understanding of the idea. For example, it is easy to teach the spelling and sound of the word *atom,* but it is much harder to teach the concept of *atom* (Graves, Juel, & Graves, 2007.) To put this another way, it is usually easier to teach students to recognize in print words that they already know (in their writing/speaking vocabularies) then to teach words students have never encountered before.

Other categories of words include the following:

- **Environmental print:** words encountered frequently in print in daily life. Examples include street signs and product and company names. These make wonderful collages.

- **Content/academic words:** words that are key to science, social studies, math, literature, and the arts. See the Online Resource box for a downloadable list of academic words.

Academic Words

http://www.victoria.ac.nz/lals/staff/Averil-Coxhead/awl/

ONLINE RESOURCE

- **Survival words:** words needed to manage daily life, such as warning signs and labels, directions, and information on banking and employment forms.

- **Personal words:** words that vary from child to child but are important to each individual, such as one's street address, relatives' names, and vocabulary for interests and hobbies.

For additional word *categories,* see *The Teacher's Book of Lists* (Fry & Kress, 2006), which includes important words in content areas, among its many categories.

Word Lists

The Dolch List is based on high-frequency words from children's literature available in 1948. (www.dolchsightwords.org)

The Fry Instant Word List includes one thousand words for use with grades one through three, remedial reading, and ESL and adult education. The first three hundred words are available for download. (www.usu.edu/teachall/text/reading/Frylist.pdf)

Word Zones lists include 5,586 frequently used words for different grades, as well as a list of Spanish–English cognates. The lists were compiled by Elfrieda Hiebert, a Berkeley professor and reading specialist. (www.textproject.org/resources/word-zones-list)

Tampa Reads has produced researched lists of words chosen according to frequency of use at each grade level, as well as by use on standardized tests. Lists for kindergarten through fifth grade are available for download. (www.tampareads.com/trial/vocabulary)

The state of **Indiana** offers a listing for grades one through eight. (www.literacyframework.ips.k12.in.us/reading_vocabulary/default.aspx)

Academic Word Lists were created by Averil Coxhead in 2000. The lists include the most important words students should know for successful progress in school. These words are particularly important for English language learners. (http://www.victoria.ac.nz/lals/staff/Averil-Coxhead/awl/)

Rebecca Sitton has compiled a list of 1,200 high-frequency words, in frequency order. (http://school.elps.k12.mi.us/donley/classrooms/berry/sitton_spelling_activities/4thgrade_spelling/sitton_word_list.htm)

The Wall Street Journal provides lists of the top 100 high-frequency words used in conversation, newspapers, the Oxford English corpus, and the British National corpus, as well as Edward Fry's top 100. (http://s.wsj.net/public/resources/documents/info-numbguy-sort.html)

Well-known children's author **Jan Brett** provides lists in batches of twenty. (www.janbrett.com/games/high_frequency_word_list_main.htm)

Teaching Students to Figure Out Unknown Words

Take care of the sense and the sounds will take care of themselves.

LEWIS CARROLL

The term *decoding* has become synonymous with word identification and recognition. Decoding is about figuring out unknown words. Instruction in decoding is an essential aspect of the literacy curriculum, because word-based print text comprehension is limited when readers lack a repertoire of flexible and automatic decoding strategies.

Decoding is not merely using the spelling–sound (graphophonic) features of words to arrive at meaning. Indeed, concentration on these surface-level aspects can detract from comprehension. Short-term memory can handle only about seven chunks of information (Miller, 1956), so a reader who is fully occupied by surface-level decoding has scant thinking power available for processing big ideas (Block & Pressley, 2007). Decoding that increases comprehension stresses *meaning.* Comprehension is about communication, not "phonication" (Harste, 1997).

INSTRUCTIONAL APPROACHES

Approaches to teaching students how to decode unknown words all come down to teaching problem solving, but they differ in their methods, especially their starting points. It is important for teachers to understand differences among these approaches and integrate aspects of all. Brief summaries of the most common approaches follow. Elements of these approaches are present in the teaching strategies described in the remainder of this chapter.

Analytic. This approach starts with whole words. Students examine spelling patterns and word parts, such as rimes, roots, and affixes, to figure out the sound and meaning of the word. For example, *unzipped* = un + zip + ed. Un = not, zip = close, ed = past tense, so *unzipped* means "not closed."

Synthetic. This approach starts with specific aspects of words, such as spelling patterns, affixes, and roots. Students pull parts of a word together to create a whole word. For example, *bio* means life and *ology* means study of, so a word meaning "the study of life" would be "biology."

Implicit. Implicit teaching involves students in discovering patterns that give clues to sound or meaning. For example, the teacher might ask, "How are these words related: *geology, biology, anthropology, astrology?*" Because the implicit approach starts with whole words and requires students to analyze them, this method is often associated with the analytic method.

Explicit. As discussed in Chapter 5, in explicit instruction the teacher tells and shows students exactly what they are to do and how to think. For example, "Today I'm going to teach you how to figure out the meanings of words using affixes. Listen to how I problem solve the unknown word in this sentence: I was *unpreading* the dog's collar when he bit me." (Use a real word students don't know or a nonsense word, like this one, with a prefix and suffix.)

TEACHING WORD-SOLVING FIX-UPS

To unlock unknown words, students need a full toolkit of strategies that targets finding the *meaning* clues *inside* words and *around* them. To interpret the clues inside words, students need a foundation in word sub-skills such as phoneme segmentation, blending, and common spelling–sound or graphophonic patterns. Indeed, phonics (short for graphophonics) can help a student decode a word's meaning: the student uses spelling patterns to arrive at a word's sound and then recognizes the word's meaning. That is the limit of phonics: the student must already know the word (i.e., remember hearing it before). Quick, accurate word recognition can facilitate comprehension, but sounding out a word does not guarantee that the word will be understood. Effective instruction in using graphophonics to decode certainly has a place, as long as

- the instruction occurs in short amounts of time.
- the teacher is clear about the purpose: phonics is one tool that can contribute to comprehension if the spelling pattern cues a sound approximation that the reader recognizes.
- instruction is immediately followed by opportunity to use the specific phonics skill with running text, so students practice decoding words with worthwhile materials.

Word-level components of comprehension should be taught systematically, with different degrees of explicitness, depending on student needs. A Phonics Framework may be found in Appendix J. Ready Resource 8.11 lists Word Fix-Ups students can use to problem solve unknown words. The Word Fix-Ups go beyond use of spelling–sound patterns (phonics) *within* words to include use of context clues *around* words, as well as structural or morphemic analysis. Ready Resources 8.13 and 8.14 list key morphemes (meaning units). Appendix F provides Spelling Fix-Ups for use during writing.

Word Fix-Ups.

READY RESOURCE 8.11

These strategies help readers figure out unknown words. Cross-check with more than one strategy to confirm meanings.

SENSE context (clues *around* the word): What makes sense?
- Skip the word, read to the end of the sentence, and come back.
- Plug in a word that makes sense. Use a synonym.

SLICE word parts (look *inside* the word): What parts do you know? (structural/morphemic analysis)
Slice into meaning units:
- prefix
- suffix
- root
- compound words
- contraction parts

SPELL TO SOUND (graphophonics): What's another word it looks like? (compare–contrast)
- Spell the word out loud to notice the letter/spelling pattern.

- Frequent vowel patterns:
  - open syllable = v (long vowel)
  - closed syllable = vc (short vowel)
  - silent e = vce (first vowel long)
  - vowel digraph = vvc (long first vowel/ second silent)
  - r controlled = vrc
- Frequent pattern for sounds of *c* and *g*:
  - soft or hard c or g? (e, i, y after signals soft)
- Check beginning and ending letters.
- Look for chunks you know: onsets, rimes.*
- Ask yourself: If the word is _____, what would it start with? End with?
- Cross-check with meaning in the sentence!

SOURCES (*outside* the word and your head): glossary, dictionary, word wall, reference charts.

LAST IS ASK!

* See Ready Resource 8.17 for a list of 61 rimes.

Readers use problem solving repeatedly, at the word, paragraph, and passage levels (Block & Pressley, 2007). Students can learn to initiate and sustain flexible use of Word and Comprehension Fix-Ups if teachers

1. demonstrate problem solving of words, including showing how to detect and correct problems.

2. provide opportunities to practice fix-ups with content-rich texts.

3. coach students to apply word-decoding strategies during reading (Taylor et al., 1999). Ready Resource 8.12 provides example questions for coaching word decoding.

Morphological/structural analysis

Examining a word's structure to figure out its meaning is called structural or morphological analysis. Carlisle and Katz (2005) report that some 60 percent of unfamiliar words students encounter are based on words whose meanings can be figured out through structure and context. Furthermore, a large percentage of words learned after third grade derive from familiar word parts (e.g., *dis-heart-en-ing*), making morphological or structural analysis an important tool for figuring out meanings of unknown words.

Critical to use of structural analysis is understanding that words are made up of meaning units called *morphemes*. Morphemes are either "free"—they can stand alone (e.g., cognates or root words)—or "bound"—prefixes and suffixes that must be affixed to a root (affixes). A student who can find some known part of an unknown word has a start on decoding. It is important that teachers demonstrate use of word morphology (especially roots and affixes) to make meaning. High-frequency roots and affixes should be taught explicitly to all students.

Cognates. Many languages share the same roots. For example, the French, Spanish, and Italian words for "possible" all derive from the Latin *possibilis*. Many English words are similar in both form and meaning to common Spanish words (e.g., *tranquil/tranquilo*). It is not surprising that bilingual students who use cognates (words that share a root) tend to have better comprehension (Jiménez, García, & Pearson, 1996). This suggests that teachers should teach the concept of cognates and coach students to find and use cognates to unlock unknown words. Explicit teaching is appropriate and should be accompanied by charts and personal student references

Questions for coaching word decoding.

> What have you tried?

> What word would make sense?

> What do you know about the word?

> What parts of the word look familiar?

> What do the familiar parts mean?

> What sources can you use to confirm or reject ideas about the meaning of the word?

READY RESOURCE 8.12

that include cognates. To teach the root word *auto*, for example, explain to students that *auto-* comes from the Greek word for "self" and occurs in words like *automobile*, *automatic*, and *autograph*. Once a root is demonstrated, students should immediately be asked to problem solve new words presented in context, such as *autonomous* and *autocratic*. High-frequency Greek and Latin roots appear in Ready Resource 8.13.

An explicit lesson on using roots to figure out unknown words might be used as follows:

> "Today we are going to learn how to use Greek and Latin roots to figure out unknown words. I'll go first and do a think aloud to show you how to figure out the meanings of words that have the same root. This is the word *geothermal*. I know *geo-* means "earth" and *therm* has to do with heat. So *geothermal* is probably heat from the earth. Now it's your turn. The word is *geology*. Remember we did *-ology* before. Turn to your partner to define the word."

Short explicit lessons should be followed by opportunities for students to construct meaning actively using the concepts and skills just taught. Explicit

Latin and Greek roots.

Knowing common roots will help students decode for meaning when they encounter unknown words. This skill is especially helpful for English learners.

READY RESOURCE 8.13

ROOT	MEANING	EXAMPLES
-anthrop-	human	*anthropology*
-chron-	time	*chronological*
-dem-	people	*democracy*
-dict-	to say	*dictate*
-duc-	to lead, to take	*produce, reduce*
-gress-	to advance	*digress*
-ject-	to throw	*reject*
-morph-	shape, form	*anthropomorphic*
-path-	feeling	*empathy*
-ped-	child	*pediatric*
-pel-	to drive	*compel, repel*
-pend-	to hang	*pendulum, depend*
-phil-	love	*philanthropy*
-phon-	sound	*phonics*
-port-	to carry	*support*
-scrib-, -script-	to write	*prescribe*
-tract-	to pull, to drag	*contract, extract*
-vert-	to turn	*revert, divert*

vocabulary instruction is a recommended part of any teacher's strategy repertoire, but it is important to remember that good readers usually use an analytic or implicit approach to figure out meanings of unknown words. They synthesize the parts they've analyzed into a whole word that they confirm or reject based on (1) whether it sounds familiar and (2) whether it makes sense in the immediate context.

Affixes. Affixes change the meaning of the root word to which they attach. Students should be taught to recognize affixes and attach meanings to common ones as a tool for decoding unknown affixed words (see Ready Resource 8.14). Affixes

Affixes: Prefixes and suffixes.

PREFIXES
High-frequency prefixes that should be taught explicitly are:

PREFIX	MEANING	EXAMPLES
un-	not	*unhappy*
re-	repeat	*rewrite*
in-,im-, ir-, il-	not	*irrelevant*
in-, im-	in/into	*immigrant*
dis-	not	*dislike*
non-	not	*non-example*
over-	too much	*overspend*
mis-	not	*misspeak*
sub-	under	*submarine*
pre-	before	*pretest*
inter-	between	*interpersonal*
fore-	before/first	*forefront*
de-	reverse/remove	*decommission*
trans-	across	*transatlantic*
super-	greater	*superman*
semi-	half	*semicircle*
anti-	against	*anti-Semitic*
mid-	*middle*	midyear
under-	too little	*underestimate*
Less frequent but important:	a-, anti-, bio-, bi-, co-, geo-, hyper-, inter-, micro-, mono-, neo-, pan-, post-, sub-, techno-, therm-	

(continued)

READY RESOURCE **8.14**

Affixes, continued.

SUFFIXES

Suffixes are categorized as "inflectional," those that change the part of speech, and "derivational," those that have more effect on meaning. The following should be taught explicitly:

SUFFIX	MEANING	EXAMPLES
INFLECTIONAL		
s (-es)	plural	*dogs*
-'s (-s')	possessive	*Sarah's*
-ed	past tense	*tapped*
-ing	present participle	*eating*
-en	past participle	*eaten*
-er	comparative	*bigger*
-est	superlative	*biggest*
DERIVATIONAL		
-ly	having the characteristic	*lovely*
-ish	noun to adjective	*foolish*
-al	verb to noun	*dismissal*
-ness	adjective to noun	*happiness*
-ment	verb or adjective to noun	*contentment*
-ive	noun to adjective	*active*
Less frequent but important:	-able/ible, -ation, -fy/ify, -gram, -graph, -ise/ize, -ism,- ist, -logue, -logy, -meter, -oid, -phile, -phobe, -phone, -ty/ity	

Source: White, Sowell, & Yangihara, 1989.

READY RESOURCE **8.14**

include prefixes, added to the front of a word, and suffixes, affixed to the end of a word. The following four prefixes alone account for 58 percent of prefixed words in English: un-, re-, in-, and dis-. These suffixes account for 85 percent of suffixed words: -s, -es, -ed, -ing, -ly, -er, -or, -ion/tion, -ible/able, -al/ial, -y, -ness, -es, -less, and -es.

A tool for teaching affix meanings, *word expansion* motivates students by showing them that knowing one word can quickly become knowing ten words. Floriani (1979) recommends displaying the following affixes and showing students how to attach them to a known word to make many new words. A webbing format is useful for this (see Ready Resource 8.15). The suffixes are ordered from easy or frequent to more difficult and less frequent.

Level 1: -s, -ed, -d, -ing

Level 2: -y, -ies, -ly, -es, -er

Level 3: -un, -re, -est, -en, -ful

Level 4: -ex, -pre, -be, -dis, -in, -ion, -tion, -sion, -cian, -ous, -ness, -ture, -ment, -ish, -less

Word expansion using important words from content texts is an appropriate independent station activity.

Context clues

Instruction in and actual practice with context clues can improve students' ability to figure out word meanings (Kuhn & Stahl, 1998). But context can be tricky. Although students need the ability to use context in their word-solving toolkit, context clues are not surefire, any more than phonics is.

Students need to be shown how to use the words around an unknown word, including the syntax (word order), to narrow the pool of words that might make sense. Explain the strategy and do think alouds showing how to predict the meaning of a word using clues such as syntax combined with graphophonics. For example, read aloud a sentence and show that the number of words that would make sense is limited:

"The dog ran down the _____." 'Street,' 'road,' 'path,' and 'lane' all make sense. A check against the spelling of the unknown word shows the word starts with the letter *s*, which rules out all but 'street.' Since the word also ends in *t*, it only takes a check on the word's middle to confirm the missing word. If I recognize the -eet- chunk from known words like *feet* and *meet*, it is almost certain the right word is *street*. It sounds right, looks right, and, most important, it makes sense.

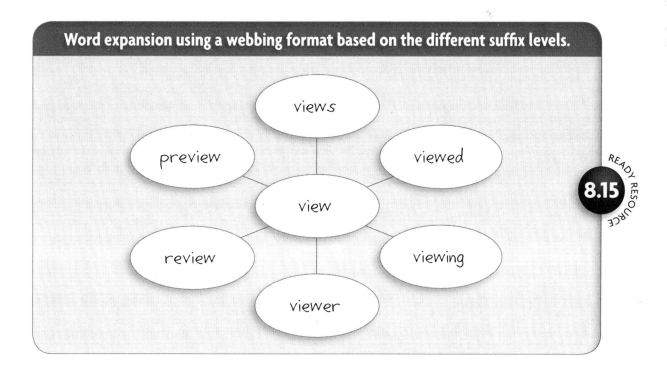

Word expansion using a webbing format based on the different suffix levels.

8.15

READY RESOURCE

Be aware that English learners have more difficulty with context than do native English speakers (Nagy, McClure, & Montserrat, 1997). Of course, English learners who simply need to learn words as labels rather than new concepts have an advantage.

Short explicit lessons should be followed by opportunities for students to construct meaning actively using the concepts and skills just taught. Ideas for explicit word lessons, focusing on context clues, appear in Ready Resource 8.16.

Background knowledge

Background experiences and knowledge are important resources for decoding word meanings. Look for opportunities to demonstrate how students can use what they know to figure out unknown words. For example, think aloud about the word *autocrat* in the sentence, "Mussolini was an autocratic leader." Your thought process might be something like,

> "If I know that *auto* has to do with *self,* I can get clues to meaning. I might connect a known word like *autoimmune* that I relate to HIV and think about how a person's own self (own immune system) is the problem. The word *autocrat* would likewise seem to mean a leader who focused on himself—one who must make decisions by himself, decisions that helped himself."

EXTERNAL RESOURCES

Although students should use clues inside and around words first, tools that are external to the text may also be helpful for figuring out unknown words. A dic-

---

READY RESOURCE 8.16

Teaching context clues.

Types of context clues:

1. **Definition:** *Puling* is crying weakly or whining.
2. **Example:** The students were *puling* about having too much homework.
3. **Description or synonym:** They were *puling,* or whining, about all the work.
4. **Compare/contrast:** The workers were *puling* because they had so much work, when they could have been celebrating that they had jobs.

Teaching suggestions:

- Explicitly teach how to use the four types of context clues.
- Post the list of types of context clues to help students find word meanings in texts.
- Ask students to find examples of clues in classroom texts, on the Internet, or in newspapers or magazines.
- Note that context clues are often more helpful in nonfiction texts than in fiction, because these texts have an informational purpose.

tionary or thesaurus can confirm meanings and refine and expand understanding. Computer resources and the Internet offer important word-learning aids. English learners should be taught not to expect one-to-one mapping between English and their first language. This misconception hampers ELs' use of the dictionary (Fischer, 1994), and it may lead students to dislike using reference books.

Although looking up words and copying definitions remain popular, there is no evidence such work improves comprehension. In addition, these common activities can lead to "superficial understanding and a rapid forgetting" of words (Irvin, 1990, p. 9). Word comprehension is complex and entails integrating context parameters with background knowledge to make sense. Dictionaries are wonderful tools, but teachers should abandon the outdated and ineffective practice of assigning looking up and copying definitions. Instead, focus on engaging students in inferring meaning from context. Once learners have used "in your head" word fix-ups, dictionary work may then be used to confirm or narrow down meaning.

Word Fluency: Freeing the Mind for Comprehension

Fluency is not a new concept, but in the past decade high-profile research reports have placed it more prominently on the national radar screen. The National Reading Panel observed that "Slow, effortful reading is a labor-intensive process that only fitfully results in understanding" (2000). No Child Left Behind legislation, implemented through Reading First grants, took the NRP report to heart and defined fluency as one of five critical areas of reading (2002).

Teachers commonly think of fluency as fast and accurate word recognition. Speedy and accurate pronunciation of words can be helpful to comprehension. But the concept of comprehension first goes further to magnify a rather neglected aspect of fluency: adding expressive elements to words that reflect the reader's interpretation of their meaning. In addition, fluency involves using CPS strategies with ease, including monitoring strategies that trigger comprehension repair, when needed. Such an expanded concept of fluency helps teachers keep comprehension at the fore. However, in its most common usage in professional literacy contexts, fluency is restricted to words.

WHAT IS FLUENT READING?

Most people can recognize oral reading that is fluent. The words just flow, because they are given musical qualities. The reader changes tempo, dynamics, and pitch to convey meaning. Skilled actors are known for their ability to read fluently. Teachers know fluent reading when they hear it, and they also know when students do not have it. These students are slow, choppy readers, who stumble over words and disregard punctuation. Non-fluent reading is unpleasant to hear and may indicate that the reader is not making sense of the words.

The goal isn't to make all students into actors or skilled oral readers, especially since, outside of school, reading is usually done silently. The goal is comprehension. Non-fluent readers can be explicitly taught to be more fluent, and such instruction can increase comprehension—if it focuses on helping students develop a clear understanding of the components of fluency and if it places emphasis on using those components for comprehension purposes. Fast and accurate pronunciation is not enough. Students must know that the goal is to invest words with meaning, which requires the reader to use a *flexible* rate of reading speed and attach expressive features to words. What's more, the distinctive pronunciation of some words (especially vowel sounds) reflects dialect, and Americans closely guard this aspect of heritage and community. We value diversity in all its dimensions, so we appreciate and enjoy dialects that, for example, turn one-syllable words into two, as my friends in South Carolina do so lyrically.

Fluency helps readers to make sense of print materials when it permits them to read words with ease, expressiveness, accuracy, and appropriate pace and phrasing (Kuhn & Rasinski, 2007). Skilled readers acquire fluency as they move through the literacy development process, which is marked by the simultaneous acquisition of words, word-decoding strategies, and a repertoire of comprehension strategies. The key is for learners to understand that these are all tools for comprehension. Fluency is the result of how these words and strategies are put to use.

An acronym for remembering the three major elements of word fluency—expression, accuracy, and rate—is EAR. EAR is useful in clarifying the goal of oral reading and rehearsing for performances.

E = expression

It is significant that EAR begins with expression, because expression encompasses accuracy and rate. Indeed, expressive reading is impossible without accurate pronunciation and the ability to change speed to suit the message the reader wants to convey. Expressiveness is much more than speed and accuracy. Expressive reading draws upon phrasing, word emphasis or stress, pauses, changes in pitch, intonation or inflection, volume changes or dynamics, and rhythm and beat. Expressive reading may even include clipping and stretching words and using dialect to add meaning. The term *prosody*, a synonym for expression, refers to the musical aspects of how we use language (Kuhn & Raskinski, 2007). It isn't surprising that arts-based strategies like Reader's Theatre are often used to motivate reading rehearsal to develop fluency.

Children begin to develop the expression aspect of fluency when they have opportunities to hear fluent reading. Parents who change their voices as they read dialogue among characters in folktales and teachers who invite children to move or clap to the beat in poetry are providing rich soil in which fluency can grow. It is easy to involve children in expression practice; a sentence can be pulled from any text for practice. I regularly use a short Read Around circle activity as part of my opening routine: students take turns reading aloud a sentence like "Mary had a little lamb," using expressive elements to indicate various meanings the sentence could imply. It is easy to coach students with questions such as, "What animal did she have?" "Who had the lamb?" "What was the lamb like?"

A = accuracy

Fluent readers know a lot of words and can pronounce them automatically. Beginning in kindergarten, children are taught to say high-frequency words like *a*, *the*, *an*, and *to* instantly. A growing body of words that the student can pronounce without effort allows thinking power to be available for comprehension. Students also need to become fast and accurate at using problem-solving strategies to figure out words they don't recognize automatically. Chunking unknown words into known parts can speed decoding. Such chunks are termed phonograms (also called rimes). Examples are *-at, -eet*, and *-op*. Using knowledge of phonograms, novice readers can chunk to decode words that are not sight or instant words—words like *bat, mat, sat, feet, meet, top, cop*, and *mop*. Chunking speeds decoding and contributes to fluency, in contrast to slower letter-by-letter sounding out. Chunks may be taught in daily routines such as webbing or listing words that share a chunk. Ready Resource 8.17 lists high-frequency phonograms.

R = rate

Comprehension often is anything but fast (Pressley & Afflerbach, 1995). It "involves considerable reflection and reaction, sometimes rereading, and pausing to think about the images conjured by the text and the big ideas in the text" (Pressley, 2006). However, speed is important to reading, in that words must be combined with other words in a timely way so the reader has enough information in mind simultaneously to make sense. Knowing words in isolation isn't enough: for flu-

Sixty-one common phonograms.

1. -ack	10. -an	19. -eak	28. -ent	37. -in	46. -oke	55. -uff
2. -ail	11. -ank	20. -eal	29. -est	38. -ine	47. -one	56. -ug
3. -ain	12. -ap	21. -ear	30. -ice	39. -ing	48. -ool	57. -um
4. -aim	13. -are	22. -eat	31. -ick	40. -ink	49. -oom	58. -ump
5. -ake	14. -ash	23. -eek	32. -ide	41. -ip	50. -op	59. -un
6. -ale	15. -at	24. -eep	33. -ig	42. -ir	51. -or	60. -unk
7. -all	16. -ate	25. -eet	34. -ight	43. -ob	52. -ore	61. -ust
8. -am	17. -aw	26. -ell	35. -ike	44. -ock	53. -ub	
9. -ame	18. -ay	27. -end	36. -ill	45. -og	54. -uck	

READY RESOURCE 8.17

Sources: Wylie & Durrell, 1970; Fry & Kress, 2006.

ent reading and comprehension, words must be understood, given their context, and then connected by meaning in a smooth and thoughtful fashion.

The optimal reading rate depends on both learner characteristics and the nature of the text. In fact, the learner's background and the specific purpose for reading should result in a flexible rate. For example, I might read aloud parts of *In a Dark Dark Room* by Alvin Schwartz (1985) slowly, using a staccato rhythm, to evoke a scary mood. Then I might speed up to advance the plot. Learners do need to become capable of reading at greater speeds in order to mature. The caveat is that rate has to be adjusted mindfully. Some texts, such as expository ones, may be conceptually more difficult, with more unknown words and ideas. Such texts have to be read more slowly. Students must be taught the integral relationships among reading rate, specific purposes for text use, and text characteristics.

Ready Resource 8.18 gives guidelines for words correct per minute (WCPM) that can serve as general targets. These are only estimates, and should be used with "comprehension first" in mind. If rate is stressed over meaning, comprehension will suffer. At times, it may feel like juggling—up goes the speed, down comes the comprehension, up goes the word accuracy, down comes the rate. Good teachers choreograph lessons that help students become skilled at the many facets of reading, without ever losing sight of the goal: comprehension through active making meaning.

Composite recommended rates: Words correct per minute (WCPM).

Target rates vary from author to author, and any benchmark must be a general goal, measured under many circumstances, with diverse texts, over time. Trend patterns in student performance are more important than one-shot measures. Of particular importance is the need for students to use reading rate flexibly to suit the immediate purpose of text use and the nature of the text.

INSTRUCTIONAL LEVEL	ORAL RATE	SILENT RATE
Grades 1–2	50–100	75–100
Grades 2–3	70–110	115–140
Grades 3–4	80–140	130–175
Grades 4–5	100–150	160–200
Grades 5–6	110–160	185–225
Grades 7–8	130–180	200–250

NOTES:

1. Kuhn and Rasinski (2007) report fall, winter, and spring norms.
2. Students who read at ≥130 wpm had the highest average performance on the NAEP Integrated Reading Performance Record (Fountas & Pinnell, 2001).

Sources: Allington, R. (unpublished); Fountas & Pinnell, 2001; Kuhn & Rasinski, 2007.

ASSESSING FLUENCY

Oral and silent reading are processed differently by the brain; obviously, the former engages a vocal response, while the latter does not. Every reader has different degrees of fluency attached to his or her oral versus silent reading. However, fluency skills, as well as the use of decoding strategies, are normally assessed by teachers listening to students read aloud. Oral reading makes thinking visible, to a degree, providing a window into how a reader interprets print. Is it possible for a person to be a fine silent reader and a less than fluent oral reader? Of course. The reverse is true, as well. Most of us could, with a bit of practice, make the following sentence sound fluent: "Undreated, the trogmer clomed the spet and grudded the moin." We could pronounce the words according to English phonetics, and we could use expressive elements such as changes in pitch and emphasis to make this nonsense sound like sense—all without understanding.

Hence, although fluent-sounding oral reading is considered evidence that a reader is thinking about meaning and is thus able to make the words sound like sense (Kuhn & Rasinski, 2007), this evidence is not conclusive. The more limited the fluency assessment, the more concerns we should have about the test's validity in representing comprehension. For example, Pressley studied children who were tested with a DIBELS assessment that measured reading rate. Even those children who met rate standards could recall only 15 percent of the ideas they read. Pressley concluded that "if you are interested in knowing about reading speed with low comprehension and memory of text, DIBELS is a great measure!" (2006). The ability to read orally often reflects comprehension, but it is not always a valid indicator.

Lack of oral fluency, alone, is not enough to diagnose a significant reading problem—especially if fluency is narrowly defined as reading rate. Instead, a broader view of fluency focuses on interpretive oral reading, in which the reader does the following *in concert*:

1. brings words to life by adding musical features that show interpretation of meaning through expression
2. pronounces words accurately, which means understandably
3. changes rate and phrasing to match the purpose for reading (e.g., slows down to study).

Readers who can do these three things are more likely to comprehend what is read, and when these skills are synchronized, we tend to interpret the resulting fluency as a sign of comprehension. This is a correlation, not a causational finding, but it is enough to justify attention to fluency in the literacy program (Pressley, 2006).

BEST PRACTICES FOR FLUENCY

Developing students' fluency is a best practice and should be integrated into the other eight best practices. Following are examples of how this may be done.

Assess to differentiate instruction

Students need to have their success made obvious in concrete ways. One way to document their progress in fluency is to record their oral readings and assess them for accuracy, rate, and expression.

Accuracy and rate. Teach students how to line-graph their WCPM based on dated recordings of oral reading. They can do this independently at a recording station by following these steps:

- Have students rehearse a text of interest that is somewhat challenging (instructional level).
- Have them read aloud a full portion into the recorder, using a stopwatch to end after one minute.
- Demonstrate how to listen and mark correct words, count them, and graph them (see Ready Resource 8.19). Limiting the time to one minute simplifies calculation.
- Have students count and mark their own correct words.

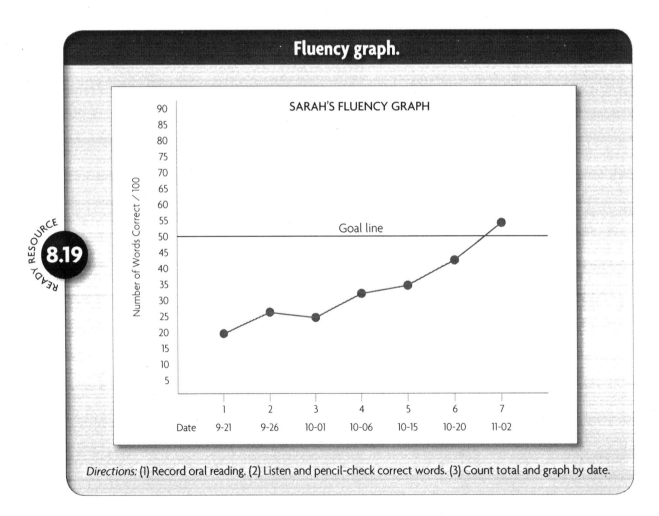

Fluency graph.

READY RESOURCE **8.19**

Directions: (1) Record oral reading. (2) Listen and pencil-check correct words. (3) Count total and graph by date.

Explicit teaching is in order for the math component of making a graph. Students need to be shown how to graph, and they need to know why they are graphing, for motivation. Increase motivation by drawing a goal line across the graph using the estimates of grade-level expectations for WCPM from Ready Resource 8.18. At least 95 percent accuracy is required for reaching an independent level with a text.

Expression. Use recorded reading to help students self-evaluate and goal set. Ready Resource 8.20 describes expression development and may be used to create a rubric. Peers can often provide descriptive feedback after oral reading performances for audiences (e.g., Reader's Theatre).

Fluency expression development.

 VERY EXPRESSIVE
- Uses meaningful phrasing.
- Emphasizes important words with volume and pitch changes and pauses.
- Uses pitch and pauses to show punctuation.
- Varies rate and pitch to suit the message.
- Has clear and accurate pronunciation.
- Presents a meaningful interpretation throughout the text.

EXPRESSIVE
- Uses a mixture of word-by-word reading and phrased reading.
- Some use of pitch and pause to show punctuation and syntax.
- Some use of emphasis or stress on important words, using volume, pitch, and pause.
- Some changes in rate and pitch to suit the message.
- Pronounces words clearly and accurately about 95 percent of the time.
- Focus on meaning is evident.
- Uses some rereading to solve problems with individual words or to adjust for meaning.

 SOMEWHAT EXPRESSIVE
- Mostly reads word by word, with some use of two-, three-, or four-word phrases.

- Little use of pitch or pause to show punctuation and syntax.
- Very little emphasis or stress is placed on important words, i.e., little variation in volume, pitch, and pause.
- Few changes in rate and pitch that show focus on meaning.
- Mispronounces as many as 10 to 20 percent of words.
- Focus on meaning is inconsistent.
- Rereads frequently, and rereading may not show thinking about word and passage meaning.

LOW EXPRESSION
- Only reads word by word.
- Does not use phrasing, or phrasing is very awkward.
- Takes long pauses between words, and pauses are not meaningful.
- Does not observe punctuation.
- Reads in a monotone, with no change in pitch (e.g., to show questions).
- Reads like a robot—no variation in rate to show meaning.
- Uses inappropriate volume (e.g., whispering).
- Does not use emphasis or stress on important words.
- Does not show focus on making sense or meaning.

READY RESOURCE 8.20

Motivate to engage

Student motivation is sparked when important goals are clear, including the purposes of fluency. Teachers should explain and discuss these purposes on many occasions. Of course, the focus should be on whether students are making sense when they read silently and orally. Furthermore, the comprehension first concept implies that teachers should allow a range of acceptability in students' expression, accuracy, and rate.

Students may rehearse oral reading with interesting texts that call for the use of CPS to make sense, which may then be expressed through EAR. Techniques like setting a goal line on a personal fluency graph and tracking progress can stimulate students to engage in thinking about fluency purposes and components. Other motivational strategies include ones that tap into the power of groups, such as teaching students how to present Reader's Theatre (see below and Chapter 9) scripts to peers and other audiences.

Provide explicit instruction

Teachers should include fluency mini lessons among teaching points chosen to introduce main literacy events. Topics for fluency mini lessons include:

- fluency: what it is and why it is important
- EAR: expression, accuracy, rate
- word accuracy: pronunciation, enunciation, decoding
- rate: speed or pace, flexible and appropriate rates, smoothness
- expression: prosody, pitch, dynamics, stress/emphasis, pausing, phrasing, stretching words, clipping words
- dialects, accents
- recording and listening to yourself read aloud
- using a fluency rubric to self-evaluate
- graphing rate and accuracy
- how to give fluency feedback to classmates (refer to Ready Resource 8.20 for guidelines)

The question of when to "correct" pronunciation (an aspect of fluency) should be answered within the context of comprehension. If a student is making sense but mispronounces, it is helpful to note the error but let the student continue without interruption, especially if the oral reading is done in front of peers. Private conferences about fluency and other word-learning targets are in order. Small groups may be formed for work on common persistent patterns of errors (e.g., mispronouncing words that contain /th/).

Offer appropriate oral reading response options

Readers' Theatre and Poetree are examples of highly motivational and appropriate ways for students to show comprehension through fluent oral reading. In Reader's Theatre, students rehearse and publicly perform scripts in the format of a radio program. Chapter 9 details how teacher Maggie Phoenix uses Reader's Theatre to motivate fluency practice. Poetree is a weekly routine during which students find, write, and rehearse poetry aloud. Students may choose from a broad range of performance techniques, including choral reading. In my classroom, every Monday was Poetree day, and students knew they were responsible for being prepared. Performances were usually done in small groups, and the poems related to current units in science or social studies.

Many other uses of oral reading are appropriate for building fluency, such as echoic reading, and some are listed in Appendix I. One to avoid is round robin (cold, unprepared) reading of a common text. This is an ineffective method that was never a part of college teacher preparation programs, but it is still used by teachers who may not know better alternatives.

Incorporate fluency instruction in literacy main events and content teaching

To become fluent, students need models and practice with feedback. Main events such as Interactive Read Alouds (IRAs) and Daily Engaged Independent Reading (DEIR) provide modeling that builds fluency concepts and provide practice. Repeated reading is effective, but for building fluency it does not seem to matter whether students read the same text or new text (Stahl, 2004). What does matter is the total amount of reading: practice counts. When it comes to fluency, practice may not make perfect, but it can make better and faster. Chapter 10 offers an extended discussion of independent reading.

Content integration across the spectrum of comprehension goals is highly desirable, and teachers should look to innovative models. In the case of fluency, arts integration is such a reform model, and the music teacher can be a particularly valuable partner. Singing well is all about fluency, so it is natural that music teachers and reading teachers should partner for the purpose of making fluency goals explicit and developing students' EAR competencies. Another key partner is the school drama teacher. For more information on arts-based literacy instruction, visit the websites of the Arts Education Partnership and Artsedge, and consult books such as *Creating Meaning through Literature and the Arts* (Cornett, 2011).

Arts-Based Literacy Instruction

Arts Education Partnership
http://www.aep-arts.org/

Artsedge, http://artsedge.
kennedy-center.org/teach/

ONLINE RESOURCES
www

Conclusion

It has long been known that a large vocabulary gap exists between low- and high-achieving students, as well as between affluent and poor students (Irvin, 1990). However, vocabulary alone is seldom the sole culprit when it comes to comprehension difficulties—recall the long list of symptoms in Chapter 1. The learner's background and interests play significant roles. Another factor is the nature of the text, although teachers must remember that texts are not easy or difficult in isolation. Vocabulary negatively influences text comprehension if the text includes many unknown important words or the reader has little background for the topic. If a reader has a strong background and the text has only a few unknown words, a reader with solid comprehension strategies may well be able to infer enough from context to leap word hurdles. If the text has many unknown words, the reader has little background, and the text is uninteresting, then comprehension may well be defeated. English language learners confront great challenges, because they encounter many unknown words that label concepts that may or may not be familiar.

Increased phonics instruction is not a panacea for comprehension difficulties. Students can be hamstrung by an overemphasis on using spelling–sound patterns to arrive at word meanings. As students move through the grades, they will encounter increasing numbers of words that they will not have heard before. The best phonics can do is yield a word's pronunciation. That is of no help if the student has not heard the word previously and lacks understanding of the concept. Some students will continue to need explicit decoding instruction, even in the middle grades, but decoding instruction should never be limited to phonics (RAND, 2002). Students need to acquire a full range of strategies to uncover the meaning of unknown words, including the use of morphemic or structural analysis to zero in on meaningful word parts, especially common roots and affixes. This aspect of decoding should be taught through high school, with a focus on particular roots related to content areas.

Vocabulary development is about relating words to ideas. Comprehension does not happen without ideas. By understanding words, readers can understand text passages and full discourses that provide resources for inquiry. This chapter offered ideas for integrating teaching of concepts and word labels and gave a set of suggested problem-solving strategies for unknown words that focus on meaning (Word Fix-Ups, Ready Resource 8.11). Other word-level skills are important, but comprehension must remain at the forefront, even for primary grade students.

Finally, the chapter addresses the role of fluency as a tool for increasing comprehension. Expression, accuracy, and rate (EAR) were explained as key components of fluency, and examples of how to integrate fluency development with comprehension best practices were provided.

CHAPTER 8 big ideas

The following are examples of big ideas from this chapter. Use them to jump-start your own personal synthesis of big ideas and guide your thinking about teaching vocabulary and fluency within the context of CPS.

1. Words are labels for concepts. "A rose by any other name . . . ."
2. Each person has many different vocabularies.
3. Vocabulary development is strongly related to comprehension prowess.

4. Vocabulary instruction should focus on teaching students to enjoy words, develop their vocabularies, and unlock unfamiliar words.

5. Word fluency is the ability to use expressive elements, accurate pronunciation, and a flexible rate to convey meaning.

6. Fluency can be an indicator of comprehension, but isolated practice of its aspects is unlikely to increase comprehension.

a look ahead

The next chapter explains how and why teachers can broaden the forms and manners through which students are able to show comprehension. The chapter develops the concept of alternative response options, including writing options and arts-based options. Finally, technology is discussed as a response option that cannot be ignored.

CHAPTER 8 response options

1. Return to the introductory questions to gauge your comprehension of this chapter's big ideas.

2. Rate your agreement with the chapter's big ideas. Create a list of ones you agree with. Modify the rest to create statements with which you agree.

3. Convert the big ideas from #2 to if–then statements of what teachers should do.

4. Describe two ideas for increasing students' interest in words that you would like to implement.

5. Use the Word Fix-Ups to decode the unknown word in this sentence: "The ungorbly girls were standing right under the bleachers."

6. Compute your own reading accuracy and rate by reading aloud for one minute and then counting the words you pronounced correctly. In a small group, discuss your concerns about focusing on such a calculation to make determinations about learner comprehension.

7. Record a student reading aloud and use the expression rubric (Ready Resource 8.20) to analyze the student's needs and strengths.

8. Start your own list of interesting words you are learning.

9. Start your own list of newly learned professional words. Practice Lisa LaTroube's Words Alive routine with colleagues, using these words.

10. Use technology to expand the experiences of your students. Use Skype to set up a partner relationship between your students and kids in other regions so they can hear other dialects.

CHILDREN'S LITERATURE CITED

Espy, W. (1982). *A children's almanac of words at play.* New York: Random House.

Schwartz, A. (1985). *In a dark dark room.* New York: HarperCollins.

Terban, M. (1985). *Too hot to hoot.* New York: Clarion.

Riddle answer: What do you call a teacher who had a shark bite off her left arm and left leg?
Always right!

Teaching Diverse Response
Options to Show Comprehension

preview

T his chapter explains how and why teachers can broaden the forms and manners through which students are able to show comprehension. The chapter develops the concept of alternative response options, including writing options and arts-based options. Technology is discussed as a response option that cannot be ignored.

Many books have been written on how to teach writing, and a growing number of them discuss how teachers can meaningfully integrate arts and technology in the regular classroom. This chapter is not meant to compete with books that do a thorough job of presenting the knowledge base and pedagogy necessary to do justice to each area of the arts and technology. This chapter is intended simply to offer "what ifs." The many Ready Resources will serve as springboards to expand the menu of response options students can use to make comprehension visible.

The chapter concludes with examples of how the best practice of offering diverse response options is linked to the eight best practices previously introduced.

important questions

1. Why are response options important to comprehension instruction?

2. How can response options serve as evidence of comprehension (product and process) for assessment?

3. What kinds of text responses both motivate students and show their progress toward comprehension standards and goals?

4. How can comprehension response options align with inquiry-based problem solving (i.e., constructionist perspectives that emphasize individual meaning making)?

5. How much and what kind of differentiated instruction should be provided to enable students to respond meaningfully?

6. Why is writing privileged over other comprehension responses?

7. How can big ideas be made the focus of the written, arts-based, electronic, and multimedia texts students create to show comprehension?

Introduction

Children have real understanding only of that which they invent themselves.

JEAN PIAGET

This chapter brings us to response, the end of the CPS process. The goal of responding is for students to learn how to *organize* and *shape*, *reflect on* and *revise* the big ideas they synthesize from texts. Today's world offers a plethora of options, including technological tools that present vast capabilities to transform big ideas, *revise* newly created comprehension products, and then make them *public* in multimedia extravaganzas.

The response portion of comprehension best practices completes the CPS process and brings teachers and students full circle: responses that show comprehension are themselves new texts created through problem solving. The intent to compose a new text sets purpose and creates motivation. The before, during, and after strategies in the CPS process are reactivated. Constructing meaning becomes creation in the literal sense, and composition choices need not be confined to traditional oral and written products. Today's communication options would fill more than one chart, but Ready Resource 9.1 lists many ideas. The Classroom Snapshot that follows shows how one teacher uses drama as an important comprehension response option.

Comprehension response options.

acceptance speech

advertisement or commercial

advice column

announcement

apology

article (newspaper or magazine)

award ceremony

blog

blurb (book cover)

book parts (e.g., table of contents, glossary, or index)

book report

brochure

bulletin board

bumper sticker

campaign speech

cartoon strip

certificate

chant, cheer, or call

chart

collage

collection (e.g., related objects)

command or proclamation

complaint

compliment

contract

dance

definition

diagram

dictionary

directions

drama (e.g., skit, pantomime)

editorial

email (e.g., expert interview)

encyclopedia entry

epilogue

evaluation

excuse

family story

films

greeting card

headline

horoscope (e.g., for a character)

humor (e.g., joke, story, one-liner)

illustration

interview

introduction

invitation

jingle

jump rope rhyme

label, tag, or caption

landscape (setting)

law

letter (friendly or business)

letters (alphabetical)

lies list

list (e.g., to-do or grocery)

literary genre

log, journal, or diary entry

love note

magic spell

map

marquee notice

menu

metaphor

mixed metaphor

mural

music

nominating speech

notes

obituary

ode

package

panel (expert discussion)

paradox

personal narrative

phone conversation

photograph or picture

play

poetry (see Ready Resource 9.5)

portrait

postcard

poster

PowerPoint presentation

prologue

propaganda (e.g., card stack)

proposal

questionnaire

ransom note

recipe

remedy

report

resume

retelling

review or critique

riddle

road sign

roast

rules

scientific report

script

sculpture or model

sign

slogan

song

table

tableau

telegram

television show

tercet

thank-you note

thesaurus

timeline

titles (e.g., for chapters)

tribute

understatement

video

visual art (landscape, portrait, abstract, 3-d, etc.)

"wanted" poster

warning

weather report

WebQuest

website

wiki

will

wish list

word list/glossary

READY RESOURCE 9.1

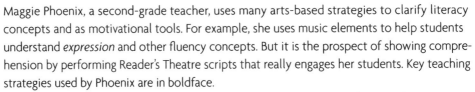

classroom snapshot

MAGGIE PHOENIX USES READER'S THEATRE

Maggie Phoenix, a second-grade teacher, uses many arts-based strategies to clarify literacy concepts and as motivational tools. For example, she uses music elements to help students understand *expression* and other fluency concepts. But it is the prospect of showing comprehension by performing Reader's Theatre scripts that really engages her students. Key teaching strategies used by Phoenix are in boldface.

It is Monday morning. After completing an opening routine (see Chapter 10), Maggie starts a mini lesson on word fluency components. The children are seated on the floor in front of a chart entitled "Fluent Readers."

"**Thumbs up** and let me see your teeth if you remember one thing that fluent readers do," Maggie says. Most smile and put their thumbs up.

"Maria, please start."

"Ah, they say—no, I mean they READ words with expression."

Maggie begins to write Maria's idea on the chart. When she gets to the word *expression*, she writes "ex" and then tells the class to "**spell the rest of the word with me.**" She leads them through "sound to spelling" stretching and reminds them about ways to spell /shun/ that they talked about last week.

"**What does *expression* mean?**" she asks next. "Rahab?"

"To make your voice have feeling. Like, you change the pitch or say important words louder."

"I'm going to put *pitch* right here under *expression*. Where in the room can we find the spelling of *pitch*?" Heads turn and fingers point to an **arts word wall** covering a large bulletin board.

"Yes! Rahab—go point to it. Now, spell it out loud, and do it with expression. We'll be your **echo.**"

Rahab grins and spells *pitch* by **grouping the letters** (p–it–ch) and making his voice higher on the "it." The class and Ms. Phoenix echo him.

"That was fun. Let's do it again. Go Rahab!" And they do.

"Why did we laugh, boys and girls?"

"Because Rahab used pitch in a funny way," a boy says.

"I liked how he put one letter and then two and two to make a pattern," another observes.

"Me, too," Maggie says. "Okay, so we have expression, which includes pitch, and Rahab also said that good readers make words or word parts louder or softer. What is the **music term** for louder and softer?"

Chorally the class chimes, "Dynamics!" Right away a boy points it out on the arts word wall, and Maggie gives him a thumbs-up.

"There was something else that goes with using your voice to show meaning and feelings that someone said. It needs to be on the chart, too."

"Expression!" several say at once.

"Yes, using your voice to show meaning and feeling *is* expression. We have listed under *expression* the ideas of pitch and dynamics. There was another idea that came up when Rahab spelled *pitch*."

"Ooh—ooh!" Several thumbs go up.

"Georgio?"

"Rahab spelled by grouping letters. If you want to show expression, you don't just read duh-duh-duh like a robot. It sounds more interesting to group the words."

"Do you remember the term for grouping words together so they make sense and have feeling?"

Georgio frowns and the class is quiet.

"I'm going to give you a clue." Maggie writes on the chart, *phr__s__ng*.

The class studies the **clozed word** but is still quiet.

"How about I **demonstrate** for you?" Maggie looks around at the class charts. "I'll use a tongue twister on the Tongue Twister Master Chart." She walks to the chart and points to *She sells seashells by the seashore.* She reads aloud, "SHE / sells seashells / by the seashore." Then she smiles and says, "Or I could read it, 'She SELLS / seashells / by the seashore.'" She makes a slash with her hand after each phrase.

"I know another way," shouts a boy with dark hair.

"Okay, let's hear it, Franklin."

"She sells SEAshells / by the seashore," Franklin reads. Maggie applauds, and others join her.

"It changes the meaning, doesn't it? Words are just dead lines and circles until we add music to them. Franklin grouped the words differently from how I did and made a whole new meaning. **Franklin, come show us** with your hand how you grouped the words."

Franklin does so, and Maggie goes over and points again at the clozed word she wrote on the chart. "Franklin used different *phrasing*. What letters do I need to fill in to finish the word *phrasing?*"

The class responds with "a" and "i" as she points to each blank and writes them in.

"Phrasing is grouping words to create the message you want," she explains. "Fluent readers do this when they read aloud and when they read silently, too."

A girl in red jeans raises her hand. Maggie nods to her.

"Franklin also used emphasis on the word *sea.*"

"**Tamara, you are absolutely right.** I'll write that here after *phrasing*. That is such an important part of expression, isn't it? **We better practice that.** Hmmm. How about I'll say a sentence and with a partner you take turns using emphasis on different words to change the message. Here's the sentence: 'Open the window, please.' Everyone turn to a partner and practice. Jerry, I'll be your partner. Go!"

There is suddenly a hubbub. Maggie listens as Jerry says, "OPEN the window, pl-eeee-aa-sse" and laughs. Maggie says, "I think that means you really want the window open, NOT closed!"

After a few minutes Maggie claps a rhythm to get attention. The class echoes it. "Listen to my question. **Who HEARD your partner** use emphasis or stress in a way that we all should hear?"

"JOHN!" says a boy, pointing at his partner.

"John, what did you say?"

"I said, 'Open the WINDOW, please.'"

"**And what was John's message?**"

"He wanted the window open, not the door or the closet," responds a girl in pigtails.

"So, *emphasis or stress, phrasing, dynamics,* and *pitch* are all ways to **use our voices to make our oral reading more fluent.** And fluent reading is more interesting, because the reader is showing how he or she made sense. It's just like when we sing a song and use the music symbols like < and >." Maggie writes the crescendo and decrescendo symbols beside the word *dynamics.*

TONGUE TWISTER CHART

She sell seashells by the seashore.

A flea and a fly flew up in a flue.

I thought of thinking of thanking you.

"In music, expression symbols are written down. **In reading, we need them in our brains. We have to remember how to use our voices to show how we think the words should sound."**

Maggie stands up and goes over to a table that holds four stacks of colored folders. **"Reader's Theatre scripts,** yeah!" a girl shouts, and many students clap.

"I'm glad you are enjoying them," Maggie says. "This week all the guided **reading groups** are doing different scripts that go with our **social studies unit** on Asia. When you get in your groups, remember to read through the scripts before you decide parts. Also, remember that more than one person can read the same part, and sometimes people will have more than one part." A hand goes up.

"Ashley?"

"Can we **read chorally** like we did with the insect poems for science?"

"Yes, or take turns. **You decide.** The important thing is to be considerate and fair AND . . ."

"Keep your focus!" the class says in unison.

"Yes, you funny bunnies. **Keep your focus on making meaning with your voice.** We've talked a lot about rehearsing— you know you need to know the words and change speed to make it interesting. Today we reviewed expression, and I think it is one of the most important things a fluent reader does."

"Because you have to KNOW the words to do IT!" Franklin points out.

"Absolutely, Franklin. I couldn't have said it more fluently!"

SNAPSHOT REFLECTION

Maggie Phoenix does much more than just assign Reader's Theatre scripts for performance. She sets her students up for success with using Reader's Theatre as a way to respond. The focus is kept on making comprehension visible. In the lesson she used these comprehension best practices that were the subjects of previous chapters:

- focus on big ideas.
- ask and invite important questions.
- explicitly teach concepts and skills.
- motivate students to engage.
- engage students in problem solving.

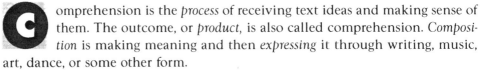

Making Comprehension Visible

Comprehension is the *process* of receiving text ideas and making sense of them. The outcome, or *product*, is also called comprehension. *Composition* is making meaning and then *expressing* it through writing, music, art, dance, or some other form.

Read the sentences that follow with the goal of comprehending or making meaning. At each X, pause and think about these questions: *What do you see and feel? What does or does not make sense? What are your predictions?*

1. The brides blushed as they waited. X

2. The fourteen-year-old went first. X
3. When all three had processed, they stood side by side and joined hands. X
4. The notary told them to turn and face the groom. X
5. The polygamist ceremony then proceeded. X

What did you notice about your thinking? Were you able to see what was going on? Did you infer that it was a wedding, even though that word was never used? When did the scene start to make sense? What questions arose? What did you do if it didn't make sense? How did your values and feelings affect your comprehension? What text evidence supports your conclusions? What information from outside the text did you use? How might your conclusions differ from those of others? Why?

Louise Rosenblatt's (1978) insightful work helps explain how readers can create multiple legitimate interpretations from texts. Background knowledge and individual reader dispositions can produce distinctly different syntheses of big ideas, all of which can be validated by text evidence. Actual harm may be done by teachers who operate on an unfounded notion that a text can have only "one best meaning" (Pressley, 2006). In the case of the wedding story, the problem was presented in the form of sentences to be read one by one, but the ultimate meaning could be understood only when the reader fit the five sentences together. Big ideas are synthesized from full texts, not single sentences and single paragraphs.

What's more, simply asking a reader to retell the events of a story leaves out much information that is necessary for understanding. For example, your personally generated comprehension of the wedding story was probably colored by knowledge of U.S. law or your moral and religious views. In the final analysis, any mindful reader has to answer the question "So what?"—which demands a personal interpretive *response* rather than a literal retelling. When individuals problem solve the wedding story using relevant background knowledge along with text evidence, varying viewpoints and conclusions emerge. When texts are discussed, the discussion itself can change participants' comprehension as individuals turn silent thoughts into oral forms and consider others' interpretations. Even with a short and simple text, the formation of immediate understanding can be complicated.

But what about *long-term* knowledge gain? Think about books, films, or music that are highly memorable. Now, consider what makes a text memorable. The memorability of a text depends on its richness (images, emotions, and insights), the degree to which CPS was practiced on the text *with self-awareness*, and the reader's opportunity to organize and shape a response in diverse ways, including discussion, writing, arts products, and electronic forms.

Comprehension is thinking, and thinking is invisible. But through written products, discussions, arts projects, performances, and exhibits, comprehension can be made visible *to an extent.* No externalized expression ever fully captures all the thinking and emotions wrapped up in a big idea conclusion. Offering students a variety of alternatives to show understanding motivates their engagement in the effort to try.

As discussed in Chapter 6, teachers can increase students' motivation in several ways, some of which have to do with the response phase of the CPS process. Response options are choices, and choice is key to motivation. Responses can make goals clearer by clarifying comprehension outcomes. What's more, response options such as Maggie's Reader's Theatre encourage students to work together and perform for, share with, and exhibit before their classmates. Collaborative and audience-focused work taps social aspects of motivation known to increase comprehension. An expanded view of response options also increases comprehension: in studies, students who were engaged in finding big ideas in texts and then graphically depicting relationships among the ideas showed improved recall and broader text comprehension (RAND, 2002).

Outside of academic contexts, people show their thinking through diverse communication forms ranging from YouTube videos to architectural drawings. Innovative products that reflect creative problem solving are highly valued. Members of the 21st-century workforce are expected to think divergently and critically, and they will need to use oral and written means to show their comprehension (Hall & Piazza, 2008). In the third millennium we have gone "back to the future" to embrace the arts as full-fledged communication tools that liberate the construction and demonstration of comprehension. No longer is communication confined to words. Non-verbal technological and arts-based communication is highly prized. For example, consider the value of visual forms like GPS systems and body-imaging devices. Students can and should be prepared for the reality of non-verbal communication.

Developing Comprehension Response Options

If they can do the worksheet, they don't need it, and if they can't do it, it won't help them.

MARILYN ADAMS

It can be argued that comprehension does not occur until constructed meaning is externalized or expressed. Certainly, teachers cannot know if students have comprehended, or the degree of comprehension, unless observable evidence is available. To assess comprehension progress, teachers need a myriad of authentic ways for students to show they know. Diverse 'externalizing' response possibilities are now available that include creating music, multimedia, and digital texts. And, the amount and diversity of text response activities can have a powerful effect on students' achievement (Guthrie, 2000; Guthrie & Wigfield, 1997). Comprehension response options also introduce to students the range of ways humans express thoughts and feelings. The success of the comprehension process depends on active mental response. Moreover, as mentioned earlier, use of diverse response options can motivate students by presenting choices that align with strengths and interests.

The success of the comprehension process depends on active mental response to incoming information from texts that may take the form of words, visual and auditory images and symbols, or touch (Scharlach, 2008). When response is driven by meaning-oriented purposes and there are a range of available options, it is more likely that comprehension will be richer. For example, consider the effect of a reader choosing to show his or her unique comprehension of big ideas through dance rather than by writing an essay. Anticipating the response form will alter the way any reader problem solves to make meaning during and after reading. Some response options engage more "what if" thinking, which employs CPS to create more novel comprehension products.

Currently, instructional response tasks are frequently geared to the questions teachers anticipate will appear on high-stakes tests. Even accomplished teachers often reduce the task of comprehension to responses that focus on recalling and retelling literal information (Taylor et al., 1999). They ask low-level questions whose answers can be found in the text, and neglect high-level questions that challenge students to construct big ideas from important details. Of course, scoring the "what," "where," and "who" questions is easier than judging responses to "why" and "how" questions that call for problem solving and yield poems, paintings, and plays.

Comprehension instruction should prepare students to do more than respond to short-answer questions and standardized test items (Pressley, 2000). When students are repeatedly told to read in order to answer questions that test recall of facts, they continually practice low-level and unengaged thinking. As the adage goes, practice doesn't make perfect, it makes permanent. Students can permanently learn that reading is a dull task controlled by a teacher's assignments.

HOW RESPONSE PROSPECTS INFLUENCE BEFORE, DURING, AND AFTER ACTIVITIES IN CPS

Making comprehension visible has many advantages. To begin with, as suggested above, how we anticipate we will respond to a text changes our thinking *before* and *during* text use. If I expect to write an expository text for teachers about comprehension, I think differently as I begin my research than if I plan to write a piece of fiction about a teacher who goes after big ideas with a vengeance—maybe something like *Pay It Forward* or the great teacher classic *To Sir with Love.*

The act of organizing and shaping big ideas synthesized from a text changes comprehension itself. The tools, media, and forms by which we choose to make comprehension concrete *after* reading, listening to, or viewing a text alter our thinking as we use them. For example, if I choose to write a novel about hurricanes, the narrative format will affect what I communicate about the topic. Alternatively, if I choose to express my thoughts and feelings about hurricanes in watercolor, the big ideas will be shaped by the brushstrokes, colors, and visual images the medium unleashes.

NATIONAL STANDARDS AND RESPONSE OPTIONS

Standards are one place teachers can find curriculum development guidance and models for instructional practices. National standards target comprehension beyond recall and can guide teachers in developing an array of response options. Ready Resource 9.2 lists the English Language Arts (ELA) standards. This resource shows the big picture rather than the small details on which schools can get hung up. Note the focus on higher-order thinking, problem solving, and use of diverse texts and responses. The ELA standards are the source document

Standards for the English Language Arts.

1 Students read a wide range of print and nonprint texts to build an understanding of texts, of themselves, and of the cultures of the United States and the world; to acquire new information; to respond to the needs and demands of society and the workplace; and for personal fulfillment. Among these texts are fiction and nonfiction, classic and contemporary works.

2 Students read a wide range of literature from many periods in many genres to build an understanding of the many dimensions (e.g., philosophical, ethical, aesthetic) of human experience.

3 Students apply a wide range of strategies to comprehend, interpret, evaluate, and appreciate texts. They draw on their prior experience, their interactions with other readers and writers, their knowledge of word meaning and of other texts, their word identification strategies, and their understanding of textual features (e.g., sound-letter correspondence, sentence structure, context, graphics).

4 Students adjust their use of spoken, written, and visual language (e.g., conventions, style, vocabulary) to communicate effectively with a variety of audiences and for different purposes.

5 Students employ a wide range of strategies as they write and use different writing process elements appropriately to communicate with different audiences for a variety of purposes.

6 Students apply knowledge of language structure, language conventions (e.g., spelling and punctuation), media techniques, figurative language, and genre to create, critique, and discuss print and nonprint texts.

7 Students conduct research on issues and interests by generating ideas and questions, and by posing problems. They gather, evaluate, and synthesize data from a variety of sources (e.g., print and nonprint texts, artifacts, people) to communicate their discoveries in ways that suit their purpose and audience.

8 Students use a variety of technological and information resources (e.g., libraries, databases, computer networks, video) to gather and synthesize information and to create and communicate knowledge.

9 Students develop an understanding of and respect for diversity in language use, patterns, and dialects across cultures, ethnic groups, geographic regions, and social roles.

10 Students whose first language is not English make use of their first language to develop competency in the English language arts and to develop understanding of content across the curriculum.

11 Students participate as knowledgeable, reflective, creative, and critical members of a variety of literacy communities.

12 Students use spoken, written, and visual language to accomplish their own purposes (e.g., for learning, enjoyment, persuasion, and the exchange of information).

[Author's note: While all the standards are connected to comprehension, those that explicitly address comprehension problem solving are 3, 7, 8, and 12.]

READY RESOURCE 9.2

for state standards, and they acknowledge that students will not understand the big ideas in the texts at hand, nor will they gain long-term knowledge, unless instruction targets problem solving to create understanding (Wolk, 2008).

The ELA standards do not stand alone in informing comprehension curriculum and instruction. A comprehension focus should drive the entire curriculum, and this perspective does underlie standards for science, social studies, math, science, and the arts. Appendix G, on big ideas in and sources for standards, provides a glimpse into these documents and suggests sources for Internet access to the complete documents. National standards overlap in their emphasis on key comprehension concepts such as problem solving, understanding, communication, construction of meaning, research, higher-order thinking (evaluation, critique), and application. Comprehension practices are well served when teachers implement the real meaning behind standards. When state and local education agencies misinterpret them or intentionally "dumb them down" for convenience in implementation or testing, no one wins, and students are the biggest losers.

National standards for every area of the curriculum support the teaching of coordinated problem-solving strategies to accomplish comprehension. The standards go further to suggest significant ways students can *show* understanding that parallel the world beyond school and help teachers develop an array of response options. In particular, the National Standards for the Arts cast the arts as communication vehicles that focus on the processes of creating, performing, and responding. Classroom teachers and arts specialists need to unite in addressing whole child needs, which entails embracing the arts as both essential learning tools and essential comprehension response options.

National Standards for the Arts

http://artsedge.kennedy-center.org/teach/standards/standards.cfm

ONLINE RESOURCE

MEANINGFUL RESPONSES

Meaningful response tasks mirror the real world. They involve synthesizing information from multiple texts, including hypertext, to *create* diverse products. High-level responses require cognitive engagement in problem solving and are student driven, with an emphasis on personal choices (Gambrell, Malloy, & Mazzoni, 2007). These responses allow knowledge to be shaped into diverse forms: oral, written, visual art, music, drama, dance, multimedia, and technology generated. The world outside school walls demands knowledge shapers, not knowledge consumers, which requires problem solving, not simple direction following.

Responding by Creating Written Texts

urrently, the most common comprehension responses are word-based written products. Observations of "accomplished" teachers show they engage students in written responses to texts 48 percent of the time, as compared to 18 percent for teachers whose classes have a pattern of lower achievement (Taylor et al., 1999). Writing enjoys privileged status when it comes to literacy, since school texts traditionally are made of printed words. Indeed, integrating writing with reading, including using writing to learn in all content areas, has been shown to improve reading achievement. Quantity of writing, however, is an inadequate measure when it comes to comprehension, especially if the writing consists solely of responses that involve answering questions or journaling (Taylor et al., 1999).

As teachers, we need to teach a broader range of written genres and offer them as response options. The world is rich in text forms that offer students choices to show comprehension. Students can learn to use a much greater range of forms to create original oral, written, electronic, arts-based, and multimedia products informed by reading, listening, and viewing. One way to incorporate a larger variety of written response options in a classroom is to create a station with real-life examples organized alphabetically in files. The following artifacts are easy to collect: advertisements, bills, greeting cards, letters, applications, thank-you notes, business letters, friendly letters, travel brochures, and solicitations. Students can use features of each to construct original versions. The response options listed in Ready Resource 9.1 offer additional categories. In addition, many involve taking the point of view of an important character or focusing on an important event—requiring the student to reflect big ideas from texts in order to indicate comprehension.

Ready Resource 5.10 in Chapter 5 lists genres that can be offered as writing response options for students as they organize and shape the big ideas they derive from texts. However, considering Multiple Intelligences theory (Gardner, 1993) and the reality of contemporary communication, it behooves teachers to make a greater variety of response forms available. In particular, technological and arts-based communication (e.g., visual art products, musical compositions, dance compositions, and dramatic forms) are texts used by real people in real life to shape and share thoughts and feelings. Why shouldn't the range of communication forms used in the world outside of school be made available to the people who will make their lives in that world? That said, the next sections briefly summarize writing basics and provide resources to stretch teachers' thinking about using writing and the arts to extend Comprehension Problem Solving and show comprehension. Ready Resource 9.3 lists springboards for written responses.

Written response springboards.

READY RESOURCE 9.3

Adjective addict: Brainstorm adjectives for the text or a character. Mark the top five.

Back story: Find a "hole" in the story where the character disappears (off camera). Describe what she or he does during this time.

Biography: Write a biography of a character. Include information from before, during, or after the story occurs.

Bridge: Draw a line down the middle of a sheet of paper. On one side write down important quotes from the text and on the other write how each relates to your life. See a student example in Ready Resource 7.9 in Chapter 7.

Business letter: Email or write a company or an organization related to a topic from the book.

Connect: Write about how the book connects to your life.

Copycat: Write your own story using the same title, theme, big ideas, or pattern of the book.

Cube a character (or whole text): Look at a character six different ways.

Dear Author: Write to the author and ask questions.

Diagram: Draw how the plot is organized in the book (linear, episodic, cumulative).

(continued)

Continued.

Dictionary: Compile a dictionary of special words in the book.

Email an author: Ask about why she or he wrote the text and what big ideas are hidden in it.

Email chat: Have a written conversation with a friend, classmate, or teacher about the text.

Executive summary: Use a 3 x 5 card to summarize what happened on one side; on the other, analyze the importance of the events.

Facts: List facts you learned and why they are important.

Fan mail: Write a letter of appreciation to the author.

Fast forward: Make the characters older or younger, or fast-forward the time period and write a new story.

Found poetry: Choose important and interesting words and phrases from the text (e.g., one from each chapter) and arrange them in a poem.

Gender bender: Rewrite the story, changing the genders.

Genre change: Write the book in another genre.

Graph: List the events and then graph them on a scale of good news to bad news events.

Interview: Write an interview between a character and the author or between you and the author.

KW Chart: Make a chart that lists what you now know and what you want to know about.

Letter: Write a letter about the book to a friend.

Library recommendation: List reasons why the library should buy the book.

Literature log: Make notes as you read, using these categories: Special Words, Topics/Big Ideas, Feelings.

Media comparison: Make a T-chart or Venn diagram comparing and contrasting a book with its film or TV version.

Newspaper: Work as a class to produce a newspaper with various stories, letters, cartoons, and so forth related to the text (e.g., *Three Pigs Gazette*).

Poem match: Find or write a poem that goes with the book.

Poem patterns: Write a poem about a character, setting, or big idea using a poem structure.

Point of view shift: Rewrite the story from the POV of another character.

Random poetry: Place random words from the text in an envelope and have groups use them to create poems, or use the same words for each student to write different poems about the text.

Recast: Rewrite a poem as a story, a short story as a poem or play, and so forth.

Review: Write a review of the text.

Sentence list: List the five most interesting sentences from the text.

Sentence stems: Use stems as starters to help students frame their thoughts as they respond to texts. Here are examples:

> Fortunately . . . , Unfortunately . . . , Someday I . . . , If . . . then . . . , I used to (think or feel) . . . but now I (think or feel) . . . , The important thing about . . . is . . . because . . .

Simplify: Rewrite the book for a younger reader.

Summarize: Get the plot down to one paragraph.

Telegram: Summarize the book in fifteen to fifty words.

Text message: Write text messages to a friend about the big ideas.

Trailer: Write a movie preview about the "best moments" in the text.

Venn: Compare the text to another book (using literary or art elements).

Webless blog: Partner students and designate them A and B. A starts and writes about the text. Student B responds to what A wrote with a question or an elaboration. *Variation:* involve more students by having each write an initial response and then passing it on to the next person.

Word hunt: List ten words to describe the book or ten important words in the text.

WebQuest: Research a related topic on the Internet and present it to the class.

X Chart: Draw a large X and write about four big ideas in the book in the spaces.

YouTube: Create a script for a video you could post on YouTube.

Zoom out and in: Write about the biggest idea in the text and give details to support your conclusion.

9.3 READY RESOURCE

WHY A WRITTEN RESPONSE?

How can I know what I think till I see what I say?

E. M. FORSTER

Why is written response usually at the top of the list of comprehension responses in school? There are many reasons, the first being that writing and reading are integrally related. There would be nothing to read if writers didn't author texts. What's more, each writer is first a reader. Young children observe the texts around them and proceed to make their marks with lipstick and crayon on any available surface. Writing and reading go forward in tandem, and children who read more build up a background of diverse, well-crafted models of what and how to write. Students who are encouraged to write while they are learning to read attune to the spelling of spoken sounds (phonemes) and are more likely to observe spelling–sound patterns that are key to unlocking words they read (phonics). Student writers read texts to seek inspiration and information for their own work. Finally, the world is dominated by word-based texts, including email and text messages, so writing deserves a prominent place in the literacy curriculum and on every comprehension response option menu.

THE WRITING PROCESS AND CPS

We all write for personal purposes, so it should be obvious that written composition is fundamentally an activity of constructing meaning. What is less obvious is how the written composition process and the comprehension process are parallel. Both engage a nearly identical set of problem-solving strategies, and both focus on making meaning. The writing process has before, during, and after (BDA) stages parallel to the CPS process, but the stages and processes are labeled differently. For example, the terms *prewriting*, *drafting*, and *postwriting* are used instead of before, during, and after. Both processes are set in motion by purposes that are addressed through problem solving (see Ready Resource 2.1 in Chapter 2). In drafting, as in reading, the person focuses on inferring big ideas, predicting, visualizing, monitoring, questioning, and so forth. Drafts go through the same evaluation process as texts that are read, a process that includes revision, and final products of both reading and writing are publicly shared (i.e., published in a variety of ways, ranging from PowerPoint presentations to wiki documents).

While it is unlikely the nation's educators will come to agreement about common labels, practitioners at specific schools can teach the parallel nature of the comprehension and writing processes with agreed-upon common labels. The common educational goal is for students to *use* the writing process, CPS, the scientific method, creative problem-solving, and other parallel processes. Diverse labels for the same concepts can confuse students and get in the way of use and reciprocal transfer of problem-solving strategies to every area of the curriculum. Professional development time is well spent examining all curricular standards to identify overlap, so that terms and concepts can be consolidated and consistently taught. At minimum, the writing process and the CPS process should be married in students' thinking, even if the two do not share strategy names. The success of any written response depends on students using a coordinated set of problem-solving strategies flexibly, just as with reading. All of the best practices discussed for reading, viewing, and listening to texts also apply to teaching students to construct meaning through writing, including explicit teaching about the writing process.

While there are important reciprocal relationships between reading and writing, as well as between word-based listening and speaking, all of these processes are about thinking. Thinking is the core of comprehension, and thinking is not limited to words. The world outside of school has heartily embraced a greater range of communication vehicles, especially arts-based technology, and teachers need to follow suit. Writing can help us decide what we really "think" about a topic, but so do paintings, sculptures, and photographs.

TEXT CHARACTERISTICS AND STRUCTURES

Text characteristics, including general organizational schemes called genres (see Ready Resource 5.10) and narrative and expository text structures, were discussed in Chapter 5. Knowing text genres, structures, and features and that writers choose them for specific purposes assists students' comprehension and gives them a greater range of forms in which to write. Genre conventions need to be taught explicitly, and students should be challenged to uncover common features using scaffolds such as genre charts.

Ready Resource 9.4 is an example of a genre chart that illustrates the common elements in fiction, nonfiction, and mixed genres. To make the chart for the classroom, use roll paper or cards and a pocket chart. For a specific genre (e.g., fairy tales), list common elements down the left side and titles across the top. Students can work collaboratively to find examples of elements in texts. The chart thus

Genre chart: Common elements.

ELEMENTS	FICTION	NONFICTION	MIXED GENRES (e.g., *historical fiction*)
Beginning	X	Introduction	X
Middle	X	Development	X
End	X	Conclusion	X
Characters	X	real people	X
Details	X	X	X
Setting	X	real places	X
Plot	X	real events	X
Facts/information	X	X	X
Problems/solutions	X	X	X

READY RESOURCE 9.4

becomes a response option that targets key elements, which should include big ideas. In fairy tales big ideas or themes are often explicit, and teachers can coach big idea statements from students. For example, the "beauty theme" from "Beauty and the Beast" can become "Beauty is more than how a person looks." Students may be asked to identify examples from texts to justify their responses.

Students need to have many additional text features in their writing toolkits. Ready Resource 5.9 in Chapter 5 lists text concepts, and Ready Resources 5.11 and 5.12 describe narrative and expository elements of writing.

Another writing activity that provides a creative written response option and teaches students about genre uses poetry patterns. To use poem patterns to show comprehension,

1. model the different writing patterns and do collaborative poem writing after reading common texts (e.g., in social studies).

2. encourage students to vary repetition in lines and words and to use elements such as alliteration, rhyme, imagery, and onomatopoeia.

3. make a set of poem pattern cards to serve as references. See Ready Resource 9.5.

READY RESOURCE 9.5

Using poem patterns to show comprehension.

Patterns Based on Syllable and Word Count

Haiku: Japanese nature verse using three unrhymed lines. There are seventeen syllables in the poem, distributed by line as 5–7–5.

> Hurricanes scared me.
> We moved north to be safer.
> But fierce winds still blow.

Lune: Three lines with 3–5–3 words in each line.

> The hurricane threat
> Caused my family to worry.
> We moved north.

Tanka: Five lines with 5–7–5–7–7 syllables per line.

> Fire wind rain cold quakes
> Weather can't be controlled
> But we moved away
> But the weather followed us
> Fire wind rain cold quakes still blow

Diamante: A seven-line poem shaped like a diamond. Line pattern: one noun, two adjectives, three present participles, four word phrases or nouns, three present participles, two adjectives, one synonym or antonym. The topic may be changed in the middle of line 4 to relate to the final antonym.

> Hurricanes
>
> Windy Wild
> Blowing Breaking Blasting
> Noisy Red Cross Shelters
> Snoring Crying Worrying
> Mindless Forceful
> Monsterstorm

Cinquain: Five-line poem that does not rhyme, with 1–2–3–4–1 words per line. The first line states the subject, the second gives adjectives, the third actions, the fourth a feeling or observation, the fifth an adjective or synonym.

> Weather
> Unfeeling Powerful
> Blowing, blasting, stalking
> I never know when
> Force

(continued)

Continued.

Couplet: Two lines that rhyme.

> You need a "go bag" if you live near the coast.
>
> Without food dry clothes and medicine you could be toast.

Triplet: Three lines that rhyme.

> You need a "go bag" if you live near the coast.
>
> Without food dry clothes and medicine you could be toast.
>
> It can't be everything you like, only what you need the most.

Quartet: four lines with one of several rhyme patterns: aabb, abab, abcb, or abca.

> From off the coast of Africa (a)
>
> Blow hot winds over hot sea (b)
>
> Add low pressure and bad luck (c)
>
> To get hurricanes from A to Z. (a)

Repeated lines: Any number of lines that start with the same stem:

> I wish: I wish hurricanes would not exist.
>
> I wish hurricanes . . .
>
> Is: A hurricane is a deadly force made of wind.
>
> A hurricane is . . .
>
> Red: Red is the color of high winds on the Weather Channel.
>
> Red is . . .

Five senses:

> Sounds like _____
>
> Looks like _____
>
> Tastes like _____
>
> Smells like _____
>
> Feels like _____

Preposition poem:

> Inside the storms
>
> With courage they fly
>
> Into the eye
>
> Out again to report
>
> (Hurricane hunters)

If/So or If/Then:

> If I lived in the path of a hurricane's fury,
>
> then I'd evacuate fast to lessen my worry.

Lie poems: Each line is something not true.

> Hurricanes are sticks in a rush.
>
> Hurricanes are the opposite of Slowicanes.

Then and now: I used to (think/feel) . . . , but now I (think / feel) . . .

> I used to think hurricanes were exciting,
>
> but now hurricanes scare me to death.

Riddle poems: Give three clues, with the first most general and the third most specific.

> 1. weather
> 2. high wind
> 3. funnel cloud

Concrete or shape: Words are placed to look like the poem's topic. (For example, words about hurricanes might be written in a swirling shape.)

Clerihew or bio poem: Quartet about a person.

> Barack Obama
>
> Had a Caucasian mama
>
> But his dad was African
>
> Our president is American

Limerick: Humorous five-lined verse with aabba rhyme pattern. The rhythm pattern is important.

> There once was a storm named Ike
>
> That hit Galveston late one night
>
> The houses exploded
>
> And the beach eroded
>
> Destroying like the hated Third Reich

Found poems: Cut random phrases from magazines or newspapers and arrange them to create a poem. It need not rhyme.

Acrostics: A word written vertically with a word or phrase stemming from each letter that relates in meaning; see Ready Resource 8.4 in Chapter 8.

Other pattern possibilities: Tongue twisters, jump-rope rhymes, camp songs, and advertising jingles.

9.5 READY RESOURCE

Graphic organizers such as story maps can scaffold students' efforts to identify text structure, which can enhance their understanding of text characteristics for reading and writing purposes. Students can use story maps to monitor their comprehension quality, see relationships in and among texts, and plan their own narrative writing (see Ready Resource 9.6). Other graphic organizers include character trait maps, plot graphs, Venn diagrams, T-charts (two columns), and E-charts (three rows). Graphic organizers can also serve as response options.

WRITING TRAITS

Good writing across genres shares attributes that are commonly labeled *traits*. The concept of traits was first developed at the Northwest Regional Educational Laboratory (NWREL, 1998/1999) in Oregon, and many districts now mandate trait teaching to help students grasp the concept of "good" writing.

Different authors list different traits and use a variety of labels. The following is a set based on NWREL's 6 + 1 Trait Writing framework. Instruction on traits should include explicit instruction and should engage students in long-term pursuit of their own examples from texts they read.

1. *Ideas:* The purpose and message are clear and supported with examples and details.

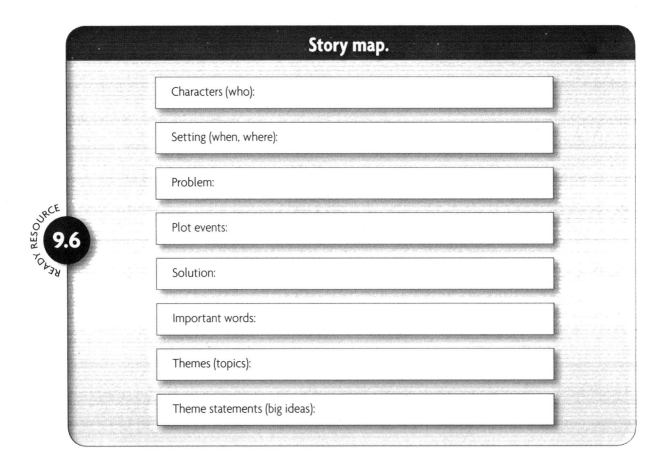

READY RESOURCE 9.6

Story map.

Characters (who):

Setting (when, where):

Problem:

Plot events:

Solution:

Important words:

Themes (topics):

Theme statements (big ideas):

2. *Style/voice:* There is a sense that a real person is writing for a specific audience.

3. *Organization:* The order makes sense, and strong transitions are used.

4. *Word choice:* Interesting words are used that both help understanding and create aesthetic response.

5. *Sentence fluency:* The sentences are constructed so that they flow smoothly when read aloud.

6. *Mechanics and conventions:* The grammar, spelling, punctuation, and so forth are appropriate for the text.

7. *Presentation:* The final product is both informative and aesthetically stimulating.

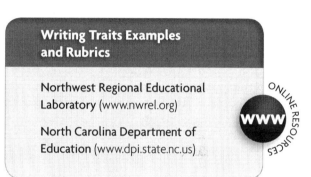

Writing Traits Examples and Rubrics

Northwest Regional Educational Laboratory (www.nwrel.org)

North Carolina Department of Education (www.dpi.state.nc.us)

State department of education websites frequently offer bibliographies of children's books that may be examined for specific writing ideas. For example, the North Carolina Department of Education site includes categorized bibliographies, a clear explanation of writing traits, and ideas for creating trait rubrics. On that site, go to the English language arts link.

Responding Through Arts Forms

The arts are fundamentally communication tools used to understand, respond to, and express ideas and emotions. They permit expression of understanding that goes beyond words. The arts are rich sources of ways to make comprehension visible. Students can *show* comprehension of big ideas by creating a sketch, painting, sculpture, song, poem, dance, pantomime, or skit.

The *creative* problem-solving process is at the core of all arts production and should be taught through comparisons to the CPS process (Cornett, 2011). The major difference is of degree. *Creative* problem solving is problem solving with greater risk-taking and experimentation, with the expectation of more surprising results.

Meaningful arts-based responses depend on teachers explicitly teaching basic arts concepts and processes (Ready Resource 9.7) and budgeting time for students to plan, rehearse, and perform. Classroom teachers usually have basic coursework in visual art and music, but they often need resources to teach arts elements, media, and tools. School-based arts specialists are the first stop, along with district curriculum guides and the National Standards for the Arts, mentioned previously. Arts professionals in the community may be willing to do short teacher training or lessons for students on arts concepts and skills. The nation's Council of Chief State School Officers (state superintendents) sponsors a website that details what classroom teachers need to know and do in visual art, music, drama, and dance. The Online Resources box lists additional websites for this information.

Fundamental arts elements, like those in Ready Resource 9.7, should be taught explicitly so students can communicate in each of the art forms. Classroom teachers are encouraged to collaborate with arts teachers to teach key

Arts elements.

MUSIC *is the intentional use of organized sounds to communicate thoughts and feelings.*

- *Rhythm:* movement of sounds through time. Includes beat or accent, tempo, meter, and syncopation.
- *Melody (tune):* a series of tones falling into a pattern. Includes pitch.
- *Timbre (tambur):* unique qualities of sound
- *Dynamics:* volume or relative loudness or softness of the sound; gives emotion
- *Texture:* layering of instruments and/or voices to create a thin or full feeling
- *Harmony:* blending of sounds, as with chords (two or more pitches played simultaneously)
- *Form:* structure, shape, or distinct pattern. Related to musical styles and genre.
- *Ostinato:* simple rhythmic or melodic content repeated over and over as accompaniment

VISUAL ART *is the intentional use of visual elements to communicate thoughts and feelings.*

- *Color:* primary and secondary hues, tints, and shades created by light and pigments
- *Light:* illusion created with lighter colors, such as white
- *Contrast:* effect created by lighter colors next to darker
- *Line:* a horizontal, vertical, angled, or curved mark made by a tool across a surface
- *Shape:* the two dimensions of height and width arranged geometrically (e.g., circles, triangles), organically (natural shapes), or symbolically (e.g., letters)
- *Texture:* the way something feels or appears that it would feel
- *Pattern:* something repeated (shapes, lines, rows, grids)
- *Space:* the areas objects take up (positive space) and that surround shapes and forms (negative space)

- *Perspective:* illusion of distance and point of view created by techniques such as size, overlapping, atmosphere, sharpness or blurriness, and angles
- *Foreground, middle, and background:* the areas in a piece of art that appear closest to the viewer, next closest, and farthest away
- *Form:* three-dimensional qualities (height, width, depth), e.g., sphere, pyramid, cube

Design Principles

Composition: arrangement of masses and spaces

Unity: sense of oneness (created by dominance, repetition)

Balance: the way parts of a piece relate (radial, symmetry, asymmetry)

Proportion: comparative relationships based on criteria such as size, number, space, shape

Emphasis: focal point, lighting, exaggeration, grouping size, repetition

Movement and rhythm: repetition, blur, types of lines, contrast

DRAMA *is created by one or more individuals taking on roles and using the body, face, gestures, and voice to communicate thoughts and feelings imaginatively.*

- *Conflict:* sets the plot in motion and creates suspension and tension. Five types:
  1. Between a character and nature
  2. Between a character and societal rules or institutions
  3. Between a character and another character
  4. Within a character (internal conflict)
  5. Between a character and technology
- *Characters:* dramatic persons who carry out the plot (action). They must be believable, and the audience must care about what happens to them. The *protagonist* is the main character or hero, who must face life, make decisions, and accept consequences. Char-

(continued)

Continued.

acters are created through actions, words, and what others say about them or how they react to them. When characters talk with each other, their words are called *dialogue*. Pantomime is non-verbal creative and mindful movement intended to express ideas and feelings with the face and body.

- *Plot:* the sequence of events set in motion by a problem or conflict. The conventional structure is beginning, middle, and end.
- *Setting:* the time and place of the action.
- *Mood:* the feeling created by the setting (including the time period, lighting, music, and place), pace, characters' use of words and body, and so forth.

Drama Skills: Body, Mind, Voice

- *Body:* control of the body, use appropriate energy, display sensory awareness and expression, use gestures and facial expressions, communicate non-verbally and interpret the non-verbal communication of others
- *Mind:*
  - *Focus:* concentration, staying involved, making others believe in the character, following directions
  - *Imagination:* flexible creative thinking, contribution of unique ideas and elaboration on ideas, spontaneity
- *Voice:* speaking clearly and using appropriate variety in volume, rate, tone and pitch, pause, stress and emphasis, inflection, and fluency, along with ability to improvise dialogue
- *Evaluation:* giving constructive feedback, using suggestions, self-evaluating, and adapting one's own behavior
- *Social skills:* working cooperatively, listening, responding
- *Audience etiquette:* attending, listening, and responding appropriately to others

DANCE *is the intentional use of body, energy, space and time to communicate thoughts and feelings.*

BEST Elements (body, energy, space, time):*
Body

- *Parts:* head, neck, torso (hips, abdomen, shoulders, back), arms and elbows, hands and wrists, fingers, legs, knees and feet (including ankles and toes)
- *Shapes:* curved, twisted, angular, small–large, flat–rounded
- *Actions or moves:*
  - *Non-locomotor:* stretch, bend, twist, rise, fall, circle, shake, suspend, sway, swing, collapse
  - *Locomotor:* walk, run, leap, hop, jump, gallop, skip, slide

Energy

Attack: smooth or sharp

Weight: heavy or light

Strength or tension: tight or loose and relaxed

Flow: sudden or sustained, bound or free

9.7 READY RESOURCE

Space

- *Level:* low, middle, or high
- *Direction:* forward, backward, sideways, up, down
- *Size:* large or small
- *Place or destination:* where we move to
- *Pathway:* pattern made on the floor or in the air (e.g., circular)
- *Focus:* where the dancer looks

Time

Rhythm: pulse, beat

Speed: time or tempo

Accent: light or strong emphasis

Duration: length

Phrase: dance sentence, pattern, & combination (e.g., twist, twist, twirl, and freeze)

*From Randy Baron, dance educator, New Mexico

Source: Cornett, 2011.

vocabulary and concepts, along with particular skills (e.g., figure drawing). Ready Resources 9.8, 9.9, and 9.10 suggest ideas for drama, music, dance, and visual art responses.

PERFORMANCES AND EXHIBITS

Of particular value in demonstrating comprehension is the regular use of student performances and exhibits for audiences. In fact, some experts argue that nothing is truly learned until it is performed—similar to the dictum that if you want to learn something, teach it. These response options can drive learning by motivating students to prepare for their peers and parents. In the classroom snapshot, Maggie Phoenix used a drama form, Reader's Theatre, for its power to motivate.

Using Reader's Theatre

Reader's Theatre (RT) is a drama-based text response option that offers students a purposeful way to participate in meaningful repeated readings in a motivating context (Cecil, 2007). Unlike traditional plays, with costumes, sets, and memorized lines, in RT students read aloud from a script. As in a radio play, voices are the only communication vehicle.

Importance of rehearsal. RT can motivate students to think about the most important meanings in texts and demonstrate their interpretation (comprehension). RT develops fluency through the rehearsals necessary to prepare for the performance. Students read scripts multiple times, focusing on using expressive vocal elements. For example, Maggie Phoenix built rehearsal time into her daily schedule. Her students were motivated to practice the oral reading because each group would perform in front of an audience—their classmates. No props were used, although Maggie did permit sound effects and music, as appropriate. She taught them that Reader's Theatre is "theater of the mind" and is like hearing a play on the radio. Expressive oral reading was the focus, and audience etiquette was also emphasized. Students regularly recorded themselves as they rehearsed to monitor their oral reading progress. Maggie had taught them how to compute their reading rate, mark phrases, and graph their accuracy independently. There was a special station in the room dedicated to fluency recording and graphing.

Most important, Maggie worked with small groups to ensure they understood the material they would perform. She asked them to discuss the mood of each piece, the point of view, and how the characters could show their motives through the "music" of their voices. Sometimes the students traded parts to experiment with different voices. The students had learned to do point of view (POV) retellings from different character viewpoints. They retold the story as if they were a character, using beginning, middle, and end (BME) plot events. From these retellings, the students eventually transitioned to writing their own scripts.

Reader's Theatre

FictionTeachers.com

LiteracyConnections.com

Scripts. To begin, Maggie converts texts she already has (e.g., from a literature anthology) to script format. She tries to create scripts that are somewhat challenging—just above the instructional reading level of most students. She has purchased some commercial collections and downloaded scripts from the Internet, as well. Scripts and lesson ideas may be found at websites hosted by Aaron Shepard and Rick Swallow. Teachers may write scripts by adapting poems or any story.

About once a month, the student groups choose a favorite script to perform for an outside audience, such as another class or invited guests. They've even sent CDs to the local radio station. For example, during the local Gullah Festival, a celebration of African American heritage, they performed African folk tale scripts on the radio.

Script Sources & Scriptwriting

Aaron Shepard's Home Page,
www.aaronshep.com/rt/

Rick Swallow,
www.timelessteacherstuff.com

One goal of RT is that eventually students will write their own scripts. During the second semester, Maggie teaches her students to write scripts by adapting poems, stories, and expository material related to science and social studies units. Guidelines for scriptwriting may be found at Aaron Shepard's website. This site offers ideas for roles, cuts and changes, narration, and script formats.

The results. Maggie Phoenix says, "The children love RT. And I think the love comes from their success. Because I start with explicit lessons on fluency and do lots of demonstration, they know exactly what to do with their voices. I heavily emphasize active making meaning, with the students deciding how to use musical elements to interpret the words. It is such an advantage when students expect to perform. They are so motivated to do well for the audience. This gives purpose to oral reading, and I have to say that every child is having success. I've never had this kind of response from any other repeated reading method."

There is proof in the assessments, too. Maggie uses a fluency expression rubric (see Ready Resource 8.20 in Chapter 8) and tracks her students' progress against grade-level accuracy and rate targets. Maggie's students show excellent comprehension through their fluency (expression, accuracy, and rate), and the gains have been steady. Every student has been checked off on top high-frequency words. The students also keep personal word rings of interesting words they choose from the scripts. Some of the students have hundreds of words on their rings and in alphabetized word boxes. All of them use Word Fix-Ups (Ready Resource 8.11) to decode unknown words during rehearsals. Maggie has demonstrated how students can prompt each other to use the strategies versus just telling each other unknown words.

"They have gotten the point that independent problem solving makes them proud and increases motivation to read." Maggie says. "They also understand that RT is a group effort. They all need to do well to please the audience on Friday. They really are ready to write their own scripts, and it is only November. I just keep thinking, how did I ever teach without RT?"

Ready Resource 9.8 provides drama performance springboards, and Ready Resource 9.9 lists music and dance performance springboards. Because the role performances and exhibits can play such an important role in motivating use of CPS, Chapter 10 will revisit them as "main literacy events." Ideas for poetry performance appear in Ready Resource 10.12 in Chapter 10.

Comprehension made visible: Drama springboards.

READY RESOURCE 9.8

Most of the following options can be used during or after reading, viewing, or listening to a text. Some can be adapted as "before" activities. Collaborate with a drama teacher, if possible, to teach drama concepts, such as actors' tools.

DRAMA *is the communication of thoughts and feelings by pretending to take the role of another person or a character. It uses the tools of imagination, voice, body, gestures, and facial expressions.*

- *Author:* Become the author and tell why you wrote this story.

- *Be the Book:* Pretend to be the book and advertise yourself.

- *Be a Character:* Tell about the events of the text and what you learned.

- *Biography:* Pretend you visited a person in the text. Tell about the visit.

- *Book Review:* Be a critic. Evaluate the text and the art in terms of content and format.

- *Censored:* Imagine the text has been challenged. Write a letter defending it.

- *Censor It:* Imagine you are someone who feels this text should be removed from the school. Write a letter presenting your argument.

- *Chalk Talk:* Draw on the board or use objects to retell plot events, and explain how they reveal big ideas.

- *Character Interview:* Write an interview between two characters, with one character asking the questions.

- *Character Meeting:* Choose a character from the book and one from a previous text. Create a dialogue between them.

- *Charades:* Play charades based on characters and their traits.

- *Clothesline:* Pin up props or pictures on a clothesline to retell key events.

- *Commercial:* Create a one-minute ad.

- *Court Trial:* Put a character on trial. Students can be witnesses, judge, jury, bailiff, and reporter.

(continued)

Continued.

- *Dear Diary:* Pretend to be a character and write about events and your reactions.

- *Dinner Date:* Create a menu that reflects the character's preferences.

- *Dress-up:* Create a costume for a character. You may use a doll. Explain how the costume reflects character traits.

- *Flannel Board:* Make felt characters and, using them, retell the main events and describe the ideas you learned by the end.

- *Interrogation:* Pretend to be a character or the author, and answer questions from the rest of the class.

- *Interview:* Interview people who have a background related to the text's central problems.

- *Introduction:* Pretend you are at an important meeting. Introduce a character or the author to the group.

- *Minor Character:* Become a minor character and tell the story from your point of view.

- *Movie Producer:* Evaluate the book as a possible film. Explain what would make it a good film.

- *Movie Version:* Compare the film or TV version with the book, focusing on literary elements (see Ready Resource 5.9 in Chapter 5), as well as the acting, musical, and visual features.

- *Mystery:* Put an object that is related to the text inside a box. Give clues to help classmates guess the book.

- *News Update:* Pretend to be a newscaster and update your partner on what just happened in a text.

- *One Liners:* As a class, list key moments from the text. Each student becomes a character and says what she or he is thinking and feeling at that moment and why. This activity may be expanded to include spoken or written monologues.

- *Oprah:* Create a talk show, with students playing the host, author, and cast of characters. The audience should prepare questions for the guests.

- *Pantomime:* Do a slow-motion pantomime of a character in an important scene.

- *Poetry Alive:* Perform a poem, using an idea from Ready Resource 9.5.

- *Postcard:* Write to a friend, the author, or a character, or write in the role of a character or the author.

- *Pretend and Write:* Take the role of a character and write to another character about your problems, or keep a diary.

- *Puppets:* Make a character puppet. In a small group, create dialogue for an important scene and present it to the rest of the class.

- *Reader's Theatre:* Transform the text into a script and present it.

- *Reporter:* Be a TV reporter. Choose the most important or exciting part for a "live on the scene" report.

- *Retell:* Pair up to recall events, piece together important ideas, and clarify the text for each other.

- *Scene Mime:* List important scene titles. In a group, draw a title and plan at least three actions to pantomime for the audience. "Scenes" may be moments in history, science, or literature.

- *Sequel:* Write what happened after the story ended.

- *Tableau:* Students stage an important scene, arranging their bodies in a freeze frame. The class discusses what they see and what it means. *Variation:* Each actor "comes alive" and tells what he or she is thinking.

- *Web:* Web how a character looks, acts, and feels, and what he or she says, to get inside the character's head.

READY RESOURCE 9.8

Comprehension responses: Music and dance springboards.

Partner with a music, dance, or PE teacher to teach basic music, dance, or movement elements to increase students' communication tools in these areas.

MUSIC *is the use of musical elements and formats to communicate ideas and emotions.*

- *Background Music:* Find music that would be appropriate to play while an important part of the text is read.

- *Favorites List:* List songs and music that the main character would like, and tell why.

- *Historical Fiction/Nonfiction:* Find music that was popular during the period of the text. Explain how the music connects to big ideas.

- *Music Mesh:* Brainstorm ways music connects to the book: songs, music, rhythm, melody, instruments, and so forth.

- *Musical Score:* Record music from CDs that would suit each chapter if the text were made into a movie.

- *Operetta:* Retell a folk tale or fairy tale through songs.

- *Piggyback:* Use a favorite melody and write new lyrics about big ideas in the text.

- *Rap:* Write a rap or read aloud an important part of the text to a rap beat.

- *Sing Me a Song:* Write a song or ballad about the story, a character, or an event in the book.

- *Songwriting:* Write a song using literary elements, especially themes, in the book.

DANCE *is the use of body, energy, space, and time to express thoughts and feelings.*

- *Cultural Dance:* View an ethnic dance linked to the text. (Use the Internet to find one.) Discuss how the dance reveals themes and big ideas from the text.

- *Dance Chart:* Brainstorm different types of dance (e.g., twist, jitterbug, salsa). List them down the left side of a sheet of paper and write character names across the top to create a chart. Mark the intersections with an X where a character matches a dance. Explain your choices.

- *Dance Moves:* List key movements in the story. Show them with different body parts, especially head, hand, and fingers.

- *Dance Revolution:* Choreograph a dance with three parts—beginning, middle, and end—related to the text. Teach the dance to the class.

- *Dancing Characters:* List dances a character might do, and explain why.

- *Period Dance:* Learn a dance from the period when the text takes place. Discuss how the dance reflects the time period and why.

- *Slow Motion:* Show a character in slow motion at three important moments in the text.

- *Three-Part Dance:* Choreograph a dance with the pattern frozen shape–movement–frozen shape about a big idea in the text. Work as a group.

READY RESOURCE **9.9**

VISUAL ART RESPONSES

Like all meaningful comprehension responses, visual art products should reflect big ideas supported by important details. Springboards for a variety of visual art products appear in Ready Resource 9.10. Students may "docent" their products by explaining how their art communicates their thinking. The comprehension rubric in Ready Resource 4.1 in Chapter 4 provides assessment ideas along with criteria related to art forms. Talk with visual art specialists and check the district's curriculum guide for more suggestions.

Comprehension responses: Visual art springboards.

VISUAL ART RESPONSES *use various art media, subject matters, styles, and techniques to convey ideas and emotions.*

- *Abstract:* Create a painting that shows key emotions, without trying to represent "real" images.
- *Art Gallery:* Find art (e.g., on the Internet or on art print cards) related to the book's time or themes. Display and discuss them.
- *Board Game:* Design a game based on the text. Include question cards.
- *Bookmarks:* Make a bookmark with quotes from the text and a blurb.
- *Business Card:* Brainstorm important character attributes. Use computer software or art materials to create a business card for the character.
- *Cards:* Make a greeting or postcard that conveys big ideas from the text.
- *Cartoon:* Draw a strip of important scenes.
- *Clay Model:* Create a character or special object in the book out of clay.
- *Collage:* Create an individual or class collage around big ideas from the text.
- *Diorama:* Create a shoebox scene of an important event.
- *Draw It:* Create a storyboard that summarizes important scenes.
- *Etching:* Use crayon resist to make portraits, landscapes, or abstract drawings about big ideas.
- *Flannel Board:* Make shapes from flannel and use them to retell key events or important information.
- *Landscape/Seascape/Cityscape:* Paint a key scene or moment within its setting.
- *Lifeline:* Make a timeline of the events in a character's life.
- *Lost and Found:* Create a lost or found advertisement.

- *Mandala:* Make a circular image conveying important ideas.
- *Mapmaker:* Sketch important events at different locations, or make a route map.
- *Media and Style:* Experiment with the style and techniques used by the artist of a non-verbal text.
- *Mobile:* Make a mobile of key characters, objects, or other text elements.
- *Model:* Make a model of an important idea.
- *Mosaic:* Use seeds, buttons, or cut paper to create a character portrait or show a setting.
- *Movie Time:* Make a hand-rolled movie using shelf paper.
- *Mural:* Create a mural to show events that shaped big ideas.
- *Open Mind:* Draw an outline of a head of one of the characters, and inside it draw symbols or words or images to represent the character's thoughts and feelings.
- *Painting:* Use watercolor, tempera, or any pigment to paint an image from the text.
- *Paper Dolls:* Cut out and dress paper dolls of the main characters.
- *Photography:* Take pictures that relate to the text.
- *Plot Graph:* Plot events on a line graph to show ups and downs in tension, emotion, or excitement.
- *Portrait:* Paint or draw the main character.
- *Poster or Banner:* Create a poster that sells the book.
- *Puppets:* Make hand, finger, bag, or sock puppets to represent characters. Create monologues or interviews between the characters about big ideas.
- *Quilt:* Fold a sheet of paper into eight sections. Illustrate each square to show characters, setting, plots, and themes.

(continued)

Visual arts springboards, continued.

- *Scrapbook:* Collect and label items and pictures related to a big idea.
- *Scroll:* Create a scroll that will show important ideas as it is unrolled.
- *Sculpture:* Make a 3D model. For example, carve an important character out of soap or make a relief map of a setting from dough.
- *Sketch:* Draw an action sequence and make into a flipbook.
- *Stage:* Design a miniature stage setting in a box.
- *Storyboard:* Make small sketches that show important moments.

- *Timeline:* Create a timeline that includes both the events in the novel and historical information for the time.
- *Travelogue:* Use pictures, postcards, and magazine clippings to show the settings of a text.
- *Video:* Create an author interview, documentary, or any other television or film genre, using key ideas as inspiration.

Wordless Book: Make a book about the story, using no words. Use any media and techniques.

Responding Through Technology

Tens of thousands of years ago, early humans communicated by drawing, pantomiming, and making sounds with primitive drums and bones. Only about five thousand years ago, written language appeared, so we know people had been listening to and speaking words by then. By the year 1900, individuals who were "literate" could sign their names versus marking an X. By 1950, war and industrialization had forced major changes in the expectations for literacy, especially for reading and writing printed communication. The concept of literacy continues to evolve, but it has always referred to communication competence, whose core is the ability to receive and understand (comprehend) and express thoughts and feelings. Today, a wide variety of technologies has added yet another layer to our possibilities for communicating, including responding to texts.

The term *multi-literacies* encapsulates the current state of communication. Large percentages of people now receive most of their information and entertainment from television and the Internet, and the number of computers sold each year now exceeds television purchases. Technology has transformed how we communicate with families and friends, and email, text messaging, and social networking have even become an addiction for some. Technology has also transformed the world of work and politics; it is routinely used to lobby for cultural change. With technology has come the ability to transmit and act upon ideas with dazzling speed. This dramatic worldwide phenomenon inundates us with electronic documents and multimedia texts.

TECHNOLOGY AND DIFFERENTIATION

For kids who have grown up with earbuds, iPods, and Wii games, school literacy may seem irrelevant. More than three quarters of students have a computer at home, and half are online at least an hour per day (Casey, 2008). Millions of youth use instant messaging, and 25 percent report they pretend to be other people online (Lenhart, Rainie, & Lewis, 2001). It is no longer sufficient to limit comprehension instruction to how to read books (McKenne et al., 2007). Response options differentiate ways students can choose to show what and how they comprehend, and those options must include technology. The electronic feast of options available as I write includes graphic packages to illustrate texts, digital morning messages on Smartboards, language experience stories written using speech synthesizers, WebQuests, and wikis.

School literacy must reinvent itself, and there is abundant evidence that "if we build it, they will come." Youth are interested in and capable of working with diverse symbolic systems. Teachers who demonstrate how to organize and shape ideas with electronic means have hungry audiences with varying degrees of computer savvy. The very students who appear at risk of failure in the school literacy arena may be the most adept at using electronic texts. For example, in a longitudinal study of at-risk adolescents, O'Brien observed that many were quite capable of creating multimedia documentaries and using multiple forms of visual texts to critique (1998, 2001). When print is not privileged over other forms of literacy, many more students can deftly communicate important thoughts and feelings. A study of an after-school program for thirty low-achieving students reached the same conclusion (Alvermann et al., 2000).

> **Using Web 2.0**
>
> **ReadWriteThink.org** offers resources for teachers using Internet technologies, including example lesson plans for blogging, wikis, podcasts, and publishing video clips.

WHEN TO CHOOSE TECHNOLOGY

Of course, when selecting and designing comprehension response options, teachers must decide whether computers are the right tool. Is the technology merely an expensive worksheet or tricked-out white board, or does it genuinely link and expand concepts (Gambrell, Malloy, & Mazzoni, 2007). Does time spent learning computer gadgetry and visiting diverse Internet sites lead students to high-level comprehension responses, or does it leave them little more than entertained? How can technology be put in service to well thought-out standards that support important comprehension process and product goals? These questions can be answered only by teachers who use problem solving to address them, keeping criteria like those in the comprehension rubric in mind (Ready Resource 4.1). Worthy examples of technological response options are:

- PowerPoints that attract attention for their ideas, not just the animations and transitions from slide to slide. Criteria should direct students to include their inquiry questions, big idea conclusions, supporting facts, examples, and logic.

- WebQuests that direct Internet research using problem-solving strategies.

- E-mails to experts asking genuine, thoughtful questions that cannot be answered at their websites.

What Is a WebQuest?

A WebQuest is inquiry-based study designed to engage students in the kind of comprehension problem solving needed in the 21st century. Bernie Dodge developed the concept over a decade ago and now thousands of teachers worldwide use WebQuests to direct student work that is done primarily on the Internet. WebQuests often entail creating a document with hyperlinks; the document may be created in any of a number of programs including Word, PowerPoint, and even Excel. Worthy WebQuests address real-world tasks that require authentic problem solving, not just summarizing. Excellent resources to practice creating and using WebQuests can be found at WebQuest.org:

www.webquest.org/index.php
http://webquest.org/index-resources.php

- Informed blogging that provides supportive evidence for conclusions.
- Wiki documents that reflect thoughtful research and include big ideas supported by evidence.
- Use of word processing tools to strengthen focus on good writing traits, especially organization of important ideas. The assistance word processors provide with spelling and grammar can help students focus on content, and cut/paste features speed revision.

Using Response Options as Best Practices

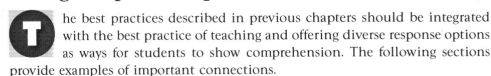

The best practices described in previous chapters should be integrated with the best practice of teaching and offering diverse response options as ways for students to show comprehension. The following sections provide examples of important connections.

BIG IDEAS AND IMPORTANT QUESTIONS

To create meaningful comprehension responses, students organize and shape explicit and implicit ideas they have derived from texts. The kinds of important questions that students use to produce big ideas in the before and during stages of text use can also be employed to create new compositions to show comprehension. Chapter 2 gave examples of big ideas and important questions that propel inquiry-based problem solving, including the *creative* problem solving that generates original response options.

ASSESSMENT

Before children acquire print decoding fluency, their print text comprehension can be assessed through read-aloud experiences followed by interviews, discussions, and observation of arts-based products. Children comprehend non-verbal texts even before they reach school age, so—at any reading level—texts such as visual art and music can serve as comprehension problem solving texts *and* as response options.

The variety of response options that can cause students to organize and transform ideas from texts is endless. The only limitation seems to be questions around how to judge novel expressions of comprehension. Teachers can address these questions by creating checklists and rubrics to specify criteria for evaluating diverse products. Even in schools where traditional letter grades are used, evaluation of novel expression forms is entirely possible.

Classroom teachers should not be stymied by worries about assessing arts-based responses. The idea that assessing artistic work automatically crushes creativity is a myth (Baker et al., 2004). Artists generally don't have this attitude. Arts products that embody comprehension evidence can certainly be graded without squashing student creativity—it all depends on making task response criteria explicit before students choose their response form and making sure students have the necessary concepts and skills to work in the art form. For example, a mural project may have to show evidence of three big ideas from the text it reflects, as well as be constructed to meet visual art criteria.

Arts products are very valuable sources of information about students' comprehension. Teachers may develop criteria collaboratively with students to ensure that artistic work reflects specific comprehension processes, demonstrates big ideas, and enlarges the student's creative experience. Appendix B and Ready Resource 4.1 in Chapter 4 give guidance on developing rubrics and checklists. Informal assessment tools (assessment *for* learning) can also help structure student work on comprehension responses and may be used to assess and evaluate student products. Use these resources to create age- and stage-appropriate checklists students can use to select and shape their responses. Such tools ensure that any response, from poetry to dance, meaningfully employs text conventions and shows substantive content learned.

MOTIVATION

Response options are all about using choice and interest to help children show comprehension of ideas worth knowing. Options that involve group work and sharing of comprehension responses go further to engage the power of the audience to motivate work. Performance, sharing, and exhibition routines—from a special "author's chair" for students to read aloud their writings, to classroom art galleries and weekly Reader's Theatre—are examples of important events.

EXPLICIT TEACHING

Meaningful student response doesn't happen without direct instruction. Students must be explicitly taught how to write in diverse forms, choose appropriate arts subject matter, and use tools, media, and styles congruent with the big ideas being communicated. Simply telling students they can draw a picture or perform a skit is not meaningful. Arts and technology-based responses have worth only when students are explicitly taught the *how* and *why* of these communication options. Scaffolded practice is needed to support students' use of writing, technological, and arts concepts, processes, and product forms. Teachers must coach students during response creation, set up reference centers for poetry patterns and other real-world texts, and provide many other forms of scaffolding and support. See Ready Resources 9.1, 9.3, and 9.5.

Collaboration with specialists is of particular importance for explicit teaching of arts and technology components. The concept of arts integration (AI) is now a guiding force in thousands of schools across America, as well as schools in the United Kingdom, Canada, Finland, and other countries. Curriculum models that rely on arts instruction only by specialists are being reformed. Teachers who are not in AI schools can approach specialists about working together to teach specific concepts and skills students need to respond *meaningfully* in a variety of communication forms (Cornett, 2011).

VOCABULARY DEVELOPMENT

Each type of response option is part of an area with its own vocabulary. Because students need to understand special terminology to use technology, music, visual art, dance, drama, music, and writing, teaching these diverse response options allows for continuous and natural vocabulary development. Many key words are polysemous (have multiple meanings) and present rich material for discussion. For example, take the word *play*, which students generally understand. It takes on new meaning in music and theatre. The same is true for dozens of other words (e.g., *line, act, light*). Concepts are shared across many types of text, including labels for literary elements, such as *plot, character,* and *theme*, which are used in literature, drama, music, and dance. Different text forms share common topics and motifs as well (e.g., Cinderella variants), whose labels can be uncovered to give students insight into response possibilities.

For students, learning how to respond differently means learning new words and new meanings for known words (Cornett, 2007). The key arts concepts listed in Ready Resource 9.7 should be explicitly taught and posted as references.

EXPERT QUESTIONS AND DISCUSSIONS

Discussion involves extending meaning making and sharing oral responses to text. All of the guidelines described in Chapter 7 for asking important questions apply to ideas about showing comprehension suggested in this chapter. As students create new response products, these products themselves become perfect material for further discussion facilitated by expert questioning. Of course, the entire process of response generation depends on asking good questions in the first place: the quality of response products depends on the questions that guide the problem solving to make the products.

Conclusion

This chapter explained why and how teachers can and should increase response options by which students show comprehension. The conventional wisdom that puts written response at the top of worthy options was supported, with qualifications. In particular, the chapter presented problems with focusing on increasing writing quantity and discussed what makes for quality written responses. This chapter also gave arguments to support the teaching of meaningful arts-based responses. Arts integration returns the arts to their rightful place as essential communication tools. Finally, the chapter explored the reality of attempting to meet the needs of children who will spend their lives in a technology-dominated world.

The resources in this chapter included extended lists of springboards to help teachers create a broad menu of response options for making comprehension visible. Finally, the chapter traced connections between the provision of diverse comprehension response options and other best practices, including the intersection with assessment.

CHAPTER **9** **big ideas**

Using this list, synthesize your own list of high-priority big ideas about using response options to increase students' text comprehension.

1. Comprehension is invisible, but responses to texts can make it visible, to an extent.
2. Offering response options for comprehension has motivational power.
3. Student responses provide assessment evidence that teachers should use to design future instruction.
4. The quality of comprehension responses is heavily dependent on instruction in how to use components of good writing, arts forms, and technology.
5. Written response deserves particular emphasis because of its integral relationship to reading.
6. Creating responses to texts recycles students' thinking back to the start of comprehension problem solving.

a look ahead

Chapter 10, a synthesis chapter, will describe how teachers can embody all nine comprehension best practices within main literacy events and content blocks.

9 response options

1. Rate your agreement with each of the big idea statements for the chapter, on a scale of 1 to 5 (1 = low and 5 = high). Rewrite the statements as necessary to align them with your own thinking. Compare your list with those of other readers.

2. Return to the Important Questions at the opening of the chapter to evaluate your comprehension. Select several questions you would like to discuss or investigate further.

3. Create a visual organizer as a response to this chapter. For example, you might draw a map, web, outline, or even a set of cartoon images. Be prepared to explain your visual response with a group.

4. Choose one response option from Ready Resource 9.7 and explain how this arts-based response form could be used to make comprehension visible.

5. Create a piece of visual art, write a poem, or compose a song that reflects one or more big ideas in the chapter.

6. Create a five-minute dramatic scene about a big idea in this chapter. Be sure your scene includes a problem and has a definite beginning, middle, and end. List criteria for evaluating how well your scene reflected comprehension of the chapter. For example, "Big idea was made clear through use of dialogue and body language."

7. Examine RT scripts on the Internet and then write a short script about a teacher who is using diverse comprehension responses.

8. Write a poem about key ideas related to comprehension response options, using one of the patterns described in Ready Resource 9.5.

9. Interview an art teacher about how to assess content (such as themes and big ideas) in art products.

10. Analyze the national standards provided in Appendix G and give examples of how they address aspects of comprehension (e.g., problem solving). Choose a response option to organize and shape a summary of your examples.

11. Turn to the lists of response options for writing (Ready Resource 9.3), visual art (Ready Resource 9.10), music/dance (Ready Resource 9.9), and drama (Ready Resource 9.8), and circle three to five ideas in each area that you would like to try—either with students or to show your own comprehension.

12. Develop a wiki about using arts-based responses to show comprehension.

Organizing Main Events with Embedded Comprehension Practices

This final chapter brings together the full picture of how to put comprehension first by coordinating nine recommended practices. At the chapter's core is the concept of both integrating and embedding literacy instruction with best practices. All nine practices described in this book also need to become integral to teaching in content area instruction. The chapter provides descriptions and a rationale for embedding best practices in seven main instructional events.

important questions

1. How can excellent inquiry-based comprehension instruction be embedded in literacy time blocks and content instruction, using texts relevant to the 21st century?

2. What do "integration" and "embedding" have to do with comprehension best practices and main literacy events?

3. What does amount of reading have to do with comprehension?

4. What are high-priority literacy events?

5. How and why should comprehension instruction be embedded in the following seven events? (1) opening routines, (2) interactive read alouds, (3) daily engaged independent reading, (4) small group and independent work, (5) writing workshop, (6) content units, (7) performances and exhibits

Introduction

This book began with a description of the problems that beset comprehension achievement in the United States. Inquiry-based teaching of the CPS process was presented as a powerful means to foster comprehension development for all students, particularly the most needy. This chapter describes ways comprehension problem-solving strategies, a focus on big ideas, and the other comprehension practices may be integrated into the time frame of a typical school day.

The main literacy events described in this chapter are key ways to organize instruction. They are based on the premise that no single instructional program or method will be effective in teaching all children to read. This conclusion was ratified by the International Reading Association and reflects the consensus of decades of research. However, certain evidence-based best practices do promote high rates of achievement. The question is how to put comprehension research into practice.

International Reading Association

Position statement, www.reading.org/ General/About IRA/PositionStatements/ MultipleMethodsPosition.aspx

No one schedule or combination of whole- and small-group instruction has emerged as superior. Many fine, artful efforts draw upon various best practices in an effort to boost student success. The set of best practices in this book (focus on big ideas; teach inquiry-based problem solving; use varied assessments to plan differentiated instruction; *explicitly* teach comprehension problem solving and key literacy concepts; use motivation strategies to engage comprehension; use and teach questioning to promote "high-level" conversations and discussions; teach vocabulary and fluency for comprehension; teach diverse response options to show comprehension; and embed best comprehension practices in literacy main events and content teaching), marked by a focus on CPS and inquiry-based teaching that targets big ideas, joins other models in the cause of improving students' comprehension.

It is clear that comprehension instruction is not effective in isolated bursts separated from content, and that it cannot happen solely during a literacy block (NCTE,

2004). No one comprehension best practice stands alone. All nine addressed in this book must be integrated with one another, with assessment laying the foundation. Embedding is intense integration. The goal is for best practices to become deeply ingrained in the curriculum, making comprehension the number one priority.

Implementation of comprehension best practices demands an "artful orchestration" of literacy events (Gambrell, Malloy, & Mazzoni, 2007, p. 22). This chapter assembles the nine practices discussed thus far (Ready Resource 3.5, p. 70, lists the practices and the chapters in which they are predominantly discussed). My hope is that teachers will integrate them into classrooms, with artful orchestration in mind.

Beyond Balanced: Comprehensive Instruction

When the facts change, I change my mind. What do you do, sir?

JOHN MAYNARD KEYNES

The concept of "balanced" instruction is evolving into "comprehensive" instruction that embraces 21st-century conditions. Today, literacy instruction needs to include the diverse text forms that typify third-millennium life and teach the problem-solving strategies students need to access these texts (Gambrell, Malloy, & Mazzoni, 2007). Reading of print texts may be the grand foyer for the house of literacy, but this house has many important rooms. Comprehensive instruction is a response to a redefinition of literacy that puts today's myriad communication forms at the center. Comprehensive instruction goes beyond balance to emphasize the personal, intellectual, and social nature of literacy, taking a constructivist perspective. The focus is on developing students' cognitive abilities, such as critical thinking and decision making, while building on prior knowledge, which is the "best predictor of what student will learn" (p. 22). It is about teaching students to use a repertoire of thinking strategies to make meaning from print, arts-based, and technological texts.

FITTING COMPREHENSIVE INSTRUCTION TO LEARNER NEEDS

Chapter 1 proposed that the comprehension development of individual learners depends on meeting the specific needs of those individuals. Learners' needs are preeminent among the Five Factors that determine any comprehension outcome, but comprehensive literacy instruction acknowledges that all five factors interact.

Literacy instructional events facilitate comprehension when learner characteristics and the other four factors are addressed within every time block. The *context* of instruction must be a classroom that is physically and psychologically supportive of inquiry-based problem solving, including a culture of respect created by the teacher's disposition. (Review Chapter 3 and the classroom checklist in Ready Resource 3.4.) Instruction must provide large blocks of time for engaged reading and interaction with a variety of content-rich *texts*. The primary *task* must be explicit teaching of comprehension problem-solving strategies, with a focus on big ideas. Finally, students need *teachers* who are literacy models, who show they enjoy reading and can demonstrate how to comprehend well. In terms of teaching, students need

- organizational routines that support literate habits.
- engagement strategies directed at intrinsic motivation.
- instruction differentiated for individual students' strengths and needs.
- high-level talk about important content.
- tools that allow them to participate in gauging their own progress.
- to be held accountable for responding to texts in ways that show high-level comprehension.

GETTING INTO THE LITERACY HABIT

Routines create habits. Students need to develop a literacy habit that puts comprehension first, and effective teachers facilitate this goal by establishing a set of organizational and management routines that ensure a minimal amount of disruption and a maximum amount of time on task. Most classroom time is spent in engaged learning. Taylor and colleagues found that the most accomplished teachers engaged 96 percent of their students. In contrast, less skilled teachers averaged engaging 63 percent of students on task (1999). Effective teachers use a wide range of motivational strategies and have well-established procedures for handling behavior. They make quick transitions between activities and maintain a rapid pace of instruction, thus creating high instructional density.

Of course, time should be budgeted in proportion to the importance of learning tasks and student needs. In the case of comprehension, many students are experiencing a major time deficit. Studies of classroom practice continue to find a dearth of time devoted to focused comprehension instruction that helps students learn to approach texts strategically (see Chapter 1). A real comprehension revolution has to increase the quantity of time devoted to comprehension and the quality of instruction provided within that time.

ORGANIZING TIME BLOCKS

The nine best practices (see Ready Resource 3.5 in Chapter 3) are mega-teaching strategies to be used purposefully to solve learning problems—in contrast to common activities that often are not so purposeful and may be merely time fillers. Effective literacy instruction involves students in actual reading, listening to, and viewing of content-rich texts, active listening to teachers as they model fluent reading, and use of CPS strategies to create thoughtful responses to texts. Key literacy events are planned as settings for students to apply the CPS process to extract and construct big ideas.

Dedicated scheduled time blocks help ensure that best practices are implemented. A typical full dedicated literacy block lasts from ninety minutes to three hours. In addition, comprehension best practices must be embedded in content instruction if all students are to become expert comprehenders. Daily schedules need to include both teacher-directed and independent comprehension work designed to cause students to learn to self-initiate and use problem-solving strategies to make meaning.

Organizing literacy instruction in blocks is common, but the use of the time within blocks varies. Fountas and Pinnell (2001) recommend three events within the block. Cunningham, Hall, and Sigmon (2000) advise that four are needed, and Reutzel (2007) recommends five. Despite these variations, all models overlap in the kinds of instruction recommended. The order and the amount of time should be flexible and respond to students' needs and strengths, determined by ongoing assessment. Effective teachers use a combination of whole-group, small-group, and individual instruction. In addition, all models consider integration of literacy with content area instruction crucial.

Seven Main Literacy Events

The following seven main events organize daily classroom time with focus on implementing comprehension best practices. While other models present literacy instruction in ninety-minute or two- to three-hour blocks, the plan presented here shows how comprehension can be a focus of the entire school day. The plan

- addresses the Five Factors that influence comprehension.
- embeds all of the comprehension best practices in all events.
- provides flexibility in the order of activities and allocation of time to fit learners' needs.
- focuses on content units, usually based on science or social studies, but integrates math and the arts.
- builds in an inquiry orientation with focus on giving choice to students.

The following sections describe the seven main literacy events and their key features. Note that students are engaged in different events at the same time, so the amounts of time given here are not discrete—because of integration and embedding, the times cannot be simply added up. Ready Resource 10.1 summarizes the events and provides an example of order and time allowances for quick reference.

Seven main comprehension instructional events.

Note: The order and time allotments are examples that should be used flexibly.

1 Opening Literacy Routines (OLR): daily, whole group (10–15 minutes)

2 Interactive Read Aloud (IRA): daily, whole group (20–30 minutes)

3 Daily Engaged Independent Reading (DEIR): daily, whole group, small group, and/or individual (30–40 minutes, total minimum daily requirement for each student)

4 Small Group/Independent Work: daily, with teacher working with two or three groups each day while others work at centers and on independent work. Individual conferences and tutoring as needed (60 minutes)

5 Writing Workshop: daily, whole or small group (30+ minutes)

6 Embedded Comprehension Instruction in Content Areas: daily, whole group, small group, and independent (2+ hours)

7 Performances and Exhibits: weekly, whole group, one to two hours per week (e.g., Friday Reader's Theatre). Includes whole-group discussions and may replace small-group work one day each week.

READY RESOURCE 10.1

Event #1: Opening Literacy Routines

pening Literacy Routines (OLRs) are hands-on, heads-on activities that engage students in using language and arts-based communication (e.g., drama and dance). Students practice and apply literacy concepts, strategies, and knowledge they have learned previously, including vocabulary knowledge. Morning Meeting and opening circles may be used as OLRs. Examples of activities include song and poem charts, tongue twisters, riddle-a-day, word wall, and warm-ups. Students may perform poems using strategies listed in Ready Resource 10.12 on page 346. This time may also be used for word-based routines, such as Lisa LaTroube's Words Alive, discussed in Chapter 8.

PURPOSES

OLRs are diverse and serve many purposes:

- Energize students to get mental and physical juices flowing
- Increase motivation, especially interest, in communicating through alternative media
- Provide practice in CPS, including fix-ups
- Teach and boost attention, focus, and concentration (see box on p. 331)
- Increase vocabulary and thinking fluency
- Provide time for experiencing fun, which builds community

STRUCTURE

The teacher

1. gives brief directions,
2. states purposes,
3. engages students in doing the activity, involving students quickly,
4. repeats the activities to build a sense of the familiar, and
5. leaves a minute or so to debrief students about what they learned and *how* they thought and felt during the activity.

RESOURCES

Build a collection of song and poem charts, tongue twisters, riddles, and energizers/warm-ups for your classroom (Cornett, 2011). An Internet search for warm-ups for drama and dance will yield many strategies that require students to be active physically and mentally.

ADAPTING ROUTINES

Many opening routines are also worthy ways to wrap up the school day. Consider establishing closing routines that will have students depart with "learning on their lips." Otherwise, when parents ask, "What did you learn today?" kids may just say, "Nothing."

Event #2: Interactive Read Alouds: Reading *With* Students

The principal arrived for a surprise observation. Several of my students had their heads buried in their arms. Others had tear-streaked faces and red noses. I could barely speak and had to keep stopping to compose myself. I was reading aloud the end of *The Incredible Journey.*

CLAUDIA CORNETT

Reading aloud to children has long been an instructional staple, as evidenced by the date of the above journal entry: 1975. Nearly 90 years ago, the *English Journal* advised teachers that "the ear must be appealed to" through expressive read alouds if students are to understand literature (Fisher, et al., 2004, p. 12). Reading aloud in fact has an ancient history extending back to storytelling.

A comprehensive literacy program without daily teacher read alouds, interspersed with guest readers, is unimaginable. Children gather on rugs, scoot up chairs, or follow the teacher to sit under a shade tree. The setting is usually a classroom, however, and read alouds may occur at any time in the school day. The best involve memorable texts, such as *The Incredible Journey*, that are connected to units under study or real-life events. For example, when our guinea pig, Dirty Harry, died, I read aloud *The Tenth Good Thing About Barney* and applied principles of bibliotherapy, or book therapy, to make it interactive (Cornett, 1980). Students' interaction during the read aloud is key to teaching comprehension during this event.

PURPOSES

For decades literacy experts have sung the praises of reading aloud. Anderson et al. (1985) called reading aloud the *single most important activity* to build knowledge students need for success. We read aloud for all the same reasons we talk to one another: to inform, explain, create interest, satisfy curiosity, and reassure. Teachers use read alouds for more reasons. Additional purposes include:

- To present themselves as literate models who make visible what skilled readers do
- To build community through a shared social experience
- To increase students' purposeful use of comprehension problem-solving strategies to make meaning
- To increase students' vocabulary by allowing them to hear new words in context
- To build a rich content knowledge background that is beyond students' independent reach (Fisher et al., 2004)
- To promote focus and concentration through active engagement

- To increase students' knowledge of text characteristics and help them learn the functions of written language
- To influence students' future interests and text selections
- To provide context for observing students' comprehension (assessment)
- To build students' comprehension through discussion
- To improve students' memory, visualization, and language
- To experience a variety of writing styles and discuss their attributes
- To develop students' imagination and creativity by fostering inquiry
- To motivate students to read on their own and associate reading with a pleasurable experience. (Children's independent reading declines co-incident with the decline in the amount of time adults read to them [Trelease, 2006].)

GUIDELINES

Read-aloud guru Jim Trelease says that reading aloud "is fun, it is simple, and it is cheap" (Trelease, 2005). I agree that reading aloud is enjoyable and cheap. And while a read aloud can be a simple activity in which teachers read and students listen, interactive read alouds (IRAs) are not as simple. What's more, educators need more reasons than "fun and cheap" to budget a significant percentage of the school day for IRAs.

All read alouds are performances, but *interactive* read alouds go further to involve the audience. For example, the stops are planned at predetermined points to ask provocative questions or discuss key concepts. The resultant cognitive, emotional, and physical engagement deepens understanding and elevates read alouds above entertainment.

IRAs are not one-time or occasional events; they must be integral to literacy and content learning. Key features are:

- Interactive read alouds are used daily, sometimes more than once.
- They involve reading *with*, not *to* the audience (Fountas & Pinnell, 2001).
- Student participation is planned based on teaching points (e.g., the teacher models or directs use of a CPS strategy such as inferring or synthesizing).
- The teacher acts as a literate model by reading fluently and responding thoughtfully and aesthetically.
- The texts are diverse, content rich, and above the reading level of most students, but at their interest and cognitive maturity levels. Students comprehend more easily because they are not required to decode print.
- Connections are made between the read-aloud text and students' background, other texts, and content under study—especially science and social studies material and "real life." For example, a teacher might ask students to relate a previously read narrative book to today's informational book read aloud.

Ready Resource 10.2 provides more guidelines for read alouds.

Interactive read alouds: Guidelines.

1 Set up the physical space. Consider gathering students on a rug, while you sit on a low chair. Be sure you can make eye contact with every student and that they have a clear view.

2 Introduce the text. Choices include:

- *Mood-set:* Change the lighting, play background music.

- *Attention-get:* Show the book's cover and tell about the author and/or illustrator; use objects and pictures.

- *Purpose-set:* Tell students what to listen for. Explain the response that will be expected at the end. Relate the book to other texts, activate or build student background, and connect to content units.

- *Vocabulary:* Introduce key words and concepts related to big ideas.

- *Teach:* Explicitly teach a CPS strategy or text characteristic.

- *Etiquette:* Review audience etiquette, including active listening.

3 For a picture book, hold the book at the bottom center with your non-dominant hand so you can track the print and point with your dominant hand (to model left-to-right line reading).

4 Read expressively: change your pitch (high–low), tone (gentle–rough), and volume (soft–loud) to show different characters or create a mood. Vary the pace and use pauses. Pay special attention to verbs, and be careful with dialect and names.

5 Use facial expressions to show your response to the content, and make eye contact with students.

6 Gesture using your body and arms to help convey the message (but don't overdo it).

7 Encourage active participation. Invite students to repeat refrains and use oral cloze—ask students to supply missing words when you pause. Stop and use a plastic mike to interview students, who pretend to be characters, asking, "What happened?" Use EPR (Every Pupil Response) cards or signals such as thumbs up and down. Include vocabulary discussions as needed for comprehension.

8 After reading, return to the purposes set earlier. Ask thought-provoking questions—not "Did you like it?" but "What did you learn? What did you notice? What was it really about? How did it make you feel? What did the author or artist do that worked? Why? How?" Engage students in written and arts-based responses (see Chapter 9).

READY RESOURCE 10.2

TROUBLESHOOTING

- Prevent problems by explicitly teaching students how to attend, concentrate, and listen actively.

- If any children say they have already heard the book, tell them to listen for new ideas.

- Lower your volume and pause to retrieve attention. Stop and wait, if necessary, for attention to recenter.

- Seat students who are easily distracted closer to you.

STRUCTURE

The best way to understand IRAs is to see one in action. The following snapshot is of Doug Brown's fourth-grade class, which is in the midst of a social studies unit inquiring into the important question, "How do people from different countries and cultures solve common human problems?" Doug's read aloud is a classic picture book, *Crow Boy* by T. Yashima, which received the Caldecott

Award for its art. The story, set in Japan, and features a teacher who uses several of the best practices described in this book, including varied assessments and diverse response options. It is a story about courage and risk and many other themes that can develop into big ideas.

classroom snapshot

DOUG BROWN'S ARTS-BASED INTERACTIVE READ ALOUD

Students are seated on the carpeted steps of a mini performance area in Doug Brown's class-room. Doug sits in the stage area where all the students can easily see and hear him. Students sit beside their **"learning buddy,"** and each pair has a **clipboard** with paper on it. **Flute music plays** from a CD player. The students seem to be listening attentively until Doug pushes the pause. He speaks softly, as if he is reflecting the mood of the music.

"Take a minute and talk with your buddy about **what you heard and how it makes you feel.** I'll set the **timer.** Use your clipboards to record ideas. Any questions?"

There are none, so he turns an apple-shaped timer to sixty seconds. Pairs talk in whispers as **Doug circulates.** Sometimes he just sits besides a pair on a step and listens. At other times he **coaches with questions** like, "What makes you think it is a violin?" and "Why does it make you feel sad?" Students use the clipboards to write on a **T-chart with HEARD/WHY? and FEEL/WHY?** written at the top of the two columns. When the timer buzzes, Doug tells the students to finish their last thoughts. He waits until he has the full attention of the group.

"Who would like to go first?" he asks. Two boys volunteer.

"We heard one instrument. We thought it was a flute, because it sounded high and like someone was blowing it. It was sad because it was alone, but it was clear and strong, too."

Other pairs volunteer, and there is consensus that it is some kind of flute. Doug finally tells them the title of the CD is "Mysterious Sounds of the Japanese Flute." Students disagree about how the flute music feels. No one thinks it is happy, because it has a slow tempo, but some pairs disagree about it being sad. Doug **often uses music to set mood** for read alouds, so it is not surprising when a girl, without being asked, says she thinks the book is about a lonely character.

"I can understand that prediction," says Doug. **"You can either confirm or reject it** during the read aloud. For now, let's use Kelly's prediction to think about an **important question** that relates to our social studies question about human problems, 'Why are people left alone or lonely?' Let's begin with a **keyword** that has to do with that. The word is *isolation.*"

Doug flips open a chart. At the top is written, *Isolation is being alone or separated.* Doug tells the students to talk about examples of isolation and use the next page on their clipboards to take notes. It is another **T-chart** with *Definition of Isolation* written across the top and the two columns labeled **EXAMPLES/FEELINGS** and **NON-EXAMPLES/FEELINGS.** Doug resets the **timer,** for two minutes this time. Doug begins to circulate.

"We can't think of an example," a pair tells him. Doug looks around the room and sees that most eyes are on him. He realizes this is a common problem.

"Hey, everyone. **Let me give you an example of isolation** to get you started. When I was in sixth grade, my family moved. At the new school I had to eat alone in the cafeteria. I was isolated. I hated it. Does that help?"

"Yeah," says a girl, and many shake their heads in affirmation. Doug resets the timer to two minutes. He continues to circulate. **Some pairs need additional examples.** Others are on the right track, and Doug tells them so. **He compliments a pair who wrote down feelings** associated with times the two remember being left out of sports activities.

Debriefing

The class reassembles to share examples, which Doug writes on a **big T-chart.** Students have many personal examples, and some include examples from **"alternative" texts** such as the movie *Home Alone* and the television show *Lost.*

"Some of you jumped ahead and included *feelings.* That's great. Let's brainstorm more of those, and I'll write them beside the experiences," Doug says. Students call out feelings: *sad, afraid, sick to my stomach,* and *discouraged.* Doug turns to the Non-example/Feelings section of his T-chart.

"Let's do this as a whole-group brainstorm," he says. **"What's the opposite of isolation?"** Students call out ideas:

"Being a member of a group."

"Having friends or at least one friend."

"Being on a team, like soccer."

"A family."

Doug then asks for feelings associated with these experiences. Ready Resource 10.3 provides examples of the students' responses.

T-chart for interactive read aloud.

Isolation is being alone or separated.

EXAMPLES/FEELINGS	NON-EXAMPLES/FEELINGS
Eat alone	Popular kids
Sad, afraid, shy, hopeless	Confident, happy, being special
Not included on a team	Big family
No friends	Best friend
Being the new kid	Choir
Weird kids	Drama troupe
Parents leave you at home	Family reunions
Plane wreck on island	Sleepovers and parties
Being an only child	Scouts

10.3

READY RESOURCE

Book Introduction

Doug moves on to focus on today's book.

"I'll turn the music back on while you do **Close Looking** at the art on the cover of today's book," he explains. "Remember to concentrate on the colors, lines, shapes, and textures and how they make you feel." He sits in a low chair and holds up the cover of *Crow Boy,* with the title obscured. The flute music plays as he slowly moves the cover from side to side so all get to see the details. After a couple of minutes he pauses the CD again. He flips to a **3-Part Chart headed by SEE, FEELINGS, WHY?** (See Ready Resource 10.4.) They brainstorm as a group.

Doug then asks **how the cover art might relate to isolation.** Students offer their ideas:

"There is just one person on the cover."

"The scratchy lines make it look like she is in pain."

"There is a lone black bird on the stump."

"His skin is yellow. Maybe he or she is sick, because of the white bandage on his head. Maybe he is contagious."

Doug listens as each student shares. Finally, he flips back to the chart on isolation. **"Listen now for examples and non-examples from the story. I'll stop a couple of times for buddy talk."**

Doug takes time to show the **endpapers** and asks what students see. There is a single white butterfly on a rough-textured background. He reads the dedication and points to the Japanese characters on the title page. He runs his finger vertically and tells them it says "Crow Boy." He reads the name of the artist/author in a whisper.

Doug reads aloud, using his voice to "make music" with the words. He holds the book in his left hand so he can track the text with his right. Sometimes he reads the text and then shows the artwork afterward. On the page about the boy being called names he has placed a **red sticky tab.** He stops.

"Examples of isolation?" he asks, turning to the T-chart.

"Left alone," says a girl.

"Hides under the floor."

"He is afraid," says a boy. "Put that under 'feelings.'"

"Can't make friends."

"He is different because he is so little."

READY RESOURCE 10.4

3-part chart: Close looking at art.

SEE	FEELINGS	WHY?
Lots of black lines	Worried	Yellow skin and bandage
Yellow and red on face	Afraid	character may attack
Black in mouth	Wondering	Mouth open; sees something
Black bird on stump	Evil	Omen?
White bandage on head	Sad	Looks poor or beat up

"He is 'forlorn.' That's a feeling, but I'm not sure what that means," offers another girl.

Doug writes down *forlorn*. He holds up a **dictionary,** and a boy comes up and takes it. Doug continues to write down students' ideas until Josh says he has it.

"Abandoned, desperate, and alone," Josh summarizes.

"Thanks, Josh. Clear **synonyms** show the meaning in this context."

Doug reads on. There is another red tab on the page where Mr. Isobe, the new teacher in the book, spends time talking to Chibi. **The class now lists non-examples** of isolation found in the book as Mr. Isobe finds ways to include the child.

Doug reads on. The talent show scene is very dramatic, as Doug makes sounds of the different kinds of crows. He comes to a **final red tab** at the end of Chibi's performance.

"I'm now going to do **Teacher in Role drama,**" Doug says as he produces a large plastic microphone. "In a minute I'll become a TV reporter covering this school event. **What roles can you choose? Who is at the talent show?**"

Mr. Isobi
School Janitor
Student
Talent Show
Host

Students list possibilities, including students, parents, teachers, and the principal. Doug reminds them to think about how to shape their bodies and how their voices will sound.

"Use imagination to *become* your character," he coaches.

Doug stands and turns his back. When he turns around he says, "I'm Doug Brown from Channel Seven here at the Talent Show. Let me start over here. **What has happened?**" He holds the **mike** in front of a boy sitting up straight.

"That little kid I thought was stupid. But he's really pretty cool. He knows all about crows," the boy says.

"So, is he a friend of yours?" the reporter asks.

"No way. He was just a slowpoke. But, now, I might like to get to know him. Maybe we will be friends," the boy explains.

Doug moves around the room and interviews a half dozen students. One is pretending to be Mr. Isobe, who is "so proud." Another is the school janitor, who says he was like Chibi when he was a kid.

The interview takes about five minutes, and then Doug signs off. "Stay tuned to Channel Seven for up-to-the-minute news. I'll stay here on the scene and there will be an update at eleven. Until then, this is Doug Brown reporting."

Doug turns around. When he turns back he smiles. The class applauds and he bows. A teacher once again, he picks up the book and starts reading. When he comes to the last page, he reaches over to the CD. *La Mer* **plays in the background** as he reads the final page. The music soars as Crow Boy stretches "his growing shoulders proudly like a grown-up man, and he makes another crow call, 'the happy one.'"

The students spontaneously applaud, and Doug bows again and smiles. "Let's do some **Quick Mimes,**" he says. "Get a personal space on the stage." Students scramble to fill up the area.

"Afraid," Doug says, and the students crouch, fold up their arms, and cover their faces.

"Isolated," Doug says, and some make their bodies tall and tight, while others hang their heads or turn their backs.

Then Doug says, "Mr. Isobe displays your work." The students smile, raise their arms, point, and peek up humbly at an invisible display.

"Being called Crow Boy," he says finally. The students stand tall, some walk in place, others turn and wave. One girl cups her hands and pretends to call out.

Follow-up

The next day the students complete an **Inference Chart** on isolation (Cunningham & Smith, 2008). They work in groups of four or five to infer and then list important events or actions, reasons, results, and connections to the concept of isolation. Doug compiles ideas from each group on a class chart (see Ready Resource 10.5).

Doug then asks the groups to work together to **write a sentence that summarizes** what they have learned about isolation. He emphasizes that using full sentences helps make the big idea clearer. He coaches them as they work. For example, when a student says "feeling afraid," Doug asks, "How does isolation connect?" Their completed theme statements (big ideas) include:

Any person can feel isolated because he or she is afraid or shy.

If you get to know an isolated person, you can find what they are good at.

No one wants to be alone all the time, and good teachers help people be a part of groups.

It takes courage to be a friend to an isolated person.

People need each other, and everyone can help to include another person.

Doug draws students' attention to the class **CPS chart,** and they debrief about which thinking strategies they used to solve the comprehension problem in *Crow Boy.* As they reach the "after" part of the CPS chart, Doug describes an assignment at the Art Center. He asks the students about the colors, lines, shapes, and textures associated with *isolation* (Whitin, 2002). He also asks them to brainstorm an opposite key word for "isolation," and they end up with *integration.* He shows an example of an abstract watercolor he has done on another concept, "fear." He asks them what makes good art and what criteria should be used to grade this assignment. The rubric they settle on is:

- Make original art about isolation or integration.
- Fill up the paper with colors, lines, shapes, and textures.
- It can be abstract or representational.
- Experiment: use tools and media to mix colors and show textures.

Class inference chart.

Text: *Crow Boy—Connection to Isolation*

IMPORTANT EVENTS/ACTIONS	REASONS AND RESULTS
Chibi hides.	He is afraid, left alone.
Mr. Isobe talks to Chibi.	Good teacher. Chibi has a friend, so not alone.
Chibi in Talent Show	Mr. Isobi believes in Chibi.
Audience applauds.	Chibi feels part of the group.
Crow Boy nickname	Shows his talent and kids like him.
Problem solved.	He is not all alone.

READY RESOURCE 10.5

- Make a tag giving the title, artist, date, and media.
- Use a frame to prepare your art for the Brown Gallery (a carpeted wall outside Mr. Brown's class).

Postscript

Doug Brown connects his read alouds to social studies or science units. In this way he ensures focus on important content and big ideas. Most of Doug's teaching of CPS strategies has been done through read alouds, allowing students to focus on thinking to problem solve without the constraints of print. Teacher read alouds support a level of success for all students that they would not feel if they were asked to grapple with thinking and decoding print at the same time. This is especially true for his English learners. Doug feels the daily read aloud also bonds students together emotionally because of the aesthetic power of literature (Cornett, 2011).

Preparation for interactive reading alouds

IRAs are performances, and they require preparation, planning, and rehearsal. Preparation includes selecting texts and planning before, during, and after strategies that address students' needs. To rehearse, the teacher practices oral reading with a focus on expression, accuracy, and rate (see Chapter 8).

Text selection. A quality read aloud begins with a text selected because its content is rich and because the teacher wants to read it out loud. The book may connect to a unit under study and offer valuable information for the whole class, as *Crow Boy* did in the snapshot. Often the books that are read aloud would be too difficult for students to read independently but contain ideas that are well within their understanding. Chapter books like *Hatchet* or *Because of Winn Dixie* may be read aloud over time, with students using writing and arts responses to build comprehension (Cornett, 2006).

Along with connections to content units and current events, consider students' cognitive, emotional, and social maturity in text selection. The goal is to read high-quality texts by different authors and from diverse genres, including picture books appropriate for older students and nonfiction narratives about people and historical events. Look for opportunities to integrate other types of text, such as videos, CDs, arts prints, art in books, and Internet sites. The Online Resource box on page 318 lists Internet resources for selecting texts. Intermediate and middle-school students enjoy picture books, and many are perfect tie-ins to science and social studies. Examples with more mature subject matter include *Faithful Elephants*, *Fly Away Home*, *The Wall*, and *I Never Saw Another Butterfly*.

IRAs are excellent venues to introduce informational (expository and narrative) texts from science, social studies, math, and the arts. IRAs with expository texts allow you to present new concepts and content vocabulary in an interesting and accessible context. Abstract concepts in science and math can be made more concrete, especially when they invite conversation, generate questions for discussion and further student investigation, and are examined for both information and artistry. IRAs also provide opportunities to model CPS strategies and compare these to problem-solving methods in science, social studies, and math. See the box on page 320 for information about text recommendations by national organizations.

Rehearsing and planning teaching points. Reading aloud does not come naturally even to teachers—success depends on practice. Strive to bring the words to life like a good actor, not hamming it up, but using expressive elements honestly to show comprehension through the interpretation of the words. Rehearsal is essential, and recording oneself is a helpful means of self-assessment.

Plan teaching points related to students' needs. Preview the text and use stickies to mark points where you will stop to question, discuss, and point out specifics (see Ready Resource 10.6).

Comprehension teaching points might include

- CPS strategies (see Ready Resource 2.1)
- Comprehension or Word Fix-Ups (see Ready Resources 5.5 and 8.9)
- vocabulary, word, or fluency concepts (see Chapter 8)
- text characteristics and features (see Ready Resources 5.10, 5.11, and 5.12)
- narrative and expository elements (see Ready Resources 5.11 and 5.12)
- genre characteristics (see Ready Resource 5.10)

Selecting Texts

The following sites provide bibliographies organized by genre, subject, author, and artist for read alouds and for creating text sets.

American Library Association, www.ala.org/ala/alsc

Carol Hurst's site, http://carolhurst.com

Children's Book Council, www.cbcbooks.org

The Center for Children's Books, http://ccb.lis.uiuc.edu/collection_development.html

International Reading Association, www.reading.org

Kathy Schrock's Guide for Educators, http://school.discovery.com/schrockguide/edlearn.html

National Council for Teachers of English, www.ncte.org

University of Calgary, http://acs.ucalgary.ca/~dkbrown/authors.html#atoj

Center for the Improvement of Early Reading Achievement, www.ciera.org

For articles about read alouds and more, Cengage's Gale research website (www.gale.com) should be available through your library's reference desk.

Bibliographies of fiction and nonfiction books recommended for teaching content areas may be found at the sites of professional associations. See the websites listed in Appendix K.

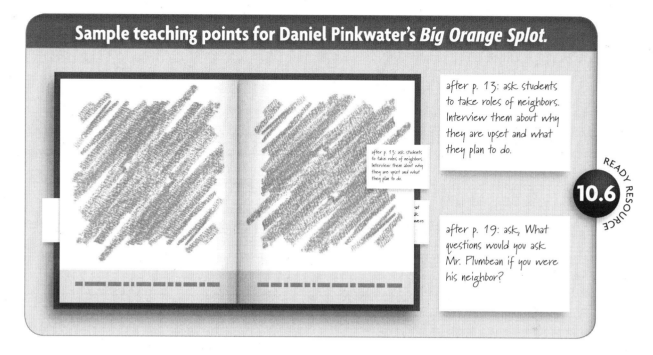

Sample teaching points for Daniel Pinkwater's *Big Orange Splot*.

after p. 13: ask students to take roles of neighbors. Interview them about why they are upset and what they plan to do.

READY RESOURCE
10.6

after p. 19: ask, What questions would you ask Mr. Plumbean if you were his neighbor?

Text introduction

A text may be introduced in many ways, as long as the focus remains on comprehension and the introduction does not slip into pure entertainment. Following are suggestions for text introductions:

- Use objects and pictures to build background.
- Assign students roles for listening: give each of them an index card labeled with a character's name and ask them to prepare for an after-reading drama (Fisher & Medvic, 2000).
- Play music to set the mood.
- Ask students to make three-part predictions from the cover related to characters, the setting, and possible problems.
- Introduce informational books with a virtual tour of a historical period or place, and involve students in pantomiming dressing and packing for the trip.

Other important considerations for a short (three- to five-minute) introduction are:

- Introduce key concepts or vocabulary. See "how to" recommendations in Chapter 8.
- Explicitly teach CPS strategies and other literacy concepts.

Look back to Ready Resource 10.2 for many suggestions for setting up the space and introducing the text, including ideas to get attention, set mood, establish the purpose for listening, and connect the text to content units.

Resources for Expository Texts That Can Be Used for IRAs

The **National Science Teachers Association (NSTA)** and the Children's Book Council identify Outstanding Science Trade Books for Students K–12 each year. Access extensive lists from 1973 forward at www.nsta.org/publications/ostb/. The list of recommended books is organized by subject and grade level, with annotations. Here are examples:

Camp, C. (2004). *American women inventors*. Enslow. Super book about women who created inventions like the square-bottom paper bag.

Skurzynski, G. (2004). *Are we alone?* Random House. Scientists search for life in space.

The **National Council for the Social Studies (NCSS)** and the Children's Book Council produce Notable Social Studies Books for Young People each year. Access the extensive annotated bibliography at www.socialstudies.org/resources/notable/. Examples are:

Bates, K. (2003). *America the beautiful*. Putman. Lines of poetry match places in United States.

Lasky, K. (2003). *The man who made time travel*. Farrar, Straus & Giroux. Timepiece for longitude revolutionizes sea travel.

Lester. A. (2006). *Are we there yet?* Miller. Journey around Australia from a child's perspective.

The **National Council of Teachers of Mathematics (NCTM)** has reviews of more than 550 titles with analyses of book content and accuracy, illustrations, style, and included activities. The NCTM publication *The Wonderful World of Mathematics: A Critically Annotated List of Children's Books in Mathematics*, 2nd ed., is available at their website, www.nctm.org. Examples are:

Burns, N. (2008). *Greedy triangle*. Scholastic.

Ellis, J. (2010). *Pythagoras and the ratios: A math adventure*. Charlesbridge.

Schwartz, D. (2006). *How much is a million?* HarperCollins.

During the read aloud

Orchestrate the students' oral performance in terms of both strategies and content, integrating modeling fluent reading with using ways to generate active participation. Point out text elements, ask questions, and use purposeful stops to discuss words, ask for inferences, and conduct drama activities. Use of every pupil response (EPR) will allow all students to participate simultaneously through signals (e.g., cards or hand signs). Quick "turn and talk to your neighbor" moments give students opportunities to extract information, construct meaning, and respond aesthetically to words and pictures. Students may be asked to make connections to their own lives and other texts and to share mental images. Generally, the number of stop points is about three.

Throughout the read aloud, be alert to students' reactions, especially confusion, and respond in an appropriate fashion. The goal is to deal with behavior without interrupting the flow. An old adage advises, "Don't raise your voice when raising an eyebrow does the job." A change in volume or a simple touch on the arm can work wonders to regain attention. To keep students focused and hold their attention, use questions or activities that invite participation from the whole class. For example, before reading, ask them to take the perspective of a character, and at planned stops interview them in a talk-show format. Invite echo responses, choral reading, and sound effects, or ask students to supply missing words (cloze) or pantomime verbs.

After the read aloud

After reading, return to the purposes set in the introduction. Questions that direct students to discuss big ideas and respond to those ideas facilitate meaning making. Refer to the guidelines for discussion in Chapter 7 and the suggestions for response options listed in Chapter 9. For example, ask students to brainstorm topics from the read aloud that they would like to research on the Internet and then to conduct research on one topic, gathering enough information to create a response.

DIFFERENTIATION

A learner who confronts a text with many unfamiliar concepts represented by unknown words is doomed to comprehension failure. Students need texts that they can access. Much of the comprehension instruction for novice readers must occur during interactive read alouds and with wordless texts, such as visual art and music. Shared Reading, a variation of interactive read alouds, scaffolds reading for novices (see Ready Resource 10.7).

Shared or co-reading with students.

WHAT IS SHARED READING?

- Shared Reading (or co-reading) is a variation of interactive read alouds during which students *see* the text in enlarged charts, big books, or individual book copies.

- Students look at the text as the teacher reads aloud and prompts students to participate through choral reading, oral cloze, and other engagement strategies.

- Materials are at the students' instructional level (85 to 90 percent word accuracy).

WHY DO IT?

- To scaffold or support students, by allowing them to use both print and pictures to participate in oral fluent reading

- To help students transition to solo reading

- To provide context for demonstrating or reviewing literacy concepts and strategies through modeling (thinking aloud)

- To simulate "lap reading," which has positive associations

- To put literacy in a social context and motivate through meeting students' belonging needs

HOW?

1. Choose materials at students' instructional level, so that they can subsequently reread them.

2. Use diverse, interesting texts related to content units.

3. Be sure all students are able to see the print easily, whether you are reading to the whole class or a small group.

4. Plan teaching points (e.g., tracking print, word matching, comprehension strategies).

5. Purpose-set before reading, and use engagement strategies during reading. Review the guidelines in Ready Resource 10.2.

6. Offer diverse meaning-oriented response options after reading.

7. Provide time for students to reread the text (e.g., at a station).

10.7 READY RESOURCE

Shared Reading

Montgomery County Public Schools, www.mcps.k12.md.us/curriculum/english/shared_reading.html

University of West Florida, www.uwf.edu/cohelp/id97/lcuric/lori/shared.htm

Galudet College, http://clercenter.galudet.edu/products/perspectives/may-jun99/corrado.htm

Interactive read alouds naturally provide many of the supports English Learners need. Modifications that can further help ELs include (Freeman & Freeman, 2001)

- Teach language, words, text concepts, and strategies fundamental to successful comprehension in the student's first language.
- Introduce the English words for vocabulary and concepts that are vital to understanding the themes and may interfere with comprehension.
- Exaggerate: emphasize words or specific events in both languages.
- Partner students with shoulder buddies seated next to them for turn-and-talk activities.
- Use visuals: show pictures from the book being read or related visuals. Use pictures or objects to explain key vocabulary from the text.
- If a dual language book is available, use the book on two days reading the students' first language on the first day and English on the second.

Read Alouds

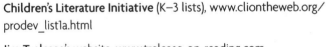

Children's Literature Initiative (K–3 lists), www.cliontheweb.org/prodev_list1a.html

Jim Trelease's website, www.trelease-on-reading.com

Mem Fox's homepage, including the 10 "Commandments for Reading Aloud" from *Reading Magic*, www.memfox.com

Public Broadcasting System, http://pbskids.org/lions

Read Aloud Nebraska, www. readaloudnebraska.org

Read Aloud Books Too Good to Miss, www.ilfonline.org/AIME/ReadAloud/ReadAloudlist.htm

About.com, http://childrensbooks.about.com/od/readalouds/

Event #3: Daily Engaged Independent Reading

The more you read, the more you know; and the more you know, the smarter you grow.

JIM TRELEASE

Practice increases learning, and reading is no exception. Examine the data in Ready Resource 10.8. The conclusion is inescapable: good readers read a lot, so they get good. Indeed, comprehension test scores are "more influenced by amount of engaged reading than any other single factor" (Guthrie, 2002, p. 382). Amount of reading outweighs intelligence, economic background, and gender as a predictor of comprehension. Guthrie concludes that if "a fifth grader is facing a high stakes test in April, the best thing the student can do is begin reading widely and frequently in October" (p. 383). Put bluntly, students who read widely become high achievers; those who read narrowly and rarely become low achievers.

Referring to the biblical passage about the rich getting richer, the "Matthew Effect" describes the fact that students who read the most read the best (Stanovich, 1986). Kids who read the most also achieve at higher levels and stay in school longer. Those who don't read much tend to spiral downward (Stanovich). Little reading leads to big failures, and failures lead to loss of motivation and interest. Struggling readers read less and less, so they get further and further behind. Prolonged reading failure then results in huge practice deficits (Torgesen, 2004).

Gaps in reading amount and comprehension achievement.

FACTS

- Good readers spend about 500 percent more time reading than struggling readers (Guthrie, 2004).

- Top readers read 219 more hours, or 2.25 million words, more per year than poor readers (Torgesen, 2004; Trelease, 2006).

- According to an NICHD study of 155 fifth-grade students, each day

    those at the 90th percentile read 37 minutes outside of school

    those at the 50th percentile read 11 minutes outside of school

    those at the 10th percentile read 1 minute outside of school

- Less motivated students read ten minutes per day, while highly motivated students read thirty minutes per day—three times as much (Guthrie, 2002).

- Lack of engaged reading stunts vocabulary, which is key to comprehension for English learners and struggling readers (Stanovich & Cunningham, 1992; Torgesen, 2004).

- The percentage of seventeen-year-olds reading daily for fun dropped from 31 percent to 22 percent between 1984 and 2004.

- Reading scores show steady declines. Between 1992 and 2003, the percentage of college graduates who tested as "proficient in reading prose" declined from 40 percent to 31 percent (NEA, 2007).

READY RESOURCE 10.8

Without sufficient reading practice, students do not develop the vocabulary and thinking strategies they need in order to comprehend. The longer students continue to read little, the worse the problem gets. The amount of practice they need to catch up becomes prohibitive, because their practice time has to be greater than that of good readers (Torgesen, 2004; Trelease, 2006). Do the math: a fourth grader who is at a second-grade reading level needs to grow two years in a year to reach grade level. That means reading more than three hours per day, because

- below-level fourth graders read only thirty minutes per day.
- on-grade-level fourth graders read two hours per day (to get one year's growth).
- above-grade-level fourth graders read three to six hours per day.

Illiteracy is connected to aliteracy. Aliterates can read but choose not to. Voluntary reading is dramatically decreasing in the United States, while scores on assessments, such as the National Assessment of Educational Progress, show only slight improvement. Aliteracy is blamed for declines with "serious civic, social, cultural, and economic implications" (NEA, 2007). Fewer than one-quarter of seventeen-year-olds read daily for fun, and young people aged fifteen to twenty-four average ten minutes or less. Where will future reading models for next generations come from if this trend continues? What are the consequences if America becomes "a nation in which reading is a minority activity" (NEA Chairman Dana Gioia, in Tompson, 2007)?

Students who read little and are not motivated to read extensively and diversely are ill equipped to use the broad array of texts they will encounter inside and outside of school. The effects of shorting reading occur even for students who have no basic cognitive deficits or deficits in reading sub-skills or oral language development.

How might teachers increase the amount of students' engaged reading? First, we have to rule out points, coupons, grades, and tests; when extrinsics such as these are removed, the behavior tends to extinguish (e.g., see Alfie Kahn's books and articles; Eisner, 2002). As Jim Trelease points out, the goal is lifetime, not just school-time readers (2006).

EMERGENCE OF SUSTAINED SILENT READING

Research has established that "reading comprehension is an outgrowth of a *wide range of purposeful, motivated* reading activities" (emphasis added) (Guthrie, 2002, p. 82). Hence, in the 1970s, Sustained Silent Reading (SSR) programs were developed in the belief that selecting their own reading materials would motivate students to read, and practice would improve their reading. Whole schools designated time each day when everyone read silently for fifteen to thirty minutes. Teachers read, principals read, custodians read, and students were supposed to be reading. Many did, but some were not engaged. SSR's focus on reading choice texts for pleasure often was interpreted to mean teachers could not hold students accountable.

Despite high correlations between amount of engaged reading and comprehension achievement, the National Reading Panel (2000) determined there was no benefit to comprehension from SSR programs, based on lack of supportive "experimental" studies. This conclusion unleashed a flood of criticism. In a rebuttal, Krashen (2001, 2005) charged that research was misinterpreted. He unearthed forty studies of which thirty-eight showed that SSR students equaled or outperformed comparison students on comprehension tests. Results were even more positive for studies longer than seven months. Marzano confirmed that programs lasting for at least a year showed more impact (2004). The benefits even extended beyond formal schooling. Adults who had participated in independent reading at school reported reading more (Tunnell & Jacobs, 1989)—and adults who read more participate more in society and enter the workforce at higher levels (Guthrie, Schafer, & Wang, 1995).

Today, many teachers include independent reading in the daily schedule, and some school-wide programs still exist. Students in the most effective schools spend over twenty-five minutes per day reading independently (Taylor et al., 1999). That takes care of quantity—but what about instructional quality concerns (e.g., accountability)?

SSR continues to evolve as practitioners experiment with different combinations of factors to increase comprehension. A focus on uninterrupted time led to USSR (Uninterrupted SSR). The thought that silence was critical produced SQUIRT: Sustained Quiet Independent Reading Time. DEAR, Drop Everything and Read, suggested reading was a priority. DIRT, Daily Independent Reading Time, targeted regularity and offered the natural kid-appeal of the word *dirt*. Research on good-reader strategies and the effects of motivation on comprehension support another revision: that the goal be daily purposeful engagement with diverse texts. This implies use of comprehension problem-solving strategies to extract and derive big ideas that are of consequence to individual students and are related to curricular content. The result: Daily Engaged Independent Reading, or DEIR.

EMERGENCE OF DEIR

There is solid research to support the conclusion that "reading comprehension is an outgrowth of a *wide range of purposeful, motivated* reading activities." DEIR grew out of Sustained Silent Reading.

DEIR, the natural partner of interactive read-alouds, is so powerful that no comprehension instructional schedule can be considered effective without it. If essential educational factors are in place, students will acquire the habit of active engaged reading. Qualifiers such as "engaged" and "motivated" tell the tale: engagement implies attention, concentration, focus, and purposeful mental activity. Opportunities to read must be coupled with an inquiry stance—an intention on the part of the learner to use problem-solving strategies to make sense of the text at hand.

In the following classroom snapshot, Lois Kelly is doing explicit teaching to introduce Daily Engaged Independent Reading. In addition to explicit instruction, Lois embeds other best practices in this lesson. In particular, she coaches students to pull out literary themes and turn them into big ideas. They will practice doing this on their own during independent reading.

classroom snapshot

LOIS KELLY EMBEDS BEST PRACTICES IN DEIR

Lois Kelly's second graders have been reading different versions of "The Three Little Pigs" during a literary genre unit on fairy tales. Today Lois has planned a **mini lesson** before DEIR to teach students how to think of big ideas derived from universal themes. The children are seated pretzel-style on a rug.

Lesson Introduction

"Look at the book covers of all the Three Pigs stories up here. Let's count together how many we have read together," says Lois. The students count to thirteen. Many smile.

"Wow!" exclaims one boy.

"That many?" asks a girl.

"Yes, that many," says Lois. "For each book, we've discussed the literary elements to make sense of the stories. Lois puts a "Literary Elements" card in the top of a **pocket chart.**

"Listen in on my brain thinking about literary elements, and help me fill in the gaps. As a reader I think about WHO is in the story. That is . . ." (**oral cloze** strategy).

"Characters!" the class says in unison, and Lois puts a **"character" card** in the chart.

"I think about what characters do—all the actions and events in the story. Now I want you to **whisper this time.** This is called the . . ." Lois whispers.

"Plot," they whisper. Lois puts a "plot" card in the chart.

"When I read I also keep thinking about where and when the story is happening. I even **make pictures in my head** of places. This time I want you to stretch the sound of the first letter. This is called . . ."

"S-s-s-s-s-setting," the class responds.

"I really enjoy how different authors use special words or use rhyme and onomatopoeia. Put your thumb up if you know this literacy element."

Lois points to three students. "On the count of three."

"Style!" the three say.

"But most important, as a reader I'm always asking myself, **What is this story really about?** and What have I learned that will help me in my life? Show me **the sign language** you learned for this." Students immediately use their hands to make quote marks.

"Can we do all the signs?" a boy asks.

"Sure." Lois points to each element, and students use American Sign Language (ASL):

- Character is represented by the sign for C against the left palm.

- Setting is a P for "place," with both hands circling and middle fingers touching.

- Plot is represented by the word "story," made by interlocking circles with the thumb and index finger of both hands and pulling them apart.

- Word use is signed by showing an inch with the right thumb and index finger, touching the left index finger, which is pointing up.

(For more information on ASL, visit www.ASLPro.com.)

"You read some of the books to us," points out one boy.

Lesson Development

"Yes and you did some in your **Book Clubs**," Lois responds. "Think about the last **literary element**. She signs "theme." **What do you know about the theme?**" Many thumbs go up. Lois **waits about five seconds** before calling on children.

"It's not just retelling the plot," says a girl.

"It is what the story is *really* about," offers another.

"Sometimes the author tells you the theme, like in the moral of a fable," says a boy.

"Yeah, but when the author doesn't write it in the story, you have to think it up," says a girl. "You have to use your own experiences. That's harder!"

Lois laughs and says, "Yes, that is harder, but remember we've talked about how **expert readers make their own sense?**"

"To make reading more fun!" says a boy.

"Absolutely!" says Lois. "When have you felt that?"

"Even in the pigs stories I like thinking up my own **big ideas**," explains one girl. "But it *is* sorta hard."

"I like that you remember about big ideas," Lois says. "Today we are going to practice with big ideas, which come from story themes, so it won't be as hard. Let's start by **brainstorming** what the Three Pigs story you just read was *really about.*"

Students call out ideas and Lois begins a **web on the overhead**. It is soon full of words and phrases: *listening to your mother, being foolish, using hard materials, don't listen to wolves, smart pigs, wolves eat pigs,* and *we need a house.*

"That's a lot of ideas! I know you have more, but this is enough for our mini lesson. Listen as I read aloud each of these, and **tell me what you notice.**"

"Some are sentences," one boy says immediately.

"You really did close looking," says Lois. "What else?"

"It's like *what about* being foolish or listening to your mother?" says a girl.

"What do you mean, Lia?"

"Well, like Joe said, some are sentences—a whole thought. The ones that aren't need more ideas," Lia explains.

"Let's do just that," says Lois. "Which one should we practice?"

"Being foolish. It was my idea," says one boy.

"Okay. **What does the author want us to learn about being foolish?**" asks Lois.

"That you shouldn't take the easy way—the straw or the mud. It would also be the cheapest," another boy answers.

"Who can say that another way?" asks Lois.

"Don't use foolish building materials?" asks a girl in almost a whisper.

"What about that? How is the story telling us that?"

"The sticks and straw were foolish because they didn't last. Brick is hard and costs more, but it won't blow down. I live in a white brick house," explains a boy.

"So, is the story *really* about building houses?" asks Lois.

"Yes, but it is more," says a girl. "The author could mean about building anything, maybe even a mobile or a puppet."

"Ella, say more about that," suggests Lois.

"Like when you make a mobile, you have to have a sturdy hanger thing to start. If you just use a straw or something flimsy all your stuff just falls down."

"That is a clear example, Ella. **Who else has an example?**" asks Lois. Three thumbs go up.

"It's like cooking, too. If you just used some rotten meat and old potatoes then your vegetable soup would stink!" The class laughs, and the boy who said this smiles widely.

"When you go somewhere you need to choose wisely," explains another girl. Lois nods. The girl continues, "You have to have good directions, write them down, and use a map."

"My dad has a GPS," says another girl.

"**The idea that we need to make wise choices about tools is a clear example,**" says Lois. She continues to take more examples and then begins to wrap up.

"All these examples of 'You need to choose materials wisely' are from so many different places. **Now let's look back at where we started.**"

"Being foolish. It was not a sentence," says a boy.

"Right," says Lois. "Why does a sentence help?"

"Being foolish is like, about what?" says a girl.

"It isn't a full idea," says another.

"**So, to get to big ideas in stories, where can you start?**"

"Brainstorm about what the story is *really* about," says a boy. Lois turns and writes this on chart paper.

"What next?" she asks.

"**Make the themes BIG by turning them into sentences,**" suggests a girl. Lois writes this down on the chart.

"How can you turn theme ideas into big ideas?" she asks. She waits, but there are no thumbs up. Finally a girl volunteers: "Keep asking yourself questions like how and why until it sounds done?" she asks.

Explicit Teaching with a Think Aloud

"Sounds like the Five W's and H!" says Lois. "Let me do another **think aloud** to demonstrate. I'll use questions. Listen to me think. I'll use one of the ideas from the brainstorm. I'll do 'listening to your mother.' Hmmm. I'm thinking, what about *listening to your mother?* 'It is important to listen to your mother'—sounds like a sentence, almost. But I want to make it better. How? Let's see, I could say it is important to listen to your mother *because* . . . . Then I ask myself why, and I think, she loves you and has more experience, so she would give good advice. That is long, but I think it is true. **What do you think?**" Lois writes the sentence on the chart and looks around.

"It is true about my mom and my grandma," says a boy. Several other kids nod their heads in agreement.

Lois smiles and asks, "**What did you notice about *how* I turned the idea into a true sentence—a big idea?** Turn and talk with a partner. I'll set the **timer** at thirty seconds."

Students **partner**, and when the buzzer goes off Lois asks for volunteers. Some of the responses are:

"We talked about how you asked questions about the idea nugget."

"You had to think about your own mother—your background."

"You asked how to make your first sentence better, more true. You added 'because' details."

Lois adds their ideas to the chart and asks, "What can we use as a **chart title** that pulls all these ideas together?"

"Making Big Idea Sentences!" shouts one boy as if he has been struck with an ah-ha. Lois laughs. She writes his title down, dramatically points at it like Vanna White, and says, "Ta-da!" She smiles and continues.

Conclusion: Preparation for Student Practice

"Let's use Doug's title and **try these steps during independent reading** today. We'll **debrief** afterward so you can **share one theme idea that you made big.** Later we'll learn about how some big ideas are more important than others. One more thing—**we will also discuss how thinking about big ideas and using self-questioning change *how* you read.** What questions do you have right now?"

"Should we write our ideas down?" asks a boy.

"Sure. That will help you remember what you are thinking," says Lois. "Use your DEIR logs and stickies to mark places."

"Can we sketch how we change as readers?" asks another boy.

"Sketching is another way to record your ideas, so yes. Do quick sketches if that works for you. Remember, the goal is to prepare for our **after DEIR discussion** about big ideas and how thinking about them changes your reading. Today I will only read with you half the time, then I'll be calling up the **diamonds** for conferences. I'll put on the Enya CD for **background music.** We'll start in one minute, so places, everyone!"

Lois goes over to a CD player while her students scramble. Some sit in a carpeted area, some on a couch beside a floor lamp, and others choose their desks. Lois picks up *Like Jake and Me* (Jukes) and sits in a rocker. She nods to a boy, who sets the plastic **timer** and then sits on a cushion. DEIR has begun.

> **MAKING BIG IDEA SENTENCES**
>
> Brainstorm about what the story is <u>really</u> about.
>
> Make themes BIG by turning them into sentences.
>
> What do <u>you</u> think?

PURPOSES

DEIR is intended to build students' confidence and increase their comprehension competence. It broadens background, builds vocabulary, and creates interests. It also fulfills the need for students to practice CPS every day. DEIR retains SSR's focus on motivation by sustaining students' involvement with content-rich, interesting texts. Desire to read springs from interest; desire makes reading fun—and fun is fundamental to motivation and learning (Cornett, 2002).

STRUCTURE

DEIR is based on the premise that regular and extended practice matters. Students should begin in kindergarten with five to ten minutes per day and by third grade should sustain engagement for at least thirty minutes each day. Once or twice a week is not enough; distributed practice over the whole week is necessary. Of course, sustained engagement depends heavily on how the teacher implements and manages DEIR, including how well the teacher instructs students in the why and how of independent reading.

DEIR has a before/during/after structure. The "before" should be short, but should include purpose-setting to focus on big ideas and CPS use, explicit teaching of new strategies or review of familiar ones, and a clear statement of responses expected after reading. During reading, students should stay in one place and remain engaged during the entire time period. They may use stickies to mark certain places in a text or make brief notes to prepare for responding, but the focus is on staying engaged. After reading, students need to participate in some kind of response. Daily responses are usually brief, with a focus on sharing strategies used and big ideas found or constructed. The response period may involve the whole class together, or students may break into small groups or pairs. Responding often is preceded by some kind of writing. Explicit teaching is used before reading, and discussion and response strategies are used after (see Chapters 7 and 9). Ideas for DEIR responses may also be found in the section on interactive read alouds.

GUIDELINES

The following guidelines are key to ensuring DEIR is an integral part of developing students' comprehension.

Integrate content

Reading and writing now demand much more of the school day, while social studies and science are being squeezed out. At the same time, increasing state standards require that students learn more social studies and science content. The only solution is integrating reading and writing with content (Pressley, 2006). DEIR is a time for that to happen. The ideal is for students to read texts related to content units. Teachers increasingly tie independent reading to science and social studies units by requiring students to select from reading lists or from a bin of books color-coded to indicate reading level. A great diversity of genres, authors, and levels makes it possible to give students choice, within the limits of unit study.

Enhance motivation

Because DEIR involves reading and responding in a group context, it taps the motivational power of groups. It also enhances motivation through choice. Students are allowed to choose when, where, and what to read, within limits. Students are directed to select texts of interest, and it is helpful to teach them how to select books that are not too difficult. Of course, students need scaffolds such as short book reviews and chalk tray displays to help them select books. For additional scaffolding, schedule short book talks at least monthly, and involve other students and the librarian in giving book talks. A simple recipe box can hold alphabetized cards for short student reviews.

Students can develop independence at selecting books by learning to do a preview, including reading the back cover, flyleaf, and table of contents. They can also learn to estimate difficulty (readability), using the "Rule of Thumb." Instruct the students to follow these steps:

1. Open to the middle and start reading.
2. Put up a finger for each unknown word.
3. If they get to their thumb, the book may be too hard.

A text's level of difficulty can be reduced with media-amplified texts, such as CD-ROMs that allow the reader to click on words for pronunciation, cues, and meaning.

Use modeling

Experts agree that it is crucial for teachers to be role models during independent reading. Students need to see you reading regularly and excited about ideas in texts. DEIR is not the time to grade papers or plan lessons, although you may use DEIR time on some days to hold conferences with students. Show engagement by reading diverse texts, including children's literature and adults' books, both fiction and nonfiction. If students write in logs after reading, you should do so, too. During debriefing, serve as a model by talking about strategies used, text characteristics, important concepts, and big ideas. For example, talk about how the main character is changing, about the author's intent, and about surprises and confusing points.

Students need to learn to be engaged and to respond to books. They must be taught how to share their thoughts and feelings about texts with others. Modeling prepares students to carry on book conversations in pairs or small groups. If the teacher models engaged reading, the students will follow.

Phase to independence

Initially, use explicit teaching to instruct students how to think strategically and respond aesthetically during DEIR. Teaching needs to include lessons on engagement, especially concentration and focus. See the accompanying box on teaching concentration and focus.

Teaching Concentration and Focus

The ability to focus and control one's attention by concentrating is invaluable. Teach students to concentrate by

1. clarifying what it means to concentrate by defining it, demonstrating, and giving examples and non-examples.
2. discussing its importance in life.
3. setting a goal for students to improve their concentration (target on-task behavior).
4. giving frequent descriptive feedback to encourage students' inclination to concentrate.
5. using frequent warm-ups, attention-getters, and games that help develop concentration, as well as debriefing discussions about students' progress.

Appendix H gives examples of brief lesson warm-ups that focus on developing concentration and focus.

PREVENTING PROBLEMS

Students need comfortable, distraction-free spaces in which to read. They also need to be explicitly taught how to engage and sustain engagement. Role playing is useful, as are regular debriefings after DEIR about engagement problems and concerns. Other ways to sustain students' engagement are:

- Use a clock or timer everyone can see.
- Give students bookmarks, such as the one on the back cover of this book, to mark spots and keep CPS strategies in front of them.
- Monitor students by sitting so you can see the whole class. Use eye contact, signs and signals, and proximity to refocus students who are off task.
- Schedule private conferences to discuss engagement problems with students who have difficulty.
- Make rules clear ahead of time (see Ready Resource 10.9).

DEBRIEFING AND ASSESSMENT

Budget at least five minutes for debriefing and recordkeeping after each DEIR session. A whole-group debriefing should focus on big ideas, key concepts, strategies used, and general sharing. This can be made special with a share chair and a microphone. Debriefing sessions may be prefaced with Write Right Away to help students prepare. These written responses, also called "quick-writes," may be prompted by a question, and you may write your own response publicly on an overhead.

If students are keeping response journals, plan to respond to students' journal entries frequently, often including another question to prompt deeper

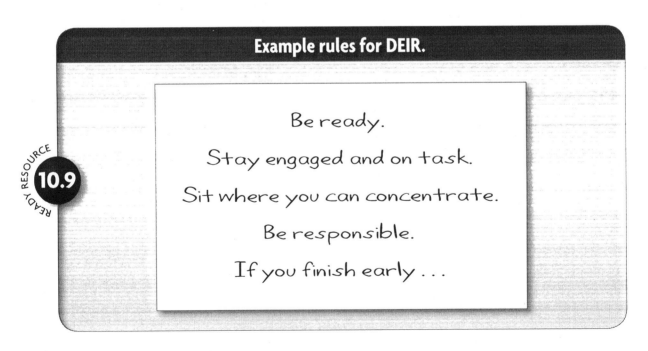

Example rules for DEIR.

READY RESOURCE 10.9

Be ready.

Stay engaged and on task.

Sit where you can concentrate.

Be responsible.

If you finish early . . .

understanding of the material. Journals take many forms, including bridge journals (students write about connections between the text and their background), sketch journals (these include drawings), and dialogue journals (partners read the same book and write back and forth).

For long-term responses, students may engage in full-length discussions of books on common topics, write, conduct Internet research, or create arts products. The classroom snapshot in Chapter 7 gives ideas; also see Chapters 7 and 9, as well as the section later in this chapter on performances and exhibits.

Giving students responsibility is key to accountability. You should state clear expectations for how students can show comprehension and use tools to track progress. For example, a dated list of books read, with brief comments by the student, shows growth. To express their comments, students may use a variety of formats, such as the frames described in Chapter 7 (EPC, IQU, and LWL). At minimum, students should be expected to keep logs of what they read, to be reviewed in short weekly individual conferences. These conferences should be regularly scheduled with each student. If four or five students are conferenced each day, the whole class can be done every week. Use a timer to keep them short (three to five minutes), and cue students about what the conference will target (e.g., CPS strategy use, big ideas). See Appendix B for checklists and Ready Resource 10.10 for a DEIR rubric.

Rubric for Daily Engaged Independent Reading.

Name _____   Dates ___ / ___ / ___ / ___ /

Scale: 0 = never, 5 = always

CRITERIA	SCORES	NOTES
Chooses text appropriate to the task	_/_/_/_/_/	_____
Begins immediately	_/_/_/_/_/	_____
Sustains concentration on the text	_/_/_/_/_/	_____
Respects others engaged with texts	_/_/_/_/_/	_____
Sets goals for strategy use and research	_/_/_/_/_/	_____
Responds thoughtfully to texts	_/_/_/_/_/	_____
Shares big ideas and strategies used	_/_/_/_/_/	_____
Treats texts with respect	_/_/_/_/_/	_____
Keeps dated records of big ideas and evidence	_/_/_/_/_/	_____
Keeps accurate records of CPS strategies used	_/_/_/_/_/	_____

Conference Dates and Student Goals:

_____   _____

_____   _____

_____   _____

READY RESOURCE 10.10

DIFFERENTIATION

You can differentiate DEIR using all the PARTICULAR aspects from Chapter 4, including altering time, texts, text use, and group size. Young children can be shown how to sustain engagement in reading the pictures in books long before they have print fluency. They can also learn to predict, infer, and summarize using art. You may decide it is appropriate for students to whisper read or even read into a recorder or to a buddy. A pair might select a book to read together and take turns whisper reading pages aloud. As students read, they should be encouraged to talk about their expectations, surprising events or facts, and what they are learning. Buddies sometimes spontaneously look back through a book together, retelling poignant parts. As always, the focus should be on finding and constructing big ideas using text evidence. Students may do DEIR in small groups on some days while you work with other groups; responsibilities remain the same as previously discussed. Students may be expected to debrief and discuss after a timed reading, using your questions to begin with and then phasing into student-generated questions. See Ready Resources 7.3 and 7.4.

You can differentiate DEIR through technology integration by allowing students to listen to books at their instructional level using software that provides supports, such as CD-ROM texts with buttons to click to hear a word or get its definition. *Note:* Computer programs such as Accelerated Reader and Scholastic's Reading Counts aim at increasing the amount of student reading, but they are controversial for many reasons (including use of extrinsic reinforcement and a focus on answering questions that are "scorable"). A critique is available at Jim Trelease's website.

Event #4: Small-Group and Independent Work

Whole-group instruction cannot address all learner needs. At times, all students need to work in small groups or individually with the teacher. Small-group and independent work can occur simultaneously as some students work together on improving specific skills or at specific centers while others work on their own.

SMALL-GROUP WORK

For small-group work, convene small bands of students based on a variety of needs. Sometimes students are grouped by interest, other times by a common struggle with a strategy or literacy concept. At times, students are grouped randomly.

Terms like "homogeneous" and "heterogeneous" grouping have taken on new meaning. Homogeneous grouping no longer is about long-term ability grouping, criticized for stigmatizing students. Traditional "bird" groups lumped students who were low achieving and minority students together and then subjected them to detrimental differentiation (Fountas & Pinnell, 2001). Grouping is now used as a tool for positive differentiation, and students in effective schools spend an average of sixty minutes each day in small groups (Taylor et al., 1999). The most successful groups are flexible and based on needs, with students frequently changing groups as assessments reveal the need to do so.

Purposes

Whole-class instruction marginalizes those who need closer contact with the teacher to make steady comprehension progress. Whole-group instruction also makes it too easy for some students to tune out and become wallpaper. Flexible grouping, an effective way to address learner passivity, allows students to be appropriately challenged and avoids labeling a student's development as static. Even students who are high achieving benefit from working with diverse groups. While they may prefer work with intellectual peers, they need to learn to be a part of a community where each person is different and can make a different contribution.

Guidelines and structure

Although studies of effective schools showed their students spent more time in small-group instruction, this instruction need not occur all at once nor occur only during the literacy block. Small-group instruction guided by comprehension best practices should take place throughout the curriculum. In particular, since CPS parallels the scientific method and historical reasoning (Parker, 2009), science and social studies classes are ideal settings for small-group work on aspects of problem solving.

Effective use of small groups depends on a teacher's organizational skills and the independence of students not in the group. Asking students to work independently is insufficient. During the first month of school, teachers need to model concentration and focus explicitly, post rules, discuss consequences, and only then gradually start groups. For example, begin with five-minute group sessions to accomplish a specific task. Debrief the whole group on how they did. Increase the time until students work for thirty minutes without direction. Of course, supervision is always needed. Effective teachers position themselves to monitor the entire room and periodically scan for off-task behavior.

Small-group procedures and rules work to prevent problems and facilitate on-task work. For example, teach students independent fix-ups (see Ready Resources 5.5 in Chapter 5 and 8.11 in Chapter 8) so they can solve their own problems. Discuss what students should do when they finish early. Inquiry-based classrooms involve students in ongoing studies of interests that can always be pursued (Wolk, 2008). Students who finish early may also choose to work at choice centers and stations if they are available.

Organizing and managing small groups involves deciding who will be in what group and when and where groups will meet. Groups that are not teacher-led must know that they are expected to produce clear evidence of task accomplishment. You may use a pocket chart and large index cards to post the location of centers and the order of groups working at each center. Groups may be numbered, lettered, or color-coded. For example, the green group might meet first with the teacher and then proceed to the Book Nook and then the Response Center. If each group spends twenty minutes at each center, students can visit three centers in an hour (the teacher counts as a center). Some students may need to meet with you every day, others just two or three days each week, depending on their needs.

Group members may rotate each week, every two weeks, or every month, but group composition does need to change periodically because needs change. Small groups can be invaluable if they are regularly reconstituted based on common comprehension needs and interests. This entails ongoing assessment to keep track of comprehension strategy needs and other key aspects of literacy. Assessment tools may be found in Chapter 4 and Appendices A through D. The positive effect of small needs-based groups depends on regular monitoring of student progress coupled with ample time for students to read and practice new strategies.

Types of groups

The purpose of a small group will determine its type. Common types of comprehension groups are:

- Literature circles and book clubs, which may be of mixed ability.
- Interest or project groups: mixed-ability groups formed for purposes of research and creating responses, often used in science and social studies.
- Guided reading groups, which are teacher led and formed to address assessed needs of learners. These groups are called "guided" groups because the teacher provides explicit instruction and scaffolded practice to guide students through a text at their instructional level. A key focus is comprehension strategies instruction, including how to use fix-ups and text characteristics. Teachers often use leveled books or material in a basal series, but it is ideal to match these texts to content units when possible.

All small groups benefit from learning how to work cooperatively. Chapters 7 and 9 gave guidelines, and teachers can consult many cooperative learning references and websites.

INDEPENDENT WORK AT CENTERS AND STATIONS

While some students work in groups, others can be working independently at centers and stations.

Purposes

Centers and stations are designated classroom areas that provide interesting, meaningful opportunities for independent work. Some are assigned and others are open to student choice. Centers are broad based, while stations focus on one task. Some teachers start the morning with fifteen minutes of choice center time, especially if students arrive at different times, and then conduct individual conferences and attend to morning tasks. Working at centers and stations may also be an option as students finish other work during the day. Some centers and stations are required—for example, every student may be scheduled to come to the Conference Station with the teacher once a week to discuss progress and set goals.

Structure and guidelines

Each center or station needs a title and a clear purpose. Tasks should be very clear and should be self-checking when possible. Rules should be posted (e.g., number of students), and a sign-in sheet can be useful. Students should have individual folders for completed work, unless a special bin is provided at each center. For assigned stations and centers, make clear that students' ability to work independently and to complete tasks will both be evaluated. You may work collaboratively with students to create a rubric for this purpose.

The possible centers and stations that focus on independent practice and research are almost endless. Many teachers have a Vocabulary or Words Center that includes activities for sorts, webs, ladders, and word making. The following are other examples specific to comprehension.

Arts Response Center. This center makes arts-making ideas and sources available for students to create visual art, music, drama, and dance products. The center offers resources such as example script formats, a prop box, and music CDs. See Chapter 9 for a list of arts concepts and arts-based comprehension response options.

Writing Center. Writing centers should provide resources including writing forms (see Ready Resource 9.1), poetry forms (Ready Resource 9.5), Spelling Fix-Ups (Appendix F), a poster of writing traits (see Chapter 9), dictionaries, and writing materials. Envelopes and stationery may be included. Computers for word processing are often located here.

Book Nook. A Book Nook is a comfortable area where students can do independent reading and hold group discussions. Books that relate to a current classroom unit might be displayed, with teasers ("What if a committee decided what you would be when you grow up? Read *The Giver* to find out more.").

Computer/Research. At this Internet-connected computer station, students can focus on doing research for specific projects (e.g., WebQuests).

Fluency Station. Here, students digitally or tape record passages to monitor their progress with expression, accuracy, and rate. They can practice, listen, and then graph their accuracy to show progress.

Portfolio Station. The Portfolio Station can be as simple as a shelf to store portfolios and a place for students to sit to look at their work. Keep portfolios in alphabetical order.

Word Play Station. Include at least ten books that have different kinds of word play (e.g., *Too Hot to Hoot* is composed of palindromes). Here students find examples of categories to put in their own word play books. Teachers may change the focus of the station each week. Espy's *A Child's Almanac of Words at Play* gives a different type of word play for each day of the year.

Tongue Twister Station. Post a new tongue twister each week for students to practice. When someone thinks she or he can read it five times perfectly, the teacher or another student listens, and the successful student's name is written on a "Tongue Twister Master" chart. Students can compile their own tongue twister books here.

Observation Station. A window is the perfect place for an Observation Station. Students write down what they see and are encouraged to record details. Use a common book so others can read what their classmates write. Have students date their entries.

Proud Put-Ups. Give each child wall space the size of a piece of construction paper to post whatever he or she is proud of during the week. Students are responsible for dating the items and changing them each week.

Skills and Strategy Station. This station can change according to students' needs. For example, if students are having trouble with plot order, provide a set of episode cards to arrange. Episodes can come from a common read aloud text or common independent reading.

Conference Station. To monitor a differentiated program, teachers need to meet with each child about five minutes weekly. Students may be assigned a regular day and instructed to bring a book they are reading or have just finished. Cue students to be prepared to talk about or offer

- how the book related to them
- the most important event in the book and why they chose it
- what the book was really about (big ideas)
- questions about the book that they would like to discuss
- interesting words found and added to a ring or box
- a passage to be read aloud with expression
- what they liked or disliked and tell why

During the oral reading, jot down observations of the student's needs and use this information for needs-based groupings. If the student has finished the book, discuss response options. Keep a loose-leaf notebook with a page for each child to note observations, goals, and progress.

Event #5: Writing Workshop

The writing workshop is an important focus of literacy instruction because of the strong connection between writing and reading. Both reading and writing focus on meaning making, and they have parallel three-part structures (pre-write/plan, draft, revise for writing; before, during, after for reading). Both use spelling/phonics in the service of words: spelling is important for encoding sounds in writing, and phonics is used to decode sounds of letters in reading. Writing is about expressing thoughts and feelings that take shape as they are written; comprehension is about receiving and responding to thoughts and feelings from texts others have created. Both writing and reading are about the construction of meaning.

PURPOSES

The word *workshop* is key to this event. Students are to spend most of the allocated time actually writing. They write for diverse reasons, using diverse forms and diverse tools, for diverse audiences. Ready Resource 9.1 in Chapter 9 lists many examples of diverse writing forms.

Writing workshop is a critical main event to ensure that students learn how to compose ideas and express them in the various written forms used in the world outside school. Writing is also a key tool to engage students and allow them to show comprehension before, during, and after text use within other literacy main events; writing workshop devotes time specifically to this complex skill.

GUIDELINES AND STRUCTURE

Writing workshop has a before (an introduction), a during (development), and after (conclusion) structure, just like IRA and DEIR. In the introduction, the teacher uses explicit teaching to address common needs of the whole group. Here are examples of topics for mini lessons to open a writing workshop:

- aspects of the writing process, such as how to get ideas and overcome writer's block
- traits of good writing (see Chapter 9)
- writing forms (e.g., narrative, descriptive, and persuasive)
- spelling patterns and tools (e.g., spell check functions on the computer, dictionary use, Spelling Fix-Ups (Appendix F)
- conventions for grammar, usage, capitalization, and punctuation
- mechanics (e.g., handwriting, keyboarding)

Students are then given a sustained period of time to write while the teacher conducts conferences with individuals or works with small groups who share common writing needs. The workshop ends with debriefing, which may take the form of a range of activities, from whole-group sharing to partners responding to each other's writing. Many classrooms have an author's chair, where students sit to read aloud what they have written. Peers then ask questions or give constructive feedback about the piece shared.

DIFFERENTIATION THROUGH ASSISTED WRITING

With the assistance of the teacher or technology, almost any student can learn to write clearly. The Language Experience Approach (LEA) involves a teacher writing or scribing for students as they dictate. It is frequently used in primary grades and reading clinics to show students how to translate their thoughts into written form. LEA may be used with groups or individual children. Following are suggested steps to follow in LEA.

1. Select a topic students know something about. For example, ask them to tell about a recent field trip. ("Yesterday we visited the Glendower Museum. Think about the most important things you heard and saw so we can write about them.")

2. Write down students' ideas on a chart or a white board so everyone can see what is scribed.

3. As you write, ask students to help spell some of the words that relate to teaching points you want to make. For example, point out common spelling patterns. You may also take time to discuss punctuation, capitalization, and other conventions and mechanics very briefly.

4. After each idea is scribed, ask students to choral read it with you. Repeat the choral reading as often as you feel is needed, and use a variety of fluency EAR elements. For example, "Let's read it again and group the words in phrases. Where should I put a slash mark in this sentence?"

5. When the draft is finished, ask students to think of ways to organize their ideas. For example, a LEA about a museum visit might be organized according to narrative elements and structure, in the form of a news article, or even as song lyrics. This is exactly what happened for one fifth-grade class that visited the Hunley submarine in Charleston, SC. Their LEA became "The Hunley Submarine Song," to the melody of the Beatles song "Yellow Submarine."

Other important forms of assisted writing are shared writing or co-writing and the use of speech synthesizers. *Shared writing* or *co-writing* nudges students toward independence by inviting them to spell words and actually write (in handwriting) with coaching by a teacher. Speech synthesizers allow students to dictate words to a computer, which turns them into written form in the manner of LEA.

Event #6: Content Area Embedding

 ntegration is not a 21st-century innovation. Combining academic areas for interdisciplinary study has long been considered beneficial for many reasons, one being that integration better reflects real life than isolated study. It makes sense to integrate the language arts with content areas such as science and social studies since the language arts are communication processes and need to be connected to content. One has to read *something*, write about *something*, listen to *something*, and talk about *something*. When that something is literature, science, social studies, math, or the arts, students have authentic contexts for strategy use. A treasury of big ideas waits to be discovered by students who know how to inquire into these disciplines.

The nine best comprehension practices should be integrated with one another (e.g., explicit instruction should be used to teach students how to ask good questions, discuss, and respond to texts), but the first eight best practices should also be *embedded* in main instruction events. Embedding goes further than integration. It involves ingraining processes such as the CPS process in the fabric of instruction, especially content study. Content learning doesn't just happen; it depends on students' use of comprehension strategies to derive big ideas and shape them into meaningful forms.

Integration and embedding allow teachers to "get time in a bottle." For example, in a study, when social studies and science were embedded with literacy instruction, engaged reading was extended. Students spent 40 to 120 minutes a day actively reading to learn in content areas, writing to express understanding, interpreting narratives, and using multiple texts (Guthrie, 2004). Teachers who provide comprehension strategy instruction that is deeply embedded in subject matter learning (and vice versa) foster students' comprehension development (Guthrie et al., 1998). Students learn to use strategies independently and flexibly, gradually increasing their strategy repertoires over time (Gambrell, Malloy, & Mazzoni, 2007).

GUIDELINES

Keep the following guidelines in mind when undertaking the embedding of comprehension instruction within content area study.

■ Balance embedded comprehension instruction with the teaching of the content itself. Of course, science class should not be overtaken by long lessons about how to use comprehension strategies, but there is a place during science, social studies, math, and arts study for comprehension problem-solving strategy instruction (e.g., review of a strategy introduced during literacy block). Content learning happens only when students know how to comprehend. The CPS process summarizes the thinking needed to comprehend any subject matter. The relationship between CPS and content instruction is mutually beneficial, since both target gaining knowledge and constructing meaning (RAND, 2002)

■ Embed eight comprehension best practices in both the literacy block and content area instruction. For example, read alouds and independent reading can easily be integrated or fully embedded in a science unit on plants. The content area teacher can provide explicit strategy instruction and review CPS strategies so students can more capably use texts that deal with big ideas related to plants. Important concepts in the plant unit, such as germination and photosynthesis, should be taught using best practices in building vocabulary that lead to comprehension (see Chapter 8). Discussions should follow the principles of high-level talk discussed in Chapter 7. Offer response options that will show growth in science knowledge and give responses a high learning profile by coupling them with public performances or exhibits.

■ Use content area units as meaningful contexts for students to use comprehension strategies. Explicitly teaching students how to use CPS to find and construct big ideas in social studies, science, math, and the arts can increase students' awareness of and deliberate use of strategies as means for learning (Brown, 2008). If comprehension strategies are not closely linked to knowledge and understanding in content areas, students are unlikely to learn the strategies fully, and they will be less likely to transfer use of the strategies to new texts.

UNIT TEACHING

Units are the most common way teachers structure science and social studies learning and address standards. The many types of units are distinguished by their central focus:

- people studies (e.g., authors and other notable people)
- topical studies (e.g., plants, communities)
- genre units (e.g., poetry, fairy tales)
- core work (e.g., a single book, painting, or song)

Increasingly, teachers are taking the unit center further and stating the big idea understandings to be gained up front. Big ideas help teachers plan units that are guaranteed to have important content to motivate students (Guthrie et al., 2004). Units built around studying and constructing big ideas are natural contexts for CPS use. As you develop these units, the question you need to ask is, "What is worthy of understanding?" The big ideas that emerge from the answer

Comprehension as Process and Product

Comprehension process. Embedding comprehension strategy instruction in content learning is an effective way to cause strategies to be learned to a "high level of competence" (Guthrie et al., 1998). Students become both more proficient and more self-regulated strategy users (RAND, 2002). If strategies are taught in isolation or with a narrow base of content, then students do not transfer them to new texts. In addition, interdisciplinary learning is more motivating to students, and motivation boosts comprehension.

Comprehension product. Content-embedded comprehension strategy instruction increases content understanding. It is only through thinking that students learn content, and CPS strategies cause students to think more. Students need to learn that strategies are an important means for understanding the content of texts, especially the big ideas. Strategy use is not the main point of reading: the main purpose is to make sense of texts.

to this question serve as unit centers and starting points for students' inquiry. Refer to Chapter 2 for a discussion of big ideas.

Teachers involved in planning units that target understanding big ideas find that a few ideas go a long way in organizing a year's worth of instruction. Big ideas have repeated applicability. Planning units that inquire into big ideas through important questions requires a thorough reading of content material (including standards), with an eye toward recurrent relationships and patterns that create big ideas. Ready Resource 10.11 summarizes the unit planning process.

Understanding by Design (UBD) is a popular planning process that has a big idea focus. In this process, the teacher identifies "enduring concepts" and core processes that are "transferable to new situations, have lasting value beyond the classroom, are at the heart of the discipline"(Wiggins, 2007).

Understanding by Design

www.ubdexchange.org/

www.ascd.org/research_a_topic/ Understanding_by_Design.aspx

ONLINE RESOURCES

WWW

Event #7: Performances and Exhibits

Ask adults about memorable school moments and they will talk about times they performed or put on an exhibit: sports events, band concerts, choir performances, plays, student art displays, and publications of writing. Early on, children vie for attention and want to be noticed. Schools that make public sharing of student responses a central feature of education are harnessing fierce motivational urges.

PURPOSES AND GUIDELINES

Performances and exhibits take many forms; some teachers make them integral to the daily routine, while others set a weekly schedule. I scheduled Reader's Theatre and Poetree performances each week, and both were always connected to science and social studies units. Some schools set up schoolwide unit performances and exhibits related to grading periods. At Normal Park Elementary in Chattanooga, these events are "opening nights" during which community members are invited to come enjoy students making their learning public.

The following guidelines will help you make performances and exhibits integral to comprehension instruction.

- Performances and exhibits involve both short- and long-term preparation. It takes time for students to learn how to sustain work on projects of interest within content units, and they need coaching through the selection and execution of a comprehension response that will be performed or exhibited.

- Students must be taught how to use CPS strategies to investigate a specific problem using multiple texts, including the Internet.

Big idea units: Development process.

This process is recursive, as teachers consult back and forth during the planning steps.

1 Consult standards, curriculum guides, and goals (e.g., learning about character traits in narrative text), along with key materials to be used (e.g., social studies text or multimedia materials). Have these available throughout the planning process.

2 Select a unit organizer.
- *Concept, topic, or problem:* often from science or social studies. Examples: courage, Civil War, animals
- *Core work:* a single book, poem, painting, or song
- *Genre:* study of a form. Examples: mysteries, landscapes
- *Person:* a real or fictional person
- *Event or experience:* Examples: field trip, residency

READY RESOURCE 10.11

3 State big ideas. Use the stem *"By the end of the unit students should know/understand . . ."* Write three to five full big idea statements to force complete thoughts. Example for a unit on the family:

> Families develop different traditions that reflect ancestry and culture.

Next, list three to five key important questions. Example:

> Why do families celebrate certain holidays in different ways?

Additional questions and big ideas will be solicited from students as the unit develops, and these will become important foci for learning, as well.

4 List key concepts that support the big ideas. Use resources listed in step 1. Examples:

> family roles, customs, traditions, ancestry, ancestors, relatives, culture.

Step 4 may be completed before step 3.

5 Select skills and processes. Use the stem *"By the end of the unit, students should be able to . . ."* Examples:

> . . . ask open-ended questions during discussions that lead to big-idea understandings.

> . . . create a response that shows key unit big-idea understandings and share it in a public forum.

6 Integrate and embed. Plan the use of the eight comprehension best practices and seven literacy main events to connect to the content in as many ways as possible.

7 Plan multi-factored assessment. Decide what assessments will be used, by whom, and when they will be used. Assessments should be connected to standards/goals and objectives. Examples:
- portfolios, performances, and exhibits of responses
- rubrics, checklists, and self-assessment

8 Design ways to differentiate learning for diverse student needs and interests. Refer to Chapter 4 for ten ways to differentiate instruction.

9 Create a timeline. Decide how long the unit will last, and create a flexible daily and weekly calendar of events. Set a date for culminating performances and exhibits.

10 Make lesson plans. Write key big ideas and important questions on each plan to keep them in the forefront of instruction.

- Since performances and exhibits frequently involve students in working in small groups to develop a final product, it is necessary to teach them how to cooperate. Of course, the problem solving required for cooperative group work is the heart of CPS. Many of the principles of group discussion (e.g., active listening and expert questioning) can be transferred to collaborative group work.

- Performances and exhibits are comprehension responses that can take diverse forms, ranging from poetry readings and skits to exhibits of models and artwork, songs, or PowerPoint presentations. Students need to be taught how to use a full range of responses. The response options and principles discussed in Chapter 9 are all possibilities for performances and exhibits.

Ready Resource 10.12 lists options for poetry performances that students can use to show comprehension in any content area. The following poem was written for a social studies class. The time period was the Gulf War and Dr. Seuss's poem "The Wump" was used as a pattern.

Did you ever see a scud?

I wish all scuds will be a dud.

Saddam is a man I'll call Zud.

Mr. Zud has a scud of biological mud.

So, if you don't want to be coated in chemical crud,

Stay away from the mud scud of Zud.

A poetry performance and a contribution to a class museum or display are examples of the kinds of performances and exhibits that allow students to show their understanding of big ideas. For a school or class museum, a special wall space is all that is needed. Mounting and framing student art shows it is valued. Museum plaques should accompany work, stating the artist's name and birth date, the title of the work, the media used, and the date the work was completed (Cornett, 2007). Students may prepare catalogues to go with exhibits to allow visitors to learn about the art and the artists. Students can act as "tour guides," explaining the contributions in the manner of a museum docent.

Schedule events in advance to motivate students with the expectation of the performance or exhibit date. Decisions about whether the audience will be class peers or an outside audience (e.g., other classes, principal, parents, community members) may be made by you alone or in collaboration with students. Of course, as discussed in Chapter 6, the motivational effect of an audience for these comprehension demonstrations is inestimable.

Work *with* students to develop criteria for evaluating the response products. These artifacts of learning should be judged against criteria specified in advance, as has long been the tradition in the arts. Ensure that criteria include standards for how well the medium is used and how uniquely and clearly the content is communicated. Criteria should address both the comprehension product and the use of comprehension problem solving. Use the comprehension rubric in Ready Resource 4.1 as a resource.

Poetry performance to show comprehension.

Demonstrate these options to show comprehension using poetry, or share poetry that students have written in response to texts. Rehearsal is important, especially for oral fluency. Ready Resource 8.20 in Chapter 8 provides a rubric that can be adapted for use with poetry performances.

Call and Response (echoic): Students echo the leader's expression line by line. This activity gives all students practice in fluency.

Antiphonal: Form two contrasting groups, such as high and low pitch, or loud and soft, and alternate lines or sections.

Line-a-child: Each student reads one line.

Cumulative: One student reads the first line of the poem, and more voices come in with each succeeding line. Everyone reads the last line.

Refrain with groups: Repeated lines are performed by a chorus.

Character voices: Students pretend to be a character and use appropriate vocal expression.

Narrative pantomime: Students add actions the poem suggests as a narrator reads or recites.

Sign language: Use finger spelling or American Sign Language to recite the poem.

Ostinatoes: Repeat a word or phrase that is important. For example, "Listen to the mustn'ts, child"—repeat *mustn'ts three times,* or chant it throughout the reading.

Cloze: Cover predictable words, such as end rhymes, and wait for the audience to supply them.

Reader–responder: Reader reads one line and responder improvises a reply. For example: *Reader:* Jack Sprat could eat no fat. *Responder:* He will have low cholesterol.

Reader's Theatre: Adapt the poem to a script, with parts.

Background music or art: Play music or show art or slides during the performance.

Prop poems: Add musical instruments, puppets, or objects to the performance.

Sound effects: Assign sounds for repeated words.

Question and answer: Find or write poems in question-and-answer form. For example,

> Who has seen the wind?
>
> Neither you nor I (Christina Rossetti)

Assign students to recite either the question or the answer.

Memorize and recite: Students memorize a poem and then recite it in groups. Each group changes their vocal expression by adjusting musical elements to present different interpretations.

Canon or round: Read a poem the way a round is sung, with three different groups starting on different cues.

READY RESOURCE
10.12

The type of assessment used in the arts can inform classroom practice. This assessment begins with clear indicators of the kind and degree of accomplishment that is expected. Assessment of performances and exhibits should likewise begin with clear expectations. The full range of assessment tools discussed in Chapter 4 is available for assessment of performances and exhibits, including rubrics and checklists that may be used by both students and the teacher.

Conclusion

We all know the importance of routines: bathe every day, brush your teeth after eating, change the sheets on Saturday. No one would expect much from an exercise program that consisted of an occasional workout, and if bathing and brushing didn't happen on a regular schedule, well, friends are only so tolerant. Literacy is more complicated than hygiene, but its attainment also depends on routines. That's why educators have long exhorted parents to read aloud to children, not now and then, but every day. Teachers, for decades, have been taught to plan independent reading time—daily, not just on a special reading day if the "real work" gets done.

We as teachers are better educated now about literacy development than ever before. However, we may not be doing the right things often enough and in the manner that will produce the greatest gains. The purpose of this chapter was to help teachers do more right things more often and to make critical refinements that put comprehension first, beginning with time apportionment. This chapter dealt with the difficult matter of how to organize and structure instructional time to implement comprehension best practices. Seven main literacy routines were discussed, which cut across the cycles in instruction that have whipped teachers from pillar to pole. The routines are time honored, research based, and workable for students making expected progress as well as those encountering difficulties.

These main instructional routines will not solve all literacy problems, and they cannot be in place on day one. They do reflect the ideal of putting comprehension first. All of the comprehension best practices were wrapped into a vision of instruction that starts each day with a focus on motivation and problem solving. In particular, the emphasis on embedding comprehension instruction in content areas and on using content units to structure read alouds and independent reading addresses the long-standing need for instruction to reflect life. In the real world, the engine of inquiry runs the comprehension process-solving process, and the desired product is big ideas. So it should be in the classroom.

Congratulations: you are now a graduate of Comprehension First!

10 big ideas

CHAPTER

Use the following examples to synthesize your own high-priority big ideas about how to organize instructional main events that are embedded with best comprehension practices.

1. Comprehension best practices should be integrated with one another and embedded in literacy events and content units.
2. Real-life work integrates process and content, with a focus on problem solving.

3. Seven main events stand out in their potential to increase student interaction and engagement with diverse texts.

4. There are many ways to design best practice implementation.

CHAPTER 10 response options

1. List your own big ideas and compare them with the list of important questions at the start of the chapter.

2. Return to the opening important questions to check your understanding of the seven main literacy events.

3. Design and present a five-minute opening literacy routine to a small group.

4. Create a PowerPoint presentation or choose another format to present the what, why, and how of DEIR and IRA.

5. In a small group, discuss ways to embed a science or social studies lesson with DEIR, IRA, and performances/exhibits.

6. Plan a literacy block schedule that includes the seven main events and integrates the other eight best practices.

7. Make a prioritized list of possible comprehension learning centers.

8. Visit an arts-based school that holds regular performances and exhibits, or visit the websites of schools like Normal Park in Chattanooga, www.normalparkmuseummagnet.com, and Ashley River Creative Arts in Charleston, SC, http://ashleyriver.ccsdschools.com.

CHILDREN'S LITERATURE CITED

Bunting. E. (1992). *The wall.* Boston: Clarion.

Bunting, E. (1993). *Fly away home.* Boston: Clarion.

Burnford, S. (1996). *The incredible journey.* New York: Delacorte.

DiCamillo, K. (2000). *Because of Winn-Dixie.* Cambridge, MA: Candlewick Press.

Espy, W. (1998). *A children's almanac of words at play.* New York: Clarkson Potter.

Jukes, M. (1987). *Like Jake and me.* Albuquerque, NM: Dragonfly.

Lowry, L. (1997). *The giver.* New York: Scholastic.

Paulsen, G. (1999). *Hatchet.* New York: Aladdin.

Terban, M. (1985). *Too hot to hoot.* Boston: Houghton Mifflin.

Tsuchiya, Y. (1997). *Faithful elephants.* Boston: Houghton Mifflin.

Viorst, J. (1987). *The tenth good thing about Barney.* New York: Aladdin.

Volaukova, H. (1994). *I never saw another butterfly.* New York: Schocken.

Yashima, T. (1955). *Crow boy.* New York: Viking.

Appendices

Directions: This inventory can be used to

- conduct a one-on-one interview
- create an inventory for students to complete independently
- do circle discussions or warm-ups

Name/nickname _____ Interviewer _____ Date _____

Birthday _____ Favorite colors _____

Favorite foods _____

People in home _____

Books owned _____

Hobbies and/or collections _____

Computer background _____

1. What do you know a lot about? What could you teach to someone else?

   _____

2. What would you like to learn more about?

   _____

3. What makes you laugh?

   _____

4. Who are your closest friends?

   _____

5. What do you do with your friends?

   _____

6. Where have you lived?

   _____

7. Where have you traveled?

   _____

8. What kinds of things do you like to write?

   _____

9. What do you like to make? (e.g., art projects, cooking, models)

   _____

(continued)

SENTENCE COMPLETION:

1. At home I spend most of my time . . .

   _____

2. Something I think is really fun is . . .

   _____

3. Something I don't like to do is . . .

   _____

4. One thing I do well is . . .

   _____

5. I wish . . .

   _____

6. Sports are . . .

   _____

7. Animals are . . .

   _____

8. A person I admire is . . .

   _____

9. I like the television show (or movie) . . .

   _____

10. I use the computer to . . .

    _____

11. I like to read about . . .

    _____

12. I like to write about . . .

    _____

13. The best thing about school is . . .

    _____

14. I wish my teacher . . .

    _____

(continued)

15. If I could do anything I wanted to, I would . . .

_____

16. I'd like to visit _____, because . . .

_____

17. I want to be _____ when I grow up, because . . .

_____

18. What else can you tell me that would help me teach you?

_____

SUMMARY:

What interests stand out?

_____

_____

What would most likely motivate this student?

_____

_____

What needs did you identify?

_____

_____

INTERVIEW: PARENTS

1. What can you tell me about _____ (child)'s background in learning to read, both at home and at school?

   _____

2. What is she or he interested in?

   _____

3. What does he or she do well?

   _____

4. What difficulties does she or he have with reading?

   _____

5. What have you tried with him or her? What has helped the most?

   _____

6. What does he or she do when he or she has trouble during reading?

   _____

7. What kinds of reading materials are available at home?

   _____

8. Does he or she have a library card? How often does he or she go to the library?

   _____

9. Does she or he have access to a computer? How is it used?

   _____

10. Is there a place at home for him or her to work quietly?

    _____

11. How often do you personally read?

    _____

12. What would most help her or him?

    _____

13. What else would you like me to know about him or her?

    _____

(continued)

Name _____   Date _____

INTERVIEW: PREVIOUS TEACHER

1. What is _____ interested in?

    _____

2. What do you think she or he needs most?

    _____

3. What else would help me teach him or her?

    _____

4. What do you teach students about the goals of reading?

    _____

5. On what aspects of reading do you spend most of time?

    _____

6. How do you teach comprehension?

    _____

7. Do you teach comprehension strategies? If so, which ones?

    _____

8. What has worked to help students who struggle with comprehension?

    _____

9. What role does motivation play in the problems of your struggling readers?

    _____

10. How do you try to motivate your students?

    _____

11. What materials do you use to teach reading?

    _____

12. How is reading instruction organized?

    _____

13. What comprehension assessments do you use?

    _____

Name _____   Date _____

1. What does it mean to solve a problem?

   _____

2. When have you solved a problem?

   _____

3. How is reading like solving a problem?

   _____

4. What does it mean to make sense of something?

   _____

5. What does it mean to comprehend?

   _____

6. How do you think when you read?

   _____

7. How do you know if you have understood something?

   _____

8. What would you tell someone to do if she or he didn't understand what she or he was reading?

   _____

9. What do good readers do before reading? During reading? After reading?

   _____

10. What do *you* do before you read to get ready to comprehend?

    _____

11. What do *you* do during reading to comprehend?

    _____

12. What are ways you can show you understand or comprehend?

    _____

Name _____   Date _____

BEFORE *reading, viewing, or listening to a text*

Purpose-set and motivate.

1. What are the main reasons or purposes to read?
   _____

2. How can you get interested in a book?
   _____

Predict and connect (to self, to other texts, to the world).

1. Why would you look through a book or story before reading it?
   _____

2. What would you look for in a book overview?
   _____

3. What are different ways books and texts are organized? What would you expect in the beginning of a book or chapter? In the middle? At the end?
   _____

4. How would you think differently during reading a story versus a science book?
   _____

5. How is fiction different from nonfiction?
   _____

6. Why would you think about what you already know about a topic before starting to read a text about it?
   _____

7. How can you tell what a text or book might be about before reading it?
   _____

8. What does it mean to connect what you know to what you read? Why would you try to do that?
   _____

DURING: *Data gathering by taking and making meaning*

Determine important ideas.

1. How can you figure out what the author's most important ideas are?
   _____

(continued)

2. What are big ideas?

_____

3. What in the text helps you find or create big ideas?

_____

Infer conclusions.

1. What does it mean to infer conclusions?

_____

2. What does it mean to predict?

_____

Image.

1. When you read, do you make pictures in your head?

_____

2. What other senses do you use when you read? What else happens in your brain?

_____

Question and wonder.

1. What are the Five W + H questions? How can you use them during reading?

_____

2. What does it mean to confirm or reject predictions?

_____

Monitor.

1. How do you know if what you are reading is making sense? If what you are reading is not making sense, what can you do?

_____

2. What can you do if you don't know a word?

_____

Analyze/critique.

1. How does it help to zoom in on details?

_____

(continued)

2. How do text features and structure (e.g., story elements or paragraph structures) help comprehension?

_____

3. How are text details related to big ideas?

_____

Incubate.

1. Why might it help to take time out from reading and then come back to it?

_____

AFTER _reading, viewing, or listening to a text_

Summarize and synthesize.

1. How do you decide what a book or text is really about? (final big ideas, themes, generalizations, conclusions)

_____

Organize and shape.

1. What is an example of how you have used big ideas from a text to create something?

_____

2. How can you put ideas from a book together to show you understand the book?

_____

Reflect and revise.

1. What can you do if what you write or create from a text doesn't work or make sense?

_____

Publish.

1. What are ways to share your comprehension with others? Why would you do that?

_____

Name _____ Date _____

BEFORE *reading, viewing, or listening to a text, the student*

Purpose-sets and is motivated

- ☐ Explains that the purpose of reading is to make sense
- ☐ Can give specific reasons to read (e.g., for information or pleasure)

Predicts and connects (to self, to other texts, to the world)

- ☐ Does an overview of the text to see how it is organized (structure and features)
- ☐ Compares text with other texts and personal background
- ☐ Connects previous knowledge to the problem or topic
- ☐ Predicts information the text might provide

DURING: *Data gathering by taking and making meaning from the text*

Determines important ideas

- ☐ Explains the author's big ideas and gives support

Infers conclusions

- ☐ Constructs his or her own big ideas and gives evidence to support the conclusions (facts or details)

Images

- ☐ Describes mental images constructed from texts, as well as other sensory images

Questions and wonders

- ☐ Confirms or rejects predictions and makes new predictions and connections

Monitors

- ☐ Checks to make sure the text is making sense. If not, uses comprehension repair strategies and word fix-ups.

(continued)

Analyzes/critiques

- ☐ Zooms in and out to notice important words, text features, and structure (e.g., story elements or paragraph structures)
- ☐ Relates details to the big ideas

Incubates

- ☐ Takes time out to review and reconsider

Summarizes and synthesizes

- ☐ Pulls together big ideas, themes, generalizations, conclusions

AFTER *reading, viewing, or listening to a text*

Organizes and shapes

- ☐ Organizes big ideas into a form that is coherent

Reflects and revises

- ☐ Evaluates the product for what works or makes sense
- ☐ Makes changes to improve the product

Publishes

- ☐ Shares the comprehension product

BEFORE *reading, viewing, or listening to a text*

Purpose-set and motivate:

- What's the problem?
- Why am I using this text?

Predict and connect (to self, to other texts, to the world). Overview the text and activate prior knowledge.

- How is the text organized?
- What do I already know about this problem or topic?
- What information might this text provide?

DURING: *Data gathering by taking and making meaning*

Determine important ideas.

- What does the author want me to think?
- What do I think are the big ideas? What evidence supports these ideas (facts or details)?

Infer conclusions. Use clues to decide.

- What do I predict?

Image. Use all five senses. Explore and experiment.

- What images can I make in my head?

Question and wonder. Ask yourself the Five W + H questions.

- What predictions are confirmed?
- Rejected?
- What new predictions and connections can I make?

Monitor.

- Is this making sense?
- If not, which Comprehension or Word Fix-Ups should I use?

Analyze/critique. Zoom in and zoom out. Notice text features and structure (e.g., story elements or paragraph structures).

- What are the important details?
- How are the details related to the big ideas?

(continued)

Incubate. Take time out, then review and reconsider.

Summarize and synthesize.

- What are the final big ideas, themes, generalizations, conclusions?

AFTER *reading, viewing, or listening to a text*

Organize and shape.

- How can I pull the big ideas together to show the meaning I've made?

Reflect and revise.

- What works or makes sense?
- What doesn't work?
- How can I make it better?

Publish.

- How can I share my comprehension product?
- With whom? When and where?

Sources: Baker & Brown, 1984; Block & Pressley, 2007; Cordón & Day, 1996; National Reading Panel Report, 2000; Pearson & Dole, 1987; Pearson & Fielding, 1991; Pressley & Afflerbach, 1995; RAND, 2002.

BEFORE *reading, viewing, or listening to a text*

Purpose-set. Create motivation, by focusing on the goal of comprehension.

- What's the problem? Why am I using this text?

Predict and connect. Overview the text to activate prior knowledge. Link the text to your own experiences, to other texts, and to what you know about the world.

- What is the text like, and how is the text organized?
- What do I already know about this problem or topic?
- What information or experiences do I predict this text will provide?

DURING: *Gathering data by taking and making meaning from the text*

Determine important concepts. Use text clues as evidence.

- What does the author want me to think? Why?
- What do I think are key concepts or topics that might lead to big ideas?
- What facts or details (evidence) make me think these concepts or topics are key?

Infer conclusions. Use previous evidence to decide.

- What do I predict so far?

Image. Use your imagination to think about the text.

- What visual images can I make in my head?
- What feelings, smells, tastes, and sounds do I connect to the text?

Question and wonder. Speculate by questioning.

- Ask the Five W + H questions (who, what, when, where, why, and how).
- What predictions about important ideas are confirmed? Which ones should be rejected?
- What new predictions can I make about what is most important in the text?
- What new connections can I make (text–self, text–text, text–world)?

Monitor. Check whether you are making sense.

- Am I understanding? If not . . .
- Which Comprehension or Word Fix-Ups should I use? (See Ready Resources 5.5 and 8.11).

(continued)

Analyze/critique. Zoom in–zoom out. Use text features and structures.

- If the text is narrative: What do I know about the characters? What are the problems? Where and when is the story happening? How are problems being resolved? What themes are emerging?
- If the text is expository: How is it organized (e.g., sequential, cause/effect, comparison)?
- If the text is non-verbal: What stands out? How does the text feel? Why?
- Overall: What are the important details and features? How are they related to the big ideas I'm finding and creating?

Incubate. Take time out.

- How can I take a break so I can review and reconsider from a fresh perspective?

Synthesize. Pull big ideas together.

- What are the most important concepts, themes or generalizations, and conclusions?
- What big idea statements are most important?

AFTER *reading, viewing, or listening to a text*

Organize and shape. Transform the big ideas.

- How can I best show my understanding of the most important big ideas?

Reflect and revise. Think about the comprehension product.

- What works or makes sense? What doesn't work?
- How can I better show my comprehension?

Publish. Make your comprehension public.

- How can I share my comprehension "product"? With whom? When? Where?

Sources: Baker & Brown, 1984; Block & Pressley, 2007; Cordón & Day, 1996; National Reading Panel, 2000; Pearson & Dole, 1987; Pearson & Fielding, 1991; Pressley & Afflerbach, 1995; Pressley et al., 1989; RAND, 2002.

TEXT–LEARNER MATCH

Consider these factors when deciding whether a book is appropriate for a particular student.

- *Maturity level:* What cognitive and emotional development assumptions are made by the text?
- *Conceptual difficulty* (ideas behind words): How much and what kind of background experience is assumed by the author? How densely packed are the concepts?
- *Vocabulary:* Are most of the words decodable using a combination of context and phonics? How many multisyllabic and affixed words are used? Is there repetition of words/phrases and ideas?
- *Structure/genre (pattern):* Is the text narrative (story) or expository (primarily meant to convey information)?
- *Features:* Which of the following are present to help the reader: table of contents, index, glossary, subheads, graphs, pictures, summaries?
- *Language/sentence structure:* How many sentences are on each page? What kinds of sentences are used (mostly simple or complex)?
- *Style/language:* Is the word usage familiar and natural, or is it more literary?
- *Predictability:* How easy it is to anticipate the language use, character actions, plot, and theme?
- *Length:* How long is the text?
- *Layout:* How much print is on each page? Is the font size appropriate? Are the words consistently in the same place, or is there variance?
- *Punctuation/capitalization:* Are uncommon marks used, such as ellipses or unconventional capitalization?
- *Format:* Is the text print only, or are visual art and music integrated, as in web-based texts, CD-ROMs, and picture books?
- *Art/illustrations:* Do art and illustrations match the text message or extend it? How much detail do they provide?
- *Readability level:* See Appendix C.3 for Lexile information and a correlation chart.
- *Purpose:* Does the author's purpose match the student's purpose or reason for using the text?

LEARNER INTERSECT

- How much does the student know about the topic?
- How familiar are the genre and format?
- How interested is the student in the text?
- How much does the student know about using text features?
- How much of the vocabulary is familiar to the student?
- Is the length appropriate?

The following is an example of how a school can organize books by using colored tape plus a number on each book's binder. Books were leveled using

- teacher judgment.
- bibliographies (e.g., *Guided Reading*, which shows instructional level).
- publishers' catalogues.
- readability formula, e.g., Flesch Kincaid on Microsoft Word (*independent levels*).
- lexile.com.

COLOR	RDG. RECOVERY	GUIDED READING*	GRADE LEVELS	LEXILE**
1 red	1	A	K/1	‹200
2 red	2	B	K/1	‹200
3 red	3–4	C	1	200–300
1 yellow	5–6	D	1	200–300
2 yellow	7–8	E	1	200–300
3 yellow	9–10	F	1	200–300
1 green	11–12	G	1	300–300
2 green	13–14	H	1	300–400
3 green	15–16	I	1 (late)	400
1 blue	17–28	J	2 (early)	400–500
2 blue	19–20	K	2	400–500
3 blue	21	L	2	400–500
1 orange	22	M	2	400–500
2 orange	—	N	3	500–700
3 orange	—	O	3	500–700
1 black	—	P	3	500–700
2 black	—	Q	4 (early)	700–800
3 black	—	R	4 (late)	700–800

(continued)

COLOR	RDG. RECOVERY	GUIDED READING*	GRADE LEVELS	LEXILE**
—	—	S, T	5–6	800–1000
—	—	—	6	900–1000
—	—	—	7	960–1050
—	—	—	8	1050–1090
—	—	—	9	1050–1100
—	—	—	10	1100–1180
—	—	—	11	1120–1200
—	—	—	12	1200–1300
—	—	—	college 1–2	1230–1400
—	—	—	college 3–4	1280–1410
—	—	—	GRADUATE	1480–1700

*Pinnell, G. and Fountas, I. (1998). *Guided Reading*. Portsmouth, NH: Heinemann.

**(1995). *The Lexile Framework*. Durham, NC: Metametrics. 75 percent comprehension and 90 percent word accuracy.

Lexiles are a measure of text difficulty calculated by a computer program. Text factors considered are semantic (word meaning) and syntactic (sentence structure) complexity. Lexile levels assume a need for 75 percent comprehension and 90 percent word accuracy to read a book.

Learners may also be assigned Lexile numbers, allowing the learners to be generally matched with texts. Many standardized tests are linked to the Lexile Framework, including the SAT and Stanford 9 Achievement Tests. A student at 900 Lexiles, for example, should look at 900-level titles, such as *The Red Badge of Courage* and *Huckleberry Finn*.

Tens of thousands of books have been assigned Lexile levels, and publishers sometimes print the Lexile on the book. Examples include:

Frog and Toad All Year: 210

Ira Sleeps Over: 310

Sarah, Plain and Tall: 540

How to Eat Fried Worms: 690

Boy Scout Manual: 780

Sounder: 830

The Lion, the Witch and the Wardrobe: 920

USA Today: 1080

Most newspapers: about 1200 (*New York Times* and *Washington Post* are higher)

Little Women: 1100

Scholastic Aptitude Test (SAT): 1200

1040 tax instructions: 1240

US News and World Report: 1300

Work manuals (how-to guides): 1400

Gettysburg Address: 1480

Declaration of Independence: 1570

New England Journal of Medicine: 1630

Rate the degree to which you do each of the following. Use a scale from 0 to 5, with 5 being "I do it all the time." Give examples to support high ratings.

LEARNER

_____ I assess to identify learner strengths and needs, including CPS strategies.

_____ I design instruction to capitalize on learner strengths and address identified comprehension needs.

TASK OF COMPREHENSION

_____ I teach a definition of reading that is synonymous with comprehension.

_____ I teach comprehension as a problem-solving process to make meaning from verbal and non-verbal texts.

_____ I teach students to find and construct their own big ideas.

TEXTS

_____ I use a wide variety of quality fiction and nonfiction print texts (e.g., narrative, informational, poetry).

_____ I select texts that coordinate with science and social studies units, match student interests and background, and are of appropriate difficulty.

_____ I match texts with students to facilitate their comprehension.

_____ I teach students to comprehend non-verbal and multimedia texts.

CLASSROOM CONTEXT

_____ I create a safe psychological classroom climate for problem solving and a stimulating physical environment that invites students to work collaboratively to solve problems.

TEACHER

_____ I show enthusiasm for reading diverse texts.

_____ I believe comprehension is a problem-solving process that focuses on extracting and constructing meaning.

_____ I use the Comprehension Problem Solving process when I read, and I share with my students examples of when, how, and why I do this.

TEACHING: BEST COMPREHENSION PRACTICES

_____ I integrate best practices with one another and embed the first eight practices in the ninth:

_____ I use varied assessments to plan differentiated instruction.

(continued)

_____ I focus on big ideas (comprehension product).

_____ I teach inquiry-based problem solving (CPS process).

_____ I explicitly teach comprehension strategies (CPS) and key literacy concepts, including text characteristics.

_____ I use motivation and engagement to increase comprehension.

_____ I use and teach expert questioning to promote "high-level" talk: conversations and discussions.

_____ I teach words and fluency _for_ comprehension.

_____ I teach diverse response options to show comprehension: written, arts-based, and digital texts.

_____ I embed best comprehension practices in literacy main events and content teaching:

    1. opening and closing literacy routines

    2. interactive read aloud (IRA)

    3. daily engaged independent reading (DEIR)

    4. small-group and independent work (e.g., centers)

    5. writing workshop

    6. content units: science, social studies, and math

    7. performances and exhibits

TEACHERS SHOULD NOT . . .

Set low-level goals

- implicitly or explicitly define reading as pronouncing words, answering literal questions, and recalling through retelling.
- neglect to make the comprehension goal clear.

Give ineffective assignments

- assign independent reading without a discussion of purposes.
- use oral or written questions *after* reading that students did not know about *before* reading.
- fail to give choices about what to read, when, or where.
- assume that if students "just read" a lot, their comprehension will improve.

Use technology poorly

- use computer software that is little more than an electronic worksheet (RAND, 2002).

Use bad timing

- delay instruction in comprehension strategies until students are fluent in decoding (pronouncing words quickly and accurately).
- assume primary students cannot do higher-order thinking; ask only literal questions that require memory of story facts and explicit main ideas.

Provide ineffective instruction

- limit decoding instruction to phonics and assume phonics skill ensures comprehension.
- drill students on sight words with cards and word sheets.
- provide independent reading time for the whole class without clear purposes *before* and follow-up *after* reading time.
- use "round robin reading": calling on students in turn for cold unprepared read alouds, usually in front of other students.
- use only whole-class instruction.
- routinely start discussions with "Did you like the story?"

Offer no or low strategy instruction

- assume that question asking and testing are ways to *teach* comprehension.
- assume the meaning is in the text or on the page, not connected to the reader's prior knowledge and ability to make meaning.

(continued)

- tell students to use a comprehension strategy (e.g., "Let's make a prediction from the picture") without explicitly teaching them *how, when,* and *where* to use it.
- model a comprehension strategy in isolation and expect students to apply it in context (i.e., assume automatic transfer).
- explicitly teach specific comprehension strategies but neglect to teach *when* and *where* to apply them.
- correct oral reading too often and interrupt unnecessarily (with regard to comprehension).

Misuse texts

- assume all texts are equal, without considering students' background or interests.
- use fiction and narrative texts exclusively in kindergarten and first grade.
- confine reading to decodable and leveled texts.

Misuse assessment

- neglect to assess students' interests and connect instruction to their interests.
- assign paper or computerized worksheet-type practice, which focuses on questions with one right answer.
- focus on plot retellings and recall of character names and actions instead of big ideas, such as literary themes.
- use limited ways to assess comprehension, such as filling in blanks, writing short answers to literal questions, computerized multiple choice tests, or plot retellings.
- assess comprehension after reading and assume this assessment is instructive.
- test too often (e.g., every story or book).
- focus on testing word accuracy and rate to assess fluency.

Misuse questioning

- ask most of the questions instead of teaching students how to select questions in the before, during, and after stages of reading and generate their own questions.

Neglect content

- neglect to cause students to transfer comprehension strategies to content learning.

If you can't spell a word . . .

- Write down all the sounds you hear.
- Write the beginning and ending sounds. Example: H___ ___ T
- Write it different ways to see which one looks right.
- If it still looks wrong, circle it and look it up later.
- Use a synonym or draw a picture.
- Check the dictionary or word wall.
- If none of the above work, ask someone.

SPELLING STUDY STEPS

1. Look at the word and say it carefully.
2. Spell it aloud in a pattern. Example: *bus i ness*
3. Picture the spelling.
4. Cover the word and write it yourself.
5. Check your spelling.
6. Correct your spelling.
7. Repeat until you can write the word three times correctly.

SPELLING TIPS

- *Rhyme:* Link the word with one spelled with the same pattern. Example: *unless* and *mess*
- *Problem spots:* Mask the rest of the word so the hard spot is all you see, and really look at the letter order. Spell the part out loud. Write it in another color.
- *Mnemonics* (memory aids): Use these to remember hard words. Create your own! Examples:

    Tell the *mosquito* to *quit* biting me.

    I before E except after C, as in *receive.*

    The *principal* is my *pal.*

    There is a "*rat*" in se*parate.*

    Take the "*bus*" to your *business.*

- *Meaning pairs:* Pair the word with a related word you know. Examples: *act–action, mean–meant*
- *Group:* Chunk letters in twos and threes. Examples: *re pet i tion, nec ess ary*
- *Pronounce:* Spell out loud to hear the letter names. Examples: *Feb ru ary, bus i ness*

SCIENCE STANDARDS (National Science Teachers Association [NSTA], www.nsta.org)

Standards are organized around:

1. Unifying Concepts and Processes
2. Science as Inquiry (find out how and why things happen through careful observation, data gathering, hypothesis making, prediction, and experimentation)
3. Physical Science
4. Life Science
5. Earth and Space Science
6. Science and Technology
7. Science in Personal and Social Perspectives
8. History and Nature of Science

SOCIAL STUDIES STANDARDS (National Council for the Social Studies [NCSS], www.Socialstudies.org)

The standards are:

1. Culture
2. Time, Continuity, and Change
3. People, Places, and Environment
4. Individual Development and Identity
5. Individuals, Groups, and Institutions
6. Power, Authority, and Governance
7. Production, Distribution, and Consumption
8. Science, Technology, and Society
9. Global Connections
10. Civic Ideals and Practices

Important ideas: relationships among human beings, use of natural resources, investigations into cultural diversity and global understanding

Special questions: How did it used to be and why? Why is it like it is today? What can I do about it?

Important thinking processes: use cause and effect, sequence, gather data, discover relationships, make judgments, draw conclusions, problem solve about issues

Use of primary source material such as newspapers, art, music, diaries, letters, journals, books, and artifacts, rather than textbooks, and gathering data through interviews, surveys, and other investigatory strategies social scientists use

(continued)

MATH STANDARDS (National Council of Teachers of Mathematics [NCTM], www.nctm.org)

Goals are established in the content areas of:

1. Number and operations
2. Algebra
3. Geometry
4. Measurement
5. Data analysis and probability

The standards also describe goals for the processes of:

1. Problem solving
2. Reasoning and proof
3. Connections
4. Communication
5. Representation

Instruction targets concepts and processes such as:

- Daily living situations involving counting, measuring, probability, statistics, geometry, logic, patterns, functions, and numbers
- Problem solving through the use of skills (e.g., raising questions and answering them, finding relationships and patterns)
- Concepts about numbers and operations, and concepts such as bigger, longer, greater than, less than, even, and odd

ARTS STANDARDS (music, visual art, theatre/drama, and dance)

The *National Standards for Arts Education* is available from The National Association for Music Education, 1806 Robert Fulton Drive, Reston, VA 20191 (www.menc.org; 800-336-3768). The arts are basically communication vehicles (Larson, 1997) that focus on creating, responding, and performing. The arts standards address content. Standards in each area deal with comprehension of the body of content and essential use of materials, techniques, and tools.

ENGLISH LANGUAGE ARTS STANDARDS (National Council of Teachers of English [NCTE], www.ncte.org, and the International Reading Association [IRA], www.reading.org)

See Ready Resource 9.2 for a summary.

The ability to focus and control attention by concentrating is invaluable. Teach students to concentrate by

1. clarifying what it means to concentrate by defining it, demonstrating, and giving examples and non-examples.

2. discussing its importance in life.

3. setting a goal for students to improve their concentration (target on-task behavior).

4. giving frequent descriptive feedback to encourage their inclination to concentrate.

5. frequently using warm-ups, attention-getters, and games that target developing concentration, followed by debriefing discussions about their progress.

Attention Getter: Use signals that remind students about concentrating. The following chant may be done chorally with motions:

> 5-6-7-8
> Pay attention, Concentrate, Focus!

Invite students to create motions for "attention," "concentrate," and "focus."

Balloon Body: Tell students to imagine their bodies are like balloons. Talk them through the following warm-up:

> Imagine someone is blowing you up. You are expanding and getting bigger and bigger. Feel yourself become lighter. While staying in your personal space, float up. Oops, you have developed a slow leak. You are beginning to lose air and slowly shrink. You get smaller and smaller. Now you are going limp. You melt down and sit in your space.

Debrief by asking students what happened in their heads and what they can share about keeping their focus.

Imaginary Balls: Form a circle and designate one person the leader. The leader holds an imaginary ball (show its size with hands) and calls someone's name before throwing it, saying, "Bob, baseball." The receiver says, "Thank you, baseball." The receiver now calls a name and throws the pretend baseball. After a few throws, the leader interrupts with a second ball, saying, "Julie, ping pong ball," and Julie responds, "Thank you, ping pong ball." Continue to add more balls as appropriate to the group's ability. At the end, call "stop" and ask everyone with a ball to hold it. The class guesses the kind of ball each person is holding by its size and how it is held. Each time this game is played more balls can be added, if students grow in concentration.

Sock It to Me: You will need two clean socks, each tied in a knot. Stand in a circle. Say your name and the name of a student, then throw one sock to that

(continued)

student. For example, say, "Claudia to Colette." Then Colette chooses another student and throws the sock to him or her. As soon is the sock is being passed in a smooth fashion, introduce the second sock by saying your name and a student's name. For example, say, "Claudia to Charles." Play proceeds, but now there are two socks in motion. The challenge is to concentrate on hearing your name called so you can catch the sock. At any point the leader can call "stop."

Remember: Assemble a tray of five objects. Direct students to concentrate and picture the objects in their heads for one minute. Cover the tray. Ask students to partner up and list all they remember. This game has many variations. For example, over time more objects can be added, students can close their eyes while an object is removed, or objects can be rearranged to challenge participants' memory. This game can also be played in teams. With small wipe-off boards, students can write down items and then show the boards on a signal.

Word by Word: Sit in a circle. The leader says one word to start a sentence. The next person says the next word, and so on. This requires concentration to make as long a sentence as possible that actually makes sense.

No N Stories: Sit in a circle. The leader starts a story about anything, and the person to the left picks up the story and carries it forward. The hitch is that no words can contain the letter N. If a person uses an N, the story must begin again. The goal is to tell a story that makes sense and get it all the way around the circle. *Variation:* Choose another consonant to prohibit.

Change Up: Pair students and ask them to face each other and choose to be A or B. A concentrates on details of B's appearance for one minute, then the leader signals time and the pairs turn back to back. B makes a change in her appearance. The pairs turn around, and A gets three guesses to figure out what was changed. Then it's B's turn.

Mirror Images: Brainstorm a list of people or characters. Ask students to line up in two facing lines or in a double circle. Partners face each other. Partner A pretends to be a character or real person, and B becomes A's mirror. The goal is for the pair to align their actions so that an observer can't tell the "real" from the "reflection." Start in slow motion. For example, Student A pretends to be Red Riding Hood getting ready to go to Grandma's house. After a while, the pairs switch roles.

Rewind: Sit in a circle. Agree on a story everyone knows, such as "The Three Little Pigs" or a recent shared book. Explain that the idea of this game is to tell the story backward, starting at the end. Tell the story backward.

(continued)

Jumping Beans: Students find a personal space. The teacher pretends to open a can of jumping beans and tells students to get ready to catch them. Toss the imaginary beans and direct students to catch and eat them. Now they are full of jumping beans and have to keep jumping in their space. On "freeze," the students stop. Repeat with half the class being the audience who gives feedback to those who focus and control their bodies with the most skill. Then reverse halves.

Silent Sounds: Brainstorm ways to pantomime sounds. For example, mime applauding, laughing, yelling, or coughing. Ask students to divide one of the sounds into three consecutive actions (e.g., the steps in a sneeze). Next, form small groups and have each plan a three-part pantomime of a sound to perform in slow motion. Groups perform for the class, and the audience gives feedback on the evidence of concentration they see.

Hand Focus: Partner students. One moves his or her hand and the other must keep her or his eyes on the hand, no matter what it does. The person moving the hand should move it at different speeds and levels. After a minute, change places.

Slow-Mo Concentration: Each student picks an everyday continuing movement, such as washing dishes, vacuuming, or setting the table. On signal, everyone performs the action in slow motion and continues until the leader says "stop." *Variations:* (1) Students choose three actions and number them 1, 2, and 3. When the leader calls a number, the student starts that motion and continues until the leader calls another number or says "freeze." (2) Split the class in half and have one half perform while the other observes and gives feedback about concentration. Reverse roles.

Hop and Pop: On signal, students walk around the room, trying to fill the space. When the leader signals "one," each student chooses a person to track with his or her eyes. Students keep walking, and whenever they come near the chosen person, they hop. Next, the leader says "two," and each student must track a second person, while still tracking the first. When the second person is passed by, students must say "pop" and freeze for a split-second. Everyone is now walking around hopping and popping.

As the students grow better able to sustain engagement, you can be more flexible. For example, the 30-minutes-a-day goal can be achieved by small groups reading independently while you work with one group on some aspect of comprehension. Emphasize the importance of DEIR by continuing to personally participate; maintain a schedule by which the class reads together at least once a week. This will likely happen during second semester, after students have established concentration and focus skills.

Children should not hear poor oral reading. It is discordant for the ear and presents a distorted concept of what reading is.

MARY HARBAGE

The following strategies are recommended for appropriate oral reading practice:

1. Use repeated reading strategies that focus on meaning making and sharing meaning through oral reading with an audience (e.g., Reader's Theatre).

2. Partner children and let them read chorally or in parts (e.g., read dialogue or just take turns).

3. Let a good reader read to a poorer reader while the poorer reader follows and "chimes" in for words he or she knows (neurological impress method).

4. The teacher or a good reader reads aloud while children follow with the tips of their fingers or a marker.

5. The teacher or a good oral reader reads a line and children echo, while following along with a finger. This also presents a model for the use of musical elements.

6. Each child chooses a part of the story, practices reading it, records it, and listens to it.

7. Have a child read aloud to the teacher alone (usually used for diagnostic purposes).

8. The teacher reads aloud the beginning of the story as children follow along, and the children finish reading silently.

9. Each child reads silently but prepares to read an important portion aloud to the group. The teacher asks purpose-setting questions that can be answered by reading aloud the part of the story that is the answer. Example:

    Read aloud the part that tells . . .

    what the main character was like.

    what the place was like where the story happened.

    how the problem of the story was solved.

    the most exciting, puzzling, or connecting-to-your-life part.

10. Give children purpose-setting questions before reading and then have a discussion after the reading. A discussion is a form of oral expression, as is oral reading, and this type of discussion focuses on teaching comprehension, since students prepare for the discussion by thinking about the questions as they read.

11. Have each child rehearse by reading aloud to the wall. Show them how to put a pencil check above unknown words but continue reading with the intent of getting the general gist of the story. They can study the checked words after the reading.

(continued)

12. Have parents, older students, or volunteers record stories so children can follow along with the recording.

13. Let children rehearse and then read texts to younger students.

14. Have a whole group read chorally. The overall effect is good oral reading, since poor reading is drowned out.

Note: The following are general groupings. Very brief descriptors are provided to help teachers start thinking about teaching these concepts. The teaching sequence should be flexible, depending on the strengths and needs of individual children.

Key concept: Phonics is a problem-solving process where the reader uses spelling patterns to arrive at an approximate pronunciation of a word. Sounds of words correspond to spelling patterns. Meaning results only if the reader recognizes the sound as a familiar word.

PHONOLOGICAL AND PHONEMIC AWARENESS SKILLS

- recognize and produce rhymes
- recognize and produce alliteration (same beginning sounds)
- understand concept of beginning and ending sounds in spoken words
- segment and count sounds in words
- blend sounds into words
- delete and substitute sounds

CONSONANT CONCEPTS

- **m, n, p,** and **b** have basically one sound. It is important to separate the teaching of **b, d,** and **p** because of similar letter shapes. This is also true for **m** and **n.**
- **h,** and **w** each have only one sound, but the letter name is very different from the sound.
- **hard c** and **g** are more difficult because their letter names are so different from their sounds.
- along with consonant sounds, teach the concept of where letters occur in words: beginning, end, or middle.
- **f, l, r,** and **s** are harder to articulate and less consistent than other consonants.
- **soft c** and **g: e, i,** or **y** triggers the soft sound, as in *city* and *giraffe.*
- **q, v, x, y,** and **z** are less frequent and more inconsistent than other consonants. *Note:* **y** has different sounds when not in initial position (acts as a vowel in words like *baby* and *my*)

Two- and Three-letter Consonant Clusters and the Blending Process

Concept of a **cluster of consonants** (all sounds are heard during blending).

Two-letter examples: **tr, pl,** and **st.**

Three-letter example: **str**

(continued)

Consonant Digraphs

ch, sh, th (voiced and unvoiced), ph, wh, and **ng** are all two consonants that occur together and make a sound that is different from the sounds the two separate letters usually represent.

VOWEL CONCEPTS

Short Vowels

One-syllable words with the **vowel–consonant** pattern (closed syllable) often have short vowels. **Short a** and **short e** are articulated similarly, so it is best not to teach them back to back. Mnemonics for the short vowel sounds are: *An ostrich egg is ugly* and *An egg is on us.*

Long Vowel Sounds

These are caused by the **silent e** pattern, vowel digraph, and open syllable patterns.

R-Controlled Vowels

There are three basic r-controlled sounds:

1. **er, ir, ur**
2. **ar**
3. **or**

Diphthongs

Special vowel sounds: **oy/oi** (as in *boy* and *boil*), **ou/ow** (as in *out* and *owl*)

SYLLABLE CONCEPT

A syllable is, at least, a vowel sound in a word. The sound may be caused by more than one vowel, and a syllable can include one or more consonants.

RIMES (PHONOGRAMS) AND ONSETS

Thirty-seven phonograms are found in the almost five hundred words encountered in primary grades (Wylie & Durrell, 1970): **ack, ail, ain, ake, ale, ame, an, ank, ap, ash, at, ate, aw, ay, eat, ell, est, ice, ick, ide, ight, ill, in, ine, ing, ink, ip ,it, ock, oke, op, ore, ot, uck, ug, um,** and **unk**. *Note:* Start with two-letter rimes such as **an, it, ot,** and **ug,** because they are easier and regular (cvc short vowel structure).

STRUCTURAL/MORPHEMIC ANALYSIS

- Contractions
- Suffixes added to base/root words: **-s, -ing, -ed, -er, -est, -ly, -y, -es, -ies**

(continued)

- Spelling "rules":
  1. Change y to i pattern.
  2. Double final consonant for short vowels.
  3. Drop silent e.
- Compounds
- Prefixes: **re-, dis-, un-, in-**

CATEGORIES OF WORDS

- **Antonyms:** words with opposite meanings, such as *black* and *white*
- **Synonyms:** words with similar meanings, such as *small* and *little*
- **Homonyms:** words that are spelled that same and sound the same but have different meanings (also called multiple meaning words), such as *pool* our money together (verb) or jump into the *pool* (noun)
- **Homographs:** words with the same spelling but different sounds and meaning, such as *read* (long e) and *read* (short e); *minute* (unit of time) or *minute* (meaning very small)
- **Homophones:** words with the same sound, but different spelling and meaning, such as *pear, pare,* and *pair.*

WORD-SOLVING PROCESS

1. What word would make sense? (use synonyms and syntax)
2. What part(s) of the word do I know? (roots/affixes)
3. Use **graphophonics:** Look at the spelling to get the sound. What words start the same? End the same? Are there familiar chunks (rimes or phonograms)? Use the five vowel spelling patterns (silent e, vowel digraph, open and closed syllables, r-controlled) and consonant patterns.
4. Check sources: dictionary, glossary, word wall.

Government and Professional Organizations

American Educational Research Association (AERA) www.aera.net

American Federation of Teachers www.aft.org

American Library Association www.ala.org

Arts Education Partnership http://dep-arts.org

Campbell Collaboration www.campbellcollaboration.org

Council of Chief State School Officers (CCSSO) www.ccsso.org

Council for Exceptional Children (CEC) www.cec.sped.org

ERIC Clearinghouse on Elementary and Early Childhood Education www.eric.ed.gov

ERIC Clearinghouse on Reading, English, and Communication www.eric.ed.gov

Institute for Education Sciences http://ies.ed.gov

International Reading Association (IRA) www.reading.org

National Assessment of Educational Progress (NAEP) http://nces.ed.gov/nationsreportcard

National Association for the Education of Young Children (NAEYC) www.naeyc.org

National Center for Educational Statistics http://nces.ed.gov

National Council of Teachers of English (NCTE) www.ncte.org

National Early Childhood Technical Assistance Center (NECTAC)/Para Los Niños www.nectac.org

National Education Association (NEA) www.nea.org

National Institute for Literacy www.nifl.gov

National Reading Conference (NRC) www.nrconline.org

National Research and Development Centers http://research.cse.ucla.edu

National Writing Project www.nwp.org

Office of Educational Research and Improvement (OERI) www.ed.gov/offices/OERI/index.html

What Works Clearinghouse http://ies.ed.gov/ncee/wwc

(continued)

General Literacy Websites

A Teacher's Guide to Fair Use and Copyright http://homeearthlink. net/~cnew/research.htm

Babel Fish Translation http://babelfish.altavista.com/babelfish

Bookhive www.bookhive.org

Google for Educators www.google.com/educators/

Carol Hurst's Children's Literature Site: Curriculum Areas Index to Internet Sites http://falcon.jmu.edu/~ramseyil/biochildhome.htm

Invention at Play http://inventionatplay.org

Kathy Schrock's Guide for Educators http://school.discovery.com/schrockguide/index.html

Literacy & Technology www.oswego.org/staff/cchamber/literacy/index.cfm

Merriam-Webster Online: The Language Center www.m-w.com

PBS TeacherSource: Arts and Literature www.pbs.org/teachersourcearts_lit.htm

Publishing with Students www.publishingstudents.com

Reading Rockets www.readingrockets.org

Read Write Think http://readwritethink.org

StoryPlace: The Children's Digital Library www.storyplace.org

Travlang's Word of the Day http://travlang.com/wordofday

techLEARNING www.techlearning.com

Teacher's Guide to International Collaboration on the Internet www. ed.gov/teachers/how/tech/international/index.html

The Electronic Classroom www.readingonline.org/electronic/elec_index.asp?

Vocabulary University www.vocabulary.com

It is a poor sort of mind that can only think of one way to spell a word.

BENJAMIN FRANKLIN

ABBREVIATIONS

A/S/L what is your age, sex, and location?

ADDY address

AFAIK as far as I know

AFK away from keyboard

ASAP as soon as possible

B I'm back

B4 before

BBFN bye bye for now

BBL be back later

BF boyfriend

BD big deal

BFN bye for now

BG big grin

BML biting my lip

BO brain overload

BRB be right back

BTW by the way

CMIIW correct me if I'm wrong

CU see you

CUL8R see you later

CUL see you later

CYA see ya (good-bye)

Dnt B L8 don't be late

F2F face to face (in person)

FAQ frequently asked question

FITB fill in the blank

FOFL falling on the floor laughing

FUBAR fouled up beyond all recognition

FWIW for what it's worth

FYI for your information

G2G I've got to go

GFI go for it

G grin

GAL get a life

GF girlfriend

GG good game

GMTA great minds think alike

HAGO have a good one

HB hurry back

HHIS hanging head in shame

HRU how are you

HTH I hope this helps

IANAL I am not a lawyer

IC I see

ICBW it could be worse

ICWUM I see what you mean

IDK I don't know

IIRC if I remember correctly

IM instant message (can be a verb)

IMO in my opinion

IOW in other words

IRL in real life

JK just kidding

LDR long distance relationship

LMAO laughing my ass off

LOL laughing out loud

MOTOS member of the opposite sex

MOTSS member of the same sex

NE1 anyone

NM never mind

NP no problem

OIC oh, I see

OMG oh, my gosh!

OS operating system

OTOH on the other hand

OTTOMH off the top of my head

PAW parents are watching

PDA public display of affection

PM private message

POV point of view

PUTER computer

RL real life

ROFL rolling on the floor laughing

RPG role playing game

SO significant other

THX thanks

TIC tongue-in-cheek

TMI too much information

TTFN ta-ta for now (good-bye)

TTYL talk to you later

TTYS talk to you soon

TY thank you

TYVM thank you very much

WB welcome back

WTH what the heck

WU? what's up?

WUF? where are you from?

EMOTICONS (*also called* smilies)

:-)	smile, happy
;-)	wink
:-d	big smile, laughter
:-(	sad, unhappy
:-o	shocked, surprised
:-/	skeptical
>:-(	angry
:'-(	crying
:~-(	weeping
:-x	my lips are sealed
:-^)	tongue in cheek

Sources: www.smilies.cz/, http://smileys.antville.org, http://paul.merton.ox.ac.uk/ascii/smileys.html, www.muller-godschalk.com/emoticon.html

References

Alexander, P., & Murphy, P. (1998). Profiling the differences in students' knowledge, interest, and strategic processing. *Journal of Educational Psychology, 90*(3), 435–447.

Allen, J. (1999). *Words, words, words.* Portsmouth, NH: Heinemann.

Allington, R. (1983). The reading instruction provided readers of differing reading abilities. *Elementary School Journal, 83,* 548–559.

Allington, R. (2002a). Research on reading/learning disabilities interventions. In A. Farstrup & J. Samuels (Eds.), *What research has to say about reading instruction* (3rd ed., pp. 261–290). Newark, DE: International Reading Association.

Allington, R. (2002b, June). What I've learned about effective reading instruction. *Kappan, 83*(10), 740–747.

Allington, R. (2005a). What counts as evidence in evidence-based education. *Reading Today, 23*(3), 16.

Allington, R. (2005b, February). *What really matters for struggling readers.* Keynote address presented at South Carolina Reading Association, Myrtle Beach, SC.

Allington, R. (2005c). The other five "pillars" of effective reading instruction. *Reading Today, 22*(6), 3.

Allington, R., & Baker, K. (2007). Best practices for struggling readers. In L. Gambrell, L. Morrow, & M. Pressley (Eds.), *Best practices in literacy instruction* (3rd ed., pp. 83–104). New York/London: Guilford.

Allington, R., & McGill-Franzen, A. (1989). School response to reading failure: Instruction for Chapter 1 and special education students in grades 2, 4 and 8. *The Elementary School Journal, 89,* 529–542.

Allington, R., & Walmsley, S. (2007). *No quick fix: Rethinking literacy programs in America's elementary schools.* New York: Teachers College Press.

Almasi, J., O'Flahavan, J., & Arva, P. (2001, April/May/June). A comparative analysis of student and teacher development in more and less proficient discussions of literature. *Reading Research Quarterly.*

Alvermann, D., Hagood, M., Heron, A., Hughes, P., Williams, K., & Jun, Y. (2000). After-school media clubs for reluctant adolescent readers. *Report to the Spencer Foundation.* Chicago: Spencer Foundation.

Amabile, T. (1996). *Creativity in context.* Boulder, CO: Westview Press.

American Federation of Teachers. (1999, June). *Teaching reading is rocket science.* Retrieved from http://www.aft.org/pubs-reports/downloads/teachers/rocketsci.pdf

Anderson, L., Evertson, C., & Brophy, J. (1979). An experimental study of effective teaching in first-grade reading groups. *Elementary School Journal, 79,* 193–223.

Anderson, R., Wilson, P., & Fielding, L. (1988, Summer). Growth in reading and how children spend their time outside of school. *Reading Research Quarterly,* 285–303.

Anderson, R.C., Hiebert, E.H., Scott, J.A., & Wilkinson, I.A.G. (1985). *Becoming a nation of readers: The report of the Commission on Reading.* Washington, DC: National Academy of Education, Commission on Education and Public Policy.

Armbruster, B.B., & Armstrong, J.O. (1993). Locating information in text: A focus on children in the elementary grades. *Contemporary Educational Psychology, 18,* 139–161.

Aston-Warner, S. (1986). *Teacher.* New York: Simon & Schuster.

Au, K. (2002). Multicultural factors and the effective instruction of students of diverse backgrounds. In A. Farstrup & J. Samuels (Eds.), *What research has to say about reading instruction* (3rd ed., pp. 392–414). Newark, DE: International Reading Association.

Badke, W. (2009). Stepping beyond Wikipedia. *Educational Leadership, 66*(6), 54–58.

Baker, L., & Brown, A.L. (1984). Metacognitive skills and reading. In P.D. Pearson, R. Barr, M. Kamil, & P. Mosenthal (Eds.), *Handbook of reading research* (pp. 353–394). White Plains, NY: Longman.

Baker, R., Boughton, D., Freedman, K., Horowitz, R., & Ingram, D. (2004, April). *Artistic production as evidence of learning in interdisciplinary contexts.* San Diego, CA: American Educational Research Association.

Barr, R., & Dreeban, R. (1991). Grouping students for reading instruction. In P.D. Pearson, R. Barr, M. Kamil, & P. Mosenthal (Eds.), *Handbook of reading research* (pp. 353–394). White Plains, NY: Longman.

Barr, R., Kamil, M., & Mosenthal, P. (Eds.). (1996). *Handbook of reading research,* Vol. 2. Mahwah, NJ: Erlbaum.

Baumann, J., & Kameenui, E. (1991). Research on vocabulary instruction: Ode to Voltaire. In J. Flood, J. Jensen, D. Lapp, & J. Squire (Eds.), *Handbook on teaching the English language arts* (pp. 604–632). New York: Macmillan.

Bear, D., Invernizzi, M., Templeton, S., & Johnston, F. (2006). *Words their way: Word study for phonics, vocabulary, and spelling instruction* (4th ed.). Upper Saddle River, NJ: Pearson, Merrill, Prentice Hall.

Beck, I., & McKeown, M. (1998). Comprehension: The sine qua non of reading. In S. Patton & M. Holmes (Eds.), *The keys to literacy* (pp. 40–52). Washington, DC: Council for Basic Education.

Beck, I., & McKeown, M. (2006). *Improving comprehension with questioning the author: A fresh and expanded view of a powerful approach.* New York: Guilford.

Beck, I., McKeown, M., Hamilton, R., & Kucan, L. (1997). *Questioning the author.* Newark, DE: International Reading Association.

Biancarosa, G., & Snow, C. (2004). *Reading Next—a vision for action and research in middle and high school literacy: A report to Carnegie Corporation of New York.* Washington, DC: Alliance for Excellent Education.

Biemiller, A. (2005). Size and sequence in vocabulary development: Implications for choosing words for primary vocabulary instruction. In E. Hiebert & M. Kamil (Eds.), *Teaching and learning vocabulary: Bringing research to practice* (pp. 223–242). Mahwah, NJ: Erlbaum.

Biemiller, A., & Boote, C. (2006). An effective method for building meaning vocabulary in primary grades. *Journal of Educational Psychology, 98,* 44–62.

Blachowicz, C., & Fisher, P. (2007). Best practices in vocabulary instruction. In L. Gambrell, L. Morrow, & M. Pressley (Eds.), *Best practices in literacy instruction* (3rd ed., pp. 178–203). New York/London: Guilford.

Block, C. (2004). *Teaching comprehension: The comprehension process approach.* New York: Pearson/Allyn Bacon.

Block, C., Gambrell, L., & Pressley, M. (Eds.). (2002). *Improving comprehension instruction: Rethinking research, theory, and classroom practice.* San Francisco: Jossey-Bass.

Block, C., & Mangieri, J.N. (2003). *Exemplary literacy teachers: Promoting success for all students in grades K–5.* New York: Guilford.

Block, C., Mangieri, J., & Fowkes, L. (1997). *Reason to read: Thinking strategies for life through learning.* Colorado Springs, CO: Innovative Learning.

Block, C., Paris, S., & Whiteley, C. (2008). CPMs: A kinesthetic comprehension strategy. *Reading Teacher, 61*(6), 460–470.

Block, C., & Pressley, M. (Eds.). (2002). *Comprehension instruction: Research-based practices.* New York: Guilford.

Block, C., & Pressley, M. (2007). Best practices in teaching comprehension. In L. Gambrell, L. Morrow, & M. Pressley (Eds.), *Best practices in literacy instruction* (3rd ed., pp. 220–242). New York/London: Guilford.

Bloom, B. (1956). *Taxonomy of educational objectives.* New York: Longman.

Braunger, J., & Lewis, J. (2006). *Building a knowledge base in reading* (2nd ed.). Newark, DE: International Reading Association.

Bromley, K. (2007). Best practices in teaching writing. In L. Gambrell, L. Morrow, & M. Pressley (Eds.), *Best practices in comprehensive literacy instruction* (3rd ed., pp. 243–263). New York: Guilford.

Brophy, J. (1986, October). *On motivating students* (Occasional Paper No. 101). East Lansing, MI: Institute for Research on Teaching, Michigan State University.

Brown, R. (2008). The road not yet taken: A transactional strategies approach to comprehension instruction. *Reading Teacher, 61*(7), 538–547.

Brown, R., Pressley, M., Van Meter, P., & Schuder, T. (1996). A quasi-experimental validation of transactional strategies instruction with low achieving second grade readers. *Journal of Educational Psychology, 88,* 18–37.

Cambourne, B. (2002). Holistic integrated approaches to reading and language arts instruction: the constructivist framework of an instructional theory. In A. Farstrup & J. Samuels (Eds.), *What research has to say about reading instruction* (3rd ed., pp. 205–242). Newark, DE: International Reading Association.

Carlisle, J., & Katz, L. (2005). Word learning and vocabulary instruction. In J. Birsch (Ed.), *Multisensory teaching of basic language skills* (2nd ed.). Baltimore: Brookes.

Carlo, M. (2007). Best practices for literacy instruction for English-language learners. In L. Gambrell, L. Morrow, & M. Pressley (Eds.). *Best practices in literacy instruction* (3rd ed., 104–126). New York/London: Guilford.

Carr, N. (2008). Is Google making us stupid? *Atlantic Monthly, 301*(16). Retrieved from www.theatlantic.com/doc/200807/google

Casey, J. (2008). Students "power down" for school: Technology left behind. *Reading Today, 25*(6), 40.

Cecil, N. (2007). *Focus on fluency: A meaning-based approach.* Scottsdale, AZ: Holcomb Hathaway.

Center for the Improvement of Early Reading Achievement. (undated). *Improving the reading comprehension of America's children: 10 research-based principles.* Retrieved from http://www.ciera.org/library/instresrc/compprinciples/index.html

Chiapetta, E., & Koballa, T. (2002). *Science instruction in the middle and secondary schools* (5th ed.). Upper Saddle River, NJ: Merrill Prentice Hall.

Coiro, J. (2003a). Reading comprehension on the Internet: Expanding our understanding of reading comprehension to encompass new literacies. *Reading Teacher, 56,* 458–464.

Coiro, J. (2003b). Rethinking comprehension strategies to better prepare students for critically evaluating content on the Internet. *The NERA Journal, 39,* 29–34.

Coiro, J. (2005). Making sense of online text. *Educational Leadership, 63*(2), 30–35.

Coiro, J., & Dobler, E. (2007). Exploring the online reading comprehension strategies used by sixth grade skilled readers to search for and locate information on the Internet. *Research Quarterly, 42*(2), 214–257.

Collins, A., Brown, J., & Newman, S. (1989). Cognitive apprenticeship: Teaching the craft of reading, writing, and mathematics. In L. Resnick (Ed.), *Knowing, learning and instruction: Essays in honor of Robert Glaser* (pp. 453–494). Hillsdale, NJ: Erlbaum.

Cordón, L.A., & Day, J.D. (1996). Strategy use on standardized reading comprehension tests. *Journal of Educational Psychology, 88,* 288–295.

Cornett, C. (1980). *Bibliotherapy: The right book at the right time.* Bloomington, IN: Phi Delta Kappa.

Cornett, C. (1997, March). Beyond plot retelling. *Reading Teacher,* 527–528.

Cornett, C. (2000). Beyond plot retelling. In T. Rasinski (Ed.), *Teaching comprehension and exploring multiple literacies* (pp. 56–58). Newark, DE: International Reading Association.

Cornett, C. (2002). *Learning through laughter II.* Bloomington, IN: Phi Delta Kappa.

Cornett, C. (2006, November). Center stage: Arts-based readalouds. *Reading Teacher, 60*(3), 234–240.

Cornett, C. (2007/2011). *Creating meaning through literature and the arts.* Upper Saddle River, NJ: Merrill/Prentice Hall.

Cornoldi, C., & Oakhill, J. (1996). *Reading comprehension difficulties: Processes and intervention.* Mahwah, NJ: Erlbaum.

Costa, A., & Kallick, B. (Eds.). (2000). *Discovering and exploring habits of mind.* Alexandria, VA: Association for Supervision and Curriculum Development.

Cuban, L. (1993). *How teachers taught.* New York: Teachers College Press.

Cunningham, P., Hall, D., & Sigmon, C. (2000). *The teachers' guide to the four blocks: A multimethod multilevel framework for grades 1–3.* Greensboro, NC: Carson-Delosa.

Cunningham, P., & Smith, D. (2008). *Beyond retelling: Toward higher-level thinking and big ideas.* New York: Pearson/Allyn Bacon.

Daniels, H. (2001). *Literature circles: Voice and choice in book clubs and reading groups* (2nd ed.). Portland, ME: Stenhouse.

Daniels, H., & Bizar, M. (2005). *Teaching the best practices way.* Alexandria, VA: Association for Supervision and Curriculum Development.

Darling-Hammond, L. (2000). Teacher quality and student achievement: A review of state policy evidence. *Educational Policy Analysis Archives, 8*(1), 1–42.

Deasy, R. (Ed.). (2002). *Critical links: Learning in the arts and student academic and social development.* Washington, DC: Arts Education Partnership.

deCharms, R. (1976). *Enhancing motivation.* Irvington, NY: Irvington.

DeMoss, K., & Morris, T. (2002). *How arts integration supports student learning: Students shed light on the connections.* Available at http://www.capeweb.org/rcape.html

Deshler, D., & Schumaker, J. (1990). *Learning strategies model.* Lawrence, KS: University of Kansas Institute for Research in Learning Disabilities.

Dewey, J. (1997). *How we think.* Mineola, NY: Dover Press.

Dodge, B. (no date). WebQuests.org. Retrieved from http://webquests.org/index.php

Dole, J., Duffy, G., Roehler, L., & Pearson, P.D. (1991). Moving from the old to the new: Research on reading comprehension instruction. *Review of Educational Research, 61,* 239–264.

Drake, S., & Burns, R. (2004). *Meeting standards through integrated curriculum.* Alexandria, VA: Association for Supervision and Curriculum Development.

Dressel, P. (1983). *On teaching and learning in college: Reemphasizing the role of learners and the disciplines.* Ann Arbor, MI: ProQuest.

Duffy, G., Lanier J., & Roehler, L. (1980). Improving reading instruction through the use of responsive elaboration. *The Reading Teacher, 40,* 514–521.

Duffy, G., Roehler, L., Sivan, E., Rackliffe, F., Book, C., Meloth, M., et al. (1987). Effect of explaining the reasoning associated with using reading strategies. *Reading Research Quarterly, 22,* 347–368.

Duke, N. (2001, September 22). *Building comprehension through explicit teaching of comprehension strategies.* Presentation at the Second Annual MRA/CIERA Conference. Retrieved from http://www.ciera.org/library/presos/2001/2001MRACIERA/nduke/01cmndk.pdf

Duke, N. (2004). *Strategies for addressing comprehension difficulties.* Presentation at the International Reading Association Reading Research Conference, Reno, NV.

Duke, N. (2007, April). Content-rich comprehension instruction. Presentation at the International Reading Association Reading Research Conference, Toronto.

Duke, N.K. (2000). For the rich it's richer: Print environments and experiences offered to first grade students in very low and very high-SES school districts. *American Educational Research Journal, 37,* 456–457.

Duke, N.K., & Pearson, P.D. (2002). Effective practices for developing reading comprehension. In A. Farstrup & J. Samuels (Eds.), *What research has to say about reading instruction* (3rd ed., pp. 205–242). Newark, DE: International Reading Association.

Duke, N.K., Pressley, G.M., & Hilden, K. (2005). Reading comprehension difficulties. In C.A. Stone, K. Apel, B.J. Ehren, & E.R. Silliman (Eds.), *Handbook of language and literacy development and disorders.* New York: Guilford.

Durkin, D. (1978–1979). What classroom observations reveal about reading comprehension instruction. *Reading Research Quarterly, 37,* 734–744.

Durkin, D. (1993). *Teaching them to read* (6th ed.). Boston: Allyn & Bacon.

Ebenezer, J., & Connor, S. (1998). *Learning to teach science: A model for the 21st century.* Upper Saddle River, NJ: Prentice Hall.

Edelsky, C., Altwerger, A., & Flores, B. (1991). *Whole language: What's the difference?* Portsmouth, NH: Heinemann.

Eisner, E. (2000). Ten lessons the arts teach. In *Learning and the arts: Crossing boundaries.* Chicago: Amdur Spitz & Associates. Retrieved from www.giarts.org/usr_doc/Learning.pdf

Eisner, E. (2002a). *The arts and the creation of mind.* New Haven, CT: Yale University Press.

Eisner, E. (2002b). What can education learn from the arts about the practice of education? *Journal of Curriculum and Supervision, 18,* 4–16.

Esquith, R. (2008, July). Keynote address for the Value Plus Summer Teacher Institute, Renaissance Center, Dickson, TN.

Fader, D., & McNeil, E. (1976). *The new hooked on books.* New York: Berkeley.

Farstrup, A., & Samuels, S.J. (Eds.). (2002). *What research has to say about reading instruction* (3rd ed.). Newark, DE: International Reading Association.

Ferguson, R.F. (1991). Paying for public education: New evidence on how and why money matters. *Harvard Journal of Legislation, 28*(2), 465–498.

Fetters, M., Beller, C., & Hickman, P. (2003). *When is inquiry problem solving and when is problem solving inquiry?* (PowerPoint presentation). Retrieved October 2008 from http://homepages.wmich.edu/~mfetters/grants.html

Fischer, U. (1994). Learning words from context and dictionaries: An experimental comparison. *Applied Psycholinguistics, 15*(4), 551–574.

Fisher, B., & Medvic, E. (2000). *Perspectives on shared reading: Planning and practice.* Portsmouth, NH: Heinemann.

Fisher, D., Flood, F., Lapp, D., & Frey, N. (2004). Interactive read-alouds: Is there a common set of implementation principles? *Reading Teacher, 58*(8), 8–17.

Fitzgerald, J., & Graves, M. (2004). *Scaffolding reading experiences for English language learners.* Norwood, MA: Christopher-Gordon.

Flavell, J.H. (1977). *Cognitive development.* Upper Saddle River, NJ: Prentice Hall.

Floriani, B. (1979, November). Word expansion for multiplying sight vocabulary. *Reading Teacher, 33*(3).

Fountas, I., & Pinnell, G. (1998). *Word matters: Teaching phonics and spelling in the reading writing classroom.* Portsmouth, NH: Heinemann.

Fountas, I., & Pinnell, G. (2001). *Guided readers and writers grades 3–6.* Portsmouth, NH: Heinemann.

Fountas, I., & Pinnell, G. (2006). *Teaching for comprehending and fluency: Thinking, talking, and writing about reading, K–8.* Portsmouth, NH: Heinemann.

Francis, K., Shaywitz, W., Stuebing, K., Fletcher, J., & Shaywitz, B. (1996). Developmental lag vs. deficit models of reading disability: A longitudinal individual growth curves analysis. *Journal of Educational Psychology, 1,* 3–17.

Freeman, D., & Freeman, Y. (2001). *Between worlds: Access to second language acquisition* (2nd ed.). Portsmouth, NH: Heinemann.

Fry, E., & Kress, J. (2006). *Teacher's book of lists.* San Francisco: Jossey-Bass.

Gambrell, L., & Koskinen, P. S. (2002). Imagery: A strategy for enhancing comprehension. In C. B. Block & M. Pressley (Eds.), *Comprehension instruction: Research-based best practices.* New York: Guilford Publications.

Gambrell, L., Malloy, J., & Mazzoni, S. (2007). Evidence-based practices for comprehensive literacy instruction. In L. Gambrell, L. Morrow, & M. Pressley (Eds.), *Best practices in literacy instruction* (3rd ed.). New York/London: Guilford.

García, G.E. (1991). Factors influencing the English reading test performance of Spanish-speaking Hispanic children. *Reading Research Quarterly, 26*(4), 371–392.

Gardner, H. (1993). *Multiple intelligences: The theory in practice.* New York: Basic Books.

Gaskins, I. (2003). Taking charge of reader, text, activity, and content variables. In A. Sweet & C. Snow (Eds.), *Rethinking reading comprehension* (pp. 141–165). New York: Guilford.

Gersten, R., & Baker, S. (2000). What we know about effective instructional practices for English-language learners. *Exceptional Children, 66,* 454–470.

Gersten, R., Fuchs, L., Williams, J., & Baker, S. (2001). Teaching reading comprehension strategies for students with learning disabilities: A review of research. *Review of Educational Research, 71,* 279–320.

Graves, M., Juel, C., & Graves, B. (2007). *Teaching reading in the 21st century* (4th ed.). New York: Pearson/Allyn Bacon.

Graves, M., & Watts-Taffe, S. (2002). The place of word consciousness in a research-based vocabulary program. In A. Farstrup & J. Samuels (Eds.), *What research has to say about reading instruction* (3rd ed.). Newark, DE: International Reading Association.

Grover, M. (2008, November 19). Study of reading program finds lacks of progress. *Washington Post,* p. A06.

Guthrie, J. (2000). Contexts for engagement and motivation in reading. In M. Kamil, P. Mosenthal, P. Pearson, & R. Barr (Eds.), *Handbook of reading research,* Vol. III. New York: Erlbaum.

Guthrie, J. (2002). Preparing students for high stakes test taking in reading. In A. Farstrup & J. Samuels (Eds.), *What research has to say about reading instruction* (3rd ed.). Newark, DE: International Reading Association.

Guthrie, J. (2004). Motivating students to read. In P. McCardle & U. Chhabra (Eds.), *The voice of evidence in reading research.* Baltimore, MD: Brookes.

Guthrie, J. (2007). Foreword. In L. Gambrell, L. Morrow, & M. Pressley (Eds.), *Best practices in literacy instruction* (3rd ed.). New York/London: Guilford.

Guthrie, J., Schafer, W., & Wang, Y. (1995). Relationships of instruction to amount of reading: An exploration of social, cognitive, and instructional connections. *Reading Research Quarterly, 30*, 8–25.

Guthrie, J., Van Meter, P., Hancock, G., Alao, S., Anderson, E., & McCann, A. (1998). Does concept oriented reading instruction increase strategy use and conceptual learning from text? *Journal of Educational Psychology, 90*(2), 261–278.

Guthrie, J., & Wigfield, A. (Eds.). (1997). *Reading engagement: Motivating readers through integrated instruction.* Newark, DE: International Reading Association.

Guthrie, J., Wigfield, A., Barbosa, K., Perencevich, K., Taboada, A., Davis, M., Scafiddi, N., & Tonks, S. (2004). Increasing reading comprehension and engagement through concept-oriented reading instruction. *Journal of Educational Psychology, 96*, 403–421.

Guthrie, J., Wigfield, A., & Perencevich, K. (2004). Scaffolding for motivation and engagement in reading. In J. Guthrie, A. Wigfield, & K. Perencevich (Eds.), *Motivating reading comprehension: Concept-oriented reading instruction.* Mahwah, NJ: Erlbaum.

Guthrie, J., Wigfield, A., & Von Secker. (2000). Effects of integrated instruction on motivation and strategy use in reading. *Journal of Educational Psychology, 92*(2), 331–341.

Gyselinck, V., & Tardieu, H. (1999). The role of illustrations in text comprehension: What, when, for whom and why? In H. van Oostendorp & S. Goldman (Eds.), *The construction of mental representations during reading* (pp. 195–218). Mahwah, NJ: Erlbaum.

Hall, L., & Piazza, S. (2008). Critically reading texts: What students do and how teachers can help. *Reading Teacher, 62*(1), 20–31.

Hallett, V. (2005, July 25). The power of Potter. *U.S. News and World Report,* pp. 45–49.

Harris, R. (2007). *Evaluating Internet research sources.* Retrieved from http://www.virtualsalt.com/evalu8it.htm

Harris, T.L., & Hodges, R.E. (1995). *The literacy dictionary.* Newark, DE: International Reading Association.

Harste, J. (1997). *Whole language.* Talk given at summer institute. Indiana University, Bloomington, IN.

Hart, B., & Risley, T. (2003, Spring). The early catastrophe: The thirty million word gap by age 3. *American Educator, 27*(4). Retrieved Sept. 23, 2008 from http://www.aft.org/pubs-reports/american_educator/spring2003/catastrophe.html

Hoffman, J.V. (1991). Teacher and school effects in learning to read. In R. Barr, M. Kamil, P. Mosenthal, & P. Pearson (Eds.), *Handbook of reading research,* Vol. II (pp. 911–950). New York: Longman.

Housen, A. & Yenwine, P. (2000). *Visual thinking strategies, basic manual K–2.* New York: Visual Understanding.

Institute for Educational Sciences. (2008). Reading First: Impact study: Interim report. Washington, DC: U.S. Department of Education.

International Reading Association. (2002). *Using multiple methods of beginning reading instruction.* Newark, DE. Retrieved from http://www.reading.org/downloads/positions/ps1033_multiple_methods.pdf

International Reading Association/National Council of Teachers of English. (1996). *Standards for the English language arts.* Author.

IRA issues statement on Reading First report. (2008). *Reading Today, 25*(6), 1.

Irvin, J. (1990). *Reading and the middle school student: Strategies to enhance literacy.* Needham Heights, MA: Allyn & Bacon.

Irwin, J. (2007). *Teaching reading comprehension processes.* New York: Pearson/Allyn Bacon.

Isakson, R., & Miller, J. (1976). Sensitivity to syntactic and semantic cues in good and poor comprehenders. *Journal of Educational Psychology, 68,* 787–792.

Israel, S., Block, C., Bauserman, K., & Kinnucan-Welsh, K. (Eds.). (2005). *Metacognition in literacy learning: Theory assessment, instruction, and professional development.* Mahwah, NJ: Erlbaum.

Jiménez, R., García, G., & Pearson, P.D. (1996). The reading strategies of bilingual Latina/o students who are successful English readers: Opportunities and obstacles. *Reading Research Quarterly, 31*(1), 90–112.

Johnson, R., & Johnson, D. (2002). *Circles of learning* (5th ed.). Edina, MN: Interaction.

Joyce, B., & Showers, B. (1996). Staff development as a comprehensive service organization. *Journal of Staff Development, 17*(1), 2–6.

Juel, C. (1988). Retention and non-retention of at-risk readers in first grade and their subsequent reading achievement. *Journal of Learning Disabilities, 21,* 571–580.

Kamil, M. (2004). Reading comprehension. In P. McCardle & U. Chhabra (Eds.), *The voice of evidence in reading research.* Baltimore, MD: Brookes.

Kamil, M., Mosenthal, P., Pearson, P.D., & Barr, R. (Eds.). (2000). *Handbook of reading research,* Vol. III. Mahwah NJ: Erlbaum.

Keene, E., & Zimmerman, S. (2007). *Mosaic of thought: The power of comprehension strategy instruction.* Portsmouth, NH: Heinemann.

Kiernan, L. (2000). Lesson 1: what is differentiated instruction? In *Differentiating instruction: An ASCD PD online course.* Alexandria, VA: Association for Supervision and Curriculum Development.

Klinger, J., & Vaughn, S. (1999). Promoting reading comprehension, content learning, and English acquisition through Collaborative Strategic Reading (CSR). *The Reading Teacher, 52,* 738–747.

Knight, J. (2009, March). What can we do about teacher resistance? *Phi Delta Kappan*, 90(7), 508–513.

Koestler, A. (1964). *The act of creation*. New York: Macmillan.

Krashen, S. (2001). More smoke and mirrors: A critique of the National Reading Panel report on fluency. *Phi Delta Kappan*, 83(2), 119–122.

Krashen, S. (2005). Is in-school free reading good for children? Why the National Reading Panel is (still) wrong. *Phi Delta Kappan*, 86(6), 444–447.

Krathwohl, D.R. (2002). A revision of Bloom's taxonomy: An overview. *Theory into Practice*, 41(4), 212–218.

Kucan, L., Lapp, D., Flood, J., & Fisher, D. (2007). Instructional resources in the classroom: Deepening understanding through interactions with multiple texts and multiple media. In L. Gambrell, L. Morrow, & M. Pressley (Eds.), *Best practices in literacy instruction* (3rd ed., pp. 285–312). New York/London: Guilford.

Kuhn, M., & Rasinski, T. (2007). Best practices in fluency instruction. In L. Gambrell, L. Morrow, & M. Pressley (Eds.), *Best practices in literacy instruction* (3rd ed., pp. 204–219). New York/London: Guilford.

Kuhn, M., & Stahl, S. (1998). Teaching children to learn word meanings from context: A synthesis and some questions. *Journal of Literacy Research*, 30, 119–138.

LaBerge, D., & Samuels, S.J. (1974). Toward a theory of automatic information processing in reading. *Cognitive Psychology*, 6, 293–323.

Ladson-Billings, G. (1994). *The dreamkeepers: Successful teachers of African American children*. San Francisco: Jossey-Bass.

Langer, E. (1989). *Mindfulness*. New York: Addison-Wesley.

Langer, E. (1997). *The power of mindful learning*. New York: Addison-Wesley.

Larson, G. (1997). *American canvas*. Washington, DC: National Endowment for the Arts.

Lawless, K., & Kulikowich, J. (1996). Understanding hypertext navigation through cluster analysis. *Journal of Educational Computing Research*, 14(4), 385–399.

Lee, D., & Allen, R. (1963). *Learning to read through experience* (2nd ed.). New York: Meredith.

Lenhart, A., Rainie, L., & Lewis, O. (2001, June 21). *Teenage life online*. Retrieved from http://www.pewinternet.org/Reports/2001/Teenage-Life-Online.aspx

Leslie, L., & Caldwell, J. (2006). *Qualitative reading inventory* (4th ed). Boston: Allyn & Bacon.

Leu, D., Castek, J., Henry, L., Coiro, J., & McMullen, M. (2004). The lessons that children teach us: Integrating children's literature and the new literacies of the Internet. *Reading Teacher*, 57, 496–503.

Leu, D., Leu, D., & Coiro, J. (2004). *Teaching with the Internet: Lessons from the classroom* (4th ed.). Norwood, MA: Christopher-Gordon.

Lindstrom, R. (1999, April 19). Being visual: The emerging visual enterprise. *Business Week, special section*.

Lipson, M., & Wixson, K. (1997). *Assessment and instruction of reading and writing disability* (2nd ed.). New York: Longman.

Lotherington, H., & Chow, S. (2006, November). Rewriting Goldilocks: In the urban, multicultural elementary school. *Reading Teacher*, 60(3), 242–252.

Lukens, R. (2006). *Critical handbook of children's literature*. Boston: Allyn & Bacon.

Mantione, R., & Smead, S. (2003). *Weaving through words: Using the arts to teach reading comprehension strategies*. Newark, DE: International Reading Association.

Manzo, A. (1969). The ReQuest procedure. *Journal of Reading*, 12, 123–126.

Marzano, R.J. (2004). *Building background knowledge for academic achievement: Research on what works in schools*. Alexandria, VA: Association for Supervision and Curriculum Development.

Marzano, R.J. (2007). *The art and science of teaching: A comprehensive framework for effective instruction*. Alexandria, VA: Association for Supervision and Curriculum Development.

Maslow, A. (1968). *Toward a psychology of being*. Princeton, NJ: Van Nostrand.

Mathis, W. (2005, April). Bridging the achievement gap: A bridge too far? *Phi Delta Kappan*, 590–593.

Mayer, R. (1997). Multimedia learning: Are we asking the right questions? *Educational Psychologist*, 32(1), 1–19.

Mayer, R., & Moreno, R. (1998). A split-attention effect in multimedia learning: Evidence for dual processing systems in working memory. *Journal of Educational Psychology*, 90, 312–320.

McCardle, P., & Chhabra, U. (Eds.). (2004). *The voice of evidence in reading research*. Baltimore, MD: Brookes.

McDermott, R., & Varenne, H. (1995). Culture as disability. *Anthropology and Education Quarterly*, 26, 324–348.

McGregor, T. (2007). *Comprehension connections: Bridges to strategic reading*. Portsmouth, NH: Heinemann.

McKenne, M., Labbo, L., Reinking, D., & Zucker, T. (2007). Effective use of technology in literacy instruction. In L. Gambrell, L. Morrow, & M. Pressley (Eds.), *Best practices in literacy instruction* (3rd ed., pp. 344–348). New York/London: Guilford.

McKown, B., & Barnett, C. (2007). *Improving reading comprehension through higher-order thinking skills*. Saint Xavier University, Chicago. (ERIC Document Reproduction Service No. ED 496222). Retrieved from http://www.eric.ed.gov

McLaughlin, M., & Allen, M. (2002). *Guided comprehension. A teaching model for grades 3–8*. Newark, DE: International Reading Association.

McTighe, J., & Wiggins, G. (2004). *Understanding by design professional workbook*. Alexandria, VA: Association for Supervision and Curriculum Development.

Miller, G. (1956). The magical number seven, plus or minus two: Some limits on our capacity for processing. *Psychological Review, 63*, 81–97.

Moats, L. (1999). Reading is rocket science: What expert teachers of reading should know and be able to do. Washington, DC: American Federation of Teachers.

Moats, L. (2004). Science language and imagination in the professional development of reading teachers. In P. McCardle & U. Chhabra (Eds.), *The voice of evidence in reading research* (pp. 269–282). Baltimore: Brookes.

Morrow, L., & Gambrell, L. (2001). Literature-based instruction in the early years. In S. Neuman & D. Dickinson (Eds.), *Handbook of early literacy research* (pp. 348–360). New York: Guilford.

Morrow, L., & Pressley, M. (Eds.). (2007). *Best practices in literacy instruction* (3rd ed.). New York/London: Guilford.

Nafisi, A. (2003). *Reading Lolita in Tehran*. New York: Random House.

Nagy, W.E., McClure, E.F., & Montserrat, M. (1997). Linguistic transfer and the use of context by Spanish-English bilinguals. *Applied Psycholinguistics, 18*(4), 431–452.

Nation, K. (1999). Reading skills in hyperlexia: A developmental perspective. *Psychological Bulletin, 125*, 338–355.

Nation, K., & Snowling, M.J. (1998). Individual differences in contextual facilitation: Evidence from dyslexia and poor reading comprehension. *Child Development, 69*(4), 996–1011.

National Council of Teachers of English (NCTE). (2004). *On reading, learning to read, and effective reading instruction: An overview of what we know and how we know it*. Retrieved from http://www.ncte.org/positions/statements/onreading

National Endowment for the Arts (NEA). (2007). *To read or not to read: A question of national consequence* (Research Report #47). Washington, DC: Author. Retrieved from http://www.nea.gov/research/ToRead_ExecSum.pdf

National Reading Panel (NRP). (2000). *Teaching children to read: An evidence-based assessment of the scientific research literature on reading and its implications for reading instruction*. Washington, DC: National Institute of Child Health and Human Development.

National Research Council. (2000). *Inquiry and the national science education standards*. Washington, DC: National Academy Press.

National Staff Development Council. (2001). *NSDC's standards for staff development*. Oxford, OH: National Staff Development Council.

NCLB legislation (2002). Retrieved from www.ed.gov/legislation/ESEA02/

Neeld, E. (1986). *Writing* (2nd ed.). Glenview, IL: Scott, Foresman.

Northwest Regional Educational Laboratory. (1998/1999). *Assessment and accountability program*. Portland, OR: Author.

Norton, D. (2007). *Through the eyes of a child: An introduction to children's literature*. Upper Saddle River, NJ: Pearson.

O'Brien, D. (1998). Multiple literacies in a high-school program for "at-risk" adolescents. In D. E. Alvermann, K. Hinchman, D. Moore, S. Phelps, & D. Waff (Eds.), *Reconceptualizing the literacies in adolescents' lives* (pp. 27–49). Mahwah, NJ: Erlbaum.

O'Brien, D. (2001). "At-risk" adolescents: Redefining competence through the multiliteracies of intermediality, visual arts, and representation. *Reading Online, 4*(11). Available at www.readingonline.org/newliteracies/lit_index.asp?

Ogle, D. (1986). K-W-L: A teaching model that develops active reading of expository text. *Reading Teacher, 39*, 564–570.

Olshansky, B. (2008). *The power of picture: Creating pathways to literacy through art*. San Francisco: Jossey-Bass.

Palincsar, A., & Brown, A. (1984). Reciprocal teaching of comprehension—fostering and monitoring activities. *Cognition and Instruction, 1*, 117–175.

Palincsar, A., & Duke, N. (2004). The role of text and text-reader interactions in young children's reading development and achievement. *The Elementary School Journal, 105*, 183–196.

Paris, S., Carpenter, R., Paris, A., & Hamilton, E. (2005). Spurious and genuine correlates of children's reading comprehension. In S. Paris & S. Stahl (Eds.), *Children's reading comprehension and assessment* (pp. 131–160). Mahwah, NJ: Erlbaum.

Paris, S., Cross, D., & Lipson, M. (1984). Informed strategies for learning: A program to improve children's reading awareness and comprehension. *Journal of Educational Psychology, 76*, 1239–1252.

Paris, S., & Stahl, S. (Eds.). (2002). *Children's reading comprehension and assessment*. Mahwah, NH: Erlbaum.

Paris, S., Wasik, B., & Turner, J. (1991). The development of strategic readers. In R. Barr, M.L. Kamil, P. Mosenthal, & P.D. Pearson (Eds.), *Handbook of reading research*, Vol. 2. (pp. 609–640). New York: Longman.

Parker, W. (2009). *Social studies in elementary education* (13th ed.). Boston: Pearson.

Partnership for 21st Century Skills. (2008). *21st century skills, education, and competitiveness*. Retrieved on February 26, 2009, from www.21stcenturyskills.org/documents/21st_century_skills_education_and_competitiveness_guide.pdf

Pearson, D., & Dole, J. (1987). Explicit comprehension instruction: A review of research and a new conceptualization of instruction. *Elementary School Journal*, 88, 151–165.

Pearson, P., & Gallagher, M. (1983). The instruction of reading comprehension. *Contemporary Educational Psychology*, 8, 317–344.

Pearson, P.D., & Fielding, L. (1991). Comprehension instruction. In R. Barr, M. Kamil, P. Mosenthal, & P.D. Pearson (Eds.), *Handbook of reading research*, Vol. II (pp. 815–860). White Plains, NY: Longman.

Pearson, P.D., Harvey, S., & Goudis, A. (2005). *What every teacher should know about: Reading comprehension instruction* [DVD]. Portsmouth, NH: Heinemann.

Pearson, P.D., Roehler, L., Dole, J., & Duffy, G. (1992). Developing expertise in reading comprehension. In S. Samuels & A. Farstrup (Eds.), *What research has to say about reading instruction* (2nd ed., pp 145–199). Newark, DE: International Reading Association.

Pennsylvania Department of Education. (2004). *Pennsylvania reading requirements for school, workplace and society: Executive summary of findings*. Available at http://www.pde.beta.state.pa.us/career_edu/lib/career_educ/pennsylvania_reading_requirements_for_school_summary_repora.pdf

Perkins, D. (2004). Knowledge alive. *Educational Leadership*, 62(1), 14–18.

Perkins, K., & Blythe, T. (1994). Putting understanding up front. *Educational Leadership*, 51(5), 4–7.

Peterson, R., & Eeds, M. (1999). *Grand conversations: Literature groups in action*. New York: Scholastic.

Piaget, J., & Inhelder, B. (2000). *The psychology of the child*. New York: Basic Books.

Pinnell, G., & Fountas, I. (1998). *Word matters*. Portsmouth, NH: Heinemann.

Pressley, M. (2000). What should comprehension instruction be the instruction of? In M. Kamil, P. Mosenthal, P.D. Pearson, & R. Barr (Eds.), *Handbook of reading research*, Vol. III (pp. 545–561). Mahwah, NJ: Erlbaum.

Pressley, M. (2001, September). Comprehension instruction: What makes sense now, what might make sense soon. *Reading Online*, 5(2). Retrieved from http://www.readingonline.org/articles/art_index.asp?HREF=/articles/handbook/pressley/index.html

Pressley, M. (2002). Meta-cognition and self-regulated comprehension. In A. Farstrup & J. Samuels (Eds.), *What research has to say about reading instruction* (3rd ed.). Newark, DE: International Reading Association.

Pressley, M. (2006). *Reading instruction that works: The case for balanced teaching* (3rd ed.). New York: Guilford.

Pressley, M. (2006, May). *What the future of reading research could be*. Paper presented at the International Reading Association's Reading Research Conference. Chicago.

Pressley, M. (2007). Achieving best practices. In J. Guthrie, L, Gambrell, L. Gallow, L. Morrow, & M. Pressley (Eds.), *Best practices in literacy instruction* (3rd ed., pp. 397–404). New York/London: Guilford.

Pressley, M., & Afflerbach, P. (1995). *Verbal protocols of reading: The nature of constructively responsive reading*. Hillsdale, NJ: Erlbaum.

Pressley, M., Allington, R., Wharton-McDonald, R., Block, C., & Morrow, L. (2001). *Learning to read: Lessons from exemplary first-grade classrooms*. New York: Guilford.

Pressley, M., Brown, R., Van Meter, P., & Schuder, T. (1995). Trends: Reading/transactional strategies. *Connecting with the Community and the World of Work*, 52(8), 81–82.

Pressley, M., El-Dinary, P., Almasi, J., Gaskins, G., & Brown, R. (1992). Beyond direct explanation: Transactional instruction of reading comprehension strategies. *Elementary School Journal*, 92, 513–555.

Pressley, M., Hilden, K., & Shankland, R.K. (2006). *An evaluation of end-grade-3 Dynamic Indicators of Basic Early Literacy Skills (DIBELS): Speed reading without comprehension, predicting little*. East Lansing, MI: Michigan State University, College of Education, Literacy Achievement Research Center (LARC). Available at www.msularc.org/dibels%20submitted.pdf

Pressley, M., Johnson, C., Simmons, S., McGoldrick, J., & Kurita, J. (1989). Strategies that improve children's memory and comprehension of text. *Elementary School Journal*, 90, 3–32.

Pressley, M., Rankin, J., & Yokoi, L. (1996). A survey of instructional practices of primary grade teachers nominated as effective in promoting literacy. *Elementary School Journal*, 96, 363–384.

Purkey, W., & Novak, J. (1996). *Inviting school success: A self-concept approach to teaching, learning, and democratic practice* (3rd ed.). New York: Wadsworth.

RAND Reading Study Group. (2002). *Reading for understanding: Toward an R & D program in reading comprehension*. Santa Monica, CA: RAND Corporation. Available from www.rand.org/publications/MR/MR1465/

Raphael, T., Au, K., & Highfield, K. (2006). *QAR now: Question answer relationship: A powerful and practical framework that develops comprehension and higher-level thinking in all students*. New York: Scholastic.

Reinking, D. (2007). Toward a good or better understanding of best practices. *Journal of Curriculum and Instruction*, 1(1), 75–88.

Reutzel, R. (2007). Organizing effective literacy instruction: Differentiating instruction to meet the needs of all children. In L. Gambrell, L. Morrow, & M. Pressley (Eds.), *Best practices in literacy instruction* (3rd ed., pp. 313–343). New York/London: Guilford.

Reutzel, R., Smith, A., & Fawson, P. (2005). An evaluation of two approaches for teaching reading comprehension strategies in the primary years using science information texts. *Early Childhood Research Quarterly*, 20, 276–305.

Richardson, W. (2009, March). Becoming network-wise. *Educational Leadership*, 66(6), 26–31.

Riekehof, L. (1987). *Joy of signing.* Springfield, MO: Gospel.

Roberts, T. (2004, September 29). The discipline of wonder (editorial). *Education Week.*

Rosenblatt, L. (1978). *The reader, the text, the poem: The transactional theory of the literary work.* Carbondale, IL: Southern Illinois University Press.

Rumelhart, D. (1982). Schemata: The building blocks of cognition. In J. Guthrie (Ed.), *Comprehension and teaching: Research reviews* (pp. 3–26). Newark, DE: International Reading Association.

Sadoski, M., & Paivio, A. (2001). *Imagery and text: A dual coding theory of reading and writing.* Mahwah, NJ: Lawrence Erlbaum Associates.

Samuels, J. (2002). Reading fluency: Its development and assessment. In A. Farstrup & J. Samuels, *What research has to say about reading instruction.* Newark, DE: International Reading Association.

Scharlach, T. (2008). START comprehending: Students and teachers actively reading text. *Reading Teacher, 62*(1), 20–31.

Sebesta, S. (2003). Reading, interest and preferences. In J. Flood, D. Lapp, J.R. Squire, & J.M. Jensen (Eds.), *Handbook of research on teaching the English language arts* (pp. 835–842). Mahwah, NH: Erlbaum.

Shankweiler, D., Lundquist, E., Katz, L., Stuebing, K., Fletcher, J., Brady, S., Fowler, A., Dreyer, L., Marchione, K., Shaywitz, S., & Shaywitz, B. (1999). Comprehension and decoding: Patterns of association in children with reading difficulties. *Scientific Studies of Reading, 3,* 69–94.

Silverstein, S. (1981). The Bridge. *A light in the attic.* New York: Harper and Row.

Smolkin, L., & Donovan, C. (2002). *The contexts of comprehension: Informational book read alouds and comprehension acquisition* (CIERA Report). (ERIC Document Reproduction Service No. ED 450351). Retrieved from http://www.eric.ed.gov

Snow, C. (2004). Introduction. In P. McCardle & U. Chhabra (Eds.), *The voice of evidence in reading research.* Baltimore, MD: Brookes.

Snow, C., Burns, M., & Griffin, P. (1998). *Preventing reading difficulties in young children.* Washington, DC: National Academy Press.

Sparks, R. (2004, June). Orthographic awareness, phonemic awareness, syntactic processing, and working memory skill in hyperlexic children. *Reading & Writing, 17*(4), 359–386.

Stahl, S. (2004). *The promise of accessible textbooks: Increased achievement for all students.* Wakefield, MA: National Center on Accessing the General Curriculum.

Stanovich, K. (1986). Mathew effects in reading: Some consequences of individual differences in the acquisition of literacy. *Reading Research Quarterly, 22,* 360–406.

Stanovich, K., & Cunningham, A. (1992). Studying the consequences of literacy within a literate society: The cognitive correlates of print exposure. *Memory & Cognition, 20,* 51–68.

Stark, J. (1985). *Don't cross your bridge before you pay the toll.* New York: Price Stern Sloan.

Starko, A. (1995). *Creativity in the classroom: Schools of curious delight.* White Plains, NY: Longman.

Stebick, D., & Dain, J. (2007). *Comprehension strategies for your k–6 literacy classroom: Thinking before, during and after reading.* Thousand Oaks, CA: Corwin.

Stephens, T. (1970). *Directive teaching of children with learning and behavioral handicaps* (2nd ed.). Columbus, OH: Merrill.

Stiggins, R. (2004). New assessment beliefs for a new school mission. *Phi Delta Kappan, 86*(1), 22–27.

Stover, L. (2003). Mind the gap: Bridging into difficult texts. *English Journal, 92*(4), 77–83.

Strickland, D. (2001). Early intervention for African American children considered to be at risk. In S. Neuman & D. Dickinson (Eds.), *Handbook of early literacy research* (pp. 323–332). New York: Guilford.

Suchman, J., & McCombs, L. (1968). *Problem book: Cases for geological inquiry.* Chicago: Science Research Associates.

Sunal, D.W., & Sunal, C.S. (2003). *Science in the elementary and middle school.* Upper Saddle River, NJ: Merrill Prentice Hall.

Tauber, R. (1997). *Self-fulfilling prophecy: A practical guide to its use in education.* Westport, CT: Greenwood.

Taylor, B., Pearson, P.D., Clark, K., & Walpole, S. (1999). *Beating the odds in teaching all children to read: Lessons from effective schools and exemplary teachers* (Research Report 1). Ann Arbor, MI: Center for the Improvement of Early Reading Achievement.

Taylor, B., Pearson, P.D., Peterson, D., & Rodriquez, M. (2003). Reading growth in high poverty classrooms. *Elementary School Journal, 104,* 3–28.

Tierney, R., Kieffer, R., Whalin, K., Desai, L., Moss, A., Harris, J., & Hopper, J. (1997). *Assessing the impact of hypertext on learners' architecture of literacy learning spaces in different disciplines: Follow-up studies. Reading Online.* Retrieved from www.readingonline.org/research/impact/index.html

Tomlinson, C. (2000, September). Reconcilable differences? Standards-based teaching and differentiation. *Educational Leadership, 58*(1), 6–11.

Tomlinson, C. (2002, September). Invitations to learn. *Educational Leadership, 60,* 6–10.

Tomlinson, C., Brimijoin, K., & Narvaez, L. (2008). *The differentiated school: Making revolutionary changes in teaching and learning.* Alexandria, VA: Association for Supervision and Curriculum Development.

Tompkins, G. (2003). *Literacy for the 21st century.* Upper Saddle River, NJ: Merrill/Prentice Hall.

Tompson, B. (2007, November 19). A troubling case of readers' block: Citing decline among older kids, NEA report warns of dire effects. *Washington Post*, p. C01.

Torgesen, J. (2004). Lessons learned from the last 20 years of research on interventions for students who experience difficulty learning to read. In P. McCardle & U. Chhabra (Eds.), *The voice of evidence in reading research*. Baltimore: Brookes.

Torgesen, J. (2006, February). *Factors that influence reading comprehension: Developmental instructional considerations.* (PowerPoint presentation). Presentation at the Core Knowledge Conference, San Antonio, TX. Retrieved from www.fcrr.org/science/pdf/torgesen/Core_knowledge.pdf

Trelease, J. (2005, February). Keynote address presented at South Carolina Reading Association, Myrtle Beach, SC.

Trelease, J. (2006). *The read aloud handbook*. New York: Penguin.

Tunnell, M., & Jacobs, J. (1989). Using "real" books: Research findings on literature-based reading instruction. *Reading Teacher, 42*, 470–477.

Tunnell, M., & Jacobs, J. (2008). *Children's literature briefly*. Upper Saddle River, NJ: Pearson Prentice Hall.

Turner, J., & Paris, S. (1995). How literacy tasks influence children's motivation for literacy. *Reading Teacher, 48*, 662–673.

USA Today. (2001). June 11. A2.

U.S. Department of Education. (1992–2000). National Center for Education Statistics. Washington, DC. Retrieved from http://nces.ed.gov/

U.S. Department of Education. (2005). National Assessment of Adult Literacy (NAAL). Washington, DC: National Center for Education Statistics. Retrieved March 31, 2008, from http://nces.ed.gov/naal/kf_demographics.asp

U.S. Department of Education. (2003–2007). National Assessment of Educational Progress. Washington, DC: National Center for Education Statistics. Retrieved from http://nces.ed.gov/nationsreportcard/

U.S. Department of Education. (2007). Washington, DC: Author. Retrieved from http://www.ed.gov/about/offices/list/ies/index.html

Vellutino, F., Scanlon, D., & Lyon, G. (2000). Differentiating between difficult to remediate and readily remediated poor readers: More evidence against the IQ achievement discrepancy definition of reading disability. *Journal of Learning Disabilities, 33*(3), 223–238.

Vellutino, F., Scanlon, D., Sipay, E., Small, S., Pratt, A., Chen, R., & Denckla, M. (1996). Cognitive profiles of difficult to remediate and readily remediated poor readers: Early intervention as a vehicle for distinguishing between cognitive and experiential deficits as basic causes of specific reading disability. *Journal of Educational Psychology, 88*(4), 601–638.

Villegas, A., & Lucas, T. (2007, March). The culturally responsive teacher. *Educational Leadership*, 28–33.

Vogler, K. (2008, Summer). Asking good questions. *Thinking Skills NOW, 65*(9). Retrieved from http://www.ascd.org/publications/educational_leadership/summer08/vol65/num09/Asking_Good_Questions.aspx

Vygotsky, L. (1978). *Mind in society: The development of higher psychological processes*. Cambridge, MA: Harvard University Press.

Walker, B. (2009, February/March). An open letter to President Obama. *Reading Teacher, 26*(4), 16–17.

Walker, H. (2009, February/March). Why Reading First has "failed." *Reading Today, 26*(4), 18.

Walmsley, S. (2006). Getting the big idea: A neglected goal for reading comprehension. *Reading Teacher, 60*(3), 281–284.

Warner, S. (1986). *Teacher*. New York: Touchtone.

Wharton-MacDonald, R., Pressley, M., & Hampston, J. (1998). Literacy instruction in nine first grade classrooms: Teacher characteristics and student achievement. *Elementary School Journal, 99*, 101–128.

White, R., Sowell, J., & Yangihara, A. (1989). Teaching elementary students to use word-part clues. *Reading Teacher, 42*(4), 302–308.

Whitehurst, R. (2008, December). *Education Update, 50*(12), 3.

Whitin, P. (2002). Leading into literature circles through the sketch-to-stretch strategy. *The Reading Teacher, 55*, 444–450.

Wiggins, G. (2007). Four things art education can teach other educators. Retrieved on June 23, 2007, from http://www.authenticeducation.org/bigideas/article.lasso?artId=48.

Wiggins, G., & McTighe, J. (2005). *Understanding by design* (2nd ed.). Upper Saddle River, NJ: Prentice Hall.

Williams, J. (2002). Reading comprehension strategies and teacher preparation. In A. Farstrup & J. Samuels (Eds.), *What research has to say about reading instruction*. Newark, DE: International Reading Association.

Wolf, M., & Barzillai, M. (2009, March). The importance of deep reading. *Educational Leadership, 66*(6), 33–37.

Wolk, S. (2008). School as inquiry. *Phi Delta Kappan, 90*(8), 115–122.

Wylie, R., & Durrell, E. (1970). Teaching vowels through phonograms. *Elementary English, 47*, 787–791.

Author Index

Subject Index